I0099637

DREAMS   OF

FLIGHT

Duke University Press   Durham and London   2022

DREAMS OF

THE LIVES OF CHINESE WOMEN

STUDENTS IN THE WEST

Fran Martin

*

FLIGHT

© 2022 DUKE UNIVERSITY PRESS
All rights reserved

Cover designed by A. Mattson Gallagher
Typeset in Garamond Premier Pro by Westchester Publishing Ser
vices

Library of Congress Cataloging-in-Publication Data
Names: Martin, Fran, [date] author.
Title: Dreams of flight : the lives of Chinese women students
in the West / Fran Martin.
Description: Durham : Duke University Press, 2022. | Includes
bibliographical references and index.
Identifiers: LCCN 2021018228 (print)
LCCN 2021018229 (ebook)
ISBN 9781478014935 (hardcover)
ISBN 9781478017615 (paperback)
ISBN 9781478022220 (ebook)
Subjects: LCSH: Chinese students—Education (Higher)—Australia. |
Women college students—Australia. | Students, Foreign—Education
(Higher)—Australia. | BISAC: SOCIAL SCIENCE / Gender Studies |
HISTORY / Asia / China
Classification: LCC LC3089.A8 M378 2022 (print) | LCC LC3089.A8
(ebook) | DDC 378.1/9829951094—dc23
LC record available at https://lccn.loc.gov/2021018228
LC ebook record available at https://lccn.loc.gov/2021018229

Cover art: Photograph by C. Zheng, 2018. Courtesy the artist.

Duke University Press gratefully acknowledges the Faculty of Arts,
University of Melbourne, which provided funds toward
the publication of this book.

This book is dedicated to Chinese women
everywhere pursuing the dream of overseas study

Contents

Preface *After Mobility?*

This book is about the international education industry, human mobilities, and neoliberal subject formation, especially its gendered aspects. Late 2020 feels like a strange time to be completing the manuscript, since, even as I write, the COVID-19 global pandemic is scrambling the conditions of possibility for each of these operations in ways that were unimaginable when this research project began.

Dreams of Flight examines the central role that geographic movement plays in shaping human lives in the era of global capitalism. It explores how transnational educational mobility—desires and potentials for it as well as representations and practices of it—has enabled young, middle-class Chinese women to elaborate and embody emergent forms of subjectivity and feminine gender. This is a particular example of a more general phenomenon: the defining influence that mobilities of all kinds have had in making the social world of capitalist late modernity and the types of human subject possible within it.

In recent decades, higher education, neoliberal rationality, and mobilities have become mutually entangled in historically distinctive ways, both in China and Australia—this study's primary foci—and globally. In many countries, amplified capacities for the transnational movement of capital, bodies, information, and technologies have been instrumental in refashioning higher education according to the principles of the market, such that degrees have tended increasingly to become framed more as a commodity for private consumption than as a public good. The young Chinese women whose stories are told in this book represent the human face of this marketization of education. Privileged to be able to opt out of the Chinese system and enter the global higher education market, they invested in expensive degrees at Australian universities in order to develop themselves as human capital for the high-paying tertiary and quaternary industries that dominate economies in late capitalism, especially finance and related fields. This book addresses their subjective experiences of that journey and the way those experiences in turn shape the women's understandings of themselves and the world.

At the time I am writing this preface, the havoc wrought by the global coronavirus pandemic has exposed more starkly than ever the reliance of the Australian higher education system on these mobile students. Their enrollments have dwindled to a trickle as a result of virus-related border restrictions, leaving a multibillion-dollar budget black hole in the national higher education sector and a question mark over its future.

Beyond the specific—and devastating—impacts of missing international student fee revenue in higher education, the immobilization enforced by the pandemic also throws into sharp relief the former taken-for-grantedness of everyday mobility capacities more generally and raises pressing questions about their sustainability and future. In many places worldwide, geographic borders are closed or heavily restricted in an effort to curb the virus's spread. Airlines and travel agencies are in an unprecedented state of crisis. This preface is being written under a "hard lockdown" that sees the residents of Melbourne, the city where I live, confined within our homes for twenty-two hours a day, and movement outside the home restricted to a five-kilometer radius. University teaching, for both domestic and international students, has moved almost completely online, obviating the need for physical movement by staff and students.

Looking back from our immobilized and uncertain present, then, this project appears like a kind of time capsule: a window back onto the not-so-distant boom times when logics of physical mobility were the commonsense grounding not only of higher education but also of virtually all aspects of late-modern life and the kind of people it enabled us to be and become. The viral crisis reminds us of the precarious fragility of a world whose incessant movement recently felt as reliable as the orbit of the planets.

Although both human mobilities and international education markets are bound to revive in some form postcrisis, many questions remain. Will nations like Australia make a decisive turn away from reliance on private international student fees to prop up public higher education? Will mobility reassert itself as our era's cultural dominant? Is neoliberal globalization experiencing a crisis that will fundamentally reshape the world we know? Does this book provide a snapshot of a lost past or an insight into forms of being that will return as a defining feature of future times? While the answers to these questions remain unclear, I hope that the book can offer some fresh understanding of ways of being, moving, and knowing oneself and the world that have been central to Chinese, Australian, and transnational middle-class cultures in the second decade of the twenty-first century.

Acknowledgments

The process of researching and writing this book has been unlike any other academic project I have undertaken. What I have learned from my engagements with the people involved has not only produced the scholarly insights that I try to relay in the pages that follow but also fundamentally transformed and enriched my own life and understanding of the world we share. This book is the product of an expansive collaborative effort involving hundreds of individuals and groups scattered across multiple cities, countries, and institutions. It is impossible to thank them enough.

My thanks, first to all, to those in various parts of the international education industry who lent their support at different stages to facilitating the primary research, including Bo Bonifacio, Joanna Buckingham, Denise Bush, Pinky Cai, Sunny Chen, Diana Crvenkovic, Melanie Duncan, Dressie Fan, Noah Feng, Chris Fyfe, Danielle Hartridge, Kang Tianfeng, James Kerley, Simon Kwok, Gary Lee, Li Yanhong, Nian Liu, Rosaline Luo, John Qiu, Lisa Renkin, Clare Shen, Andrew Shi, Liz Stinson, Cathy Su, James Sun, Jacqueline Taylor, Justin Tighe, Ben Waymire, Xu Cheng, Sherry Xu, George Yue, Venice Yun, O. J. Zhang, and Janet Zhuang. Thanks also to those who generously read and offered invaluable feedback on earlier drafts of parts of the book, especially Wanning Sun, Chris Healy, Anita Harris, Shanthi Robertson, Dallas Rogers, and the anonymous readers at Duke University Press. My thanks, too, to the many other colleagues and friends who offered various kinds of support and assistance along the way: Jon Chew, Jamie Coates, Helen Forbes-Mewett, Koichi Iwabuchi, Ka Weibo, Michael Cheng Liu, Lu Ye, Simon Marginson, Simone Meng, Jinghua, Juni, Greg Noble, Louise Olliff, Nikos Papastergiadis, Nick Parissis, Jessica Walton, Sun Wei, Meng Xu, Fan Yang, Jamie J. Zhao, and Andy Xinyu Zhao. Without the contributions of the project research assistants, this book would never have been written. Heartfelt thanks to Zheng Yue in Shanghai and to Juliet Wen Zhou, Yuxing Zhou, Carman Fung, and especially my project collaborator, Can Qin, in Melbourne. Special thanks, too, to Wang Xiaoming and Luo Xiaoming, who hosted the China-based research at the Centre for Contemporary Cultural Studies at Shanghai University.

Most of all, thanks to all of the participants in the fieldwork study. Words cannot express my gratitude for their generosity and grace in sharing their lives with me over these years. The opportunity to know them has changed me, just as this book shows that studying in my hometown changed the students.

I acknowledge the financial support of both the University of Melbourne and the Australian Research Council, which funded the project under its Future Fellowships scheme (FT140100222). It is rare for a researcher to be afforded the resources to dedicate herself full-time for several years to a single research project, and I am grateful to the Australian Research Council for that opportunity and hope that such schemes will continue to offer researchers assistance to undertake important research into the future.

Thanks to Ken Wissoker at Duke University Press for his unflagging enthusiasm and support for this project and to Ryan Kendall, Ellen Goldlust, and Liz Smith for all of their help during the production process.

Finally, my thanks to my immediate family—Peter, Tom, and Mum and Dad—for the love and support (emotional, musical, and comestible) they have lavished on me over the course of the geographic and intellectual journeys that have resulted in this book.

Some material from chapter 1 appeared in an earlier version in Fran Martin, "Mobile Self-Fashioning and Gendered Risk: Rethinking Chinese Students' Motivations for Overseas Education," *Globalisation, Societies and Education* 15, no. 5 (2017): 706–20. Some material from chapter 3 appeared in an earlier version in Fran Martin, "iPhones and 'African Gangs': Everyday Racism and Ethno-transnational Media in Melbourne's Chinese Student World," *Journal of Ethnic and Racial Studies* 43, no. 5 (2020): 892–910. Some material from chapter 4 appeared in an earlier version in Fran Martin, "Rethinking Network Capital: Hospitality Work and Parallel Trading among Chinese Students in Melbourne," *Mobilities* 12, no. 6 (2017): 890–907. Some material from chapter 5 appeared in an earlier version in Fran Martin, "Overseas Study as Zone of Suspension: Chinese Students Re-negotiating Youth, Gender, and Intimacy," *Journal of Intercultural Studies* 39, no. 6 (2018): 688–703.

INTRODUCTION

Worlds in Motion

*

Growing Up on the Move

Summer storms delay my flight from Shanghai, derailing Mr. and Mrs. Qiu's plan for us to discuss their daughter Yiruo's imminent journey to Australia over dinner.[1] *Instead, I meet the family in the lobby café at my hotel minutes after skidding in from the airport. We chat for an hour and a half, sipping tea and hot chocolate as discreet piano music tinkles in the background, punctuated now and then by the beep-beep of incoming business calls on Mr. Qiu's cell phone. The initial polite reserve between Yiruo's parents and me gradually dissolves as we realize we're the same age: all born around 1970. When Mr. Qiu learns that I studied in China in the late 1980s, he visibly warms up: "Ah, then you understand how different China was in our student days." I nod, smiling: no need for further elaboration, the changes are too obvious—from socialist state in the dusty throes of early development to rising economic superpower with a string of shining megacities like the one where we meet tonight; from everyday austerity to superabundant consumer culture; from a mainly rural to a largely urban population; from geographically static lives to people everywhere on the move; from comparative economic equality to a widening wealth gap; from relative cultural insularity to ever deeper internationalization. Illustrating some of these transformations, although today Mr. and Mrs. Qiu—both university-educated professionals—belong clearly to China's new urban middle classes, when they were their daughter's age they had virtually no chance of studying abroad: such a dream was beyond reach for the vast majority owing to insuperable economic and bureaucratic constraints. In contrast, Yiruo has already spent four years in Malaysia for high school and is about to embark on an undergraduate engineering degree in Melbourne, after which her parents expect her to remain abroad for postgraduate study and probably to live and work outside China long-term, in Australia or perhaps the United States, Canada, or Britain.*

The Qius have an easygoing manner with each other and with me, and the affection between parents and daughter is obvious, expressed in jokes and friendly banter that, as the evening progresses, reveal some interesting family dynamics.

Evidently Mr. and Mrs. Qiu think eighteen-year-old Yiruo needs to work on be-coming more independent. She is too emotionally attached to them, they say, and should concentrate on developing her own independent career and personal life. For Mr. and Mrs. Qiu, Yiruo's overseas study supports this goal, and they push the idea that she should live independently overseas after graduation. Yiruo, however, resists this narrative. While she shares her parents' vision of herself as simulta-neously a Chinese patriot and a developing global citizen—someone who is proud of her homeland but, in her words, "suited to traveling around everywhere, . . . fitting in anywhere"—she hopes to prove her worth by prospering professionally to the extent that she could bring her parents overseas to live with her and support them financially. Her father gently scoffs at this idea, interpreting it as a sign of Yiruo's immaturity. "After all, your parents do have some capacity for independent survival!" he chuckles.

Yiruo's parents' vision of how she should grow up also includes overtly gendered elements. Mrs. Qiu tells me she hopes Yiruo will grow out her hair, which is cut in a boyishly short style. "I mean, in Malaysia the weather's so hot, so she's always kept her hair short like that. But when she goes [to Melbourne], I hope she'll style it more like her mum's. . . . Grow her hair long. . . . That way it'd be more girly." Another disagreement arises over the question of marriage. Mrs. Qiu hopes Yiruo will follow gendered convention: "[One should get married] when one's finished studying and one's about twenty-five or -six. . . . As parents, we feel she shouldn't leave it too late, just follow the normal way: when you've finished studying, start a family. . . . So that [marriage] happens before age thirty." But Yiruo disagrees: "These things are impossible to plan. . . . Everything depends on whether you meet the right person. . . . If you never meet the right person, then there's nothing you can do about it, is there!" But Mr. Qiu repeatedly urges Yiruo to find a boyfriend at university to avoid finding herself left on the shelf. "You shouldn't think: this time is purely for study, I can't have a life. . . . While you are studying, you can also find love. . . . [Otherwise,] later on, when you want to find a boyfriend, . . . you're in trouble." "The good ones will all be taken," her mother concurs. Yiruo sits listening respectfully to her parents' imprecations, smiling a small, self-contained smile and nodding, saying little. But when her parents go on to foretell Yiruo's inevitable lifelong loneliness if she fails to make a timely marriage, she speaks up: "You're over-thinking it!" she chides her father, laughing. "Let's not discuss this topic. I don't want to talk about it." "She's quite attached to her parents, you see," her father interprets to me. "But," turning to Yiruo, "you can't refuse to grow up! You do have to grow up sometime."

*

This discussion, which took place shortly after the commencement of my fieldwork in mid-2015, reveals gendered tensions that surfaced repeatedly, in different forms, in my interactions with young women in the Chinese student diaspora over the next five years. At issue in the (superficially) lighthearted disagreements between Yiruo and her parents on the eve of her departure for overseas study are generational, gendered, and personal divergences in their understandings of what it means for a young woman to grow up. For Mr. and Mrs. Qiu, for Yiruo to grow up meant that she should emulate a more normatively feminine look, find a boyfriend, loosen her reliance on her parents, and exchange her ideal of long-term co-residence with them for timely marriage and a family of her own. They hoped study abroad would help push Yiruo along this route, increasing her capacity for emotional independence while also throwing eligible bachelors into her path (later Mrs. Qiu pointedly asked me about the male-to-female ratio among Chinese students at the university her daughter would attend in Melbourne).

Yiruo, however, had different opinions on these issues. This was borne out over subsequent years as I continued to meet with her during her study in Melbourne. Yiruo stuck to her tomboyish style. She kept her hair short; favored androgynous, sporty clothing; and once jokingly referred to herself as "half-girl, half-boy." Gradually, she also revealed to me her same-sex sexual preference. In these ways, while living abroad, Yiruo defied many of the rules of normative femininity that her parents held dear. A couple of years after the event, Yiruo provided some insight into our conversation with her parents that night in her home city. She told me that because she had studied abroad since the age of fourteen and before that had lived away at boarding school, her parents actually didn't know her nearly as well as they thought they did. That night she hadn't felt able to contradict them directly on the boyfriend issue and instead just tried to change the subject. Rereading the discussion in light of this, we see Yiruo tactically deflecting her parents' attempts to have her conform to their gendered ideal of how she should grow up. To circumvent the marriage question, she emphasizes instead her emotional attachment and filial duty to her parents (which by no means implies that her sense of these is not sincere). For Yiruo, then, growing up seems connected with staying true to her alternative version of gendered selfhood and finding ways to resist parental pressures pushing her toward a normatively feminine identity, while remaining filial toward her parents.

However, notwithstanding these conflicting understandings of the meaning and appropriate conduct of female youth, overseas study was able to "work" for both Yiruo and her parents and to some extent mediated the conflicts between them.[2] Both parents and daughter shared the assumption that spending some years studying abroad is a normal and desirable experience for a middle-class Chinese woman in her late teens or twenties. Yiruo's study abroad was very much a family project, with her parents financially supporting her studies; encouraging her emergent mobile, cosmopolitan outlook; and hoping that overseas study might facilitate their daughter's progress toward normative feminine adulthood. Yet, in and through these family-supported overseas study ventures, Yiruo was actually able to hew out a space and time of partial insulation from her parents' concerned efforts to mold her gendered self, sexuality, and life trajectory.

My evening with Yiruo and her parents illustrates this book's core claim: that understandings and practices of gender are inseparably entangled with middle-class Chinese students' experiences of educational mobility. Indeed, Yiruo's story prompts us to consider a whole series of questions about gender, class, and mobility in (and beyond) China today. What does it mean, and how does it feel, to grow up within the category "girl" in China's urban middle classes in the new millennium? How does the personal mobility newly available to members of these classes impact youth, women, and families? How does traveling abroad for study transform gendered practices and understandings of the transition from adolescence to adulthood for young people like Yiruo and her contemporaries? In short, how are experiences of gender and transnational educational mobility entangled and mutually transformative for the current generation of Chinese women students? These questions are all the more pressing given that since economic reform, the proportion of women leaving China for study has increased fivefold, so that today 60 percent of outgoing students are female—even though men significantly outnumber women in the birth cohorts of this generation (Kajanus 2015, 1; *Renmin Ribao* 2016).[3]

During that first month of fieldwork during which I met the Qiu family, gendered aspects of study abroad were everywhere apparent in my discussions with students and their families. I met a young woman from a lower-middle-class family who was to be the first in her circle of acquaintance to study abroad and who came to our interview accompanied by an elder female cousin who spoke at length about how she had married too young, now faced intense pressure from her mother-in-law to have a baby and devote herself to familial care work, and regretted losing opportunities for further education such as her cousin now had. I met several young women who, like Yiruo, hoped for various reasons either to delay marriage or to avoid it altogether and saw studying overseas as a means of distancing themselves from family pressure and buying some extra time. I met daughters who hoped to overcome what they saw as the gendered limitations of their mothers' lives by expanding their own geographic, cultural, and professional horizons through international education, and mothers who framed overseas study as an attempt to compensate for the gender bias in professional employment markets that might otherwise hinder their daughters' chances of landing a decent job in China. I engaged in a WeChat conversation over several months with a young rural woman whose dream of studying in Australia was shattered at the last minute by her parents' divorce and the consequent withdrawal of her paternal grandfather's financial support for her education. Of course, not everyone I met was critical of the gendered status quo. The educational choices of many reflected orthodox views about careers that "naturally suit" women, being relatively safe, stable, and undemanding (office work in the corporate sector or as a civil servant in China's government bureaucracy were the most commonly cited examples; Hoffman 2010, 121–41; J. Zheng 2016, 84). Some opted for a one-year master's course on the grounds that although it might be taken less seriously by employers in China than a standard-length degree, "that's all right for a girl." A couple put aside their hopes to remain abroad for work or further study in order to "follow" boyfriends already settled into employment back in China (Y. Hao 2019). But whether they criticized the gendered status quo or saw it as natural and inevitable, all of these women's stories point to the deep entanglement of gender with educational mobility for the generation of Chinese youth born around and after 1990 (commonly called the 九零后 *jiuling hou* or "post-90" generation). This entanglement, and the subjective and affective dynamics to which it gives rise, provides the central theme of *Dreams of Flight*.

In addition to questions about the gendered social life of the Chinese student diaspora, Yiruo's story also raises a number of broader questions. How does the Chinese educational exodus reflect China's economic rise and the attendant in-process transformations in the world order? Within this new order, what will it mean to think of oneself, as Yiruo and many of her contemporaries do, as a global citizen and simultaneously a patriotic Chinese one? How do the massive and ever-growing numbers of mainland Chinese students studying abroad impact the societies overseas where they live and study? How will Chinese students living in multicultural Western cities be interpellated, construct themselves, and interpret others around them in relation to discourses of ethnicity and race? While this book's central theme is the entanglement of gender with educational mobility, around this thread are woven concomitant questions concerning the lives of China's new middle classes, students' negotiations of the ideals of cosmopolitan selfhood and global citizenship alongside loyalties to the Chinese state, and the ways in which China's intensifying transnational reach through educational mobilities reconfigures aspects of urban social life, including the workings of race (and racism), in the Western cities where these young people study. The chapters that follow explore these gendered and other questions across the full life cycle of international study, from Chinese students' and families' hopes, expectations, and motivations predeparture, through my fifty core research participants' experiences of everyday life abroad, to their peripatetic postgraduation lives in China, Australia, and other locations around the world. The following pages provide contextual background by discussing China's transforming economy and class structure in the reforms era and the concomitant new cultural centrality of mobility as a form of value, as well as the shifts in available frameworks for interpreting gender over this same period, which have produced the tensions outlined earlier.

Market Socialism and the New Middle Classes

Following the death of Mao Zedong, from 1979 the Chinese Communist Party under Deng Xiaoping initiated a series of reforms (改革开放 *gaige kaifang*) based on market liberalization, the decentralization of economic planning, the partial privatization of state enterprises, and the opening of the nation to foreign investment. Processes were thereby set in motion that, four decades later, have thoroughly transformed the structure of class in China, both by intensifying social stratification and by complicating its underlying logics. Whereas under high socialism (1949–78) access to resources depended almost wholly on one's political and institutional relationship to the party-state, in the reforms era a hybrid of market and reconfigured state forces has enabled increasing numbers of professionals, managers, and entrepreneurs across private, collective, and state sectors to accumulate unprecedented levels of private wealth (Bian et al. 2005; Goodman and Zhang 2008; Li Zhang 2010; Goodman 2014). Today these groups may be characterized—albeit contentiously—as constituting China's new middle classes.[4] The expansion of these classes has not been autonomous from the party-state but was actively encouraged by it. Whereas, during the Mao years, the bourgeoisie was represented as the enemy of the people, and the material basis for its existence was removed through the abolition of private enterprise and property ownership, in 2002 the Sixteenth Party Congress explicitly endorsed enlarging the "middle-income strata" (中等收入阶层 *zhongdeng shouru jieceng*), framing this class as a bulwark to economic stability and a "harmonious society" (Tomba 2004; Cheng Li 2010). This stance continues to the present day (figure I.1).

FIGURE I.I Government slogan outside the Shanghai Exhibition Centre (formerly the Sino-Soviet Friendship Building), December 2017, mixing socialist rhetoric with the language of lifestyle: "It is the people's aspiration toward the good life that is the objective of our struggle." Photo by the author.

Connected with economic and income growth, urbanization, and increasing higher education and white-collar jobs in the reforms era (Chunling Li 2010), the new entrepreneurial, professional, and managerial classes to which the participants in this study belong emerged through a number of stages. Between the late 1970s and the 1990s, social mobility was relatively high as opportunities to accumulate wealth in the emerging private sector expanded (Bian 2002). Chunling Li (2010, 150) observes that most members of the first generation of China's entrepreneurial middle classes previously held blue-collar jobs. David S. G. Goodman and Xiaowei Zhang (2008, 10) trace the history behind this upward mobility in more detail: first, a wave of small-scale individual business operators (个体户 getihu) emerged in the late 1970s and early 1980s, followed in the 1980s to early 1990s by entrepreneurs in rural township and village enterprises who developed the nation's manufacturing base. The 1990s saw a third wave of entrepreneurs emerging in the construction and resource industries, followed by a fourth in the real estate and finance sectors.[5] But the high levels of social mobility supporting the emergence of today's middle classes were short-lived (J. Lin and Sun 2010). Writing in 2014, Goodman describes contemporary China as "a society characterized by its low social mobility and high intergenerational transfer of privilege and disadvantage" (33; see also Bregnbæk 2016). By now, the new class structure formed during the first two decades of reform has to a great extent solidified (Goodman 2014, 79).

In China the concept of the middle classes circulates widely in a number of linguistic forms—from the classic Marxian *zhongchan jieji* (中产阶级), or *middle-propertied class*, to *the middle stratum* (中等阶层 *zhongdeng jiecng*), *the well-off* (小康 *xiao kang*), and *the petite bourgeoisie* (小资 *xiao zi*)—and refers to a commonly recognized (and self-recognized) group associated with specific resources, lifestyle practices, anxieties, and aspirations. The middle classes as they are generally understood are largely urban, with a social status based on higher-than-average income, occupational prestige, education, and leisure consumption (Chunling Li 2010; M. Chen and Goodman 2013). They own property in the form of apartments, cars, and financial assets; use commercial financial services like credit cards; and travel internationally for tourism and education (Cheng Li 2010; Li Zhang 2010). Recent research with people belonging to these groups also points to some collective preoccupations. In particular, the middle classes seem pervaded by a fear of falling: an underlying anxiety about their capacity to maintain and reproduce their class status in the face of an uncertain economy, risks attaching to income derived through "gray" channels in a time of hard-hitting anticorruption drives, and the disappearance of socialist-era safety nets (Li Zhang 2010, 7–10; Osburg 2013). For those within them, China's new middle classes feel like a precarious place, surrounded on all sides by new risks that are the underside of the opportunities brought by economic reform (Ren 2013; Ji 2017; Zhu and Zhu 2017).

The family backgrounds of the core participants in this study reflect this sociohistorical background. Most of the students' families belonged to the professional, entrepreneurial, and managerial middle classes. They mainly lived in larger cities on the wealthy eastern seaboard and in central and southwestern provinces, although about a quarter were from smaller, less developed cities in these areas. The parents worked in state or private enterprises as managers or in a range of professional roles, including as engineers, editors, designers, teachers, doctors, accountants, and media workers; many were also entrepreneurs running their own trading, manufacturing, or other small businesses. Some were government cadres; a smaller number—largely mothers—were nonprofessional employees. But although all participants' families could be classified at the broadest level as belonging to China's middle classes, they demonstrated a spread from the lower to the upper segments of this diverse and fragmented class formation.[6] At one extreme, one or two families subsisted on income from small-scale family businesses that involved parents in hands-on manufacturing and retail activities; at the other extreme, some parents were high-ranking cadres and wealthy professionals with significant investment holdings. The class history of participants' families was also diverse, including some parents with only basic levels of education who began life as smallholding farmers (or "peasants": 农民 *nong-min*) and struck it rich as entrepreneurs in the manufacturing and construction sectors during the 1980s and 1990s, alongside other parents who were born into far more privileged situations and held postgraduate qualifications.

Despite the pervasive sense of precarity experienced by members of China's middle classes, with the state's endorsement of an expanding middle stratum and ordinary people's desires for a comfortable life, the concept of middle-class identity nevertheless has a largely positive public image: a set of idealized representations and aspirations attaching to the "good life" that is spread through government campaigns, popular media, and literary print culture (figure I.1; Y. Zheng 2014; T. Lewis, Martin, and Sun 2016). In particular, middle-class people are represented as having high levels of *suzhi* (素质): a term that originated in state discourse in relation to the goal of optimizing population quality for national development and today has taken on a life of its own in everyday speech and become deeply polysemic, broadly indicating something like cultural civility (Kipnis 2006; Hsu 2007; D. Lin 2017). As the term is popularly understood, the individual with high *suzhi* is well educated, tasteful, cosmopolitan, and cultivated and displays civic virtues including good manners and ethical engagement with others. As an exemplary norm and new form of human value, *suzhi* is indicatively associated with the urban middle classes, in contradistinction to rural and laboring populations (Bakken 2000; H. Yan 2003; Anagnost 2004; Jacka 2006; Wanning Sun 2009; Tomba 2009; Hoffman 2010).

Class, Education, and Transnational Mobility

High levels of education are central to both the image and the practices of China's new middle classes. First, the emergence of these classes is structurally linked with the expansion of educational institutions and opportunities (Chunling Li 2010; J. Lin and Sun 2010); and, second, the government-supported popular ideal of middle-class identity hinges centrally on the embodiment of *suzhi*, which is itself based in significant part on educational attainment (Anagnost 2004; Kipnis 2011, 57–89). The central place of academic achievement in China's middle-class imaginary is well established. Fengshu Liu (2008, 206) demonstrates how the academic endeavors of successful university entrants are fueled by their aspiration toward a middle-class lifestyle ideal (小资生活 *xiaozi shenghuo*) characterized by financial security, material comfort, social status, and pleasure. Other studies show how children become vessels for middle-class aspirations and anxieties, undergoing multiple forms of private training to enable them to excel academically while embodying a middle-class habitus and high *suzhi* (Donald and Zheng 2008; Li Zhang 2010, 124). Thus, argues Liu, "in present-day China, education, *suzhi*, qualifications, social mobility, and the 'good life' have become inter-related concepts," fueling the formation of a credential society (following R. Collins [1979]): "the widespread assumption . . . that one should get as much (credentialized) education as possible in order to cash in on as much career advancement as possible" (F. Liu 2008, 197–98).

A number of factors have combined in recent decades to extend the geographic range of educational credential seeking among China's middle classes to a transnational scale, producing student outflows of unprecedented size and with them a new, education-based economy of Chinese transnationalism. Overseas study at destinations including Europe, the United States, Japan, and the Soviet Union has a long modern history in China, commencing in the late nineteenth century and proceeding through a series of stages, with different destination countries predominating at different historical moments in reflection of current social, economic, and political imperatives.[7] Since the turn of the twenty-first century, though, outward student flows to Western study destinations have grown exponentially and taken on a new character reflective of their times. Chinese government statistics reveal that more than four and a half million Chinese students studied abroad between 1978 and 2016, with an annual average growth rate of 19 percent and over half a million outbound students departing China annually since 2015 (*Renmin Ribao* 2016; Xinhua's China Economic Information Service 2017). This dramatic upsurge in privately funded Chinese young people traveling overseas for education has been fueled, on the most basic level, by rising wealth and the Chinese middle classes' belief that standards of tertiary education in Western nations and Japan are in general higher than those in most Chinese universities (aside from the very top tier). "Study-abroad fever" (留学热 *liuxue re*) is also fed by the middle classes' anxieties about the reproduction of their social status in light of an ever more marketized, inequitable, pyramid-shaped, and competitive secondary education system at home. In this regard the situation mirrors Johanna L. Waters's findings in Hong Kong, where "overseas education provides a means of escape and sanctuary [from a highly demanding local education system], as well as an opportunity to acquire more valuable cultural capital" (2008, 109–10; see also Fong 2011; Nyíri 2010, 37; Kajanus 2015, 46–72). These factors have in turn driven the emergence of elite, fee-supported internationally oriented secondary school programs, encouraged by neoliberalizing state education policy, which, as Shuning Liu (2020) argues, further exacerbates class inequality in China's education system.

These interconnected contexts were reflected in study participants' educational experiences and orientations. In line with their families' middle-class privilege, the urban secondary schools that participants had attended included many selective-entry, designated key state schools and elite private and international schools and streams, as well as some mid-to-high-ranked ordinary public schools. Based on National College Entrance Exam (高考 *gaokao*) results, however, most had middling levels of academic capital. Although, unusually, two participants had actually turned down places in first-tier Chinese universities in order to study abroad, many other undergraduates had gained entry only to second- or third-tier courses and saw an Australian degree as a preferable alternative.[8] A handful had skipped the stress of the *gaokao* altogether to enroll directly in Australian foundation studies programs geared toward university entrance.

In Australia over half of the participants (twenty-eight) enrolled in degrees in business, accounting, and finance-related areas; smaller numbers majored in media, construction, health, education, design, and arts. The interest in accounting qualifications partly reflects Australian immigration policy at the time, which designated accounting as a skill-shortage area and hence a preferred occupation for skilled migrants. But the concentration in finance-related fields also reflects a broad trend among Chinese students studying abroad (Australian Department of Education and Training, International Research and Analysis Unit 2016)—with a gendered dimension. Many parents consider office-based work in finance and accounting fields an appropriate choice for women, and anecdotal reports from study participants confirm that a significant majority of the Chinese international students taking such courses are female. The most common career aspiration I heard these young women voice was to be hired by one of the Big Four multinational accounting firms (Deloitte, PricewaterhouseCoopers, Ernst and Young, and KPMG). Through their transnational education ventures, they hoped to develop themselves as human capital for the female professional labor force that fuels global finance capitalism, especially in its ongoing expansion into East Asia (Nonini and Ong 1997; Sklair 2001; Duthie 2005; A. Ong 2008; Hoffman 2010; Brown 2015, 175–200; Rottenberg 2018).

But the cultural capital students hoped to attain was not only the direct result of educational credentials that would help them land desirable jobs. It also connected to transnational mobility and cosmopolitan habitus as themselves carriers of value. As in Waters's Hong Kong example, students and parents hoped that Western education would "inculcat[e] [students] into the mores of a cosmopolitan and *hypermobile* middle-class lifestyle" (Waters 2008, 10), so that such education could be seen (drawing on Katharyne Mitchell [1997]) as "an essential component of . . . a 'self-fashioning' process, undertaken by East Asia's transnational middle-class seeking inculcation in the 'language of the global economic subject'. . . . It symbolizes the possession of more than just a credential, representing a whole host of cultural, embodied traits conducive to professional success in a global economic arena" (Waters 2006, 181; see also S. Zhang and Xu 2020). In China today, Western education has become a commodity that indicatively expresses and consolidates middle-class social status (Xiang and Shen 2009). In the case of Australia, where immigration pathways may open out from tertiary study, transnational education may also be part of a broader family strategy of flexible residence, providing a hedge against the possible economic, political, or environmental risks of remaining in China (Osburg 2013, 14, 190; Robertson 2013; Liu-Farrer 2016).

The valuation of transnational mobility as a good in itself reflects a broader context in China, where, as Pál Nyíri (2010, 6) has shown, after 1978 and particularly since the 1990s, cross-border mobility has taken a central place in state discourses of what it means to be Chinese in the modern world (see also Oakes and Schein 2006). The state's rhetorical valorization of mobility is supported by far-reaching reforms to mobility's bureaucratic regulation at both domestic and international scales. Reforms to the place-based household registration (户口 *hukou*) system during the 1990s have resulted in massive population movements from rural to urban areas as people move in search of work (Pun 2005; H. Yan 2008; Nyíri 2010, 10–34). These new domestic human mobilities are paralleled by rapidly increasing numbers of people traveling outward for tourism, education, business, and migration: annual documented international departures soared from 3 million in 1990 to 130 million by 2017 (Zhongguo Wang 2012; Xinhua She 2018).

Concurrently with this exponential growth in human mobility, as Wanning Sun (2002) illustrates, increasingly deterritorialized media enable new forms of imaginative mobility and the formation of a pervasive transnational imagination and subjectivity, even among those who have not (yet) traveled abroad. The generation of urban dwellers born since 1990 has grown up in an era of near-ubiquitous English teaching in schools and at a time when imported media have become a pervasive part of everyday life through online distribution. This affords China's current generation of youth—the nation's first digital natives (Prensky 2001)—unprecedented opportunities to develop a transnational imaginary and to dream of mobile futures. Participants in this study grew up surrounded by an omnipresent mediated imaginary of "overseas" (国外

guowai), supporting their class-bound capacity to aspire to transnational mobility (Appadurai 2004) and naturalizing educational travel as both a normal part of youth and a step toward membership in a globally extensive, transnationally mobile developed-world community (Fong 2011; Baas 2012; Robertson, Harris, and Baldassar 2018).

In broad terms, for the families supporting their children's study abroad, educational mobility functions as a transnational strategy to enhance human capital and thereby consolidate and reproduce middle-class identity and privilege. However, when Chinese students are living in Western cities, the question of their privilege becomes more complex. Students' privileged class status tends to be undercut by their racialization as Chinese: a national-racial identity more likely to be a liability than an advantage vis-à-vis self-advancement abroad. When they are corralled into underpaid, low-status jobs in Australia, Chinese students and graduates, like the Indian IT professionals in Germany studied by Sareeta Amrute, are both "nonwhite migrant workers . . . *and* upwardly mobile, middle-class subjects" (2016, 2). As well as illustrating the general point that "the impact of individuals' multiple identities is not always mutually reinforcing" (Ho 2020, 70), such complexity within the students' middle-class identity underlines the specific significance of geography for the production—and destabilization—of social privilege. Even in an era of global capitalism and ubiquitous human mobilities, *where you are* continues to matter, materially and intensely, for *who you can be.*

Making Gendered Subjects: Frameworks in Flux

One of this book's starting points is the claim that the subjectivity of China's post-1990 generation of middle-class women is conditioned by multiple historically specific, competing, and sometimes contradictory understandings of what a woman is, what being a woman means, and how one should practice this form of gendered identity. As a result of the multiplicity and fragmentation of the discursive field surrounding femininity in China today, this is the case even before these women leave the country and potentially find their understandings complicated further by experiences abroad. In the following, I delineate some of the main discursive frameworks that may condition these young women's experiences of gendered subjectivity. No single framework can provide a definitive answer about what femininity is or means; instead, it is precisely the gaps and the tensions between them that are most definitive of this generation's experiences of their own gendered situation.

The first framework is a neoliberal-style discourse of enterprising selfhood and competitive self-advancement that has arisen alongside economic liberalization, the end of the "iron rice-bowl" system of state-assigned employment, and the emergence of consumer society. The extent to which China's authoritarian governance and market-socialist economy can usefully be described as neoliberal is the subject of ongoing debate (Harvey 2005; Sigley 2006; A. Ong 2007; Nonini 2008; Dirlik 2012; Osburg 2013; C. Lee 2014). But in the realm of culture, multiple studies of state and commercial media, advertising, work practices, and ordinary people's reflections on their situation point to the pervasiveness of a structure of feeling (Raymond Williams 1977) that posits the self-governing, rational choice-making, independent, and individualized subject as the author of his or her own fate in China's market society (Anagnost 2004; Rofel 2007; A. Ong and Zhang 2008; Y. Yan 2009, 2013; M. Hansen and Svarverud 2010; Hoffman 2010; Kleinman et al. 2011).[9] This idea of the "self-animating, self-staging subject" (A. Ong and Zhang 2008, 1), loyal to the party-state yet also motivated by private accumulation and individualized desire, is central to the emergent understanding of middle-class identity.[10] Such a privatized, self-governing subject is well suited to a time when the state is withdrawing from welfare provision, leaving the individual ever "freer" to navigate both the opportunities and the risks of a rapidly transforming economy and social structure (Thelle 2004; Li Zhang 2010; Ren 2013; T. Lewis, Martin, and Sun 2016).

The model of the enterprising subject whose raison d'être is self-advancement in the market economy has ushered in a new framework for understanding youth. Youth—for both women and men—is today popularly framed among middle-class urban dwellers as a time of "striving" (拚 pin) to obtain academic qualifications, training, and capacities for self-management that will increase one's chance of success in the fiercely competitive job market and hence secure the economic foundation for one's own and one's family's future (F. Martin 2014). The idealization of striving in the reforms era is underlined by sociologist Yunxiang Yan: "Driven by the urge for success, the individual strives by all possible means to make it out there, to deal with his [sic] anxieties and to strike a balance in the torment between conflicting moral visions and values, resulting in a noticeable change in China's moral landscape, that is, as I will call it, the ethics of the striving individual" (2013, 264–65).[11] As Anders Sybrandt Hansen (2015) persuasively argues, study abroad has in recent years become stitched into this script of youthful striving.

Given the increased opportunities available to singleton daughters of middle-class families, this vision of individualized, striving selfhood exercises an allure for young women as well as men, and women's self-focus and self-reliance have been explicitly promoted by the state (Croll 1995, 150–53; Beck and Beck-Gernsheim 2002, 54–84; Wu X. 2009). The popularization of the striving-subject ideal commonly sees middle-class singleton daughters encouraged just as strongly as their male peers to acquire the independent capacities, advanced skills, and academic credentials that will enable them to compete and thrive in the market economy (Fong 2002; Kajanus 2015).[12] As we glimpse in aspects of Yiruo's story, above, for many women in the current young generation, the aspiration toward independent self-fashioning underlies their motivation to undertake transnational educational ventures (Kim 2011; F. Martin 2014; Kajanus 2015, 37–44). The arguably neoliberal cast of these ventures is evident not simply in the broad sense that study abroad is usually a privately funded strategy aimed at enhancing the individual's competitive edge in global or national job markets, but even more explicitly in parents' and daughters' frequent description of study abroad as an opportunity for self-development (自我发展 *ziwo fazhan*) and the nurturing of individual independence (独立 *duli*) in a context where, socialist-era safety nets having been largely withdrawn, success is understood to hinge significantly on one's capacity for self-reliance (靠自己 *kao ziji*) (F. Liu 2008).

The metaphor that best distills postsocialist culture's valorization of the individualized, desiring, and striving subject is that of the dream (梦想 *mengxiang*), which saturates Chinese public culture today. Throughout the nation's shopping malls, airports, train stations, and mass mediascape, commercial advertising and self-improvement rhetoric accosts one at every turn with assertions of the importance of dreaming. Authoritative (generally masculine) voices relentlessly demand that one pursue a dream—to drive a luxury car, to realize one's potential, to see the world, to achieve a beautiful lifestyle. Even political discourse has been reconfigured around the dream trope, the old modernist preoccupation with national rejuvenation now repackaged in the metaphor best suited to current conditions (Z. Wang 2013; D. Lin 2017, 127–30). President Xi Jinping's Chinese dream narrative (中国梦 *Zhongguo meng*), first articulated in 2012, aims to harness the energies of individualized desire for the collective project of nation building (Xinhua Materials 2016). The ubiquitous propaganda slogan "Chinese dream, my dream" (中国梦 我的梦 *Zhongguo meng, wode meng*) directly translates the state project of national revival into personalized subjective aspiration.

Echoing this broad public cultural insistence on the imperative to dream, the rhetoric of educational mobility as involving a kind of dreaming was pervasive throughout this study. Participants and their parents frequently framed the aspirations they hoped overseas study would advance—to land a leadership role in an international company, to get an Australian PhD, to start an import-export business, to feel at home traveling the world—as intimately personal dreams. And, as can be seen in this list of examples, many of these dreams involved forms of transnational movement: of people, of knowledge, of money, and of goods. It seems that, for these young women, to dream is to dream of global mobility. Their persistent representations of transnational movement as a deeply held, intimate desire based on the dream of individual self-transformation provide part of the inspiration for this book's title.

NEOTRADITIONALIST FAMILIALISM

However, the story at the beginning of this chapter also illustrates an alternative discourse running counter to the ideal of the striving individual. In the conflict between Yiruo and her parents over the question of her marriage, we glimpse a different discourse based on neotraditionalist understandings of adult women's "naturally" marriage-and-family-oriented disposition. This highly influential (re)emergent discourse holds that it is normal, natural, and beneficial for women to get married and exchange self-focus for family focus by age thirty. It operates through public representations, including government campaigns and popular media, as well as through family and peer pressure (Rofel 1999; Hong Fincher 2014; Kajanus 2015). Some argue that after three decades during which the Maoist state line championed gender equality, the current prominence of essentialist constructions of women's gentle, nurturing, and family-centered nature indicates that gender relations have to an extent become retraditionalized in the post-Mao era (H. Evans 2002; Ji 2015, 2017; S. Sun and Chen 2015; J. You, Yi, and Chen 2016).[13] For example, in her influential Foucauldian analysis of transforming gender ideologies, feminist sociologist Wu Xiaoying (2009, 2010) observes that in the reforms era, the market discourse of individualized self-improvement has formed an alliance with a revitalized gender traditionalism that posits that women innately have lower levels of ability than men. The concept of natural differences is reinforced by commercial culture, where young, hyperfeminine beauty is eroticized and commodified across the fields of fashion, advertising, narrative media, sports, and cosmetic surgery (M. Zhang 2012; G. Chong 2013; Hua 2013; F. Liu 2014; Zurndorfer 2016; P. Ip 2018).

Linking this neotraditionalist discourse with the self-justifying actions of the post-Mao state, Lisa Rofel names the (re)naturalization of gender from the

1980s onward the "postsocialist allegory of modernity" (1999, 217–56). Across wide-ranging examples from employment policies and government rhetoric on family planning to popular media, Rofel traces a gendered allegory about the ills of Maoism, according to which "all along . . . women have merely wished to express their natural femininity in motherhood and wedded love while men have needed to find their rightful masculinity in economic exploits outside of the state sector, in virile sexual expression, and in the mastery of political power" (1999, 219). The state does not thereby cease interceding in social life but actively works to promote gender-role essentialism, representing itself as "enabling 'natural' social relationships to come forth from the repression of Maoism" (Rofel 1999, 219; see also Huang 2018, 1–13). The neotraditional-ist gender discourse provides ideological support for a number of significant structural changes either directly led or enabled by the state. These include the government's pressure on women to return to the family in times of rising urban unemployment (H. Evans 2002; Wu X. 2009; Song 2011), increasingly open gender discrimination by employers (Croll 1995, 117–24; Human Rights Watch 2018), a widening gender-wage gap (Cook and Dong 2011; World Economic Forum 2018, 63), and the intensifying concentration of capital in the hands of husbands at the expense of wives (Hong Fincher 2014).

In recent years, one of the clearest ways in which the state has naturalized gender neotraditionalism is in its popularization of the "leftover woman" (剩女 shengnü) stigma attaching to highly educated women who remain unmarried at the age of twenty-seven and over. Leta Hong Fincher (2014) argues that in endorsing the "leftover women" label and urging women's "timely" marriage, the All-China Women's Federation (妇联 Fulian) acted to further state goals in relation to population planning and maintenance of social stability. The state's promulgation of this chrononormative stigma responds to real demographic shifts (E. Freeman 2010). In urban China women's average age at first marriage has risen steadily since 1990. As Yong Cai and Wang Feng (2014, 104) show in their study of trends in age of first marriage between 1950 and 2005, across urban China increasing numbers of women remain unmarried into their late twenties; in Shanghai the last 5 percent of women to marry do so at about thirty, marking a historical high. "Delayed" marriage among urban women correlates positively with their level of education and consequent potential for economic independence (National Bureau of Statistics of China 2012, 26). Thanks to increased government investment, tertiary education became a mass phenomenon in China in the early 2000s, and around 2008 women's enroll-ment in higher education reached, then surpassed, parity with men's (Bai 2006; World Bank 2016). In this context increasing numbers of urban women resist marriage pressure and the patriarchal power it represents, delaying marriage or avoiding it altogether (Z. Zhang 2000; Gaetano 2014; Ji 2015; Y. Chow 2019; Hong Fincher 2018). The state responds with its own particular style of gendered chronobiopolitics by stigmatizing that choice in the name of protecting social stability (E. Freeman 2010).

Popular media regularly throw up reflections on and critiques of the leftover-women discourse (SK-II 2016; S. Cai 2019), and many middle-class young women—including the study participants—are openly and sharply critical of it. It remains, however, a shaping force keenly felt by virtually all young women, even if ultimately resisted. References to the concept emerged frequently during my fieldwork, including in mild anxieties expressed by some mothers that their daughters may run the risk of "getting left over" (剩 *sheng*) as a result of their educational attainments and in some participants' ambivalent jokes about this risk.

These anxieties and ambivalences illustrate one of this study's grounding contentions: that the coexistence of the discourse of striving selfhood with the neotraditionalist gender discourse means that the post-1990 generation of women become caught in an unavoidable contradiction as they move through their twenties (Hoffman 2010, 121–41; Fong et al. 2012; J. Wu 2012; Gaetano 2014; F. Liu 2014; F. Martin 2014). As Anni Kajanus (2015, 90) neatly summarizes, while women *as daughters* are encouraged to pursue overseas study, *as wives and mothers* they are expected to focus on family care work instead. Moreover, the *anticipation* of women's (presumptively inevitable) marriage tends to frame their experiences of youth in multiple ways, including family pressure to find a fiancé (sometimes beginning as soon as their early twenties) and the shaping of educational and career choices by women's anticipated family care responsibilities postmarriage.[14] For the young, mobile women of Yiruo's generation, the imperatives of individualized striving selfhood and of neotraditionalist familialism stand in fundamental conflict, so that their self-understandings and life plans are beset at a basic level by a gendered contradiction. One of the central questions this book investigates is how time spent studying abroad affects their negotiation of this contradiction.

DAUGHTERLY FILIALITY

But Yiruo's parents' insistence on the importance of timely marriage is not the only factor complicating her identification with the ideal of striving selfhood. While on the one hand Yiruo hopes to live a life of global mobility, pursue academic excellence and professional success, and remain true to her counternormative sex-gender identity, on the other hand the apparent individualism of these aspirations is tempered by her desire to carry out a filial (孝 *xiao*) duty toward her parents by living with them overseas in the future and providing for them financially. In suggesting this, Yiruo is following a broader trend in the single-child generations whereby daughters, both rural and urban, increasingly shoulder the filial responsibilities of elderly parent care that were traditionally the province of sons (Zhan and Montgomery 2003; Fong 2004b, 130–15; Shi 2009; M. Hansen and Pang 2010; Kajanus 2015, 29–33; Ji 2017; Hong Zhang 2017). This is linked with contemporary women's independent earning capacities, simple necessity in sonless single-child families at a time when the state has retreated from elderly care, and parents' increasing valorization of a filial bond based on an emotional attachment between parents and child rather than simple moral duty—a type of attachment that is popularly assumed to be stronger with daughters than with sons (Shi 2009; Kajanus 2015, 33). Many of the young women I got to know in the course of this study expressed a similar wish to bring their parents abroad to care for them in their old age (养老 *yanglao*). Other expressions of affective filiality also arose frequently. Many participants expressed a strong sense of duty to repay their parents for their financial and emotional investments in their upbringing and expensive overseas education, for example, by earning enough to buy their parents luxury gifts and support them financially in their elderly years or by eventually moving back to China to care for them personally.

To some extent, the habitus of daughterly filiality interrupts the neoliberal paradigm of striving selfhood insofar as it complicates that model's basis in individualized self-interest. Young, mobile women like Yiruo and her contemporaries may simultaneously espouse a version of the self-enterprising model and complicate that model by understanding themselves as morally and emotionally bound to a hierarchical family collective and family interests.[15] Moreover, paradoxically, it is precisely such women's capacity to earn and control their own income independently that *enables* them to enact such new (feminized) forms of filiality. In this sense, the daughterly filiality of these middle-class women blurs the boundaries between what might initially seem like contradictory models of the autonomous enterprising self and "traditional" familial ethics.

MASCULINE *GUANXI*

One bright late-winter afternoon a couple of years after our first meeting, I was chatting with Yiruo outside a campus library in Melbourne while she took a break from studying. When I asked about her current plans for after graduation, she said her father had mentioned that his former classmate who ran a construction firm in her hometown could arrange a job for her if she wanted it. Yiruo wasn't very keen on this idea, since she hoped to remain in Australia for postgraduate study and possibly immigration, but job offers like this from an extended family member or associate of the family—usually male—were quite common for young women who had studied abroad, and some did land jobs this way. Such opportunities, referred to colloquially as *pin die* (拼爹, leaning on dad), are based on *guanxi* (关系): the particularist, instrumental influence networks that underlie many aspects of social life in contemporary China across state, commercial, and personal domains and across scales from multimillion-dollar business deals and the tendering of government contracts right down to ordinary people's negotiations to secure a child's place in a particular teacher's class or obtain other minor everyday benefits.

Some anthropologists have argued that the prevalence of *guanxi* practices among government and business elites in China evidences a fundamentally distinct structuration of governance and economy that precludes understanding the system as simply neoliberal. Donald M. Nonini (2008), for example, argues that China in the reforms era is characterized by an oligarchic state and party and the rise of a new cadre-capitalist class whose operations rely on *guanxi* ties that blur the distinction between state and market. For Nonini, the forms of subjectivity engendered by this situation cannot be described as neoliberal, with all of the individualist connotations that brings, but rather are "constructed around contextual and relational definitions of the self within a pre-existing society distinguished by status differences and . . . around a fluidity between the self and others" (2008, 168; see also Nonini and Ong 1997; A. Ong 2006, 219–39; 2008). John Osburg concurs, finding that post-Mao China does not instantiate neoliberal capitalism; rather, the end of the Maoist system "created the space for *guanxi* practices to evolve and proliferate, and the moral economy specific to *guanxi* has . . . served as an ethical counterweight to market individualism" (2013, 184–86).

In cases where graduate students rely on *guanxi* to land a job, it is not usually the type of elite-level *guanxi* studied by Osburg, who focuses on the nexus between superrich entrepreneurs and high-level government officials. Instead, it generally takes more middling forms, as when Yiruo's father's classmate offered her a job in his firm. Nonetheless, these middling forms of *guanxi* practice, like the more elite forms, still trouble some of the central tenets of neoliberal ideology as it is usually understood in Euro-American contexts, particularly meritocracy, individualism, and the subjugation of social life by market norms. Like elite forms of *guanxi*, too, they are also often markedly masculine in character, based largely on networks connecting fathers or other elder male relatives with male associates.

Thus, somewhat like daughterly filiality, for young middle-class women, *guanxi* practices overlap the seemingly contradictory models of the autonomous striving self and patriarchal familialism and trouble their opposition. When *guanxi* is leveraged to help female graduates find employment, this *both* relies on masculine, hierarchical familial and social networks *and* advances young women's independent professional careers, with all the opportunities for female individualization and posttraditional gender practice that entails.[16]

~

My aim in delineating these frameworks has been to give some sense of the heterogeneity and internal contradiction of the conceptual resources available to middle-class urban women in understanding their gendered situation. Sometimes these plural frameworks work against each other so that one may be exploited tactically to undercut another: for example, the autonomous, enterprising self as a riposte to neotraditionalist, familial femininity—seeing oneself as a proud career woman resisting pressures to become a subordinated daughter-in-law, wife, or mother. At other times, apparently contradictory discourses paradoxically reinforce one another, as with daughterly filiality facilitated by women's economic independence, or women's professional career building enabled by paternal *guanxi* (see also Kajanus 2015, 8–9). Nor do these four basic frameworks by any means exhaust the field of influences on how young women can understand their gendered situation. My naming of them is heuristic: to make the simple point that the available symbolic structures are plural and in tension rather than monolithic.

Transnational Education Assemblage

The dramatic increases over the past two decades in the outflow of students from China and the inflow of international students to Australia result from the commercialization of education in both nations (S. Liu 2020). Rising numbers of Chinese students going abroad are linked with an understanding among China's middle classes that a privately funded overseas degree is an educational commodity that facilitates the accumulation of cultural and mobility capitals. In the case of Australia, the development of education as what is widely characterized as an "export industry" results from declining government funding for universities. While between 1988 and 2014 the number of domestic students attending university more than doubled to over a million (Norton and Cakitaki 2016), from 1994 to 2004 public funding of universities fell by 27 percent per student (Marginson 2007), and by 2014 government contributions made up less than 40 percent of universities' revenue: the sixth lowest of all nations in the Organisation for Economic Co-operation and Development (OECD 2017, 193). Alongside the introduction of university fees for domestic students in the late 1980s, the marketing of degrees to international students, largely from Asia, has been a key strategy to fill this funding shortfall (Welch 2002; Ramia, Marginson, and Sawir 2013, 59–71). Governments have encouraged universities' targeting of international markets by providing pathways for students to convert to skilled-migrant visas postgraduation (Robertson 2013). Under these conditions, international student numbers have increased dramatically since the early 1990s, recording double-digit annual growth in recent years (Australian Department of Education and Training, International Research and Analysis Unit 2017c, 2018). From 2004 to 2014, the number of places for international students rose by over 40 percent. In the same period, the revenue to universities from the fees they paid—on average three times those charged to domestic students—increased by around 75 percent (Universities Australia 2015, 14; OECD 2017, 293; Universities Australia 2018; H. Ferguson and Sherrell 2019). By 2017 international fee income accounted for over 23 percent of Australian public universities' revenue, making it their single largest nongovernment revenue source (Norton and Cherastidtham 2018, 45). Australia has been recognized as having "the most organized and aggressive [international] recruitment and marketing strategy" for its universities in the world (Brooks and Waters 2011, 117) and is the world's third-largest destination country for international students after the United States and the United Kingdom (OECD 2017, 287).[17] In 2016, during the middle years of this study, the average proportion of international students in Australian universities was over 21 percent, and a third of universities had more than 25 percent international students (Australian Department of Education and Training, International Research and Analysis Unit 2017b). This places the concentration of international students in Australian universities at one of the highest levels among OECD countries (OECD 2017, 286). For many successive years, mirroring a global trend, students from China have composed the largest group studying in Australian higher education (over 38 percent in 2019), more than double the size of the second-largest group, from India (H. Ferguson and Sherrell 2019). Most Chinese students study in the big east coast cities; Melbourne, this study's primary field site, is their second-largest host city, after Sydney (Australian Department of Education and Training 2017c).

The regional aid model on which Australia's international education policy was based before the mid-1980s has thus been replaced by a market approach that has seen international student numbers and fee levels deregulated, "enabling universities to run international education as an expansionary capitalist business"

(Ramia, Marginson, and Sawir 2013, 60). As Simon Marginson and Mark Considine (2000, 4) argue, in the era of the enterprise university, Australian education institutions are driven by a "frankly commercial and entrepreneurial spirit" to compete for private income from international student markets, with the students themselves conceptualized essentially as consumers (see also Marginson et al. 2010; Kell and Vogl 2012). The language in which international education is couched by Australian governments is that of international trade. In a typical example, the Department of Education and Training reported triumphantly that activity linked with international education contributed $28 billion to the national economy in the 2016–17 financial year, making education the nation's third-largest export after iron ore and coal (Australian Department of Education and Training 2017).[18]

The serendipitous fit between ever-intensifying educational demand from China's middle classes and an Australian higher education sector characterized by increasing costs, decreasing public funding, and government support for privatization and internationalization has produced a vigorous transnational education vector linking the two countries. Indeed, extremely high concentrations of Chinese international students in some courses—participants and university staff report that in some master's courses in the business and finance fields, such students account for over 80 percent of enrollments—lead some to feel that Australian universities seem like extensions of the Chinese education system. Certain courses are designed from the outset to target these students and are direct-marketed to them by commercial education agents in China who have cooperative business arrangements with Australian universities. The Australian university classroom may feel at such times like a kind of floating, geoculturally ambiguous space: a node in a transnational education assemblage connected just as firmly to China as it is to Australia (figure I.2; Collins 2014).[19]

The social, political, and economic factors within China that have resulted in rising numbers of students studying in Australia have also increased their numbers in the United States, the United Kingdom, Canada, New Zealand, and other Western nations. While Chinese students have been studying in all of these countries since early in China's reforms era, across all of them the current cohorts differ from the much smaller numbers who studied abroad during the 1980s and 1990s in that they are wealthier and overwhelmingly funded by family rather than the state; are more likely to study business and management than earlier groups, who focused on science and technology; are younger overall, with more studying at the bachelor's degree level; and are increasingly dominated by women (C. Qin 2012, 196–200; Kajanus 2015, 54–61; L. Liu 2016b, 11–49). Although, during the period of this study, Australia was only

FIGURE I.2 Facebook meme portraying an Australian university as a Special Administrative Region of China, shared as a joke by a study participant, March 2018.

The Three Special Administrative Regions of China

Macau   Hong Kong   University of ▓▓▓▓▓

the third most popular destination for Chinese students after the United States and the United Kingdom, the proportion of Chinese students within the group of international students as a whole was and remains very similar in each country (Australian Department of Education and Training, International Research and Analysis Unit 2016), while the proportion of international students within Australia's tertiary student body is comparable to levels in the United Kingdom and significantly higher than those in the United States (OECD 2017, 286). To the extent that a broadly comparable situation exists or may develop in other Western study destinations beyond Australia, some of this study's findings may prove relevant to those contexts as well, although undoubtedly each country's (and city's) experience of educational transnationalization will also be somewhat geospecific.

Thinking beyond the Nation: Transmigration, Translocality, Liminality

To capture the pervasive transnational connections that mark students' everyday experiences, in this book I conceptualize Chinese international students in Australia as *student transmigrants*. I choose this term over other alternatives—*transient migrants*, *sojourners*, *international students*, or *student-migrants* (Robertson 2013; X. Zhao 2016; Gomes 2017; Tran and Gomes 2017)—for two reasons. On one hand, while studying in Australia, these students *are*, structurally, a type of migrant: they reside long-term in Australian cities and participate in urban social life; avail themselves of many national, state, and local services beyond education; work in local businesses; pay taxes; and in many cases ultimately become holders of Australian permanent residency or citizenship. Their residence in Australia may be transient, but it is not always or necessarily so. Recognizing them as a category of migrant brings into focus the significance of their presence in local communities while complicating traditional conceptualizations of migration-as-resettlement through attention to increasingly common practices of open-ended migration and flexible residence. On the other hand, these students also maintain links back to China and outward into the worldwide Chinese diaspora, reinforced by ubiquitous communicative connectivity through mobile technologies (Robertson 2013, 7; F. Martin and Rizvi 2014). The moment-to-moment transnational interconnections that characterize the experience of these mobile subjects resonate strongly with Nina Glick Schiller, Linda Basch, and Cristina Szanton Blanc's (1995) theorization of the transmigrant. In contrast to the traditional understanding of the immigrant as someone uprooted from one society and transplanted permanently into another, the transmigrant's experience is marked by "multiple and constant interconnections across international borders and . . . public identities [that] are configured in relationship to more than one nation-state. . . . They are not sojourners because they settle and become incorporated in the economy and political institutions, localities, and patterns of daily life of the country in which they reside. However, at the very same time, they are engaged elsewhere in the sense that they maintain connections, build institutions, conduct transactions, and influence local and national events in the countries from which they emigrated" (48). This conceptualization works well to illuminate the experience of the multiply connected student transmigrants who are the subject of this book.

Flowing from this recognition, a central argument of the book is that Chinese students produce the Australian city as a *translocality* and, more broadly, inhabit *translocal worlds*: topological geographies marked by the entanglement of near and distant locales (Amin 2002b). This argument draws on recent work in geography that advances the concept of translocality as a means of appreciating both the intensifying transborder connectedness of people's experiences of place and the persistent effects of geographic localities in everyday life (Appadurai 1996; Conradson and McKay 2007; Greiner and Sakdapolrak 2013). As Tim Oakes and Louisa Schein (2006) note, translocality provides a particularly apposite framework for understanding contemporary social life in (and beyond) an increasingly mobile China. Such an approach allows us to sidestep unhelpfully dichotomous thinking about place in globalization, for example, the opposition of the "space of flows" to the "space of places" (Castells 1996) or of global "non-place" to local authenticity (Augé 1995). Instead, translocality as a concept underlines the experiential interweaving of human and nonhuman mobilities with states of fixity, and of ubiquitous transnational connections with more grounded forms of geolocal experience. It also helpfully unsettles the primacy of the nation-state as a presumptive frame for analysis through an alternative focus on material links between specific localities such as cities or neighborhoods. Lives like Yiruo's, lived across geographies stretched between near and distant sites, may in turn produce translocal subjectivities: "the multiply-located senses of self amongst those who inhabit transnational social fields" (Conradson and McKay 2007, 168).

But exactly what difference does translocal experience make to one's sense of oneself in everyday experience? How might it reconfigure, for example, one's sense of gendered subjectivity in the present and of the gendered time of one's future life course? At the same time as I argue that participants' experience abroad produces and takes place in translocal space, I also propose that while studying overseas, these young women inhabit *liminal time*. In developing this analysis, I draw on Saulo B. Cwerner's (2001) work on the temporal dimensions of migration. In his typology of experiences of time among Brazilian immigrants in London, Cwerner describes liminal time as characteristic of transitional stages of migration, noting that such a temporality may be a central feature of the experience of migrants who are, or perceive themselves to be, temporary. Such migrants' "condition is suffused with liminality. They are 'betwixt and between' all the recognized points in the space-time of structural classification" (27). For Cwerner, liminal temporality is marked by indecision, disorientation, and often significant mental stress as migrants navigate between discordant life-course regimes in home and host societies—and this was certainly often the case with participants in this study. But, equally important, liminality also "creates a time 'out of the ordinary,' when anything can happen. The old rules do not apply, while the new ones are still to be internalized" (27). In the chapters that follow, I explore how time abroad functions as a liminal time for these mobile young women, in which they reconfigure the meanings of youth, gender, intimacy, and the life course by rescripting and sometimes contesting gendered norms that are dominant within China.

~

This book addresses emergent cultural phenomena conditioned by far-reaching in-process transformations in the character of *nation, gender,* and *space*. The educational transmigrants who are the book's focus make their journeys in a world in which the Chinese nation is deterritorializing and self-globalizing, available discourses of femininity are multiplying and fragmenting, and space and place are being remade on a translocal and topological model. By asking how it feels for young Chinese women to live and move under these volatile conditions, the book invites new conversations among China studies, gender studies, and studies of human mobility in globalization.

In the context of China's expanding global influence and increasing outward human mobilities, *Dreams of Flight* contributes to studies of Chinese transnationalism (A. Ong and Nonini 1997; A. Ong 1999) by exploring what it is like to participate in the forms of middle-class movement that characterize a globalizing China (Conradson and Latham 2005a). Attending to deterritorialized articulations of ethnonational identity by Chinese citizens abroad, the book enriches the study of Chineseness beyond the frame of the nation (Ang 2001; Shih 2007, 2011). And while Western media have tended in recent years to depict China's globalization as simply the transnational extension of state and party influence, this study unsettles totalizing views of nationhood—whether promulgated by the Chinese state itself or by its critics abroad (Mankekar 2015). It reminds us that China is not just an abstract political entity but is composed of people and their embodied experiences of place, mobility, gender, and subjectivity.

This emphasis aligns the book with materialist studies of globalization as a series of concrete social processes rather than a network of frictionless flows (Bude and Dürrschmidt 2010). In conversation with the mobilities turn in social research (Sheller and Urry 2006), the book unpacks in empirical detail the dialectics of mobility and containment—gendered, racialized, spatial, academic, and social—that shape educational transmigrants' experience, and pays attention to how these women's practices of personal, imaginative, and mediated mobility and immobility reconfigure place as translocality. Thus, while *mobilizing China* beyond the nation's geographic borders, this study simultaneously *grounds the global* through focused attention to people's embodied and subjective experiences of both locality and movement. By taking a feminist ethnographic approach that centers young women's everyday lives, the book offers a critical alternative to the masculinism and abstraction of both state discourses of nationhood and macrotheories of globalization (Dána-Ain Davis and Craven 2016). At the broadest level, this book illuminates how *gender shapes mobility* and how *mobility shapes gender*, demonstrating the inextricable entanglement of the two for Chinese student transmigrants and furthering the evolving conversation between gender studies and mobility studies (Hanson 2010; Penttinen and Kynsilehto 2017; F. Martin and Dragojlovic 2019).

Moving Subjects: Approach and Methods

As discussed earlier, the younger generations in China's middle classes draw on multiple discourses to understand and enact gender. But in addition to such shared symbolic structures, ethnography also throws up affective experiences that are far more idiosyncratic and less amenable to codification. These are highly contingent aspects of the microlevel of everyday experience that proponents of affective ethnography suggest occur at a pre- or noncognitive level, in excess of representation (Thrift 2008; Overell 2014). To take seriously the place of affect in ethnographic practice is to keep in mind the corporeality and multisensoriality of experience, both that of research participants and that shared between researcher and participants in the ethnographic encounter (Pink 2015); to pay attention to the nonverbal traffic of feeling between human (and nonhuman) bodies beyond conscious will and intentionality (Knudsen and Stage 2015); and to be alive to visceral forces other than conscious knowing (Seigworth and Gregg 2010). In Kathleen Stewart's feeling words, the "ordinary affects" that ethnography generates and uncovers are "more directly compelling than ideologies, as well as more fractious, multiplicitous, and unpredictable than symbolic meanings" (2007, 3). Moreover, "models of thinking that slide over the live surface of difference at work in the ordinary to bottom-line arguments about 'bigger' structures and underlying causes obscure the ways in which a reeling present is composed out of heterogeneous and noncoherent singularities" (4). Ordinary affects of the kind Stewart refers to here are another referent for the "dreams" in the book's title. As already discussed, on one hand, the trope of the dream connects with a structure of feeling particular to the current era. The idea of a person who "has a dream" conjures a visionary, desiring, striving subject defined by independence, aspiration, individualism, and upward and outward mobility: such dreams are the imaginative fuel of the mobile, enterprising self that takes center stage in the reforms era. On the other hand, I also intend the "dreams" of the book's title to refer to the far less structured realm of affective experience; the strange singularities of the inner worlds of sense and consciousness that make up the present from moment to moment. *Singularity* in this sense does not stand in opposition to shared cultural practices but rather designates an ineffable kernel of subjective experience—whether individual or collective—that resists capture by the generalizing abstractions of theory. Nor does singularity simply mean particularity or specificity; as Dipesh Chakrabarty reminds us, "The very conception of the 'specific' . . . belongs to the structure of a general that necessarily occludes our view of the singular. . . . 'Singularity' . . . comes into being when we look on things in such a way as not to see them as 'particular' expressions of that which is general" (1997, 42–43). The dreams on which this book focuses are in this sense double: at once the aspirational dreams consciously pursued through educational mobility and the unreflexive, half-sensed daydreams that comprise people's singular affective experiences of mobility as it is lived.

In the chapters that follow, while I do not attempt to adhere to a purely or rigorously affective method, I try to take the affective dimensions of social and subjective experience into account in order, at least, to give some sense of how educational mobility *feels*. To do this, I go beyond transcribing participants' words and describing their everyday practices, then analyzing these with reference to symbolic frameworks. I also include graphic and creative material meant to capture something of the experiential texture of these mobile women's singular experiences, as well as my own experiences while working with them. These include photos, maps, and social media posts created by participants in which they represent their worlds in ways that exceed verbal description and I hope may capture, to varying degrees, an atmosphere, a feeling, and a sense of the always ongoing, always in-motion "specificity of present being" that exceeds the fixity of symbolic structures (Raymond Williams 1977, 128). As in this introduction, many of the chapters include segments of my own nonanalytical writing about particular encounters and stories, in which I include sensory and affective elements—recollections of smell, taste, temperature, qualities of light and sound, emotional atmosphere—to augment the theorized analysis with some sense, however shadowy, of the embodied human experience that is the live core of the research.

~

This book draws on a multisite ethnographic study carried out with a core participant group of fifty Chinese women students between 2012 and 2020 across China and Australia. First, I conducted a pilot study in Melbourne in 2012 with in-depth, semistructured interviews of fifteen female undergraduate and master's degree students. This provided the basis for the main study, to which I was able to dedicate myself full-time between 2015 and 2020 thanks to funding from the Australian Research Council. Over the years of the main study, I remained in contact with seven of the pilot-study participants; reinterviewed six of them in Melbourne, Sydney, and Hong Kong; and added one of them to the core group.

In 2015, with the assistance of five Australian universities, three Chinese universities, and four Chinese education agencies, I sent out a call for participants via WeChat and email to Chinese students about to commence study in Melbourne. In mid-2015 I traveled to China for four weeks and conducted initial interviews with thirty commencing students and ten of their families in Shanghai, Guangzhou, Hefei, Kaifeng, and Shenyang. These thirty students became part of the study's core participant group. During the same trip, I also attended predeparture briefings for students run by Australian universities and Chinese education agents and gave presentations about life in Melbourne at two Chinese universities to large cohorts of students soon to depart on joint-program courses. I also conducted focus-group interviews with thirty female undergraduates at Shanghai University to get a sense of how domestic students thought about gender and educational mobility, as well as an understanding of their reasons for *not* studying abroad (overwhelmingly economic). I remained in contact with this group throughout the years of the study via a WeChat group and reinterviewed some of them on annual return trips to China. They provided an informal comparison group to the mobile students who are the main focus of the study.

Back in Melbourne in late 2015, I gathered a further twenty core participants who had already commenced studies in five universities at the (pre-undergraduate) foundation, undergraduate, or master's degree level. Over the next four years, I met regularly and often with the core group of fifty in large groups, small groups, and individually. In addition to conducting periodic recorded interviews, I hung out with participants and their friends, housemates, boyfriends, classmates, and visiting parents at activities organized by them and met them periodically for chats over coffee or meals, or at home visits. With the help of the project research assistant, Can Qin, I organized a series of eleven large-group activities to allow further participant observation, create a sense of group cohesion, and increase the group's identification with the project. These included weekend day trips to scenic spots, film screenings, barbecues, community festivals, public events, gatherings at my place, and discussions and other research activities conducted at annual meetings over a pub lunch. Between 2015 and 2019, I also maintained virtually daily contact with the group via WeChat, both in a dedicated chat group for the study and via private messaging and our shared Moments feeds (similar to a Facebook wall). Inevitably, with some participants I established a strong rapport and met and communicated with them frequently, sometimes weekly or more; with others, interactions were less frequent, perhaps once every six or nine months.[20]

When participants graduated from their courses, I remained in touch with them via social media. Between 2018 and 2019, I traveled to interview the participants postgraduation, both to Sydney and Canberra, where some were undertaking further study, and to various cities in China, where some had returned to work. On regular trips to China each year between 2015 and 2018, I also conducted interviews with a number of additional female graduates from Australian universities who had returned to China to work, and with professionals working in the international education industry. I also kept in touch with those participants who remained in Australia to work after graduation and spoke with them about their postgraduation experiences. My analyses are contextually enriched by my wider social involvement with Melbourne's diasporic Chinese communities and by my experiences teaching and supervising increasing numbers of students from China in Australian universities over the past twenty years.

Organization of the Book

Chapter 1 asks why studying abroad should be such a common aspiration for Chinese women. Drawing on initial interviews with study participants and their family members, it explores in detail the gendered risks that young women and their mothers hoped to mitigate through the daughters' transnational study. These include gendered bias in China's professional labor markets and the limitation of opportunities for personal and professional development by women's too-early corralling into marriage. Through this discussion, this chapter lays out the cultural logic underlying young Chinese women's "dreams of flight" from gendered disadvantage through transnational education. I conclude, however, with a counterstory intended to complicate a simplistic understanding of international student motivation based on an instrumentalist model of rational, agential choice making.

Chapter 2 is the first of three chapters focusing on participants' sociospatial practices in Australia. Introducing this study's primary field site, it considers participants' imagination of the city of Melbourne pre-arrival, their practices of the city postarrival, and the ways in which the city's sub/urban architectures shaped their habitation. I introduce what I call the *expatriate microworld* of Chinese student sociality in Melbourne and contextualize this with reference to students' wider sociospatial exclusion. Aiming to convey a sense of the complexly variegated experiential textures, affective ambiences, and subjective meanings of participants' sub/urban lifeworlds, the chapter shows how, for participants, Melbourne was both a translocality—a place constituted by the everyday intertwining of near and far locations—and an environment that interpreted their bodies in racialized and gendered terms. In these ways, the chapter demonstrates Melbourne's dual character as both a place of self-extension and (trans)local belonging and a site of social encapsulation and exclusion for these student transmigrants.

Chapter 3 explores how participants' uses of mobile social media decisively shaped their experiences of Melbourne. I consider how translocal media connections produced the city and what kind of place(s) and subjectivities emerged from this mediatization. Extending chapter 2's discussion of the tension between encapsulation and extension in participants' sub/urban placemaking, chapter 3 analyzes the operations of ethnicization, racialization, and class in participants' media practices in the superdiverse city. Focusing on local WeChat public accounts, it explores the tension between extension and encapsulation that is expressed in the contrast between, on one hand, lifestyle and leisure accounts' capacity to facilitate spatial extension by mapping ways into the city through consumption and, on the other, popular tabloid news accounts' tendency to cocoon students in a defensive capsule based on the essentialization of Chinese ethnicity and the racialization of classed Others, including "Africans" and "refugees."

Following the previous two chapters' discussions of how sociospatial practices of habitation and communication produce the translocal city, chapter 4 considers students' work practices through analysis of their verbal and photographic narratives. I analyze two types of feminized labor: underpaid casual waitressing work (打工 *da gong*) in Chinese-run restaurants and the microentrepreneurial activity of parallel trading (代购 *daigou*), a type of informal e-commerce in which individuals buy local goods to on-sell to customers in China via social media. I show how participants' restaurant work linked them to fixed, localized, diasporic employment networks, while their e-trading connected them to mobile, transnational, digitally mediated trade networks. Demonstrating that e-trading is often a response to students' racialized exclusion from more desirable types of local employment, the chapter develops the concept of feminine network capital to name the form of value produced through e-trading as a "weak," tactical form of transnational networking, in distinction to network capital's well-documented "strong" and strategic (masculine) forms.

Chapter 5 marks a shift from a focus on the external realm of participants' sociospatial practices (chapters 2–4) toward a stronger emphasis on the internal world of their affective and subjective attachments (chapters 5–7). It focuses on overseas study as a liminal time during which, as a result of distancing from familial and social surveillance at home, young Chinese women may reconfigure the meanings of feminine gender, life course, and sexuality. In particular, the chapter draws on participants' stories to work through three potentials of this liminal time: the creation of new forms of intimate isolation, the opening up of queer possibilities, and the scrambling of patriarchal power coordinates within families. But the examples discussed suggest that, ultimately, the tensions of gendered life-course regulation tended to be reconfigured, rather than resolved, in the liminal "time out" that educational mobility afforded.

China is home to one of the world's fastest-growing Christian populations, and some Christian churches in Western nations, cognizant of this fact, actively target international students for religious conversion. Chapter 6 explores participants' experiences of religion in Australia. It proposes that Christian churches' provision of acculturation and welfare services to Chinese international students is a function both of students' broader social exclusion and of the effective outsourcing of these services by universities and governments in the wider context of the sacralization of social services in the postwelfare state. The chapter pays special attention to the gendered vulnerabilities of female students abroad, which may heighten their need for social support and hence the potential for them to turn to evangelical churches in the absence of effective alternatives. This chapter also tries to illustrate the affective pull of spiritual practice, which tends to interrupt the secular rationality of scholarly analysis.

Chapter 7 explores national feeling as a third affective domain. The post-1990 generation has come of age in a time of contradictory influences in this regard. On the one hand, a transnational imaginary is increasingly available to them. On the other hand, since the early 1990s, the party-state has enforced a patriotic education curriculum that inculcates Chinese nationalism. In this context, this chapter asks how national feeling manifests in this generation's physical and digital mobilities beyond China's national territory. Seeking to complicate influential media caricatures of Chinese students' blind nationalism, I delineate two key logics that I argue are central to these students' national structure of feeling: a performative ethics of national representation and a developmentalist narrative of nationhood. I draw on fieldwork and interviews to analyze the gendered dimensions of this national structure of feeling, especially in the dominant metaphor of China as motherland. The chapter's final section explores changes in aspects of participants' orientations toward China during their years abroad.

Chapter 8 draws on material from the final years of the study to consider participants' postgraduation experiences seeking professional employment in Australia and China and the subjective (re)orientations that they felt several years of transnational education had engendered in them. After graduation, participants overwhelmingly remained geographically mobile, professionally oriented, and unmarried into their late twenties. This chapter explores how international education enabled the emergence of these shared attributes and shaped participants' understandings of themselves vis-à-vis mobility, work, and a gendered life course. In particular, returning to one of the book's central inquiries, I detail how overseas study appeared to strengthen participants' identification with the neoliberal ideal of enterprising selfhood while weakening their attachment to neotraditional femininity. Even those few participants who actively disidentified with the neoliberal-style self-advancement script, I show, tended still to feel that study abroad had made them more critical of neotraditional femininity and more attached to a mobile imaginary.

The conclusion summarizes findings on how feminine gender and educational mobility shaped each other in the experiences of study participants and offers some ruminations on the study's conceptual and methodological implications by interrogating the interrelationships among some key operations. I consider how we might understand the relationship between subjective neoliberalization and gender detraditionalization, underlining the class-bound character of that relation. I elaborate on the study's ramifications for thinking through the relationship between gender and globalization and for understanding how emplaced experiences of mobility speak to theorizations of large-scale transnational processes. This opens out into a broader methodological reflection on the tense relation between the macroscale focus of social theory and ethnography's more microscale preoccupations. The chapter ends with a consideration of the study's implications for our understanding of "Chinese international students" as a category in Western higher education, and a closing note on the historical specificity of this study in light of the emergent viral challenge to a world order based on neoliberal globalization and mobilities.

1. BEFORE STUDY
Dreams of Flight

*

[Studying overseas] has been a dream since I was in my undergraduate studies. Sometimes I just felt like going and giving it a try. Because otherwise . . . in China, the traditional view is that girls, when they get to this age, should settle down. Work, get married, whatever. I felt that if I didn't make this decision right now, . . . I might never be able to do it. (Xiaofen, 24, Zhejiang)

*

Xiaofen offered these reflections on her long-held dream of overseas study during our first interview, just two weeks after she arrived in Melbourne to undertake a master's degree in managerial accounting. She had already worked for two years in her home city for one of the international Big Four accounting firms and said she wanted to study abroad more as a personal challenge than for any concrete advantage it would confer on her professionally. Her reflections draw on the concept of the dream in the first of the two senses discussed in this book's introduction: as an aspiration, fuel for the self-developmental quest of the striving individual. Xiaofen's statement also sets up a series of oppositions: moving abroad for study versus settling down at home; future-oriented dreaming versus backward-looking tradition. The logic underlying her evaluation of her situation is gendered and temporal: it is girls who are encouraged to settle down and get married, and they are encouraged to do so at a certain age. For twenty-four-year-old Xiaofen, this lent a sense of now-or-never to her Australian study venture, highlighting the temporal limits that feminine gender places on the potential to dream.

This chapter addresses the question of why studying abroad should be such a common dream for Chinese women like Xiaofen. In spite of the sex-ratio skewing of the youth population in China toward males, some 60 percent of those who leave China for study, and over half those who go to Australia to attend university, are women (Australian Department of Education and

Training, International Research and Analysis Unit, private communication, February 23, 2016; *Renmin Ribao* 2016). This means that Chinese women are about 30 percent more likely to study abroad than Chinese men. Why should this be? Drawing on my initial interviews with study participants and their family members, either before participants left China or soon after their arrival in Australia, this chapter explores two answers to this question. The interviews demonstrate, first, that for female students and their mothers, transnational study ventures may be partly a pragmatic response to gender bias in China's professional labor market. In this context, it is hoped that international educational qualifications will enhance female job seekers' competitiveness. Second, some young women also voice a broader concern about life-choice restriction as a result of neotraditionalist familialism's deep influence on gendered life scripts (see the introduction). Women like Xiaofen frame international education as an opportunity for mobile self-fashioning as an alternative to the neotraditionalism of the standard feminine life trajectory. The dream of transnational movement and self-advancement becomes a form of tactical resistance to the social pressures on twenty-something women to settle down into a normative, family-focused identity. The chapter begins with a brief discussion of the general middle-class anxieties that parents and students hoped study abroad could address. It then considers the two main themes in participants' framing of transnational education's desired function vis-à-vis gender—as mitigating gendered labor market risks and as offering an opportunity for mobile self-fashioning—before ending with a counterstory that underlines the limitations of framing human mobilities as the result of rational choices and the agential pursuit of dreams.

Transnational Education and the Anxious Middle Classes

The urban middle classes from which children are sent abroad for study are keenly alert to the precarity of their own social and economic position in the context of an uncertain economy and property market, the erosion of socialist-era safety nets, and their unprotected private wealth (Li Zhang 2010, 8–9). Members of these classes also worry about maintaining their social status through academic capital in the face of China's hypercompetitive secondary education system (Donald and Zheng 2008; F. Liu 2008), and keeping up their basic physical and mental health while dealing with chronic overwork, environmental pollution, and food insecurity (Zhu and Zhu 2017).[1]

My interviews with students and their families predeparture clearly illustrated these anxieties. Many participants explained study abroad as a strategy to maximize educational and hence economic opportunities while hedging against a variety of risks they perceived as likely to affect their future lives. These included risks common across genders, like downward social mobility as a result of poor performance in China's university entrance exams, environmental and industrial risks, and risks to psychological health and well-being resulting from highly pressurized education and work settings. Environmental risks within China—especially air pollution and food contamination—were frequently mentioned by participants in the context of their long-term consideration of possibly caring for elderly parents and/or future children in Australia, if they emigrated after graduation. The clean-and-green Australian brand also connoted a relaxed, easygoing, low-stress life that contrasted markedly with what participants perceived as the stressful, exhausting, and competitive character of work life in China. Typical statements include the following:

> [I want to be] happy, I guess. . . . I mean, in China life is very high-pressure, and you can't do the things you like to do. I really like the lifestyle here. For example, the shops all close at five or six p.m., and everyone gets to spend more time with their family. (Jiaying, 21, Hunan)

> I feel my life here is very laid-back and ordinary; very suited to an unambitious person like me [*laughs*]. Because I don't really want to get ahead, and I don't really like being overbusy with things day in, day out, rushing here and there. I prefer a slower pace. (Xinling, 19, Zhejiang)

The perception of Australia as a peaceful haven also articulated, at times, with gendered considerations of its suitability as a study destination for daughters in particular. Mothers were especially unwilling to let their daughters live alone in high-pressure, "dangerous" American cities: low-stress, low-crime Australia provided a reassuringly safe alternative, they felt. Some education agents explicitly played up the gendered appropriateness of Australia as a study destination. For example, Shihong, a twenty-year-old from Henan, recalled:

> The agent said . . . the main destinations for overseas study are America and Australia, and he said that for girls, it's safer to go to Australia. . . . He said it's more suitable for girls. And he said the competition [for work] is too exhausting in America. For girls, it's better just to lead a peaceful, stable life.

In all of these instances, life in Australia, both during the years of study and in a potential postmigration future, is framed as an antidote to specific risks attendant on contemporary urban middle-class life in China (and the United States): pollution, hypercompetitive employment markets, and general life stress.

But, given that most of these risks are not gender specific, how can we explain the gender differential in families' and students' decisions to embark on study abroad? When I asked participants why they thought study abroad was more popular for female than for male students, they gave several immediate answers. Some parents felt that daughters might be seen as more reliable than sons—less likely to go off the rails when away from parental supervision (for example, drinking, taking drugs, gambling, or neglecting their studies). Both male and female students also observed that, for all the talk of gender equality in China today, there is more pressure on sons than daughters to develop a successful career as fast as possible. In particular, in cases where the parents are entrepreneurs, sons are more likely than daughters to be pressured to become involved in the family business soon after graduation, with a view to taking over the reins in the future. This suggests a certain resonance with the case of Japan, analyzed by Karen Kelsky (2001), in that women's very exclusion from aspects of male privilege vis-à-vis professional advancement at home paradoxically affords them increased freedom to explore alternatives like study abroad.

Of particular interest in this chapter, though, are gendered risks that study in Australia is seen as potentially mitigating, that is, risks pertaining to women in particular (for related discussions, see Xiang and Shen 2009; J. Zheng 2016, 86–90). One risk that emerged clearly from the initial interviews was gender bias in China's professional employment market: a phenomenon that increasingly affects the current generation of young urban women (Du and Dong 2009; Hoffman 2010, 121–41; F. Martin 2014). While the European risk-society theorists assume that in late modernity, patriarchal relations tend to weaken, allowing women to participate more freely than ever in the labor market, the situation in postreforms China paints, in some respects, an opposite picture (Mulinari and Sandell 2009, 494). As noted in the introduction, many social scientists argue that gender relations have become *re*traditionalized in the postsocialist era, along with *increasing* gendered inequalities in the labor market. The post-1979 period has witnessed a decline in married women's workforce participation as the state pushes women "back to the family" in times of rising unemployment, and women workers have become the main losers in the state policy of labor flexibilization that has been in place since 2001 (Wu X. 2009; see also Rofel 1999; J. Liu 2007; Song 2011; J. Hao 2012, 250–63; Hong Fincher 2014; on rising graduate unemployment, see J. Hao and Welch 2012). While the belief that family caregiving is women's work has persisted since the Maoist era, today's profit-motivated private-sector employers are far less inclined than state-owned enterprises to accommodate women's caregiving needs (Cook and Dong 2011). These needs are also greater than they were under the planned economy, since childcare and elderly care have been privatized. Married women workers are thus at greater risk than male workers of lost earnings; they are also popularly framed as unreliable owing to employers' awareness of their additional caregiving duties within the family (Croll 1995, 117–24). All of this adds up to a situation in which gendered labor market risks have increased considerably since the economic reforms of the late 1970s, and it is widely recognized that a significant gender bias exists in China's urban professional labor market, especially in the private sector (Goodman 2014, 50–51).

To understand how participants and their families viewed the young women's situation vis-à-vis their potential professional futures in China, I raised the issue of gender bias in the domestic job market during initial interviews. While, among the students, understandings of whether and how their gender might affect their life opportunities varied quite widely, most parents and many of the older students were well aware of this gender bias, and their responses often indicated the anxieties generated by this knowledge and the dilemmas it raised for them. Many related personal stories involving themselves, female friends, relatives, or colleagues about gender discrimination in private-sector professional workplaces. These included accounts of female white-collar workers either losing their jobs when pregnant or finding themselves unable to advance professionally after returning from maternity leave; generally higher academic grade and qualification thresholds for female job applicants than for men; female graduates taking far longer to land desirable jobs than their male classmates; employers directly questioning female job applicants about when they planned to marry and have a baby and being unwilling to hire them if that was likely to happen soon; job ads that stated directly that preference would be given to male applicants; the general understanding that it was risky for women to try to change jobs in or after their mid-twenties if they had not yet had a child; successful female applicants being asked to sign contracts committing not to become pregnant within the period of their employment contract; female employees being forced to accept unpaid maternity leave in return for a promise from their employer to keep a position open for them; and so on.

When I asked future students and their mothers how they would handle such gender bias when the time came for them or their daughters to seek work, the responses showed that they felt that high-quality overseas education could add value to young women's natural abilities, which they hoped might then balance out the structural gender disadvantage. Consider these responses from students' mothers:

I think, as long as the child has the ability—I mean, people, in general, appreciate talent. So, if you really do have the ability, then in terms of this [gender] issue, the company [employer] won't take any notice of it.... That's why people say, ability comes first, position follows.... Yes, I think that [going abroad for study] will improve [her chances]. Because I think the purpose of her going is to master her major, improve herself, increase her abilities. (Zhenghui's mother, Chongqing)

In fact, I think a person's level of ability is very important, right? What your superiors will appreciate about you is most likely your ability. So even if, say [as a female employee], you want to get married, or you are going to have a baby, if your superiors see that your abilities cannot be supplied by anyone else in your place, then under those circumstances, they'd rather give you what's rightly yours; they'll feel ... that you're worth it. To their company, you—you're completely irreplaceable, so they will value you. So I feel that a person's abilities are really key. Especially for girls. (Xiaoyin's mother, Shanghai)

[As a woman], nowadays, if you don't wear yourself out [with work], you've got no chance; nowadays the pressure is too great.... And in a way the pressure on girls is even greater; it's not so bad for boys.... [Because] work is hard to find. Because with the same educational qualifications, with the same ... major, they [employers] will take the boy and won't take the girl. Unless the girl has [qualifications] that are higher than the boy's, then maybe they'd take on the girl rather than the boy. (Liangliang's mother, Henan)

Each of these women had a slightly different take on the question of labor market gender bias in China. In our further discussions, Xiaoyin's mother, who had spent her whole working life in the state sector, tended to minimize its impact, while Liangliang's mother, who worked in the private sector, was quite outspoken about the discrimination faced by female graduates and employees. But the common thread is these mothers' hope that extra effort on the part of the individual and her family to hone her abilities might overcome the structural disadvantages she faces entering the labor market as a woman (see also Xiang and Shen 2009, 517; J. Hao 2012, 256).

A related logic can be seen in statements made by some of the daughters as well:

Well, there's always a gender problem, like in the whole world.... It's, like, really common. You have to accept this kind of thing. Like, you always want women [to] be equal to men, but sometimes [it's] just not there. You have to accept it. And there's always women trying to get to a high position, but it's not easy compared to men. . . . I think [the way is to] better yourself. . . . If you get improved and you are a better you, you are better prepared, the opportunity will come. . . . You can't change others, but you can change yourself. (Shuangshuang, 22, Chengdu; original statement in English)

If I were to experience [gender] discrimination when looking for work, well, I know it definitely exists, and as a girl, right, I'm not too, y'know [assertive]. But with this sort of thing, all you can do is rely on your own abilities. I think if I were really amazing, then even if this place didn't want me, somebody else would. So all I can do to resolve this is rely on studying hard. (Xinling, 19, Zhejiang)

The faith in meritocracy underlying such statements resonates remarkably clearly with a market-oriented discourse that Xiaoying Wu and others have identified as central to the dominant cultural logic of gender in postreforms China: one that holds that individual hard work and ability create a level playing field across gender lines (see also S. Sun and Chen 2015). Wu writes, "The market discourse [on gender] appeared in the context of the market economy that arose in the wake of reform and liberalization. At its heart, based on the principle of individualism, lie the concepts of *suzhi* [素质] and ability, and the assumption that the market can provide for anyone, whether male or female, a level playing field. If one's *suzhi* is high and one has the requisite ability, then on this playing field one can win better opportunities and flourish [发展 *fazhan*]" (2009, 8).[2] With a kind of cruel optimism (Berlant 2011), these mothers and daughters demonstrate their attachment to the central feature of this discourse: the idea that individual-level efforts to improve oneself are the most effective tool to maximize one's opportunities in the competitive market economy. What marks the statements' divergence from the state-supported market discourse, however, is the ambivalence of their shared recognition, to varying degrees, that the playing field is in fact *not* level in terms of gender and that female students and job applicants must work *extra* hard to bring themselves up to the same starting line as men. These families hoped sending their daughters abroad for tertiary study might help counterbalance their daughters' structural gender disadvantage (see also J. Zheng 2016, 86–90).

Grasping Opportunity: Mobile Self-Fashioning

In addition to gender bias in China's labor market, participants also identified other gender-related problems that they hoped international education might mitigate. In particular, several highlighted the idea that study abroad represented a means to escape—either temporarily or permanently—the social regulation of women's behavior within Chinese society (see Kelsky 2001, 85–132; Farrer 2002, 158; Kobayashi 2007; Zurndorfer 2018). While the decision to study overseas is almost always a collective family decision financially supported by parents, this aspect of international education particularly appealed to some of the students (but, interestingly, was occasionally also highlighted by parents). Like Xiaofen, many hoped that international study could provide a means for them to avoid getting "trapped" in a standard feminine life course. As discussed in the introduction, in China, while robust social norms make heterosexual marriage effectively compulsory (Kam 2012), there is currently much intensive debate among social scientists, popular media, and ordinary young women and their families about urban professional women's rising age at first marriage (Duthie 2005; *China Daily* 2012). While educated women in the large cities of eastern China are now delaying marriage, on average, until well into their late twenties, over recent years, the state media's promulgation of the *shengnü* (剩女) discourse stigmatizing so-called leftover women—a caricature of educated, professional women who remain unmarried beyond age twenty-seven—encourages women to stick to a heteronormative and marriage-focused sociotemporal template (Hong Fincher 2014; J. Zhang and Sun 2014).[3] This normative feminine life course was narrated for me, with varying degrees of irony and exasperation, by many respondents.

> Before, everyone felt, including parents, that when a woman was twenty, she should do certain things; when she was twenty-five, she should do certain things; when she was thirty, she should do certain things. Like, for example, you graduate from university at twenty, and from then until twenty-five you can start having boyfriends, falling in love, so that you definitely establish your family before you're thirty: you establish your family at twenty-eight, so that by thirty you have a baby. . . . But now I think that a lot of women, including those in my own generation, born . . . around 1990 . . . don't think that way. . . . They feel that work is more important: why . . . can't you look for [family] after you're thirty, or get married a few years later? Since after all, for example, say . . . I get married at twenty-eight and have a baby by thirty. That time is often the exact moment when you're reaching a peak in your career. I could keep working my way up a bit further. But at that moment, because I have a baby, it might mean that all I can ever do is stop at that level. (Cihui, 22, Shanghai)

Cihui at once outlines the standard feminine life progression and offers a sharp analysis of the generational shift that sees career-minded women in her own generation come into direct conflict with the still-dominant ideology of their elders. It was clear from discussions with other participants, too, that studying abroad in their twenties represented, in part, a means for them to distance themselves from the pressures pushing them toward the lockstep of that standard life course. Consider the following responses to my questions about students' motivations for studying in Australia:

P: Because I'm twenty-one now, and I know there are some girls around my age [whose families are], like, you should consider getting married.

F: So young?

P: Yes! And their parents are already really worried that they won't find a boyfriend and what will they do then. If they don't have a boyfriend, they worry about what that entails for the future. So, I don't want to be judged like that.

F: So coming overseas is a way of escaping from that pressure?

P: Yes, you could say that. (Pingping, 21, Chengdu)

To speak concretely, I guess I'll want to establish a family at around thirty, I mean establish a family and a career—actually to establish my career first and then my family. Because I think I am the—sort of independent type. I want to have my own career first. Because for girls, if you, say, after you're married, if you don't have your own career, then probably the center of your life will be your child and the home, and that would tend to lack a certain—sense of achievement, I guess. Because personally what I want to attain is to make certain achievements academically or professionally. And to have my own personal time to pursue my hobbies, because I enjoy certain sports, outdoor sports, and I like traveling, so I want to have my own time, and I want to have a rich life. (Yixin, 23, Guangdong)

For women like these, desire for overseas education connected with a desire for female individualization: a move from "living for others"—especially family members, including both elders in one's natal family and hypothetical future husbands and children—toward "a life of one's own" (Beck and Beck-Gernsheim 2002, 54–84; D. Qin 2009; Kim 2011; J. Wu 2012; F. Martin 2014). The mobile, individualized self that these women hope transnational education could help them become is marked by independence, self-determination, and cosmopolitanism: a version of the enterprising, striving self discussed in the introduction (Conradson and Latham 2005a; Elliott and Urry 2010).

Despite some participants' tendency to frame their aspiration to embody this type of selfhood in generational terms, as markedly distinct from their elders' understanding of the ideal life course (as in Cihui's statement), in fact, similar aspirations for daughters were often expressed by parents. This is perhaps unsurprising, since participants' parents, born between the late 1960s and early 1970s, came of age during the first decade of economic reform, when state feminism was encouraging women to understand themselves as independent, self-focused subjects even as the countervailing post-Mao discourse on women's "natural" family-centrism was also beginning to gain power (see the introduction; Fong et al. 2012). There is thus no radical break between the dominant discursive structures contributing to the social construction of gender in the formative years of the parent and daughter generations (Rofel 2007, 111–34; F. Martin 2014). In this context, some parents echoed and encouraged their daughters' aspirations toward mobile, individualized selfhood. They hoped that study in Australia would help their daughters to become more independent (独立 duli) and self-confident (自信 zixin) and to cosmopolitanize themselves by widening their horizons (开阔视野 kaikuo shiye) and assimilating knowledge of other cultures (Rizvi 2005). They hoped it would make their daughters better able to recognize and actively maximize career opportunities and thereby more effective in the kinds of self-entrepreneurship demanded by China's postreforms market economy (A. Ong and Zhang 2008; Y. Yan 2009, 2010; M. Hansen and Svarverud 2010; Hoffman 2010). Echoing a discourse central to China's public culture in the current era, both parents and students often linked international education with the concept of self-development (自我发展 ziwo fazhan); a few mothers also used the state's language of "improving cultural civility" (提高素质 tigao suzhi) to describe one aim of study abroad (Bakken 2000; H. Yan 2008, 187–216; J. Chen 2019).

One of the commonest responses, from both families and students, to my question about what they hoped study abroad could give them that study in China could not was independence (see also F. Martin 2014). This emphasis on the value of independence reflects not only the postsocialist context in which the state has scaled back welfare provision but also the generational specificity of children of the one-child-policy era. Two mothers explained this specificity as follows and connected it with the value of overseas education for only children like their daughters:

Children in China tend to be spoiled by their parents: parents—mothers and fathers—do everything for them, help them do everything. Especially this generation of only children. . . . When you think about it, you'll see it means they're bound to be weaker in this regard, weaker as regards independence. So parents have to let them go. To tell you the truth, as parents we're quite worried about doing this, since when our daughter goes [overseas], she's going alone. . . . Even though we're quite worried, we still hope that our daughter can become a bit stronger [as a result], since in the end she has to live her own life, isn't that right? This road in society, she must walk it, she must experience it. And on this road, she must face whatever she faces independently; [she must] support herself. So all we can do is let her go. (Xiaoyin's mother, Shanghai)

We look after my daughter a lot at home. Since her maternal grandma also lives with us—well, old people tend to spoil children. She's overprotected her ever since she was little, and I've always felt that her capacity to be independent was a bit weak. . . . If she stayed forever under the protection of the family, she'd entirely lose her capacity for independence and self-reliance; she'd become even weaker in that regard. I want to let her go, send her off, so that she can further develop her independence, her self-confidence. Because her mum and dad can't protect her for her whole life, no matter whether in terms of work, everyday life, or whatever: in all aspects she'll have to go out and create her own life. I want to give her the chance to get out early and practice. (Xiaoshu's mother, Henan)

Many of the parents I spoke with made similar statements, sometimes explicitly contrasting their daughters' situation with their own family structure growing up, when the presence of brothers and sisters, together with the straitened economic circumstances of the time (late 1960s–1970s), meant that far less parental attention was available to focus on children; hence, children developed the capacity for independence much younger than the current generation. The daughters, too, consistently emphasized independence as a capacity that they hoped studying overseas could strengthen. They frequently contrasted their experience growing up in China—where multiple adults hovered around, preparing meals and taking care of everyday logistics to allow the younger generation to focus on schoolwork—with their situation in Australia, where they had to quickly learn to cook, shop, and clean as well as deal with landlords, rental contracts, banking, transportation, the purchase and assembly of furniture, and so on.

In addition to teaching these pragmatic forms of everyday know-how, some also saw life abroad as capable of fostering a more wide-reaching form of temperamental independence and inner strength born of facing a major life challenge. The following are some examples drawn from participants' responses to my question about whether a principal motivation for study was the advantage it might confer in job seeking later on:

> I just feel that if I stayed there [in China], my life might not ever change, I'd just be walking along the same old road. I might feel that my life lacked a certain *challenge*, lacked a certain freshness. So I decided to try [studying overseas]. . . . Right now, there are so many people going out from China to study abroad. If you think you can go back and [in seeking work] rely on your *background* [of overseas study]—well, it's hard to say concretely how much of an influence that would really have. So I guess the more important point was that I wanted to go out and give it a try, have a look around. (Xiaofen, 24, Zhejiang)[4]

> [The most important thing I hope study abroad will do is] to give me a chance to research things myself, to explore things myself. It will force me to adjust myself; it will make me more hardworking: that kind of an opportunity. . . . Actually . . . it's just all about relying on yourself [靠你自己 *kao ni ziji*]. . . . It's about training myself up [锻炼自己 *duanlian ziji*], making myself more and more hardworking and stronger and stronger. I like that feeling of having a challenge. . . . Training yourself up. For me, [advantages seeking work later] are not the main point. (Shang, 22, Hunan)

Xiaofen's and Shang's strong emphasis on how study abroad would provide a "challenge" and aid in "training oneself up" was frequently repeated by other participants as well. In this rhetoric of self-strengthening and self-challenge, we hear an echo of the individualist-meritocratic discourse identified by Xiaoying Wu (2009), in which individual efforts are promoted by the postsocialist state as the universal, equalizing key to life success. In the terms proposed by Aihwa Ong and Li Zhang, through study abroad, Shang, Xiaofen, and others like them are seeking to fashion themselves on the model of the enterprising subject of the postsocialist era, whose production "begins by developing basic individual capacities to make autonomous decisions, to take initiative and risk, and otherwise act on his or her own behalf to achieve optimal outcomes. The point was never to limit such personally responsible and self-propelling behavior to the market environment but rather to embrace such a calculative logic as the ethic of subject formation" (A. Ong and Zhang 2008, 3). Far exceeding the simple instrumentalism of maximizing one's chances of landing a good job, such students' overseas study projects, seen in this light, are nothing less than expressions of this historically specific ethic of self-fashioning.

Underlying most of my initial conversations with students and their families was a strong, commonly held assumption on their part that the chance for young women to travel and cosmopolitanize themselves by integrating intercultural experience and understanding was of value in its own right (F. Martin 2014; J. Chen 2019). For example, Xiaofen spoke enthusiastically of being inspired by two people for whom she had worked in China: managers and their spouses who she felt maintained a good work-life balance while also living exciting and highly mobile lives, with professional, educational, and long-term travel experience spanning mainland China, the United States, Hong Kong, Canada, and Cambodia. Consider, too, the following statements from two mothers and two student participants:

Advantages? I think that increasing her life experiences is a great advantage. . . . I guess that Chinese children are fairly conservative, not very open, so what I mean is that we hope our daughter can become more open, and have wider horizons, and experience more things. And in terms of our daughter's own maturation, I think this is both an experience and a type of asset [财富 *caifu*]. From our point of view, as educators, we always feel: ah, the students I have taught, maybe wider experience would enrich their lives a bit more. So I also hope that my own child can go out [overseas]. And having gone out, . . . this type of experience will provide a rare kind of asset. (Xiaoyin's mother [a teacher], Shanghai)

The most important thing for me is that she should learn some things to bring back, bring back a few good things from overseas—culture, education: study those things and bring them back. It's not as if it's solely for the sake of [finding] work. (Changying's mother, Anhui)

As for travel, I hope to be able to go to new places and take a look, go to all kinds of different places and meet all kinds of different people. . . . To experience new things; that's why I like traveling. . . . It so happens that . . . my qualification will give me a sort of practitioner's license that would allow me to also do this work in England. So I've considered maybe working here in Australia for a few years and then going to work in England. And if England recognizes [my qualification], and so does Australia, then I guess a lot of other countries will recognize it too. So I thought I could go and hang out in some different places [*laughs*]. . . . Sort of like "deep traveling" [深度旅游 *shendu lüyou*]. (Shihong, 20, Henan)

I hope I will have the kind of life that, when I'm old, I can say has been truly interesting: lots of stories, lots of experiences. I think, for me, that would make it *special*. . . . Since your life is your own, right? You must live it fully, make it interesting. . . . Of course [I want to travel]. But not only to spend money *shopping*. I also want to take photos and take a look, take a look at culture and the arts in other countries. . . . That's why it's hard to say what my profession will ultimately be, in the future. I've worked as a teacher, in the past, for children in basically an impoverished mountain area [in China], and there are lots of things [I might want to do]. For example, maybe I might go to New Zealand for a *working holiday*, and maybe I might go—say, to India, or some villages in China, maybe to work as a teacher, like for one or two years. (Shang, 22, Hunan)

The two mothers use market-related metaphors to frame cosmopolitan experience as a kind of portable capital or "asset" that they hope their daughters will be able to retrieve from abroad and bring home with them. The students themselves, meanwhile, frame the value of travel as inhering in its capacity to transform one's life into a series of adventures or interesting personal experiences, imagining their poststudy futures on the model of "lifestyle mobility": ongoing voluntary geographic movement that blurs the boundaries between travel and migration, work and leisure, and home and away (Cohen, Duncan, and Thulemark 2015; King and Sondhi 2016). For mothers and daughters equally, though, a cosmopolitan outlook born of transnational mobility is a key aspect of the type of self-determining selfhood that they hope overseas education will foster.

How, though, does this focus on cultivating mobile cosmopolitan selfhood articulate more specifically with *gendered* motivations for overseas study? Some examples will help flesh out the connection. Suyin and Ruomei, both twenty-two, attended the same school in Chengdu and met again, by chance, in Melbourne, where they became close friends. They shared both a strong city-based identity and a nascent feminist consciousness: when we conducted our first interview over coffee in Melbourne, the conversation turned several times toward their bafflement at those women who give up their careers at an early age for the sake of marriage and children, a choice they said they couldn't fathom. For both of these young women, the dream of undertaking postgraduate study abroad was strongly linked with their twin desires to sidestep gendered convention in China and to fashion a more self-determined, cosmopolitan identity. Illustrating this, Suyin explained her decision to study abroad as follows:

Actually my reason at the time was very simple. I thought: I've spent my whole life growing up in Chengdu. When I was little, I went to school in Chengdu; I went to high school in Chengdu; and I went to university in Chengdu. . . . And I thought: I don't want to stay in this same place forever; I want to go out and take a look. My dad once said to me . . . : Do you want to stay in Chengdu forever? Or do you want to have your own dream? He said, if you stay in Chengdu, then after you graduate you'll work here and find someone to marry, and that will be your life. And then he said: Do you have a dream? If you have a dream, then you should follow it: go off and realize your dream yourself. . . . Actually, he said all that very casually, but at the time, I did take notice. I thought about that question a bit. And then I said: I don't want to spend my whole life there. I don't want to be like ordinary girls and just pass my life in a very ordinary way, so I thought: I want to go out, I want to take a look around, take a look at this world [*laughs*]. . . . Yes, I really wanted to see what this world is like, so I started to consider going abroad for study.

Suyin makes an especially clear connection between the desire to escape gendered life-course convention—here associated with geographic stasis in her insistent repetition of the city name Chengdu—and an educational mobility project that will let her "see what this world is like." Her statement also illustrates the complex roles played by parents in shaping young women's mobility dreams, underlining the pitfalls of assuming that the patriarchal family acts simply as a repressive force dominating Chinese women (Pun 2005, 60–63; Belliappa 2013, 68–91). While in some cases parents and other elders were indeed described as pressuring young women toward "timely" marriage, in this case the seed of an idea sown by her father directs Suyin *away from* what they both perceive as a somewhat stultifying standard feminine life course in Chengdu and toward the dream of international mobility as a means of avoiding "pass[ing her] life in a very ordinary way." Highlighting once again the paradoxically familial inflection of her own desire for individualization, later in our interview, Suyin emotionally described the deep filial gratitude she felt toward her parents as another motivating factor for her studies: she hoped her overseas qualifications would help her get a highly paid job so that she could readily buy them the things they want—a luxury bag, a pretty coat—as an expression of her love and gratitude (see also M. Hansen and Pang 2010). In an apparent paradox that echoes work done in other Asian contexts (e.g., Belliappa 2013), Suyin's narrative illustrates that the self-individualizing practices that educationally mobile young women engage in may be deeply interwoven with family connections and loyalties.

To illustrate her own motivations for studying abroad, Suyin's friend Ruomei, even more outspoken about her desire to sidestep the standard feminine life course, told two contrasting stories about older women she knew. First, she described a talented friend whose promising career had ended with marriage and childbirth before the age of thirty:

> R: I had a very accomplished elder sister [i.e., friend], and she passed the entrance exam for a very good university we have in Chengdu; it's called the Southwestern University of Finance and Economics. Then after she graduated, she went to Shanghai to work; she got a job at Deloitte. After she finished at Deloitte, she worked as an auditor, and after that, she just sort of found somebody to marry. Once she'd married, she was twenty-eight or twenty-nine, and now she has a child. And now her home life revolves completely around her child. . . . I think this is basically not—
>
> S: The life you want.
>
> R: Correct. When I heard about it, I was—because I thought, right now I'm just at that age, where if I stayed in China, I guess, you know, it's about the time when they try to force you to marry and stuff. I don't want to get match-made or anything like that, I really hate all that.

While this friend provided for Ruomei a negative example of the risks of staying in China and succumbing to the socially prescribed feminine life course, another friend provided a positive example of the benefits of self-cosmopolitanization through overseas study:

> I have a very good friend, an elder sister; the two of us have grown up together since we were little. First she went to study in Hong Kong, but then she found she didn't like Hong Kong, she found education in Hong Kong too rigid, so she . . . transferred to America, where she lived a life of struggle. Because she studied subjects in the humanities, she studied . . . philosophy and politics. Originally she'd been studying engineering, but later she felt that her own interests were more [in the humanities], so she went to study at a liberal arts college in America. I think she's influenced me very deeply. . . . After I watched her go off, I felt that each time she came back, she brought me something new. And I felt that I wanted to become someone like that, too. . . . I felt that I, too, wanted to bring those kinds of new things to other people. I felt that I needed to go out and create something new myself and then become an influence on others.

Like several other participants who similarly discussed changes they noticed in female friends after several years' study abroad, Ruomei feels that her friend has been transformed by her assimilation of new ways of thinking gleaned from other cultures, and it is this self-cosmopolitanization that Ruomei wishes to emulate.

Twenty-nine years old when we first met, Yuli from Guangzhou was among the oldest of this study's participants. Despite having already worked for several years in the advertising industry in China, Yuli had persuaded her parents to support her coming to Australia to complete a bachelor's degree in the design field. Her decision to study abroad was linked directly with her desire to escape the pressures toward marriage being brought to bear on her as a twenty-nine-year-old single woman, particularly from several male elders in her extended family who made no secret of their contempt for her unmarried state. The first time I met her, she told me:

Y: My philosophy was: I want to become [someone who does] not follow the ordinary steps. Maybe I [could] do study and go to work and get married, blah blah blah: [this] is [supposed to be] a thing for everyone. But everybody should have a different approach to their life.... So far, I think I'm right.... Most of my friends in China are now worrying about marriage, worrying about how to build the family. I'm the only one that still can chase after my dream [*laughs*]....

F: So what is the most important thing that you hope to get from studying here instead of studying in China?

Y: Freedom, I think. No, I'll say the will [to] freedom. The will [to] freedom.... The freedom of understanding the world.... Because in China, you are told. Everything is told. You are told to get married before the age of thirty. You're told. That's the point. But in Western countries you're not told.... Actually it's your choice. In China you have no choice.... People like my grandma blame my parents: why did they let me ... come to Australia? Because I'm old enough to get married. "Let her settle down." That's my grandma's words. "Why she's going away? Let her settle down, get married." ... My parents told me [she said that].... I think they told me because they have similar concerns, but they just can't say it.... So I pretend I didn't hear. I ignore it.... Because ... I compare my life with my friends' life.... I can tell I'm better [off].... Because they're busy rais[ing] their kids, which means in some respects they lose a lot of personal space, lose a lot of time.... Most of the problem is how to deal with their families. After you get married, you need to deal with your husband's parents. That's Chinese tradition. Some even live with the husband's parents, but I think it doesn't happen here in Australia.... There are invasions from their mother-in-law. They will tell you what is the good way to raise your kids [*laughs*]. Or why are you so lazy, or why are you blah

blah blah. They will criticize and judge. . . . I think my generation can escape from that. My generation can. (Original statement in English)

Yuli's account reveals clearly how, unmarried at twenty-nine, she was located at the sharp end of the pressure toward marriage and, perhaps as a result, had become highly reflexive about and critical of Chinese gendered conventions. Feeling that her married female friends had lost their autonomy as they became absorbed into their husbands' families, where they as young wives were low in the hierarchy, Yuli had chosen educational mobility as the means to "escape" and pursue "freedom" and her "dream." In the face of disagreeable gendered pressures she experienced within her own family and Chinese society more broadly, Yuli voiced a gendered occidentalist counterdiscourse (Xiaomei Chen 1995) that idealized Western nations like Australia as the locus of "choice" and "freedom" for women.

If for Yuli the potential to escape from the standard feminine life course was generational ("my generation can escape from that"), then this is partly because well-resourced women in Yuli's generation, to a far greater extent than previous generations, are able to travel outside China and thereby not only distance themselves from family pressures but also increase their reflexive understanding of the culture-bound character of gendered conventions, as Yuli saw herself doing (D. Qin 2009; F. Martin 2014). Having thus far rejected the standard feminine life course, Yuli painted a picture of her desired future life as having geographic mobility at its center. She hoped to stay and work in Australia long-term and if possible also travel to Japan to complete a master's degree; she also had travels planned for America and Spain. Like the other participants quoted so far, she saw overseas travel, whether for study or for leisure, as a means of cosmopolitan self-fashioning (Conradson and Latham 2005a). The type of lifestyle mobility she aspired to would be personally enriching, Yuli explained, as it would allow her to integrate an understanding of the different ways of thinking that underlie each culture (Cohen, Duncan, and Thulemark 2015).

The Differential Distribution of Dreams

However, overemphasizing the capacity of articulate, confident, academically successful young women like Xiaofen, Yuli, Ruomei, Suyin, Xiaoyin, Shang, and the others to align their personal dreams with the ideal of mobile, cosmopolitan selfhood may risk overstating the role of personalized agency in the process that leads students toward transnational education. I therefore end this chapter with a counterexample that illustrates transnational education used not so much to realize a dream of mobile self-fashioning but more simply to manage academic risk. I do this both to complicate the picture of tactically choosing subjects and more broadly to problematize the assumption that educational mobility is necessarily propelled primarily by decisions based on strong individual or familial agency.

For those participants who had performed poorly in China's National College Entrance Exam (高考 *gaokao*), study in Australia represented a means of mitigating the risk of downward social mobility resulting from low academic capital. One cluster of participants, in particular, illustrated this function of Australian education as a second chance to repair academic-capital deficits in China. These were students in an expensive undergraduate joint program between a Chinese and an Australian university. When I spoke with a rowdy roomful of departing students in this program in China and asked them why they wanted to complete the final two years of their degrees in Australia, they chorused candidly that it was "because we messed up the *gaokao*" (因为高考靠烂了 *yinwei gaokao kao lan le*). As I packed up after my presentation, while the students' guidance counselor (辅导员 *fudaoyuan*) gave one student a public talking-to about his failing grades, I chatted with an administrative assistant in the program.[5] She told me frankly that some of their students were clearly unsuited to academic pursuits and would have been better off taking technical or vocational courses but had been pushed to enroll in a university degree program by anxious parents. While the program to which these students had gained admittance in China was ranked as third-tier, their parents hoped that two years' undergraduate study at the midranked partner institution in Australia would act as a springboard to a master's degree at a more prestigious ("Group of Eight") Australian university, which would increase their social status and employability back in China. Indeed, all eight study participants who were part of this joint program remained in Australia after graduating with their bachelor's degrees in order to follow this route.

Yaling was one of this group. A quiet young woman from Anhui, she had attended ordinary public schools before her admission to the third-tier university course and struggled academically first in China and then also in Australia. She seemed not to make friends easily, although underneath her social reticence she was a warm, considerate, and thoughtful person. During our initial interview in Anhui, Yaling frankly encapsulated the logic of the academic risk management that motivated her study abroad:

> [Graduating] from a third-tier course, you can't get anything. I mean, when you come out, you can't find good work. And they [my parents] think that overseas universities are on sort of a slightly higher level. . . . If

you stay in China and take a third-tier course, you've got no prospects. You could say that it was out of helplessness [无奈 *wunai*] that we chose this [study abroad] route. . . . They [my parents] were pretty helpless [to make any other decision].

Yaling's description of her parents' helplessness in the face of her low *gaokao* score stands in sharp contrast with the statements of other parents and students quoted earlier, with their representations of study abroad as a positive choice made to foster autonomous, self-directed personhood (albeit a choice necessitated, in part, by the risks attaching to feminine gender). Instead, Yaling presents herself and her parents as moved by forces beyond their control: things happen *to* them that mean she must go to Australia, rather than the family actively choosing this route in the optimistic mode of maximizing opportunities and chasing dreams. During her time in Australia, Yaling continued to experience herself as helpless. Struggling with poor grades and, later, debilitating personal safety fears during a spate of street crime in her neighborhood (see chapter 2), Yaling wished she could simply leave and go back home—but was helpless to do so, faced with her parents' insistence that she stay in Australia to finish her undergraduate course plus a master's degree (from which she ultimately failed to graduate). Thus, from beginning to end, Yaling's studies in Australia were pervaded by an overwhelming sense of her own helplessness.

While, through the privileging of the self-enterprising subject, "choice" has become a form of governing under China's postreforms social regime, as Lisa Hoffman (2010) among others argues (see also F. Liu 2008; A. Ong and Zhang 2008), Yaling's example illustrates the *differential distribution of choice*; that is, choice, like aspiration, not only as a practical capacity but also as an affective resource, is more available to some than to others (Appadurai 2004). This is not to deny that the capacity to choose transnational education reflects a powerful material differential based on social class (Waters 2006, 188). Certainly, at root, it is a result of privileged class status that a family like Yaling's is able to choose international education for their daughter, whereas a family without their economic resources could not. Nonetheless, at the subjective level, the examples analyzed in this chapter demonstrate that while some experience educational mobility as a choice, others, like Yaling, experience it as an expression of their own desperation and powerlessness (Bregnbæk 2016). The difference arises from multiple complex factors not limited to social class but including individuals' temperament, personal history, and levels of academic capital.

Yaling's experience of educational mobility as helplessness resonates with cultural geographer Vickie Zhang's retheorization of migration beyond "the figure of the utility-maximising, rational individual whose intentional process of decision-making becomes the causal mechanism for movement" (2018, 200; see also Kell and Vogl 2012, 2). Rather, argues Zhang, "it is possible to discern many threads affecting the choice to [move]. Any strong account of 'where' this decision is located becomes a tricky one, with theories of distributed agency looking beyond the sovereign effectivity of a given human act" (207). In Yaling's case, the human, nonhuman, and affective actants involved in pushing her toward study in Melbourne included not only her parents and herself but the *gaokao* exam, the Chinese education system with its guiding principle of academic stratification, her own distress and her parents' anxieties about her underachievement at school, the institutional structure of the joint program, the capital available to her family as a result of her father's position as a cadre, and so on. Zhang's point in reconceptualizing migration beyond the sovereign decision act is that *any* instance of migration may be understood in this way: as produced by the distributed agency of multiple interacting human and nonhuman forces. But in cases where those who move do so from a relatively weak position—as one could say, in the context of middle-class academic endeavor, of the student who has performed poorly in the *gaokao*—the capacity to experience oneself as exercising agency will be lower than for those whose stronger position is likely to afford a greater sense of autonomy.

In a time of gender retraditionalization, some female educational transmigrants identify with the ideal of cosmopolitan self-enterprising subjecthood as a way to resist the gendered limitations imposed by the normative feminine life course. But, based on a complex array of factors, some are more readily interpellated by this ideal than others. Many, like Yaling, may be excluded from full identification with the vision of the autonomous enterprising self and may experience their mobility less as a triumphant, self-directed soaring—the realization of a dream of flight—than as being tossed from here to there by forces beyond their control. Taking this into consideration forces us to recognize not only that capacities to exercise and affectively experience agency and choice are shared out unevenly between subjects with different levels of social power but that dreams, too, may be subject to the principle of differential distribution.

Mobile Self-Fashioning as a Gendered Tactic

In key respects, the ideal of the mobile, self-fashioning subject voiced by many of the participants quoted in this chapter resonates with neoliberal-style discourses on the value of self-development, self-reliance, and mobility that are prevalent in postreforms China (A. Ong and Zhang 2008; Nyíri 2010; T. Lewis, Martin, and

Sun 2016). Yet, as I hope to have reinforced throughout, the social position from which people embark on their mobility projects makes a difference. By focusing on young women's appropriations of educational mobility to manage gendered labor market risk and pursue agential self-fashioning, this chapter's analysis has highlighted "minor" uses of mobility, that is, uses of mobility by subjects who are, in at least one respect (vis-à-vis gender, albeit not class), minoritized. The statements I have analyzed by students and their families about their complex and multifactorial motivations for international study reveal that—in this respect analogously to the female labor migrants who have been written about by Arianne M. Gaetano (2015, 99–129), Pun Ngai (2005, 49–75), Leslie T. Chang (2009), and Penn Tsz Ting Ip (2018)—they try to use mobility tactically, to negotiate their gendered predicament vis-à-vis the sexism of both the labor market and the neotraditionalist discourse of the appropriate feminine life course (Certeau 1984). Within the larger system of China's postsocialist society, they thereby manage as best they can the contradictions between what this system simultaneously *demands* that they be—individualized, self-determined, self-reliant—and *blocks* them from embodying fully. In striving to embody ever more deeply the type of entrepreneurial subjecthood demanded of them, they take up the tools available against the contradictions inherent in the system, wielding the potentials of mobility against the imposed limitations of gender. However, even this minor and tactical appeal to mobility's potentials proves to be a limited resource. As we saw in Yaling's story, students' structural position vis-à-vis other kinds of capital—most glaringly financial but also academic—determines not only the extent to which they can take up transnational educational mobility as an option but also, once they have taken it up, the extent to which they are able to experience such mobility as agential: as the realization of a dream rather than as a type of forced movement. Later chapters (especially chapters 5 and 8 and the conclusion) follow up on what happens next: whether and how overseas study enabled participants like Xiaofen, Yuli, Cihui, Shang, and others to realize their dream of fashioning new modes of selfhood and life trajectories that might sidestep gendered restrictions.

2. PLACE
Welcome to Melvillage

*

The muted, air-conditioned atmosphere of the Ritz-Carlton is a relief after the muggy Shanghai afternoon outside. At the door of the meeting room where the predeparture briefing for Capital University will take place, a welcoming squadron of alumni in matching T-shirts branded with the university's logo chat among themselves and arrange brochures.[1] Cissy from Capital's Shanghai office bustles about inside the room, setting up her presentation. She wears sleek corporate attire—dark suit with pin-striped pants, kitten heels, and sterling silver designer earrings—but she's feeling hassled. A system error at the Melbourne end messed up the sending of invitations for the event, and she's worried that numbers might be down. In the end, though, a respectable crowd of about forty people materializes. Most are fashionable young people in their late teens or early twenties: future undergraduate or master's degree students. A quick poll by Cissy reveals that the majority will study finance, accounting, and related majors in business and economics. Some attend with mothers or aunties. In the row in front of me, a young woman in strappy black rhinestone sandals and a white draped top rests her head languidly on her boyfriend's shoulder. He musses her long hair absentmindedly.

During the two-hour session, we hear from a range of speakers offering information in Mandarin on various aspects of students' upcoming Melbourne experience. We listen to practical advice from Cissy and her colleague Sherry from the Singapore office on topics ranging from health insurance to housing options to Australian customs regulations. A representative of the Victorian state government's education export section, Study Melbourne, says a few words, and an ANZ bank employee promotes ANZ's transnational banking services. I make a brief, slightly awkward-feeling presentation about my research project, soliciting further participants. A panel of the logo-shirted alumni also presents, recounting their journeys from study at Capital U to employment in China and imparting friendly advice about everyday life and study in Melbourne. Like the future students, most of these alumni took degrees in finance and related areas. They are well-groomed, articulate, confident women and men in their mid-twenties who have secured well-paid corporate-sector employment in China's east coast megacities, mainly in foreign companies: the Big Four global accounting firms and international banks like ANZ and HSBC. They offer advice to the future students on how they could follow a similar path. We hear about how to seek mentorship to learn effective job interview techniques, how to choose elective classes to maximize employability, and how to enhance your professional CV by doing volunteer work in Melbourne.

Cissy also screens a short video introducing the city of Melbourne and the Capital U experience (figures 2.1 and 2.2). A series of touristic images unfolds: the Yarra River at sunset; the Arts Centre spire; Melbourne's city skyline; Flinders Street Station bathed in night lighting; the city's "iconic" laneways decorated with edgy graffiti, peopled by friendly locals and lined with quaint cafés; and the beaming faces of Anglo students on the Capital U campus. This dreamlike succession of images of a safe, welcoming, middle-class city is accompanied by a folk-pop soundtrack whose young female vocalist sings that she yearns to be taken to where the sunshine is free. At the side of the projection screen stands a vertical banner picturing a multiethnic group of students chatting on a sun-drenched lawn in front of a sandstone clocktower, beneath them the slogan of Capital U's current promotional campaign: "dreamlarge."

*

This chapter is the first of three that focus on participants' sociospatial practices in Melbourne, this study's primary field site. If the city as represented in Capital University's promotional video is a phantasmagorical Melbourne—touristic, dreamlike, utopian—then what kind of place, these chapters ask, is the Melbourne that the student transmigrants materially inhabit? My approach to tackling this question is informed by movements in current architectural theory, human geography, sociology, and urban studies toward a postessentialist, performative understanding of the constitution of space and place through human activity. This is to approach places—the city, the suburb, the rental room, the street, the shopping center, the boardinghouse, the place of work—as, in the words of architectural theorist Kim Dovey (2010, 6), "an inextricably intertwined knot of spatiality and sociality" that is produced through an ongoing process of becoming (see also Certeau 1984; Lefebvre 1991; Latham and Conradson 2003; Massey 2005; Thrift 2006; Amin and Thrift 2017). Places are understood as brought into being in their doing—although inhabitants do not make place just as they please but in ways both enabled and constrained by existing infrastructural, economic, institutional, political, racial, gendered, and other structures of power (Benson and Jackson 2013).

Following these logics, this chapter asks, *what is Melbourne*, for its Chinese student-transmigrant inhabitants and practitioners? And *what kinds of subjects*

FIGURES 2.1 AND 2.2 Dreaming of Melbourne from Shanghai: Capital University
promotional video, "Create Your Own Melbourne," 2012.

do these students become, in and through their material and affective engagements with Melbourne's sub/urban spaces? How are the places that they inhabit and traverse produced by their collective imaginings and everyday spatial practices in the context of wider institutional, infrastructural, and social structures? How do these places come into being experientially as the effect of atmospheres, routes, routines, and constraints that make them distinct in some measure from those that might comprise "Melbourne" for other groups? Through discussion of fieldwork materials—recorded interviews, stories from participant observation of students' everyday activities, a map-drawing exercise, and excerpts from participants' social media feeds—this chapter aims to convey a sense of the experiential textures, affective ambiences, and subjective meanings of these sub/urban subjects' sociospatial worlds.

It is evident from the outset that the Melbourne that these mobile students experience constitutes a *translocality* (Conradson and McKay 2007; Hepp 2009; Greiner and Sakdapolrak 2013). This term highlights the ways in which particular places concentrate multiple forms of mobility—media, human, financial, technological, infrastructural (Giddens 1990; Hannerz 2000; Urry 2007)—and thereby become extroverted and relational: constituted to a significant degree through their multiplying relationships with other places (Massey 1994, 2004; M. Smith 2001; Amin 2004). To do justice to the ways in which translocality is lived, it is important to keep in view the dimension of material geographic emplacement as well as mobility, relationality, and distal networks; indeed, the intertwining of these two dimensions defines the translocal approach (see also M. Smith 2001, 2005; Ley 2004, 2010; Conradson and Latham 2005b). Inspired by this approach, this chapter and the next two explore how student transmigrants' routinized practices of transnational travel, communication, imagination, and work sustain persistent connections between *here* and *there*. However, I also show that being connected to various distant elsewheres does not somehow remove the student transmigrants from the here-and-now of their immediate geographic locality. Rather, for these sub/urban inhabitants, those elsewheres are drawn into the scene of the local, so that they become constitutively intertwined with participants' experiential encounters with Melbourne's city and suburbs.

The chapter begins by returning to the utopian urban imaginary touched on in the opening fieldwork story in order to consider how this mode of representation in popular films and photography practices links with the aspirational dream inherent in transnational educational projects. I then consider an alternative, more ambivalent representation of the city in the "Melvillage" (墨村 Mocun) concept: a popular slang term that styles the city as a kind of (intermittently) lovable village-like backwater. This is followed by a section discussing the production of a dense capsule of Chinese student-transmigrant sociality in the city's central business district (CBD). Next, analysis of participant accounts that frame the city differently—as a space of extension, belonging, and possibility—is followed by an exploration of participants' practices of suburban habitation. The chapter ends with a discussion of sub/urban unbelonging in experiences of racism, violence, and gendered fear, preparing the ground for further investigation of these topics in chapter 3.

Utopian Imagination: The Edu-tourist City of Consumption

The promotional video from Capital University is not an idiosyncratic example. The touristic mode through which it represents Melbourne as a study and lifestyle destination is echoed in a number of other media products that are likely to be familiar to many students even before they arrive in Australia. For example, consider an emergent film subgenre that we might call the *international student film*: feature films focusing on international student life in specific Western cities. Examples include China's 2015 *Les Aventures d'Anthony*—based on a series of popular novels by An Dongni, a former international student of finance at the University of Melbourne—and the 2013 Singaporean film *3 Peas in a Pod* (Chun 2015; Chong M. 2013; see figures 2.3–2.5). These films could be seen as the latest wave in a media genre that traces its roots back at least as far as the 1990s, as Wanning Sun (2002, 67–89) shows in her discussion of the 1997 CCTV series *In Pursuit of Melbourne* (Chen Y. 1997), part of a cluster of 1990s television dramas focusing on the experiences of Chinese people living abroad. *Les Aventures d'Anthony* and *3 Peas in a Pod* mix touristic visual aesthetics with youth journey motifs to present an idealized, lightly exoticized Melbourne as the backdrop for stories of love, friendship, and coming of age among East Asian protagonists studying far from home.

Films like these enable students to engage in forms of imaginative travel predeparture (Urry 2007, 169–70). Along with a range of related media, they form a transnational mediascape that, as Arjun Appadurai argues, provides "protonarratives of possible lives, fantasies that could become prolegomena to the desire for acquisition and movement" (1996, 36; see also Kim 2011). Several participants, for instance, observed that one inspiration drawing them toward Melbourne was their enjoyment of An Dongni's (2008) first novel, a series of lyrical reflections on a young Liaoning man's experiences of self-realization while studying in Melbourne, later adapted as the film *Les Aventures d'Anthony* (figures 2.3–2.4). The aestheticized depiction of the city in such cultural products also affects

FIGURE 2.3 Flinders Street Station. Still from *Les Aventures d'Anthony*, directed by Janet Chun, 2015.

FIGURE 2.4 The Yarra River. Still from *Les Aventures d'Anthony*, directed by Janet Chun, 2015.

how students and others practice the city postarrival. Particular sights/sites like the railway station, the river, and the graffiti lanes—mythologized in prior representations as the city's most beautiful, typical, or meaningful elements—become the focus for photographic sign collecting (Urry and Larsen 2011) and social media display. This process is particularly interesting when it begins to incorporate university locations as prototouristic signs (figure 2.6). In such practices, the physical architecture of the overseas university campus becomes a collectable signifier of the dream of transnational movement.

FIGURE 2.5 Hosier Lane. Still from *3 Peas in a Pod*, directed by Michelle Chong, 2013.

FIGURE 2.6 Recently arrived project participants, enrolled at Fawkner University, photograph the prestigious Capital University, September 2015. Photograph © C. Zheng, used with permission.

Cultural products like films and promotional videos, An's popular novels, and the stylized snapshots taken by students and circulated via social media form a mediascape that visualizes what I call the *edu-tourist city*. This is an idealized, consumption-oriented vision of Melbourne that may be activated predeparture and is referenced periodically while students inhabit the actual city and circulate photographs in this style, for example, filtered shots of artistic brunches at fashionable *wanghongdian* (网红店: restaurants popularized by Chinese internet celebrities) that feature in many students' WeChat and Instagram feeds. This urban imaginary is powerful, as it crystallizes many of the central hopes that underlie students' and their families' overseas study projects. The dream of Melbourne as a bright, safe, clean, accessible, consumable, and welcoming entry point to the Western world represents overseas study's promise to secure one's position in a transnational cosmopolitan middle class. The consumerist logic underlying this vision of the city, meanwhile, echoes the interpellation of these middle-class young people by government, institutional, and commercial discourses in both China and Australia, which invite them to understand themselves principally as market subjects (G. Li 2016).

Ambivalent Imagination: Melvillage as Global Backwater

An alternative view is found in the popular term *Mocun*, a piece of internet slang that pairs the first character of the Mandarin name for Melbourne (墨尔本 Moerben) with "village" (村 *cun*). With regard to the logic behind the Melvillage name, the most upvoted answer on Baidu Zhidao, a popular Chinese collaborative question-and-answer website, reads,

> Most Melbournians live in the suburbs, and suburban houses are detached bungalows. The environment is quiet with lots of greenery, in addition to which lots of people keep dogs so in the evening you often hear dogs barking, and the whole thing feels sort of like a village. Also Chinese people in Melbourne might feel it's sort of "backward" in that there aren't as many shops, products and restaurants as in China, tech services aren't as good as in China, the population is small, the shops close early, there isn't enough nightlife, etc. (Baidu Zhidao 2018)

The Melvillage term is a relative of TuAo (土澳)—literally meaning "native Oz" and implying the cultural and economic backwardness of Australia as a whole. TuAo crops up most often in online complaints about the nation's backward infrastructure (shambolic public transport, slow broadband, overstretched public health service) and consumer culture (early shop closing times, hick fashion, underdeveloped online shopping, lack of mobile payment services). But rather than conveying a definitively negative assessment, the popular usages of TuAo and Mocun express precisely students' ambivalence. Mocun conjures up both the cozy sense of familiarity of a small city that can, at times, feel safe and friendly and the disparagement of a village-like place that feels parochial, limited, small, and backward compared with China's booming first-tier cities. Whereas the utopian urban imaginary frames Melbourne as a sophisticated front-runner and locus of global aspirations, the Melvillage concept depicts the city as a hick, slowed-down, quiet—albeit sometimes charming—backwater: the humdrum backdrop of students' sociospatially constricted everyday lives.[2]

Sub/urban Placemaking

Compared with the simplifications of these two competing city imaginaries, student transmigrants' material, symbolic, and affective placemaking through everyday practices proves far more complex. The Melbourne they experienced is characterized by a range of operations including spatial concentration and social segregation but also spatial extension and emergent forms of local belonging.

After arriving in Melbourne, student transmigrants, like anyone arriving in a new place, got to know the area in clusters of sites relating to everyday activities. These included the places where they studied and lived, their friends' and boyfriends' or girlfriends' places, the local offices of the Chinese education agents through whom they often continued to manage their Australian university enrollments, their places of work (chapter 4), shopping places, sites of leisure consumption, churches (chapter 6), and the tram, train, and bus routes linking all of these together. In terms of residence, for students studying in or near the CBD (known in Chinese student shorthand as the CT: city), the commonest choice for those over eighteen—hence legally permitted to live independently—was to share a small rental apartment in a mid- to high-rise building in or near the CBD with conational student flatmate(s). For those studying at suburban campuses, the standard model was a hybrid of student share-house and boarding-house in a detached suburban residence, sharing with Chinese (and occasionally other East Asian) student housemates and sometimes also a migrant landlord plus family. Often, students' first rental accommodation was found and paid for before students even left China via classified sites like Yeeyi.com: a Chinese-language website set up by members of Australia's Chinese diaspora.

Especially in the months or year following their arrival in Melbourne, the world that many (not all) Chinese student transmigrants inhabited was peopled largely by coethnic, conational social contacts. This was particularly the case within Melbourne's CBD. In 2014, of 37,600 higher education students living in the municipality, about 57 percent were international, the largest subgroup being Chinese (City of Melbourne 2016, 11; see also City of Melbourne 2013), and in 2016 Mandarin was the commonest language other than English spoken in central Melbourne, with 19 percent of residents speaking it at home (Australian Bureau of Statistics 2016c). Many participants in this study found that they had left China only to arrive in a subworld populated by Chinese friends, Chinese landlords, Chinese classmates, Chinese flatmates, Chinese bosses, Chinese media, and Chinese businesses. Indeed, the extent of the Chinese diasporic world in central Melbourne surprised many participants, who remarked on it—with mixed feelings—during their first months in the city. I call this world, which some referred to as a kind of "bubble," the *expatriate microworld*.[3] This microworld operated both through students' media practices and through their face-to-face social interactions, but its borders were porous rather than hermetic, and participation in it certainly did not exhaust student transmigrants' social experience in Melbourne. They simultaneously negotiated an Australian education system, Australian immigration regulations, and an Australian legal system, and these two worlds—as well as others, including the Chinese diaspora abroad and other international student communities in Melbourne—continually interpenetrated at the everyday experiential level.

Two points are worth underlining here. First, to observe student transmigrants' strong links to diasporic and transnational Chinese networks is not to claim that these students "aren't really in Melbourne": rather, to a significant extent, this diasporic translocality *constitutes* their experience of the city. Second, for those who choose to live and socialize largely within the expatriate microworld, this decision must be seen as a result of social exclusion from the city's other worlds. Such exclusion—a broader theme of this book as a whole—is the result of multiple factors, from "missing friendships" with generally polite but largely indifferent local students (McKenzie and Baldassar 2017), to structurally determined clustering in particular urban areas and types of housing (Fincher and Shaw 2009), to institutional distinctions between different types of student made by Australian governments and universities, to exclusion from jobs in non-Chinese-run businesses (chapter 4), to racist violence in public space. In the pages that follow, I explore participants' negotiations of and challenges to the expatriate microworld in their everyday practices of habitation, first in Melbourne's CBD and then in its suburbs.

Cihui's map of Melbourne (figure 2.7), drawn as part of an exercise aimed at illustrating participants' everyday sociospatial worlds, exemplifies the CBD-centric experience. I asked participants to sketch their own experiences of the city and/or suburbs, indicating some locations that they visited at least every month and some locations where memorable things had happened to them. I sought to draw out a sense of both sub/urban space as habitually practiced and the subjective significance of specific geographic sites to individuals. On Cihui's map, except for an indication of the location of the inner-urban neighborhood of Richmond at bottom right, all of the places she included are located within the CBD and adjacent southern Carlton (the site of Capital University). Her places of residence, study, exams, shopping, and leisure were all sited within a two-kilometer radius centering on the CBD, with the graphic logic of her plan placing Chinatown (Little Bourke Street) at the symbolic center.

Something of the experiential texture of this inner-urban world emerged from further conversations with CBD-dwelling participants over the duration of the study. When I was chatting with small groups of participants, when the conversation turned to who was living where in the city, it became clear that particular apartment buildings were well known to many who either had lived there themselves or knew other Chinese students who did. Examples included the "face building" (脸楼 *lian lou*: the Barak Building at the north end of Swanston Street, commemorating the Wurundjeri elder with a portrait of his face built into the architecture), the "rock-climbing building" (攀岩楼 *panyan lou*: the apartment tower over Hardrock Climbing on nearby Franklin Street), and 11 Rose Lane, part of a large new residential development in the western CBD. Along with several others, these particular high-rise apartment blocks were well known as residential hubs for Chinese students and contributed to the sense of the inner city as a geographically delimited zone of ethnonationally specific sociality. For the student transmigrants, this zone often felt like a small, close-knit community.

I meet Shang for lunch in the CBD. As I stroll through the warm midday streets to the café where we've arranged to meet, I enjoy mingling with the throngs of people Christmas shopping and sitting at tables on the pavements, basking in the late spring sunshine over lunch and drinks with friends. For me, late November in the city is always marked by the pleasant sense of a slowdown toward the Christmas season: as the weather heats up and the streets fill with people, I feel the work grind slowing down, people relaxing, deadlines being put off until next year, and

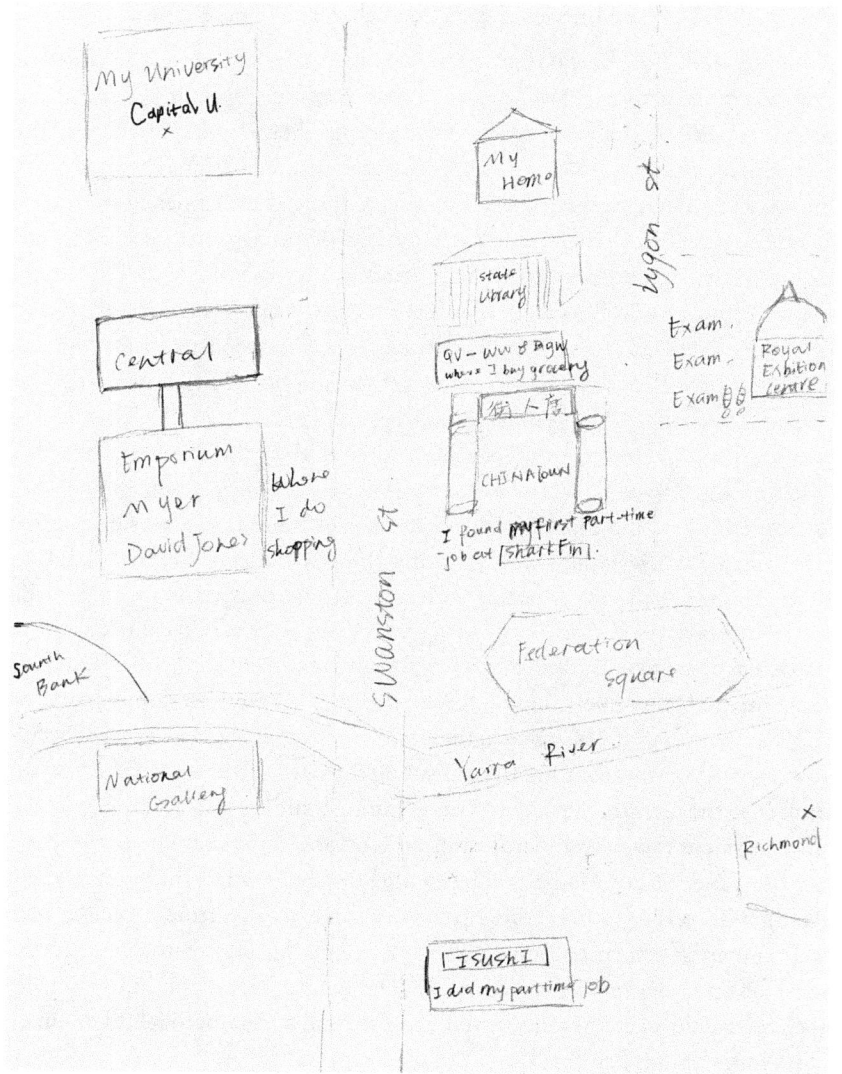

FIGURE 2.7 Cihui's map: CBD-centric lifeworld.

the long summer holiday drawing palpably near. As we eat lunch, I ask Shang if she notices anything about the feel of the city at the moment.

Yes, she replies. Every day, I notice that there are fewer and fewer people here.

Momentarily confused, I realize after a second that she is referring to the annual exodus of Chinese students, as many leave Australia for the long university vacation over summer. As my city is festively filling, Shang's is melancholically emptying.

As well as poignantly illustrating that two people walking along the same street on the same day can be experiencing two different cities (Healey 2002), Shang's remark about the city emptying out in late November also tells us something particular about the character of the city she inhabited. For student transmigrants like Shang, Melvillage is village-like not only in the frequently noted underdevelopment of its infrastructure and consumer culture but also in its perceived size. While, as a city of 4.5 million, Melbourne is indeed objectively far smaller than China's large cities, the more important point here is how small it *felt* to Shang, for whom, at least at that moment, "people in the city" seemed commonsensically to refer to fellow Chinese student transmigrants. Following that logic, for Shang, Melvillage was a village of some 55,000 inhabitants (Australian Department of Education and Training, International Research and Analysis Unit 2017b). When many of them left for the vacation period, the village became even smaller, even quieter, even emptier.

ARCHITECTURES OF SOCIOSPATIAL SEGREGATION

This urban microworld is supported by quite specific sociospatial structures. Rising international student numbers driving increased demand for housing close to the CBD and nearby university campuses have significantly transformed the architectural character of the city itself. On one hand, the past two decades have seen the streetscape of the central and northern city area transformed by a rising tide of trans-Asian consumer culture, a form of neighborhood change led by student transmigrants (K. Anderson et al. 2019, 163–85). Businesses popular with East Asian students now predominate in this area of the city, from Japanese sticker-machine parlors to karaoke complexes to boutiques selling Northeast Asian–style trendy accessories, to Chinese mail-courier services and Korean barbecue restaurants, sashimi bars, Taiwan-via-Singapore bubble tea and shaved-ice dessert shops, and Chinese dumpling and noodle bars and hotpot restaurants. These businesses are often owned by East and Southeast Asian diasporic entrepreneurs, and they both cater to international students as a major customer base and act as significant employers of international students (chapter 4). On the other hand, the cityscape has also been transformed by new forms of apartment housing (Rogers and Wiesel 2018). In a 2009 article based on an in-depth study carried out between 2005 and 2008, architecture scholars Ruth Fincher and Kate Shaw chronicle how the north end of Swanston Street, at the end of the CBD where several university campuses are located, was transformed by the rapid construction of purpose-built commercial apartments to house the international students whose numbers had risen so fast over the preceding decade (figures 2.8–2.9). Newly arriving students—largely from Asian countries—were actively channeled into these apartment complexes by advice from universities and education agents (Fincher and Shaw 2009, 1891).

In the decade following Fincher and Shaw's study, while the broad trend of rising international student numbers driving demand for inner-city apartments remained consistent, other aspects of the situation changed. After 2010, to the immediate south of the area on which Fincher and Shaw had focused, the CBD was thoroughly transformed by a boom in high-density, high-rise apartment construction (figures 2.10–2.11). While some of the new developments are student housing specifically targeting Chinese international students (like the development whose bilingual signage is pictured in figures 2.12–2.13), most are regular apartment buildings. Some sit at the high-rent, luxury end of the scale, while others—commonly disparaged as dogbox developments—are notable for the tiny size and poor amenities of their apartments.[4]

One factor contributing to Melbourne's boom in CBD apartments between 2010 and 2016 was foreign investment (Wong 2017). Overseas demand for new property peaked in the state of Victoria in 2014 at around 32 percent of the market, when Credit Suisse stated that 80 percent of offshore property investors were from China (Scutt 2017). Indeed, my discussions with participants and observation of Chinese-language social media during this period revealed that Chinese international students themselves were targeted as both sales agents and buyers for the new apartments. Numerous students discussed with me how Melbourne's Chinese-run real estate agencies employed untrained international students on a commission-only basis—sometimes using a multi-level marketing structure—to market apartments off the plan to friends and family back in China.[5] Illustrating what Shanthi Robertson and Dallas Rogers (2017, 2398) have dubbed an emerging "real estate-education-migration nexus," Chinese students were also targeted as a market for the apartments, with social media ads and direct-marketing events pushing the supposed advantages of buying an investment apartment with a low-deposit, interest-only loan. This situation shifted in late 2016, when the tightening of offshore property investment restrictions meant that overseas investors were no longer permitted to

FIGURES 2.8 AND 2.9 Early 2000s development: Midrise student apartments on the north end of Swanston Street. Photos by the author.

FIGURES 2.10 AND 2.11 Post-2010 development: High-rise construction in the CBD. Photos by the author.

FIGURES 2.12 AND 2.13 Apartment construction in the CBD targeting Chinese students, July 2017. Photos by the author.

purchase Australian property on a mortgage and existing mortgages immediately came due, leaving many student buyers scrambling either to get together the cash to pay off their Australian loans in full or to sell their recently purchased investments.

Before the regulatory changes, the spate of Chinese property investment between 2010 and 2016 had both intensified the CBD high-rise apartment construction boom and produced concentrations of Chinese absentee landlords permanently renting out their Melbourne apartments. A combination of proximity to major university campuses, the availability of parental financial support to pay comparatively high rents, a sociocultural preference for inner-urban apartment living, and easy access to local Chinese-language rental ads via phone apps made the new CBD high-rise apartments a popular choice for financially comfortable Chinese student transmigrants looking to rent. At the other end of the economic spectrum were struggling international students inhabiting what the local media dubbed "high-rise slums": dogbox apartments owned by unscrupulous landlords, crammed with bunk beds to enable illegally high occupancy rates (Dow 2015). The Melvillage inhabited by Chinese student transmigrants, then, had quite a specific architectural form, with the CBD's high-rise residential towers occupying a prominent place in their socio-spatial experiences of the city.

Fincher and Shaw (2009, 1893) explain the channeling of international students into a narrow range of housing types in the inner city in the early 2000s as the result of actions by a network of actors including the students themselves, their families, property developers, urban planners, universities, and education agents. Over a decade later, we must add to this list new social media technologies (smartphones and the apps through which students most commonly access rental ads), commercial actors within the local Chinese diaspora (real estate agencies and the social media companies that circulate the rental ads), foreign investment regulations (which channel overseas property investment toward new housing stock; Rogers and Dufty-Jones 2015; Robertson and Rogers 2017); and property investors themselves, whether Australian or offshore (who have facilitated the availability of a new style of CBD housing that is particularly appealing to international students). Despite these changes, the overall effect is very similar to what Fincher and Shaw observed in 2009: international students are channeled into a relatively narrow range of housing types in the inner city. The multiple, mutually reinforcing factors in play mean that this has become a self-perpetuating system.

Fincher and Shaw's broader point, however, concerns the social impact of such housing trends for the students. They show how the type of housing into which international students are channeled contributes to their effective sociospatial segregation, as they are "wall[ed] into fortified buildings of tiny and extremely private (rather than communally oriented) apartments" and thus are "catapulted for socializing, rather timidly and with their housemates from the apartment buildings, into certain entertainment spaces of the central city" (2009, 1890). The segregation in housing, the authors argue, also contributes to intensifying the social separation of international from domestic students (1896). If student transmigrants' own reflections are any guide, these observations still held true ten years later. When I asked participants to reflect on their experiences in and of Melbourne, they frequently spontaneously observed that, to their disappointment, they hadn't (yet) managed to "integrate into local/mainstream society" (融入当地 / 主流社会 rongru dangdi/zhuliu shehui) (X. Zhao 2019b, 201–7). On many occasions, Chinese students both within and outside the participant group contacted me to seek advice on how they could better integrate and make local friends. They expressed frustration that their main friendship group was other Chinese students but felt trapped in their own isolation and virtually powerless to expand their social world owing to significant challenges in finding both opportunities and effective means to forge durable transcultural friendships. And, echoing Fincher and Shaw's conclusions, this problem had a spatial aspect.

When I asked Mei whether, after several years living and studying in Melbourne across two separate stays for undergraduate and postgraduate degrees, she felt any sense of belonging in that city (归属感 guishugan), she paused to reflect, then told me that, instead, she felt like part of a "floating population" (流动人口 liudong renkou) of Chinese international students in the CBD.[6] With the high concentration of Chinese students, tourists, and associated services—from Chinese grocers, to Chinese student-run home-cooked food delivery services, to ubiquitous Chinese-language social media—she added that she sometimes had the sense that she and her friends in the CBD were "living in Chinatown." Several other participants independently remarked that, for them, the city felt more or less analogous to other nonhometown cities where they'd previously studied within China: you become familiar with the urban geography and comfortable enough staying there temporarily but don't develop any particular sense of belonging or identification as a resident (居民 jumin) of that city:

> I mean, there are so many Chinese people here, this place is basically on the verge of being taken over by Chinese people. So whenever I go shopping, there'll be a Chinese person there saying, Oh, can I help you with

anything? It feels absolutely no different [from a Chinese city]. . . . My sense of Melbourne is solely the physical aspect. . . . Although everyone's here together, our chemical structure is different [*laughs*]. . . . I feel I'm not integrated. Quite a few aspects of our lifestyles are different. (Xiaojuan, after one year)

In terms of a sense of belonging . . . maybe because I'm a graduate student, busy with study . . . I haven't taken part in that many activities here . . . and so, in terms of how it feels, it seems no different than when I was studying toward my undergraduate degree in another city [within China]. . . . There's no difference. . . . Some people feel, Oh, it's so far away from home, and whatever. But actually I don't really notice that. (Fenfang, after two years)

Shang made the important additional point that her (non)identification with the city was connected with her awareness of being blocked from full belonging by the bureaucratic definition and regulation of her non–permanent resident and international student status by the state and the university (Fincher and Shaw 2009):

A sense of belonging—hmmm, it's just so-so. To tell you the truth, I have a kind of feeling, sometimes, while I'm studying here . . . that I'm sort of actually traveling [旅游的那种感觉 *lüyou de nazhong ganjue*]. . . . I don't see myself as a Melbournian, because in many aspects we're very clearly restricted. Like whether you have PR [permanent residency] or not, right, and whether you're an international student . . . ; they exclude us from things [on that basis; 把我们限定开了 *ba women xianding kaile*]. Especially PR: [if you get it, then] it seems that certain things would suddenly open up to you.

In discussing their disappointment at the nonlocalized, overwhelmingly conational character of the social networks they found themselves engaging in Melbourne, participants also often underlined the dominance of Mandarin in their everyday verbal interactions in the CBD—with classmates, flatmates, shop staff, restaurant workers, and friends—and the extremely high concentrations of students from China in certain inner-city university courses. The issue of student transmigrants feeling trapped in a Chinese linguistic, educational, and social bubble and disconnected from a wider social context is certainly not restricted to the CBD: some participants living in the suburbs made related points, whereas some living in the CBD had much more diverse sociospatial experiences. However, the high concentrations of universities offering courses specifically targeting international students, Chinese students renting apartments, and Chinese-run businesses in and near the CBD made the ubiquity of the expatriate microworld a particularly palpable feature of sociospatial experience for those living in the central city area.[7]

Life in the Dogbox

I take the tram down Elizabeth Street and walk from the corner of Lonsdale. It's a bright early-summer afternoon, and the city streets bustle with shoppers and workers on their lunch break. But the cheery scene feels like a flimsy facade, the day suffused by some darker undercurrent. I am on my way to Honghong's apartment from the psych ward at Royal Melbourne Hospital.

The eldest of my participants, Honghong is a forty-six-year-old mother who'd come to Melbourne supported by loans from friends to pursue an undergraduate medical degree at the Imperial University of Technology. Finding it too expensive to have her two young sons attend school in Australia, she'd sent them back to China to live with their father, a decision that caused her deep sorrow. Over the months that followed, Honghong's behavior had become more and more eccentric. At a Mid-Autumn Festival party, she guided me into a dark corner where the crowds and loud music, she said, made it safe to talk. Someone was trying to harm her. She needed to move to another house. In subsequent conversations, her insistence that she was being watched, followed, and phone-tapped became stronger. Someone had come into her room at night and installed a spy app on her phone. Where did these bruises on her wrists come from?

The final time I saw Honghong before her hospitalization, she told me her landlords kept trying to poison her. She couldn't sleep. She'd moved six times. She'd slept rough on a city street for three nights. She couldn't tell her husband back in China about her problems because then he'd be in danger, too. Everything was connected to a vendetta by her former employer at a university in China who was angry because she'd refused to become his mistress. His spies were everywhere. Honghong was wrapped in a heavy black coat and smelled of stress and stale clothing. That afternoon, after a self-taught internet and telephone crash course on dedicated mental health services for international students—I found none—I'd put Honghong in touch with a counselor at her university, recommending that she seek professional help for her insomnia and stress. A series of events then led to Honghong being forcibly admitted under the Mental Health Act to a secure ward at the Royal Melbourne, where I visit her the day of her admission.

She is in a bad way. Her only visitor, I sit with her in a small meeting room with two worn chairs, stained carpet, and the sound of a violently abusive male patient shouting and crashing around on the other side of the door. Through an hour and a half of circular conversation, Honghong's original trust in me sours into angry accusation. It's all my fault that she is trapped there. I am in league with Them. She can't possibly stay in this hospital. How can she ever earn the money to repay her loans if she can't work? How can she come to a developed country like Australia and return home empty-handed? And she is frightened. She is refusing the antipsychotic medication prescribed for her newly diagnosed paranoid schizophrenia: it will be poisoned, obviously. Finally, she asks if I could pick up some of her things. Not realizing she was going to be hospitalized, she hasn't brought pajamas, reading matter, toiletries, underwear, or clean clothes. She asks the duty nurse to give me her electronic door key, kept in safe storage during her admission, and tells me her address.

At the west end of Lonsdale Street, Honghong's apartment is on the top floor of a tired ten-story building that seems several decades old. Photocopied informational posters in the elevator indicate that many of the tenants must be international students. The corridors are awkwardly narrow, and the tenth floor's stagnant air is suffused with a nasty smell. Nobody answers when I ring the doorbell, but after I knock and push the door open, it turns out there is a young woman in the living room—dark, owing to having been divided in two with curtains to make an extra bedroom—cross-legged on the couch, with earphones plugged into her phone. I greet her, and she doesn't respond, so I try speaking in Chinese. She isn't Chinese. She is nonplussed. Embarrassed, I apologize for my mistake, explaining that I am Honghong's friend and have come to fetch some of her things. The young woman doesn't know Honghong's name and overall doesn't seem too clear on who is living in the apartment. There are twelve people in two and a half rooms. Oh, she says, do you mean the Chinese girl? She's in the first bedroom. But she just stays in there, in bed, all the time.

She shows me to the darkened room, crammed with two sets of rumpled, white metal-framed bunk beds, and indicates one of the top bunks, piled up with clothes, covers, and things in plastic bags. Timidly, I start sifting through the pile, looking for the things Honghong requested—then realize with a start that a very small, still, quiet young woman is lying on the bunk, behind a laptop screen, plugged into earphones. She hasn't seen or heard me. After I get her attention, she tells me the older Chinese lady sleeps in the other bedroom, but neither she nor the woman in the living room knows which bunk is Honghong's. I make a lucky guess and find the things Honghong asked for on the bed and in an overflowing walk-in closet next to the en suite bathroom. As I leave the apartment, I leave my card for the landlord (actually the landlord's proxy—another international student tenant), because Honghong is very stressed about the rent—is it due? What *about her $300 bond? Should she relinquish her bunk if she is going to have to stay in the hospital?*

Back in the psych ward, Honghong is glad to have her things and seems calmer. A couple of days later, her psychiatrist calls me—I am Honghong's only known social connection in Melbourne and so have been listed as her contact person by the hospital—to tell me that Honghong's condition has improved after she agreed to medication, and she's been discharged. A social worker will visit her regularly.

Honghong contacts me once more via text message, thanking me for my help, and after that stops responding to my messages. A month or two later, her social worker calls me: Honghong has disappeared. I never hear from her again.

As temporary home to a group of strangers crowded together under one roof yet each too preoccupied with her own immediate problems to connect meaningfully with the others, Honghong's apartment seems like a textbook illustration of the potential for the CBD high-rise slum to exacerbate the social disconnection and alienation of student transmigrants like Honghong, who was extremely vulnerable financially as well as in relation to her mental health. Yet this is certainly not always the case. The following section illustrates the multiplicity and complexity of student transmigrants' sociospatial experiences, which complicate the "ethnic ghetto" stereotype.

THE EXTENSIVE CITY: BELONGING AND POSSIBILITY

Although at times those living in the CBD emphasized its frustrating tendency to reinforce the boundaries of the expatriate microworld to the exclusion of wider connections, at other times student transmigrants experienced the city as a more open geography: a place of belonging and possibility. We see this in Yixin's map of Melbourne (figure 2.14). Like Cihui's map, Yixin's also centers on the CBD, but it includes a wider range of surrounding locations as well, indicating Yixin's more extensive everyday mobility. In addition to inner-city locations, she drew in the inner-west neighborhood of Kensington, where she worked as a Mandarin teacher at a Catholic primary school; Caulfield South, the southeastern suburb where her Russian boyfriend lived; and the out-of-town destination of Wilson's Promontory, where she went camping during her first year in Melbourne with a multiethnic group of international student friends. Moreover, the whole area that Yixin drew in mid-2017—she had completed two years' study at Capital University and was on the verge of seeking work to enable her to stay on in Melbourne—seems saturated both with the intensity of good memories (romance in Flagstaff Gardens, the sociability of bars and cafés with friends, the fun of the camping trip) and with the excitement of

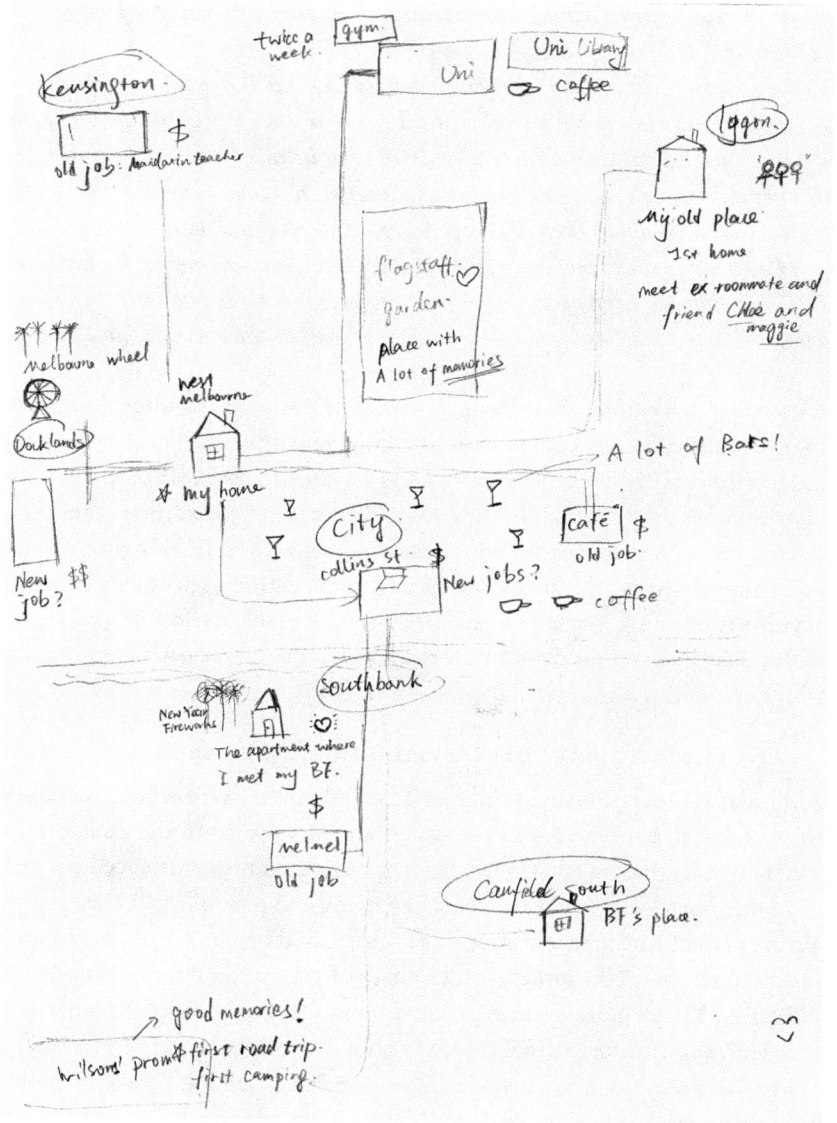

FIGURE 2.14 Yixin's city of memory and possibility.

future possibility ("new jobs?" throughout the CBD). Yixin's Melbourne seems in the process of being extended: outward in space, forward in time, and deeper in sociospatial connections.

I first met Song, then twenty-two, in the autumn of 2012, when she was studying toward her undergraduate degree at Capital University. I interviewed her in her rental room: a small, home-built wooden box attached at first-floor level to the back of a shop in Coburg, a suburb in Melbourne's north, entered via a gate onto the rear alleyway (figures 2.15–2.16). The Guangzhou-born tailor who owned the shop was evidently something of a handyman, and had illegally constructed ten such rooms, each housing a student from China, thereby bringing in a hefty tax-free income of $1,000 per week. Sunlight spilled into Song's room from the north-facing sliding glass doors as she served me boiled water from a clear plastic jug. The small room was filled with Song's things—she apologized self-deprecatingly that it was very messy, but actually, together with Song's quiet demeanor, the room exuded a somehow cloistral air of calm and orderliness. Despite the illegality of the dwelling, the obviously exploitative landlord, and safety issues such as the lack of a fire plan, Song loved her room. It was bright, quiet, private, and self-contained: the way she liked to live her life.

By the time we reconnected three years later over lunch at a café in Carlton, Song had graduated, found work, and moved to a studio apartment in the inner-city neighborhood of North Melbourne. She revealed that when we'd met the first time, she'd been in deep mourning for her recently deceased father, isolating herself socially and spatially in her small wooden room as a means of coping with her shock and grief. But in contrast to others quoted thus far, Song now spoke of a deep sense of belonging in Melbourne:

> It's interesting—I think maybe I'm different from many people. These days, although I lived in [my hometown in Jiangsu] for eighteen years of my life, I've actually developed a deep sense of belonging in Melbourne. It relates to the fact that I live by myself, and my place just feels so comfortable. Whenever I have to go back to [my Jiangsu hometown], I miss this place. And every time I go back to China, before I leave, I always go to the *Yarra River* in the evening, and walk around there. I feel a bit sad to leave, even if I'm only going for a month. It's quite mysterious. I think maybe it's because Melbourne is a place I've explored on my own. Whereas in [my hometown] there are people at home to help me, people to guide me. So I really have deep feelings for Melbourne, I feel like it's true love for me here [*laughs*]. . . . It's where I've been independent—happy or sad, I've always been by myself; I've experienced it all by myself. . . . I

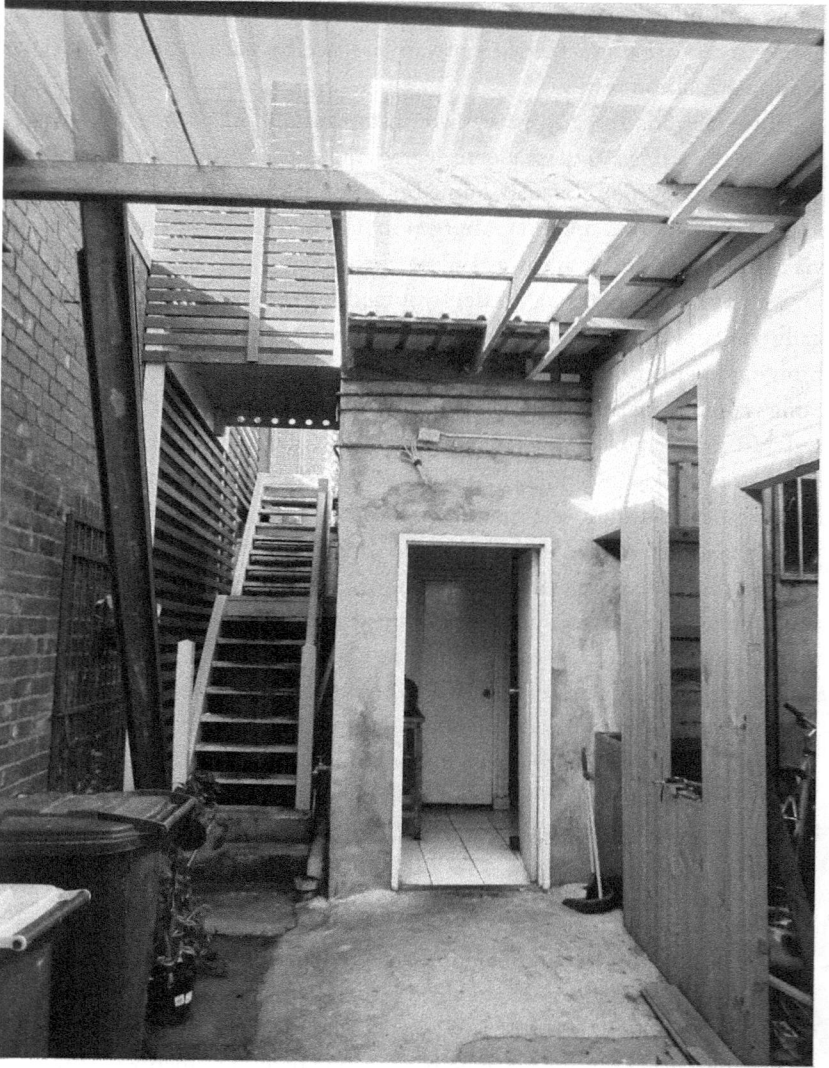

FIGURE 2.15 The home-built boardinghouse where Song lived, Coburg, 2012. Photo by the author.

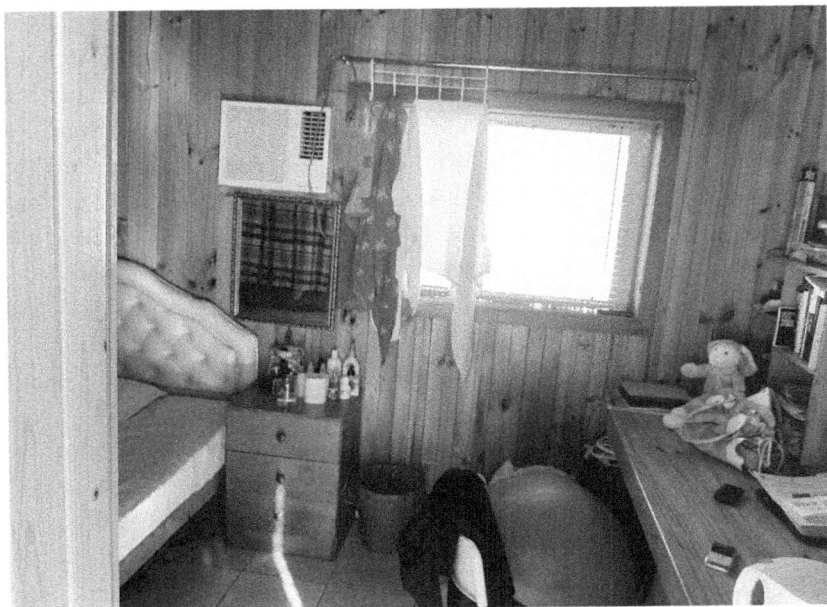

FIGURE 2.16 The home-built boardinghouse where Song lived, Coburg, 2012. Photo by the author.

think it really is true love. . . . It's a process of growing up. Sometimes it's not the place you were born that you love the most but the place where you've changed the most that you come to love more.

Typically thoughtful and considered, Song's discussion of her feelings for Melbourne is remarkable both for its reflexivity and for the intensity of the place feeling she expresses. The core of her reflection is that she feels a sense of belonging because this city is where she has grown into her independent, adult self, but the way she expresses this idea is arresting. The Chinese phrase *Moerben shi wo yige ren tansuo chulaide difang* (墨尔本是我一个人探索出来的地方) is difficult to translate directly; to translate it as "Melbourne is a place I've explored on my own" misses the implication, clear in the Chinese, that the Melbourne Song inhabits today has *arisen from* her exploration of it, as if the city didn't precede her exploring. For Song, who had lived in Melbourne for six and a half years at the time of our second conversation, the strong affective resonance of the city—productive of an intense sense of belonging, deep feeling, "true love," and sadness on leaving—arose from her intuition that the city and her adult self had been produced in and through their relation with each other.

Like Song, Anni was young—just seventeen—when she arrived in Melbourne. Pursuing an undergraduate degree at Bourke University in southeastern Melbourne, Anni lived near campus in the suburb of Caulfield, even though her parents owned an investment apartment in Box Hill. The recently constructed apartment block where she lived with one flatmate was home to a cluster of her Chinese classmates, and they often cooked dinner together and hung out in the evenings. Despite this conational clustering, Anni's map is notable for the degree of dispersion in her sub/urban geography, with each featured place floating in an independent, nonhierarchized bubble (figure 2.17). Although Anni's home in Caulfield is pictured (along with the associated places and practices of university, work, and supermarket), and the CBD makes an appearance (shopping, fireworks, Flinders Street Station), there is no strong center to her map, which appears more rhizomatic than focused. Anni includes the location of her first suburban homestay in Springvale ("totally deserted streets"; "never want to go there again"), the Box Hill "ethnoburb" (W. Li 1998) and her aunt's place ("everyone's <u>speaking Chinese</u>"), her yoga class in inner-suburban South Yarra, a beach to the south that she visited by accident after taking the wrong train, and her memory of New Year's Eve fireworks in the city, where she "said happy new year to strangers in the street"—all symbolically connected by a merrily tooting

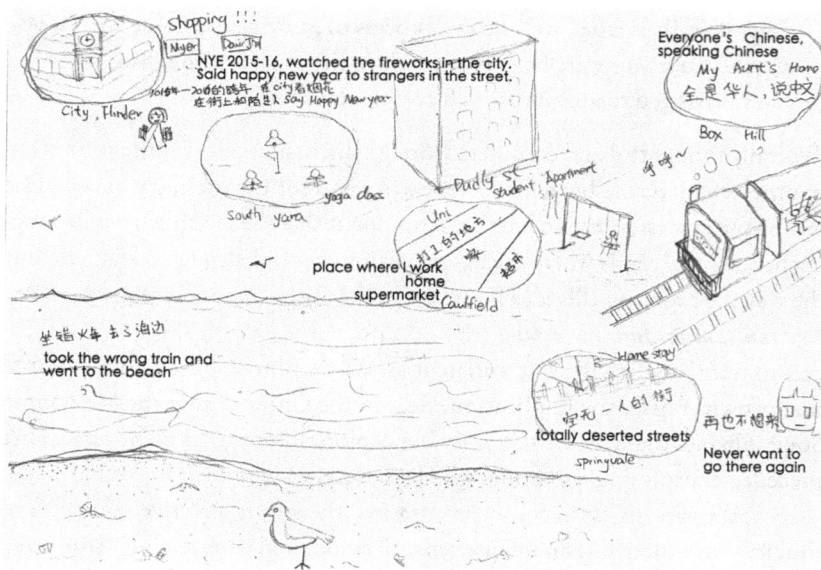

FIGURE 2.17 Anni's dispersed sub/urban geography (author's translations added).

suburban train. Not only does this map depict a dispersed geography, but it is also—like Yixin's map—rich in affect, demonstrating how Anni maps her own embodied responses onto the territory of the city and suburbs: unbearable tedium in Springvale, happy shopping in the CBD, bemusement at finding herself unexpectedly at the beach (expressed in the seagull's glassy blank eye), and joy at greeting friendly strangers during the New Year's Eve fireworks. Anni's Melbourne is extensive, extroverted, and open, both geographically and affectively. This impression is strengthened by a captioned photo she posted to her WeChat feed later on the same afternoon we did the mapping exercise, saying that she dreamed of climbing out toward the world like the vine of a potted plant on a verandah in the inner-urban neighborhood of Fitzroy where she was walking (figures 2.18–2.19). Anni's map also clearly includes suburban locations beyond the CBD. Given the number of

FIGURE 2.18 Photograph of outward-reaching potted vines from Anni's WeChat post.

阳台上种满植物，然后顺着阳台爬到外面去
大概就是我的梦想吧

1 hour ago

FIGURE 2.19 Anni's WeChat post from Fitzroy: "The balcony is filled with plants, and they climb along the balcony to the outside/That's pretty much my dream I guess."

educational transmigrants who, like Anni, choose to live near suburban university campuses, such locations are crucial to take into account in any consideration of this group's placemaking.

SUBURBAN CLUSTERS

While the dominant imagination of Chinese communities in Australia still centers the image of the inner-urban Chinatown enclave, research on Chinese diasporic life in the suburbs points to the datedness of that image (D. Ip 2005; Gao-Miles 2017; K. Anderson et al. 2019). Chinese *ethnoburbs*—defined by geographer Wei Li (1998) as suburban clusters of residential and business districts in large metropolises, with a concentration of a particular minority ethnicity—are a well-known feature of Australia's large east coast cities. With 26.6 percent of its residents claiming Chinese ancestry (compared to a state average of 4.7 percent) and 21.1 percent born in mainland China (Australian Bureau of Statistics 2016b), Melbourne's eastern suburb of Box Hill is one example.[8] Many participants—like Anni, whose parents owned an apartment there and whose aunt lived there—already knew of this area before arriving in Australia. Some enjoyed visiting it for the comforting familiarity of Chinese regional

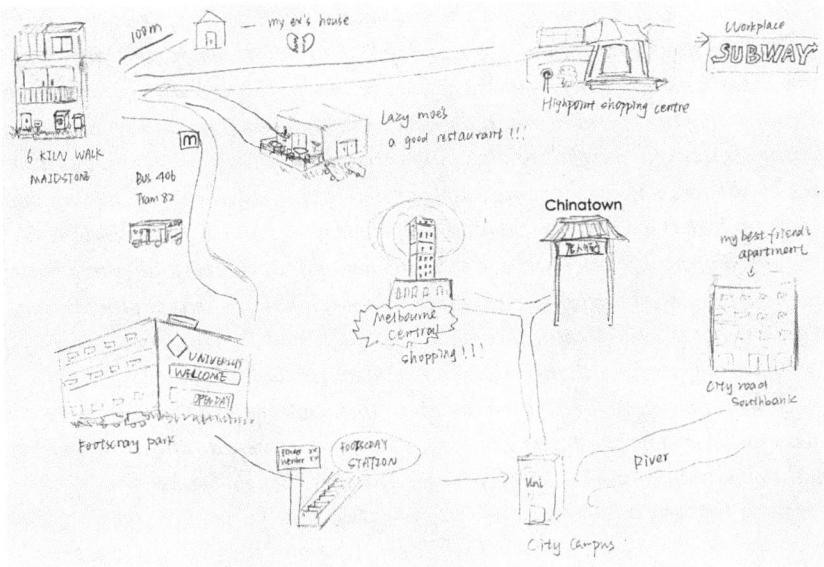

FIGURE 2.20 Zhenni's west-centric map.

cuisines, languages, and food stores. Others found jobs in Box Hill's Chinese restaurants, and a few lived in rental or family-owned apartments there.

But living in a relatively clearly demarcated "Chinese area" like Box Hill was not the suburban norm for these student transmigrants. Instead, most participants who resided outside the CBD lived in smaller, more diffuse suburban clusters near the campuses where they studied. Melbourne as experienced by these residents was less CBD-centric and more focused on suburban geographies. This is illustrated in Zhenni's map (figure 2.20). Zhenni, who studied at Queens University in the inner-west suburb of Footscray, included Chinatown and the CBD on her map, but the majority of her regularly visited and emotionally significant locations were in the inner-western suburbs: her apartment and her ex-boyfriend's place in Maidstone, Queens University's Footscray campus, Lazy Moe's restaurant in Maribyrnong, her workplace at the Subway in Highpoint Shopping Centre, and Footscray train station.

Loquats in Bundoora

The morning smells of eucalypts as I park my car in front of the newish, two-story brick-veneer house on the suburban street. Carrying the plastic bowl that Yueming asked to borrow and a package of chicken satay sticks, I crunch across the drying grass of the front yard and ring the doorbell. This house, where Yueming, Qiqi, and Xiaoyin have recently moved in, is just around the corner from where the three friends previously rented rooms in the home of a young migrant family. Xiaoqing, Yaling, and several other classmates from the same joint program at nearby Fawkner U also live within the same couple of streets. The year before, Yueming told me proudly that she orchestrated all this before leaving China: she'd found the first rental rooms in this neighborhood via classifieds on Yeeyi.com, and everyone else followed her lead. I've visited several times already and have become familiar with their neighborhood: its calm curving streets, big newish houses, native plantings, and local shopping court with several Chinese courier businesses.

One of the girls' male housemates opens the door for me and leads me into a spacious lower story with tiled floors, an open-plan kitchen/dining area, and two additional living areas walled off to make bedrooms. Six classmates from the joint program between a Chinese university and Fawkner U live here together: two men and four women. As we chat while shucking corn and hulling strawberries in the kitchen, the housemate who let me in tells me the house is an investment property belonging to a Chinese lecturer they know at the Confucius Institute at Fawkner U. Recently woken, Qiqi and Xiaoyin patter sleepily to and fro fetching items of clothing from the laundry; Yueming wanders around searching for her lost lidded cup, tossing out reckless accusations that someone must have hidden it. Eventually we load the many plastic bags of meat, salad, biscuits, chips, drinks, sauces, and plates that Yueming bought the day before into Yueming's car and set off for nearby Bundoora Park. We stop off at Xiaoqing's place on the way—she's made a sweet herbal soup for the occasion—but it turns out she's already got a ride with someone else.

Eighteen classmates from the joint program join this postexams celebration. The plan to have a barbecue was hatched the previous year, when I organized a similar event for our participant group at a park in the CBD. Qiqi's eyes had lit up; she is a keen cook:

Say, do all parks here have these free barbecues? she'd asked. Look at it! It's just like teppanyaki. You could stir-fry beef, even do fried noodles!

As we cart our bags of food from Yueming's car to one of the barbecue shelters, nearby a group of disabled people slowly exit their minivan for an outing with their caregivers, and two women in hijabs bring their young children to play on the slides. Traffic hums by on Plenty Road as the morning cloud slowly burns off.

Mirroring the Australian barbecue stereotype, the work of grilling and socializing is markedly gendered. The boys mainly man the barbecue while the girls sit chatting on plastic sheets under a nearby clump of gum trees, drifting between there and the barbecue shelter eating chips, cups of Xiaoqing's sweet soup, sandwiches, the meat as it gets cooked, and cheeks of mango from a box Yueming has brought and slices for everyone. Someone comes to grief with an overgenerous sprinkling of his classmate's homemade chili-and-rice powder brought from his hometown in Jiangxi. Yueming tries hard to get the others to eat her leafy salad (which everyone refers to as "grass")—she's become a convert to raw salads after discovering balsamic dressing—but few are convinced. After two years sharing classes in Shanghai and a further eighteen months in Melbourne, the students know each other well and call out to each other with affectionately wisecracking nicknames: Xueba (学霸: "study nerd") for five of the boys; for Yueming, Ma Wang (in sly reference to her den mother–style social role) or Tongxiang (同乡: "hometown buddy": teasing her and another classmate for their bond based on both coming from the same village in Zhejiang). American pop, hip-hop, and Chinese pop drift tinnily on the spring breeze from a speaker connected to someone's iPhone. We take selfies and circulate them in a WeChat group; there is a half-hearted attempt to play a card game based on the medieval classic Romance of the Three Kingdoms. A sweet-voiced girl quietly sings a Mandopop ballad accompanied by music from her phone.

One of the boys brings a big plate of freshly barbecued marinated chicken gizzards over and offers it to Yueming, knowing it's her favorite. She tucks in enthusiastically, explaining between mouthfuls exactly what a chicken gizzard is, for the benefit of her citified classmates:

OK, so you've killed a chicken, right? Has anyone ever killed a chicken? No? Well, you know our family's from the country, so we do it all the time. Take, say, an old hen. After you take out its digestive tract, you'll find these little things down at the bottom, below the intestine. Those are the gizzards. They're perfectly clean; the chicken shit doesn't go through them.

After lunch, we go back to the big house. The downstairs area is soon set up for an afternoon of hanging out: a mah-jongg table in the kitchen, a card game round the dining table, leftover barbecue snacks set out for grazing, and the doors and windows open to the warm afternoon, admitting clouds of tiny insects. I do my best—unsuccessfully—to help Yueming, Qiqi, and Xiaoyin figure out how to ignite their complicated gas oven: Yueming is keen to try a recipe for banana bread she got from her homestay landlady on a trip to Adelaide. She shows me the neatly written slip of yellow paper. I hang out with the three girls as they show a soon-to-be-vacated upstairs bedroom to a prospective housemate.

Afterward, we drift into Yueming's room. She's recently covered her mirrored wardrobe doors with a nifty set of miniature curtains bought online from China, and she explains to me the feng shui principle of never sleeping in a room with *mirrored surfaces. Yueming's mother is a professional feng shui consultant, so she knows all the ins and outs. I suddenly recall that once, living in Taipei, I found it hard to sleep in a bedroom with a mirrored wardrobe and ended up buying some cloth to cover it. Yes, confirms Yueming: that'll be the 阴气 yinqi (dark energy). Mirrors emit yinqi; they'll give you insomnia and nightmares. You simply can't have them in a bedroom.*

Later, Qiqi and Yueming take me out to the side garden. In the yellowing late-afternoon sun, Qiqi shows me the mini vegetable garden she's made in a raised brick bed. She's planted a tomato, spring onions, and a sprouted potato—she asks me where the new potatoes will grow on the plant. Examining her little plants, Qiqi curses lightly: the neighbor's cat has been scratching in the soil again. I sympathize: neighbor cats are the bane of our veggie garden at home. Well, I'm not too fussed, says Yueming. Back home in the country, we use cow and pig dung to fertilize the vegetables. So I'm sort of used to the idea of vegetables growing in animal dung. I tell her I'm not so sure. Cats are carnivores and share parasites with humans: their poo seems a lot dirtier to me than a nice grass-eating cow's. Pigs are pretty clean too, I ramble on, they mainly eat vegetables, although they can eat meat—Yueming swiftly interrupts: Don't worry, no pig of ours is about to get a meat dinner!

Qiqi points to the dark spreading leaves of the big loquat tree hanging over the fence, bearing bunches of small round fruit. Would you look at that: what a waste. The old Shanghainese couple next door have this great tree, but they don't pick the loquats. Their daughter married a local, and their grandchildren speak in English. They can't understand them. Yueming hops onto the garden bed and reaches up to pick some loquats. The trees grow so well here, how come nobody eats these? I say I've never tried one, and she hands one of the yellow fruits down to me. It's delicious.

With regard to suburban clusters, the clustering effect notable in some student transmigrants' sociospatial habitation patterns may not be based on ethnicity and nationality alone, or even principally. Clusters of friends and acquaintances living near one another may be linked through diverse and multiscaled facets of identity—institutional, subnational, and religious, to name a few—problematizing the reductiveness inherent in the "ethnic enclave" model (Gao-Miles 2017). The close-knit suburban neighborhood produced through the connections between Yueming, Qiqi, Xiaoyin, Yaling, Xiaoqing, and their classmates was based on their institutional links, as classmates in the same transnational degree program, rather than simply on ethnicity or nationality. In representing themselves as a group, they were more likely to frame themselves as "joint program students in Bundoora" than as simply "Chinese." And their experience of Melbourne was, in fact, primarily an experience of this suburban locality. On another occasion, Yueming reflected, "Actually, living in Melbourne, we pretty much live in Bundoora. I mean, this [the suburb] is 'Melbourne,' for us. I can't even remember how long it's been since I went to the CT." Similarly, another group who studied at Queens University in joint programs with two Chinese universities said the area near the Footscray campus where they all lived in close proximity "felt like a village."

The story from the Bundoora group illustrates how Yueming and Qiqi made their neighborhood homelike by symbolically articulating their everyday practices there with aspects of their home-based habitus. Qiqi, famous among her friends for her skills in preparing southern-style cuisine, was excited about cooking home-style dishes on the public barbecue, planting vegetables, and harvesting loquats in their suburban backyard. Throughout the day of the barbecue, Yueming's conversation proudly highlighted her self-identification as an earthy country person. Having been brought up in a small, semirural town in Zhejiang, she was familiar with disemboweling chickens, fertilizing crops, and feeding pigs, and also knew the principles of feng shui. She articulated these directly with elements of her current (trans)locality in Bundoora: barbecue, veggie patch, wardrobe.

In another example of alternative suburban clustering principles, when twenty-three-year-old Huisheng from Shandong arrived in Melbourne to pursue her master's degree, she moved in with her twin brother in the inner-eastern suburb of Hawthorn. During their first year in Melbourne, they shared a flat with a landlady from their home province and the landlady's husband, young baby, and mother, as well as another student, also from Shandong. Huisheng described the warm, family-like feeling of their apartment: she enjoyed hanging out with the landlady and the baby and preparing and eating Shandong-style dishes together. This kind of intimate social support made Huisheng feel that her time in Melbourne was relatively stress-free compared to the experiences of other international students. The communal social space these Shandongese flatmates created together stemmed not from any national-level ethnic or (even less) political "Chinese" identity but rather from a shared provincial-cultural affiliation expressed in the microlevel details of everyday living, especially cuisine and dialect. When Huisheng, her brother, and the other Shandongese flatmate ultimately left the apartment, they rented another close by and continued to visit their former landlady's family regularly to cook, eat, and hang out.

Wenling, who arrived from her hometown, a small city in Jiangsu, when she was seventeen, was by 2017 living in a neighborhood defined by connections based on religion. During her stay in Melbourne, Wenling converted to Mormonism (see chapter 6), and the church became the center of her social world, taking up most of her time on weekends with worship and Bible study activities, introducing her to a tight-knit group of similar-aged friends (American, Chinese, and Australian), and leading to a series of trips to visit Mormon youth in other parts of Australia and, later on, Salt Lake City in the United States. From 2016, Wenling lived in a rundown share-house that had previously been government housing in the working-class suburb of Heidelberg West, sharing with Mormon housemates met through her church: another Chinese student; Noah, a young Anglo man from Queensland; and Noah's younger sister. Wenling was also close with Noah's Chinese girlfriend, who often hung out at their house. In the street where they lived, there were no fewer than three other Mormon households. They had got to know one of their Chinese Mormon neighbors well: a young divorced woman with children, whom the church elders had charged them with looking after. Wenling explained this church-based neighborhood network to me one afternoon over coffee at Northland Shopping Centre in Preston, near where we both lived. Demonstrating the density and ubiquity of their neighborhood network, that day I also got to meet Noah, who worked in the café where we met, and the divorcée neighbor, who happened to pass by our table on her way to pick up her son from childcare.

City of Fear: Racism, Violence, and Gender

The rather idyllic image of student transmigrants' sub/urban connectedness painted in some of the preceding examples is, however, only part of the picture. Throughout the years of this study, a consistent thread in participants' conversations concerned their experiences of fear in urban and suburban contexts as a result of property crime, racist attacks, and what they felt to be the growing risk of violent assault.

Quotidian racist violence on the street and public transport were a not-uncommon cause of a sense of social exclusion in everyday sub/urban life for these student transmigrants (F. Martin and Rizvi 2014; F. Martin 2016). For example, Shihong told me about a friend who witnessed a Chinese man being violently attacked by a group of teenagers on a tram in Bundoora on a Saturday night for no apparent reason, to the extent that an ambulance had to be called; on another occasion, while she was walking along Plenty Road, someone yelled at her from a passing car, "Fucking Asians!" Shunqing recounted the visceral impact of a tram that failed to stop for her, then broke regulations to stop fifty meters past the stop for a white man:

The driver just ignored me. Yeah, just ignored me. . . . So I missed [the tram]. I had to walk back to my place. . . . So I walked down the street and then I thought, Why did I come here? Why feel this discrimination? Because I'd have better opportunities in China. . . . I left my parents there, and they have to bear this feeling [that] "my daughter is far away from me." It was quite sad for me.

Mei told a related story:

M: Sometimes on the street you encounter people who don't really welcome friends from overseas and yell at us to "get back to your own country!" . . . [It happened to me] once, not often. But nevertheless it—
F: —was pretty memorable, I guess.
M: Yes, because I was really young at the time. I felt very hurt.

In mid-2017 this issue erupted in a new way, specifically targeting Chinese international students, when a neo-Nazi group pasted up notices in awkward Chinese on the campuses of two of the city's large universities, on university letterhead, stating that Chinese people were barred from entering the campus under threat of prosecution and deportation (figure 2.21). Obviously, experiences of such racist abuse in public space tend to interrupt any nascent sense of sub/urban belonging.

Random—or perhaps, many suspected, at times racially motivated—street assaults became a recurrent topic of conversation in 2016–17, with participants' perceptions of the increased risk of such crimes exceeding their recorded statistical increase.[9] In late 2016 Qin related the story of a young Chinese student couple she knew who had recently been attacked in the entry courtyard of their apartment building, in the middle-class suburb of Kew. The man was stabbed repeatedly, and the woman had her cheek slashed, yet the attacker didn't rob them. "Could he have been drunk?" Qin wondered. "It's terrible: they were just about to graduate. We daren't tell our parents about this sort of thing. If I told my mum that this happened to my classmate, she'd say, 'There's no way you can stay there. Come home immediately.'" Stunned, I could think of no explanation other than that the attacker may have been mentally ill or drug affected and/or that the attack was racially motivated.

Similar cases frightened the group living in Bundoora as well. Leaving her townhouse complex one evening, Yaling witnessed a woman being assaulted with a baseball bat and robbed by a "black man" (黑人 heiren) who jumped out of a passing car; soon afterward, somebody—perhaps a homeless man, she thought—snatched Yaling's grocery bags out of her hands outside the local

FIGURE 2.21 Anti-Chinese poster at Capital University, posted by a neo-Nazi group.

supermarket.[10] These incidents left Yaling extremely fearful and reluctant to walk alone in a neighborhood where previously she had felt quite safe. She left for China the very afternoon her classes finished at the end of that semester, reluctant to spend even a single extra day in Melbourne. And when I visited Yueming and Qiqi's house seven months after the barbecue described earlier, they showed me a WeChat post from a classmate who had been violently assaulted and robbed by a group of teenage girls in Bundoora the day before (figure 2.22). Yueming told me, "It's bad. We don't dare go out after dark anymore. I used to think nothing of walking to the supermarket alone at ten p.m.; there's no way we'd do that now." I mused aloud that even though I lived nearby in a broadly similar suburb, I somehow didn't feel that way: I'd still walk to the shops alone at night. Yueming responded insightfully: "It's a question of a sense of belonging. . . . We've already lived nearly two years in Melbourne: a long time. But our sense of belonging is definitely not as strong as yours [plural]. We're still foreigners, outsiders [外来人, 外地人 wailai ren, waidi ren]." "So we feel we could be attacked," added Qiqi. They were right, of course. As a middle-class, long-term

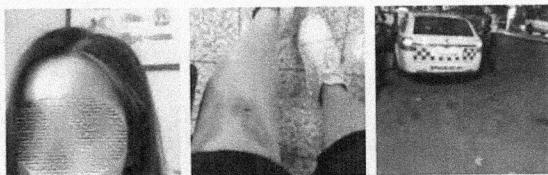

FIGURE 2.22 WeChat post from a joint program student in Bundoora, June 2017. "Just back from making a report at the police station Yesterday my bag was stolen by local youths At first I thought I could handle the beating but then four or five of them [female] pulled my hair to the point where they knocked me to the ground and the nightmare began I was so scared My eye and knee were injured My phone was broken too It really is too unsafe overseas too scary."—Melbourne, two minutes ago

Anglo resident with Australian citizenship, in my Melbourne, I implicitly trust fellow residents not to attack me, and I more or less trust other pedestrians, the police, and the legal system to protect my safety. With what appeared to be a rise in violent street attacks against Chinese students and migrants, these young women's affective relationship with sub/urban Melbourne had become very different from mine.

The landscape of fear that the city and suburbs became for participants at such times had a clearly gendered element. The generalized parental safety worries that I heard voiced during interviews with families predeparture over sending a *daughter*, in particular, to live overseas were echoed in many of my participants' gendered fears about going out alone at night, both before and—even more—after the increased social media reporting of assaults in 2016–17. In late summer in 2017, as I had lunch with a group of participants in the Southgate area next to the river, Meng—an adventurous and, in her own description, risk-loving young woman—told the other five participants about her fond memories of that area, where she'd often partied at the nearby Crown Casino entertainment complex. "Don't you have those memories, too?" she asked. Meng was met with blank looks. It emerged that, as women, none of the other five would consider going out in the city at night: they all tried to get home before dark owing to safety concerns. As well as fears of assault, these concerns were sometimes also connected to participants' sense that East Asian–looking young women could become sexual targets for non-Asian men with stereotyped preconceptions of their desirability as partners. Several participants related unpleasant experiences of unwelcome pickup attempts by Anglo men, which exacerbated their unease in public space, particularly at night.

Making Melbourne: Multiplicity and Translocality

This chapter has considered the question of what Melbourne is for the Chinese student transmigrants who inhabit, practice, and produce the city. The answers that have emerged suggest that Melbourne has multiple competing meanings centering around some core tensions: dream/disillusion, advancement/backwardness, extension/encapsulation. Melbourne is imagined ambivalently as both an entry point to the dream of transnational advancement and a village-like backwater; it is the site of social encapsulation and sometimes violent exclusion as well as a place of self-extension and (trans)local belonging; it supports an expatriate microworld based on Chinese nationality but also multiple smaller sociospatial clusters based on nonnational principles. The experiential city crystallizes out of atmospheres of hopefulness, frustration, excitement, disorientation, connection, disappointment, alienation, comfort, boredom, fulfillment, grief, melancholy, love, and fear. And it is transnationally connected at every scale, its everyday localities—bedrooms, parks, backyards, neighborhoods—constitutively interwoven with distant places through a restless tide of movies, recipes, bodies, curtains, money, chili powder, selfies, dialects, messages, and memories.

In the next chapter, I extend and complicate this chapter's closing discussion of sub/urban placemaking, fear, and racialization through a case study that underlines the role of social media in shaping student transmigrants' experiences of Melbourne, including transnational social media's potential to reinforce encapsulation along ethnic, national, racial, and class lines at the local level. Chapter 3 focuses not only on how student transmigrants are themselves racialized but also on how racializing representations of other city dwellers circulated via WeChat: the most widely used social media platform within Melbourne's Chinese student world.

3. MEDIA
Connection and Encapsulation

*

For the first few days after I arrived [in Melbourne], I didn't eat anything—I couldn't eat. . . . It was because when I came, I didn't bring my mobile phone, because my dad said I should open an account here. I didn't have the internet, and I didn't have a phone, I didn't know anything! I was completely cut off from the world! I couldn't sleep at all, either. I'd get up really early in the morning. I missed home a lot, I missed my mum and my dad, and I thought, oh, there's such good stuff to eat back home, and I have so many good friends. I had no friends at all here. Then later I got a phone account and got the internet on, and ahhhh, my life gradually got back to normal. . . . I go online to chat with my mum and . . . look at entertainment news and celebrity gossip and keep up with things back home a bit, which tends to cheer you up. . . . I could chat about how I was feeling—you feel different when you've got someone to talk to. I could hear my mum and dad's voice, and feel, ahhh, Mum and Dad are with me here all the time. (Mianmian, 19)

*

This story, which Mianmian related as we chatted in her small student apartment in Carlton in 2012 three months after her arrival, provides an arresting account of how the capacity for transnational communication may be experienced by the current generation of mobile digital natives as a condition of a place's inhabitability. In a sense, for Mianmian (to paraphrase Gertrude Stein), there was simply "no there there" in Melbourne until communication with home could be reestablished. She became a node without a network, deprived of all information and "completely cut off from the world" in a city that could not be experienced as a place at all (Wellman 2002). Indeed, the severity of the affective and bodily symptoms attending Mianmian's temporary disconnection—difficulty eating and sleeping, anxiety, intense dejection— suggests that for this mobile subject, transnational connectivity was a condition of viable subjecthood, as well as of inhabitable place.

This chapter extends chapter 2's exploration of participants' placemaking in Melbourne by focusing more sharply on how these mobile subjects' media engagements shape their experiences of the city. Rejecting the popular dichotomy in which embodied experience is conceptually opposed to technological mediation, the chapter rests on the assumption that—especially for the current generation, who have grown up in the era when digital media and communication systems constitute a taken-for-granted aspect of everyday experience (Prensky 2001; Zhang X. 2010)—embodied and mediated engagements with place are constitutively intertwined. It contends that a significant part of what *makes* Melbourne, for these inhabitants, is a proliferation of translocal media connections. Thus, the chapter focuses on the sociospatial aspects of participants' media use and the mediated aspects of their engagements with the city's social life.

My proposition that people's experiences of place are produced through the entwinement of mediated and nonmediated encounters draws inspiration from current scholarship spanning urban geography, the anthropology and sociology of mobilities, and phenomenological media studies that recognizes that the media-networked character of places is increasingly fundamental to how people experience them. An influential strand of work in media studies, for example— sometimes called a non-media-centric media studies (Morley 2009)—focuses primarily not on the content of media representations but on the way people's media engagements are articulated with the wider context of their lived experience, including their experiences of place. Along these lines, drawing on the work of phenomenologist geographers Yi-Fu Tuan and David Seamon, Shaun Moores (2012) argues for the mutually constitutive triangulation of media, place, and mobility (see also Tomlinson 2007; Couldry and Hepp 2017). For such thinkers, the ubiquity of mobile and ambient digital media conditions our experience of localities at the most basic level. In the words of Ash Amin and Nigel Thrift, the "human membrane"—the interface between outward perception and inward consciousness that constitutes the human experience of place—"has been technologized" (2017, 79, 75). Ubiquitous media may make us feel that we are "in two places at once," pluralizing place by stretching our social world beyond the constraints of geographic proximity (Scannell 1996), or that we can "take our homes with us" when we travel (Gergen 2002; Morley 2003, 452–53; Metykova 2010). They may link us to a cosmopolitan sense of a wider world or encapsulate us in inward-looking subworlds (Ding and Tian 2009; Christensen and Jansson 2015); they may provide us with both ways into and ways out of the life of the city (Georgiou 2011; F. Martin and Rizvi 2014). The intensifying mediatization of everyday life, especially through mobile devices, thus means that our sense of place becomes transformed in its very substance as physical and digital experiences intertwine, hybridize, and mutually transform (de Souza e Silva 2006; Silverstone 2008, 110–11; D.-H. Lee 2010). Most important, ubiquitous media connections intensify the effects of translocality, so that the places we inhabit come to feel less and less territorially defined and more and more marked by their interlinkage into expansive networks connecting other worlds, near and far.

If, for Chinese student transmigrants, a large part of what makes Melbourne is translocal media connections, then the questions become, *how* do these connections produce the city, in practice? *What kind of place(s)* emerge from this mediatization? And *what kind of subjectivities* are formed in student transmigrants' engagements with the mediated city? Chapter 2's discussion of participants' sociospatial practices in the city and suburbs highlighted a structuring tension between encapsulation (the expatriate microworld) and extension (wider sociospatial expansion). This chapter develops a related theme in a different register by focusing on the operations of spatial extension, ethnicization, racialization, and class in participants' media practices in Melbourne. Focusing particularly on mobile networked Chinese-language media, I argue that the tension between extension and encapsulation is expressed in popular platforms' capacity, on one hand, to open up spatial connections by mapping ways into the city and, on the other hand, in the context of users' wider social exclusion (X. Zhao 2017), to cocoon them into a defensive capsule based on the essentialization of Chinese ethnicity and the racialization of classed Others. Although encapsulation dominates over extension in the main case study of local WeChat news in the chapter's second half, I do not intend to draw definitive conclusions about the dominance of one or the other of these contradictory operations. Rather, the mobile networked media that shape student transmigrants' sub/urban lifeworlds simultaneously have both connecting and encapsulating capacities, so that their social and subjective effects are unpredictable and highly contingent, depending on multiple contextual factors.

The chapter begins with a broad overview of participants' everyday media practices in Melbourne, including their use of WeChat, their most used platform. I then consider some of the ways in which such translocal media produced the space of the city and enabled spatial extension across sub/urban geographies, before turning to these media's socially encapsulating effects. Some brief background is provided to set the scene for the chapter's main case study of a racializing panic that spread via local WeChat news accounts during 2016. The case study considers the structure, content, production, and regulation of this new form of translocal media. It also analyzes participants' engagements with the WeChat news accounts, especially the ramifications of some popular accounts' reactionary framing of "Chineseness," "Africans," and "refugees" for participants' experience of the city.

The conclusion explores how these local examples connect with broader questions about media, mobility, superdiversity, and socially sustainable urban life.

Translocal Media Worlds

Student transmigrants' media practices in Melbourne were dominated by online delivery, portability (platforms accessible by smartphone), and transnationality (connected to national and global-diasporic Chinese mediaspheres). They overwhelmingly accessed entertainment media—films, video, radio, and music—online via Chinese and other providers, including Youku, iQiyi, YouTube, KuGou, and QQMusic (F. Martin 2016). Participants generally did not engage with much Australian media: the easy and largely free availability of a wide range of familiar content via online streaming meant that their media consumption patterns following relocation were obliged to change far less than would have been the case even ten years earlier. While certain platforms clearly dominated, individuals tended to engage a polymedia bundle whose composition depended on function and personal preference (Madianou and Miller 2012). For example, QQ might be used for video calls with family, Instagram for photo sharing with friends overseas, Weibo for China-related social commentary, WeChat groups for messaging with specific contact clusters, transnational online gaming for entertainment and socializing, and so on.

By far the most popular and frequently engaged platform among participants was WeChat, an app they had generally used habitually in China and continued to use after moving to Melbourne. Released by China's Tencent Holdings Ltd. in 2011, by 2017 the WeChat "mega-app" reported 938 million monthly active users and was among the top smartphone apps both within China and among Chinese students abroad (F. Martin 2016; E. Lee 2017). WeChat's popularity rests on its smoothly integrated panoply of functions. It bundles together one-to-one and group messaging, including the capacity to share photos, links, and documents, as well as audio messaging and audio and video call options (similar to WhatsApp); a Facebook-like wall feed (the Moments function); official accounts (subscription feeds delivering a range of information and commercial products and services); live video streaming; online shopping; payment functions linked to users' bank accounts that can be used both online and in brick-and-mortar stores; a geolocative function for finding friends in the user's immediate neighborhood; a shake function facilitating hookups; integrated games; the capacity to gift digital red money packets on celebration days; a search engine; user interfaces for a range of government and community services within China; and much more.

The importance of WeChat in student transmigrants' everyday lives cannot be overstated. In a survey of Chinese-speaking international students conducted throughout Australia in 2018, 97.5 percent of 555 respondents reported that they opened WeChat several times every day, making it their most favored social media platform by a very wide margin, ahead of Chinese alternatives like Weibo and very significantly ahead of major Anglosphere platforms like Instagram and Facebook (F. Martin et al. 2019, 29). Most participants in the present study kept WeChat open on their phones twenty-four hours a day and checked their Moments feed, groups, and subscription accounts multiple times every day and night, for cumulatively significant periods of time.

The Chinese student microworld's internal networks in offline life, explored in the previous chapter, are reflected in its WeChat networks. During my project I witnessed the development and intensification of this digital network in real time. I added contacts in Melbourne's Chinese student community independently of each other as I met them in different contexts: study participants from various universities, some of my own graduate students and former students, students and early-career scholars in the field, research assistants, friends of participants, professionals working in international student services, and so on. WeChat's privacy settings in the Moments feed mean that users are only shown posts and comments from other users with whom they are already connected in the app: if I post a photo and two people like it or comment who are not already added as each other's contacts, then they will not be shown each other's responses. This feature makes it possible to track who knows whom by observing interactions on the feed. When I first added people early in their Melbourne sojourns, those I added independently of each other were typically not connected. But as the months went by, webs of interconnection spread organically: participant A's housemate liked participant B's photo, participant C's boyfriend and participant D had an exchange about a reflection posted by participant E's coworker, and so on. For users, the digital visibility of these social connections contributes to the sense that Melbourne is a small place: a close-knit, village-like community where everyone knows everyone.

Media Extension: Syncretic Spatial Experience and
Ways into the City

Notwithstanding WeChat's apparent digital replication of the expatriate microworld with all its potentials for social encapsulation, such platforms may also enable forms of sociospatial extension. In an article I wrote with Fazal Rizvi (F. Martin and Rizvi 2014), we focused on the translocal character of

Chinese social media, with an emphasis on their potentials for spatial localization in Melbourne. Apps like WeChat and Weibo are developed in and run from China and are populated by many of the student migrants' contacts and familiar media content from back home; yet they are often engaged in public space overseas, as student migrants access them via smartphone while physically traversing the city and suburbs. Accordingly, we proposed that "both 'out here' and 'back home' become fragmented and deterritorialized, woven in and through each other, as the Melbourne that this generation of international students inhabit is fundamentally conditioned by the fluctuating mediated co-presence of elements of 'back home.' Such a proposal goes beyond arguments about media's doubling or pluralization of places . . . to suggest a more fundamental transformation in the very meaning of place itself as a result of the experiential ubiquity of transnational media connections" (1018). We had in mind something that resonates with Amin's conceptualization of "topological" geographies, which emphasizes that since both local places and the spaces of global flows are produced from practices in networks, "we cannot assume that local happenings or geographies are ontologically separable from those 'out there'" (2002b, 386). Amin therefore advocates "a reading of spatiality in nonlinear, nonscalar terms, a readiness to accept geographies and temporalities as they are produced through practices and relations of different spatial stretch and duration . . . without any a priori assumption of geographies of relations nested in territorial or geometric space" (389). The translocal media connections that draw fragments of "back home" instantaneously into the very fabric of student transmigrants' everyday experiences of locality in Melbourne produce a syncretic spatial experience that resonates strongly with Amin's conceptualization of the nature of geographies in globalization (see also de Souza e Silva 2006).

This conceptualization of the syncretic spatial experience afforded by mobile networked media also resonates with work by Chinese media scholar Sun Wei, who has developed perhaps the richest theorization to date of the social and philosophical implications of WeChat's ubiquity in contemporary Chinese social life. Extrapolating from Heideggerian phenomenology an understanding of both place and subjectivity as produced through everyday practical engagements, Sun (2015) proposes that WeChat's pervasive mediation of both spatial experience and social relations means that it can be understood to constitute nothing less than contemporary Chinese people's being-in-the-world. Sun observes that the app enables a certain loosening of the user's experiential tether to static locality, as well as a relinking into a more mobile sense of being. The mobile scene (移动场景 *yidong changjing*) is an affordance that Sun theorizes as central to the experience of using WeChat, and defines as describing

> a situation where a person can be placed in multiple scenes at the same time. The scene follows people to become mobile, interwoven, collaged, and integrated. . . . The mobility to which I refer has two implications. Obviously the first one is travel between physical spaces, whereby people move, along with their mobile phones and WeChat, from one physical scene to another one. . . . The deeper meaning of [the mobile scene's] mobility is that people habitually shuttle between multiple scenes, including physical scenes, mass media scenes, and WeChat friendship circles, producing a situation in which multiple scenes are juxtaposed, crossed, and integrated. (10)

The mobile scene, in other words, is an assemblage of images, sounds, social relations, and affects composed and recomposed from moment to moment through users' WeChat-enabled interactions through text, graphics, videos, and voice. This syncretic scene "mobilizes along with people" (随着人而移动 *suizhe ren er yidong*; Sun 2015, 10) as they move from one location to another and becomes integrated with their experience of the physical spaces they are occupying. This usefully extends our conceptualization of mobile networked media's capacities for syncretic, translocal placemaking.

Rizvi and I emphasized that their capacity to syncretize "here" and "there" does not mean that translocal social media like Weibo and WeChat somehow magically lift student transmigrants out of the geographic locality of their place of study: instead, they may provide a "way in to the city" (Georgiou 2011). These overseas users' mobile scenes integrate elements of Melbourne locality and to a significant extent *become localized* in the Chinese educational diaspora in Australia. Illustrating this, among the most widely used features of apps like WeChat and Weibo are those that extend student transmigrants' spatial range in the city by helping them to navigate urban and suburban geography. In particular, students read a range of subscription-based leisure-and-lifestyle accounts that provide information on many aspects of life in Melbourne, from the weather, to current events, to food, shopping, day trips, and entertainment. For example, pilot study participants observed in 2012:

> On Weibo, there are those [groups], like Melbourne *Discounts* or Melbourne Let's Eat, and if I see lots of posts saying, hey, this place in Oakleigh

is pretty good, then I'll go there and try it with my friends.... When people say somewhere's good, we'll go and check it out. (Wenyi)

Because there are a lot of Chinese people here, we often use Weibo to exchange information. Like, where is there good food; where is there a sale on; where is a room available. (Shujuan)

Such media enable the "thickening" of locality (Andersson 2012) by providing student transmigrants with readily accessible information on where to go in Melbourne, how to get there, and how to understand and engage with the sites one encounters. Reinforcing this idea and providing a point of historical comparison, Mei remarked in late 2016:

If I compare the young students coming now for undergraduate study with myself when I came the first time [in 2006], I think... they know so much more. The information is so much more available to them. When I came, it wasn't until my third year here that I finally discovered: oh, so there are places you can go and have *brunch*! [*laughs*] Today you only have to browse through your WeChat [public accounts] to find scores of places, on your first day here.

These reflections underline how such apps enable today's student migrants to extend their geographic mobility in the city and suburbs in ways that would otherwise be (and formerly were) much more difficult.

Such observations, however, focus largely on the geospatial rather than the social affordances of these platforms. They underline the apps' capacity to provide ways into the city by mobilizing students across a wide range of geographic routes and sites, while domesticating sub/urban space by interweaving local geographies with familiar digital scenes to produce a syncretic spatial experience particular to Melbourne's Chinese student diaspora. However, as the participants' remarks suggest, the kinds of activities mapped on such city-based accounts overwhelmingly promote class-bound leisure and consumption practices: coffee culture, eating out, tourism, shopping, and large cultural events. In this sense, while extending student transmigrants' worlds *spatially*, they tend to invite users to experience the city as a site of consumption rather than promoting cross-group *social* extension.[1] This was reflected in the ways participants in this study mostly engaged these accounts in practice. The potential for socially encapsulating effects is even more evident in the way the reporting of local news in some of the most popular city-based WeChat public accounts invites readers to (dis)identify with specific racial and class categories.

Media Encapsulation: In-Grouping in WeChat's
Digital Diaspora

In her discussion of the phenomenological implications of WeChat, Sun Wei (2015) highlights the sense of belonging generated by the app's groups function, whereby conversations are established and often maintained over time in virtual communities that share specific affiliations. Sun's examples are WeChat groups based on former classmates and school alumni. The participants in the present study participated in WeChat groups based on Chinese students taking the same major at a particular university, Chinese students in specific Australian cities, group assignment partners, e-trading activities (see chapter 4), family (X. Zhao 2019a), location-based leisure interests such as foodies in Melbourne, friendships, and the study itself. With reference to the groups function, Sun writes that "the most significant characteristic of WeChat use is the ubiquity [伴随性 *bansuixing*: literally, 'accompanyingness'] of the sense of group affiliation in everyday life" (2015, 13). This sense of group affiliation, like the mobile scene, follows the user from place to place. Sun further observes that "the particularity of the sense of place created by WeChat lies in the fact that while it breaks [spatial] borders, at the same time it produces localized belonging and identity for individuals and groups" (14). These observations underline that, for Sun, WeChat enables a certain *detethering* from geographic locality (the mobile user is "followed" by WeChat's mobile scene; spatial borders around social connection are broken) at the same time as it enables a *retethering* to a different sense of belonging within particularized groups.

While Sun explicitly references a mainland Chinese national framework (albeit one complicated by the mobile scene's capacity to scramble conventional geographies), it is interesting to extend her reflections to the experiences of WeChat users outside China. In this case, users become physically mobile at a transnational scale and yet continue to participate in a digital mobile scene that is characterized by Chinese-language interactions and peopled overwhelmingly by others of the same ethnicity and nationality, whether they are physically located inside or outside China—a kind of Chinese digital diaspora. The habitual use of China-based, Chinese-language mobile social media apps in non-Chinese-dominant overseas settings may tend to amplify users' consciousness of these apps' linguistic, social, and ethnonational particularity. That is, beyond the specificity of WeChat's groups function (which produces a microlevel sense of mobile affiliation based on specific interests and subnational groupings), the general use of the app in an overseas context may conceivably produce a macrolevel interpellative effect based on mobile ethnonational affiliation. This would parallel users' own increasingly reflexive sense of ethnonational identity as a result of mobility—as one participant put it, "In China, you just feel like a person; only on coming overseas do you realize you are a *Chinese person.*"

Under what conditions will such platforms' potential for social encapsulation based on ethnicity and nationality be activated? In the following, I present a case study of a series of events in 2016 that demonstrates WeChat news's potential to act as an encapsulating force in Melbourne by shoring up exclusivist understandings of Chinese ethnicity, African race, and social class. To set the scene, I first present some contextualizing background on Melbourne's urban multiculture (including participants' engagements with it), superdiverse society, and everyday racisms.

Contexts: Urban Multiculture, Superdiversity, and Everyday Racisms

Following the adoption of multiculturalist policy during the 1970s and the overseas migration that largely drove postwar population growth, today Australia's level of cultural diversity is one of the highest among Western democracies (Harris 2013, 8). The 2016 national census revealed that 26 percent of the Australian population was born overseas—significantly higher than in the United States, Canada, or the United Kingdom—with a further 25 percent having at least one parent born overseas (Australian Bureau of Statistics 2017). Cultural diversity is greatest in Australia's large cities: during this study the City of Greater Melbourne recorded that over 40 percent of its residents had been born overseas (Australian Bureau of Statistics 2018).

A well-established body of scholarship examines the workings of everyday multiculturalism in Australian cities, paying attention to ordinary people's material practices of living in cultural diversity and the resultant production of hybrid lifeworlds and subjectivities (Stratton 1998, 2006; Ang et al. 2002; Wise 2005, 2011; Bloch and Dreher 2009; Wise and Velayutham 2009; Colic-Peisker and Farquharson 2011; J. Collins, Reid, and Fabiansson 2011; Ho 2011; Harris 2013). Referencing Steven Vertovec's (2007) conceptualization of superdiversity in Britain, Greg Noble (2009, 47) characterizes everyday multiculturalism in Australian cities with reference to an analogous process of "diversification of diversity." Vertovec argues that superdiversification occurs "not just in terms of bringing more ethnicities and countries of origin, but also with respect to a multiplication of significant variables that affect where, how and with whom people live" (2007, 1025). He points to a number of new factors changing the face of diversity in cities in the United Kingdom. These include a diversification of migration channels and immigration statuses (such that migrants include, for example, workers, students, accompanying family members, refugees, and undocumented migrants) and an intensification of migrants' transnational engagements through both new media technologies and personal travel (Vertovec 2007, 1042–44). These two features stand out in the case study that follows, which focuses on WeChat's mediation of events unfolding between different migrant groups at the local neighborhood level.

Australia's multicultural society is one of the nation's major draws as a study destination for Chinese students. It is regularly cited in the standard list of attractions of the country, both by education-industry professionals and by future students and their parents. The vast majority of future-student interviewees expressed the hope of broadening their horizons by making friends across cultures while studying in Australia. As noted in the previous chapter, following their arrival in Melbourne, many participants found themselves excluded from "local" (当地 dangdi, which in their habitual usage usually means "white") friendship circles. But several developed friendships and romantic relationships with other East, Southeast, and South Asian international students. Shihong, finding herself one of just two Chinese students in her course at the Imperial University of Technology's Bundoora campus, also developed close friendships with a group of Muslim women students: one from Syria, one from Turkey, and one Anglo-Celtic Australian woman who was married to a Muslim man and had converted to Islam. "I often look around and find that I'm the only one not wearing a headscarf!" Shihong joked, seemingly surprised (pleasantly) by this unexpected turn in the ethnocultural composition of her friendship group. Changying, meanwhile, spoke forthrightly about how her experience of the multicultural classroom in her pre-enrollment English class had changed her views about Vietnam, Malaysia, India, and the Philippines, which had previously been influenced by negative Chinese state discourse based on current political disputes: "Since leaving China, my view of China has changed a lot. I now think it's very closed off and has a lot of misunderstandings about [these] other countries." Relatedly, Meng spoke of her sense of belonging in the western suburbs of Footscray and Maribyrnong, citing the hospitability of everyday suburban multiculturalism and conviviality among friendly strangers:

> I do, I do feel a sense of belonging here. . . . Because I think there are lots of different ethnicities and nationalities here. There's not a strong sense that everyone thinks this place is only for the locals, and outsiders can't integrate. . . . I feel it's easy to communicate with the people around

me. They'll speak with you, and I think that's enough [to give a sense of belonging].

And, after two years living in the central business district (CBD) with Chinese flatmates, Niuniu moved into a multiethnic share-house in the inner neighborhood of Carlton, which she enjoyed sharing with Spanish, Iraqi, Mexican, New Zealander, and local housemates. Clearly, many Chinese students make significant cross-cultural engagements in Australian cities, challenging the stereotype that ethnic ghettos naturally form among Chinese migrants in Australia (Gao-Miles 2017).

Nonetheless, conditioned by the media worlds they inhabited, the student transmigrants' relations with other groups in the city across lines of race and ethnicity were not always so positive and unpanicked. An important corollary to the work on everyday multiculturalism is a related strand of work by some of the same scholars on everyday racism (Stratton 2006; Bloch and Dreher 2009). Drawing on the earlier work of Philomena Essed (1991), Jon Stratton frames this as "the day-to-day, common-sense ideological legitimations that . . . people . . . developed to justify their racist practices . . . [;] the formation of attitudes and understandings that are so embedded in the everyday life of a racialized culture . . . that members of that culture . . . don't even recognize themselves as making decisions based in a racialized history" (2006, 662). Everyday racism is a central theme in the discussion that follows, but the case study departs in important ways from those analyzed in extant works in this area, which have tended to frame international students exclusively as victims of racist violence from the majority culture (for example, Dunn, Pelleri, and Maeder-Han 2011). This study shows that these students are not *only* victims of racism in Australia (although they certainly are that) but are embedded in complex, transnational racial hierarchies and may themselves be complicit in racisms that morph and evolve along with educational mobility.

This case study illustrates a mediatized panic that drew on preexisting everyday anti-African racisms in both China and Australia but amplified their effects to produce a city marked by sharply heightened racial and class antagonisms. Anti-African racism in contemporary China has its historical roots in the early twentieth century: the discourse of race that formed in the writings of intellectuals in that period took on aspects of racial biologism, evolutionism, and eugenics to (re)produce a racial hierarchy with northern European and Han races at the top and darker-skinned peoples, especially Africans, at the bottom (Dikötter 1992, 61–190). Africans as a "race" thereby became associated with barbarism, backwardness (落后 luohou), uncivility, and intellectual inferiority.

Although the discourse of race was officially abolished with the founding of the People's Republic in 1949, the earlier racist discourse on hierarchized differences between ethnic groups clearly continued to shape Afrophobic popular attitudes through the Maoist era and into the present (Dikötter 1992, 191–95; M. D. Johnson 2007; Yinghong Cheng 2011; Denyer 2017). Outbursts of Chinese cyberracism in the contemporary era, for example, routinely construct Africans as primitive, corrupt, lazy, greedy, and hypersexual (Yinghong Cheng 2011; Pfafman, Carpenter, and Tang 2015; T. Liu and Deng 2020). This type of anti-African racism resonates with racist discourses worldwide (Pfafman, Carpenter, and Tang 2015), including in contemporary Australian public culture, where moral panics over Sudanese refugees have become a media staple over the past decade. Australian news reports persistently represent African-heritage youth in Australian cities as a racially othered problem group associated with urban decay, violence, delinquency, and gang-related crime (Windle 2008; Nolan et al. 2011; Abur 2012). In the real and virtual events of 2016 in Melbourne's CBD, I suggest, Chinese, Australian, and global racist frames merged and became mutually amplified.

iPhones, "African Gangs," and WeChat News

In May 2016 the anonymous poster in figure 3.1 was attached to a post near the entry to a building in inner-northern Melbourne used by a bridging program that some international undergraduate students, including those from China, had to take to gain admission to Capital University. Its simplified-character Chinese text reads, "Danger. African criminals," accompanied by photographs of unidentified but hostile-looking African-heritage young men and assertions that such men target Chinese students to "rob" and "bash" them. A photograph of the poster was circulated among Chinese student transmigrants via WeChat, where it fed into a stream of posts and news stories that had been running since February concerning the alleged targeting of Chinese students by "African gangs" in a spate of iPhone thefts in the area. Given its obvious racial vilification, photographic accusation of unidentified people, and casting of doubt on police efficacy, unsurprisingly, the original poster was swiftly removed by the police.

This poster points toward hostile engagements (allegedly physical, definitely rhetorical) between two specific ethnic groups in inner Melbourne: "African migrants" and "Chinese international students." In pitting these two groups against each other, the poster highlights class as well as "racial" differences, for example, asserting that the African migrants came from nearby public housing. While African-heritage youth in Melbourne may be the children

FIGURE 3.1 Photograph of poster on Swanston Street, Melbourne, May 9, 2016, circulated via WeChat.

of former refugees from Sudan, South Sudan, and the Horn of Africa—among the most severely disadvantaged residents of Australian cities on multiple socioeconomic indicators (Olliff 2007; Dhanji 2009; Human Rights and Equal Opportunity Commission 2009; Gatt 2011; Abur 2012)—the Chinese international students in the city generally come from middle-class and elite families in China. What is happening here? What led to this poster being produced, displayed, and circulated? Beyond the poster's wide circulation via WeChat, how else might it be connected to the media practices of the northern CBD neighborhood's Chinese student-transmigrant inhabitants?

In early March 2016, I arrange an evening film screening for study participants (the classic Australian supernatural drama Picnic at Hanging Rock, *ahead of* our own planned picnic at that scenic spot the next weekend). A day or two before the screening, Niuniu sends me a WeChat message saying there is something she wants to talk to me about, and maybe we could discuss it at the film night. On the evening of the screening, I meet at the venue on campus in Carlton with nine participants and about eight others, mainly other Chinese international students who also want to see the movie. Before we watch it, we share a meal of sushi and chat in the bland institutional meeting room, a warm wind stirring the darkness outside and rattling the window blinds. Addressing everyone around the table, Niuniu brings up what is bothering her:

You know all these stories on WeChat lately about African gangs attacking Chinese students in Melbourne? I'm just wondering whether they're actually true or not.

The whole thing is news to me, and I listen intently. Niuniu tells how she has followed up on a number of the stories currently circulating only to find that although everyone seems to know someone who knows someone who has been robbed, she can't find any eyewitnesses or any of the actual people who have allegedly been attacked. So she thinks it's all groundless media sensationalism and worries that it could be harmful both to interethnic relations and to Chinese students' sense of security in the city. Others around the table are less reflexive, simply fearing for their own safety. Shunzi tells how, as she walked to the screening, a beaming African man randomly approached her in the street and tried to hug her. Playing it for laughs, she tells everyone with her characteristic rapid-fire humor:

I told him to go away. My culture is different from yours, OK? This isn't France, OK? We don't just run around hugging strangers in the street!

Niuniu protests that the man was probably just trying to be friendly. But later that evening Shunzi leaves before the end of the film, sending me a WeChat message saying she is scared to stay out any later.

Over the days that follow, stories of Chinese students being robbed near Capital U by groups of "tall, fast black youths" come in thick and fast: in our participant WeChat group, through public news accounts, and via the Moments feed, where I have around 250 contacts in the wider Chinese student community. A sense of panic sets in, with many saying they dare not go out alone or at night in the Carlton/CBD area, and some reporting that people they know directly—flatmates, classmates—have been robbed and had underwhelming experiences with reporting thefts to the police. This culminates on the night of March 12, when a violent disturbance takes place in Federation Square during celebrations for Moomba (Melbourne's city festival) and is widely reported in local media as involving rival "African" and "Pacific Islander" gangs from Melbourne's disadvantaged outer-eastern suburbs. WeChat news accounts selectively pick up the sensationalist stories from the

Australian tabloid press, translate the headlines into Chinese, and in many cases exacerbate the racist cast of the reporting, adding photos of injuries sustained by ethnically Chinese people and referring repeatedly to "black bandits" who are "out of control" and are targeting "Asians" or "Chinese people" (figures 3.2–3.3).

Chinese student groups encourage their members to contact the Chinese consulate to voice concern over whether the police and university are doing enough to protect their safety. Students' parents back in China, many of whom subscribe to the same Melbourne-based WeChat public accounts as their daughters in Australia, send panicked messages; Jiale is even contacted by a former teacher she hadn't seen in years, "to check whether I'm still alive." Meanwhile, Victoria Police attempt—somewhat ineffectually, given their lack of access to Chinese-language media—to circulate a deracializing message that the iPhone robberies aren't targeted at Chinese people specifically and that only one-third of victims are of Asian heritage.

Just after midnight on the night of the Moomba disturbance, Niuniu posts a link to a WeChat public news account story, sourced from the tabloid Herald Sun, embellished with a wild headline: "Live video: Over 200 people from two gangs exchange fire in Melbourne's CBD, the city has become a battleground, take care everyone!" (In fact, the teenagers involved had no firearms.) Niuniu comments:

Ai—it's true. Originally I clung to my illusion that this was sensationalism by profit-driven media, but now the reality is staring me in the face, I have to accept it.

The Sunday after the Saturday night disturbance is the day we'd planned to visit Hanging Rock: we were going to meet in Carlton and take a hired bus to the picnic spot in the countryside north of Melbourne. Several participants drop out at the last minute—including Niuniu—saying they are afraid to travel the short distance from the CBD to Carlton in light of the disturbances the night before.

Several popular WeChat articles and posts around this time represent Chinese women, specifically, as the group most vulnerable to attack by African men—supposedly being smaller, weaker, and more defenseless than either white women or Chinese men. In my discussions with participants over the weeks and months that follow, many report now feeling generically afraid of "black people" and unwilling to encounter them in the street. The poster in figure 3.1 appears and is circulated a couple of months afterward.

LOCAL NEWS IN WECHAT GROUPS
AND SUBSCRIPTION ACCOUNTS

The reports on phone thefts that student transmigrants were reading via WeChat in 2016 came not only from their personal Moments feeds (朋友圈 pengyouquan), where friends post individual comments, photos, and links, but also from their WeChat groups and from their subscriptions to a range

4/18/16 12:51 PM

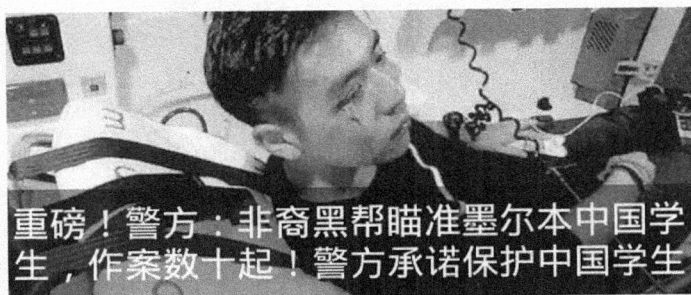

重磅！警方：非裔黑帮瞄准墨尔本中国学生，作案数十起！警方承诺保护中国学生

|今日有饭|我带着你，你带着钱，我们去吃猫本最棒的螃蟹！

【转让】墨尔本著名连锁礼品店转让了！16年老店转让，机会实在难得，千万不要错过！

【汇率】澳元一路飙涨，兑人民币汇率成功突破5元大关！

【秘密】揭密 "太阳的后裔" 乔妹冻龄的秘密！

【靠谱】谁说办公室恋情不靠谱？

FIGURE 3.2 Headlines from WeChat news account MelToday, March 2016. "Headline! Police: African gangsters targeting Chinese students in Melbourne, dozens of cases reported! Police promise to protect Chinese students."

中国女生███附近遭黑人团伙打劫！奔驰车主被撞停洗劫！非裔黑帮犯罪肆虐墨尔本！墨尔本警方："我们不可以追击"！

2016-04-26 今日墨尔本

今日犯罪

今日墨尔本今天接到爆料，一位华人女学生在███大学附近遭遇非裔黑帮团伙抢劫！面对警方"严打"，非裔黑帮不但没有分崩离析，反而好像"越战越勇"，在昨天更是采用撞车+武装抢劫的方式，在Toorak抢走了一辆奔驰用于连环犯案！

FIGURE 3.3 Headlines from WeChat news account MelToday, March 2016. "Chinese girls robbed by black gangsters near University of X [redacted]! Mercedes-Benz owner looted after stopping after a deliberate collision! African gangs out of control in Melbourne! Melbourne police: 'We cannot chase them'!"

of official public accounts. Specifically addressing amateur news production in WeChat groups, Sun Wei (2015, 14–15) observes that such groups produce news and hence truth for their members and as such constitute a significant node in the global news production network. She further notes that "a major feature of news production in the WeChat group is its closeness to the group: its location, occupation, values, institutions, and so on. It constructs the sense of 'us' from moment to moment across multiple dimensions. This news is 'ours' and is embedded in and inseparable from 'our' daily life. . . . This kind of news production . . . continuously constructs [people's] sense of place" (15). These observations are extremely pertinent to the 2016 "African gangs" panic. The in-grouping of Chinese student transmigrants and the concomitant othering of young dark-skinned men presumed to be African were reinforced not only by the content of the news being reported in WeChat groups but also by the technosocial affordances of the WeChat group itself. That is, the affiliative structure of WeChat groups—for the participants, most often based on a shared situation, language, ethnicity, and nationality and personal relationships—arguably reinforces what Sun characterizes as these groups' "cocooning" effect (2015, 16). In this case, it marked out "our"—Chinese students'—interests over and against those of ethnic, racial, and classed Others: violent African youths and indifferent white police. This process in turn produced inner-northern Melbourne as a landscape of racialized, classed, and gendered fear (Low 2001).

Unlike WeChat groups, which are informal associations based on personal or institutional affiliation and share mainly user-generated content (personal stories, rumors, and photos as well as links to publicly available content), WeChat official news accounts are a form of profit-driven subscription media produced by commercial enterprises. They offer a free daily digest of Chinese-language news and information about life and events in specific cities, sourced and translated from local media, written by stringers, or submitted by readers themselves. Scores of such accounts exist in Melbourne, providing a central source of local news and information for student transmigrants and other members of the Chinese diaspora.

Subscription accounts of this type occupy a unique emerging niche in both local and transnational media ecologies. WeChat is a Chinese-owned and -run service that is regulated almost wholly from the Chinese side: for example, state censorship of content applies, so that even when operating in Australia, content producers self-censor to avoid criticism of China's government and the Chinese Communist Party. On the Australian side, meanwhile, these public subscription services tend to be somewhat insulated from Australian Commonwealth media regulation—for example, the enforcement of laws against racial vilification, political campaigning laws, and so on—owing to the language barrier for Australian authorities.[2] Yet, in terms of content, accounts like MelToday, Melbourne WeLife, and Mel_life—three of participants' most commonly read accounts—present news and information that is almost wholly concerned with local current events in Melbourne. In this sense, WeChat news subscription accounts occupy an emergent gray area between traditional "ethnic" media (diasporic media previously exemplified by video, television, cinema, music, and Web 1.0 platforms) and new forms of transnational media; hence, I call them *ethno-transnational media* (Cunningham 2001).

Students' preference for sourcing news via mobile apps like WeChat reflects broader global trends (Bell 2016; Tang 2016; Taylor 2016). In China, WeChat is among people's top sources for news, especially via its public accounts service (WalkTheChat 2016); research in Australia confirms that a strong preference for accessing news via WeChat public accounts prevails among Mandarin speakers in the diaspora as well (Wanning Sun 2018a; Astarita, Patience, and Tok 2019). Since WeChat news in Melbourne is easy to access, tailored to the specific city and community in which students are living, and written in their first language, it becomes a ubiquitous guiding presence in their everyday navigation of the city.

MELTODAY AND TRANSNATIONAL CHINESENESS

Many Melbourne-based WeChat news accounts covered the incidents outlined above. But while some attempted to disentangle fact from fiction and offer readers a nonalarmist explanation of events, one of the most widely read subscription accounts stands out for its extensive and highly sensationalist coverage of "African gangs" stories both before the Moomba events and ever since. MelToday (今日墨尔本 Jinri Moerben), which published both of the stories in figures 3.2–3.3, is among the largest and most popular of the Melbourne-based news accounts, operating across Weibo, WeChat, a website, and a dedicated phone app. At the time of these events, its top WeChat headline stories attracted between 10,000 and 100,000 views, averaging around 35,000 views (for context, around 50,000 students from China were studying in Victoria in 2016; Herbert 2016). In 2015 MelToday reported that it had over 150,000 followers on Weibo, over 50,000 on WeChat (with 7,000–8,000 new followers each month), and over a million monthly views from 250,000 unique visitors to its website (Jinri Chuanmei Jituan 2015, 18, 21). MelToday, registered as a share limited company in 2014, is part of the Media Today Group, founded and directed by the young entrepreneur Dapeng "Roc" Zhang, a graduate of the University of Technology Sydney, following his establishment of the similar SydneyToday service in 2010 (subsequently ranked among the top ten most influential Chinese new-media platforms in the world; Cao T. 2018). Between 2014 and 2016, the Melbourne-based account grew from modest beginnings with just three staff into a successful commercial enterprise with ten employees, including five reporters.

MelToday uses tabloid-style headlines and images eliciting strong emotional responses—shock, astonishment, fear, outrage, Chinese patriotism, pathos, intrigue, and so on—to draw readers in to click on stories on a range of topics deemed to be of interest to Melbourne's Chinese diaspora, especially immigration, investment, real estate, education, entertainment, and crime. An ex-staffer told me that the focus on sensationalist stories and soft news was implemented as a policy by MelToday in 2015 following commercially unsuccessful attempts at original hard-news reporting in the company's first year of operation. Since then, clickbait churnalism in the daily headliner articles has grown alongside increasing advertorial content in the rest of the feed. MelToday's headliner news features are marked by insistent references to "Chinese people" (中国人 Zhongguoren or 华人 Huaren), constructing Chinese heroes, Chinese crime victims, Chinese concerns, and Chinese responses to current affairs, thus continually reinforcing Chinese identity as both the linchpin of reader engagement and the lens through which local events are evaluated. While Zhongguoren refers literally to citizens of China (中国 Zhongguo), the term Huaren is etymologically linked to the premodern Huaxia (华夏) concept of Chinese civilization, thereby referencing a primordial, China-centric conceptualization of Chinese ethnicity (Y. Wu 2012). Huaren commonly refers to a type of primal ethnocultural identity assumed to transcend specific national affiliation and has been popularly used online to elicit a globally extensive sense of Chineseness (Ang 2001; A. Ong 2003; Nyíri 2010).[3]

The content of MelToday is organically linked with Australian media, with a preference for sensationalist material gleaned from Rupert Murdoch's News Corp publications and other right-wing tabloids. Anglophone news producers' ongoing moral panics over "African youth" are selectively reproduced—often embellished and generally given some Huaren spin—in MelToday features (Windle 2008; Nolan et al. 2011; K. Smith 2016). The Today accounts are also transnationally networked into Sinophone communities worldwide and are cited regularly by journalists covering Australian news across mainland China and Hong Kong (e.g., *Sky Post* 2016).

Similarly sensationalist public WeChat accounts delivering local city-based news exist in China as well as abroad. There, such accounts attract vulnerable groups with limited access to alternative information channels, such as the poorly educated and the elderly; they are dismissively referred to by younger, middle-class media users as tabloids (小报 *xiaobao*) produced by hack journalists focused solely on sensational headlines (标题党 *biaotidang*). But whereas within China such accounts occupy a lowly position on the news media spectrum, with low readership and credibility among young middle-class readers, for Chinese students abroad—where higher-quality Chinese-language media are generally lacking and the students themselves become a vulnerable group vis-à-vis information access—these tabloid accounts tend to dominate local news delivery.[4]

WECHAT NEWS PRODUCTION AND THE COMMERCIAL
BOTTOM LINE

In mid-2016 I met with one of the partners in MelToday, Mr. A.—a young finance graduate from a prestigious Australian university with a background in e-retail and marketing—to discuss the company's approach to news reporting. Young people today, Mr. A. explained, want news fast, conveniently, cheaply, and in few words, and Chinese people prefer it in Chinese. And they need news media that will represent issues of particular concern for Chinese people (Huaren), to which the local media don't give a lot of attention. Mr. A. told me frankly that whereas traditional news's higher budget gives it the advantage of in-depth reporting and systematic fact checking, in contrast, social media news's advantage lies in its speed. MelToday's fact checking is minimal, he revealed, often confined to a simple web search to ascertain whether reported events actually occurred. Editors choose news topics based on an evaluation of their likely popularity: the goal is to keep up traffic to the account since the operational model is wholly commercial, relying on selling advertisers space whose value is based on traffic volume. Mr. A. observed candidly that to keep the traffic up, writers routinely take stories from the local press and "just, you know, exaggerate things a *little* bit, for the headline."

With specific reference to MelToday's reports on the "African gangs" topic, Mr. A. emphasized that MelToday's reporting did not directly incite interethnic violence and was aimed mainly at keeping the Chinese community safe from crime. Perhaps intuiting my own orientation as a liberal intellectual, he waxed thoughtful on the social needs of the children of refugees from African nations, observing that such youth need a stable life environment to keep them away from crime and that the Australian government has a responsibility to provide that. But it was clear from the overall tenor of our discussion that the first priority of Mr. A., as a businessman, was profit: delivering news content with high clickability to guarantee advertising revenue. Of course, this is not unique but part of a broader trend toward the tabloidization and "infotainment-ization" of journalism in deregulating commercial digital media environments the world over (Bennett 2004; Fenton 2010). Here, however, we see a new permutation of this trend: sensationalized local news delivered through a highly popular form of transnational commercial online media that is somewhat insulated from content regulation in the jurisdiction where it operates.

The determining influence of a nakedly commercial bottom line in WeChat's local news reporting was reinforced by accounts from participants who worked for WeChat news services in Melbourne. Yining, a media studies postgraduate student, worked part-time on the marketing side of another local WeChat public account. She told me that her boss was a bit mystified as to why on another occasion MelToday had had to apologize formally for misrepresentation in a highly sensationalist article it ran on radicalization among Muslim refugees:

> I talked about that incident with my boss and said, well, some of them exaggerate the facts and whatever. But then he—because he's never studied *media*—he said to me . . . that he couldn't really understand why anyone had to come forward and . . . clarify things. He said that actually doing so was kind of market interference [搅乱市场 *jiaoluan shichang*], because you only have to ensure that the facts are true. Actually you <u>can</u> sort of spice things up a bit, because you have to maximize your audience.

Such crude and unabashed market logic suggests a parallel with Australia's broader commercial media environment, in which, as Australia's former race discrimination commissioner Tim Soutphommasane (2018) has observed, racism has become monetized by a media industry feeling the strain of technological disruption and audience fragmentation.[5]

Yixin, also a media studies postgraduate, linked her own subjective sense of (in)security in the city in late 2017 with her work as a writer of exactly the kinds of stories that court clicks by whipping up such fears:

> Recently a lot of things happened in the city. I feel it's not that safe. . . . The terrorists and the criminals, violence, happen all the time. I never came across [it] in person. But because I'm working for the media, so I am writing about this [kind of] news all day, like [headlines that say] "*Zhenjing!*" [震惊: shock!]. [*laughs*] All the time it's just like they're trying to [convey] this kind of stress to the public. . . . Chinese media do [it] all the time. So people think, like, maybe right now it's not the safest in [the] CBD in Melbourne. . . . [The editors] think that's the things people pay attention to. . . . But actually if you emphasize it over and over again, it becomes a bubble.

Yixin's account is intriguing for her double perspective: as a news writer, she herself participated—albeit reluctantly—in the process through which stories of violent crime were selectively translated and exaggerated with shocking headlines in order to attract clicks and hence advertising revenue. Yet, despite critiquing the homogeneous "bubble" or echo-chamber effect created by the WeChat news accounts' media ecology here and on several other occasions, Yixin was also personally affected by the very stories she helped concoct, feeling that Melbourne had indeed become more unsafe.

Aftermath: Racialized Space, "Refugees," and Shattering Dreams

Suspicious about WeChat news's relentless invocation of "African gangs" in relation to the phone robberies, in mid-2016 I lodge a freedom-of-information request with Victoria Police inquiring about the backgrounds of the people arrested in connection with the incidents in Carlton and the CBD between January and May that year. After a months-long snail-mail exchange of requests, payments, receipts, clarifications, further payments, and further receipts, in late October a fat white envelope finally arrives with the information I requested. Its contents demonstrate, first, that the arrestees did not, as suggested on the poster in figure 3.1, come in from government housing projects in Carlton, Fitzroy, and Flemington but lived in a wide range of metropolitan and outer areas with no discernible pattern except a majority of poorer suburbs, from inner Melbourne to disadvantaged St Albans, peri-rural Pakenham, and the regional town of Drouin. Moreover, the police statistics on the "racial appearance" of the thirty-five arrestees show the largest group (49 percent) to be white (fourteen "Caucasian," two "northern European," and one "southern European") with only eight "African" and three "African/Middle East." Given the information already released by the police that only one-third of reported victims were of "Asian" heritage, the WeChat line on the phone robberies as a story of Africans attacking Chinese looks shakier than ever.

On a sweltering day in early March 2017, almost exactly a year after the phone robberies, I meet six participants for a gallery tour and lunch in the Southgate area, by the river. As we sit chatting around a big table in the cool, dim restaurant, I suddenly remember: I have to tell them about the police stats on the phone robbery arrestees! But when I do, instead of shock and immediate reevaluation of the previous year's reportage as I'd expected, I am met with an awkward silence. After a moment, Xiaofen offers politely:

Well, if it's true, it's certainly explosive news.

Fenfang quietly objects, seemingly voicing the unspoken thoughts of the others:

But if the eyewitnesses all said they were black—?
The topic is quickly dropped. They don't believe me.

The aftereffects of the 2016 iPhone robberies for participants' perceptions of urban public space were remarkably long-lived, kept alive by ongoing WeChat reportage of other street crime involving Chinese victims and "African" or "refugee" perpetrators. Participants regularly discussed feeling fearful upon encountering African-heritage young people in the city; in a typical statement, Xiaoshu recalled that when she saw a group of African-heritage youth at Melbourne Central Station, "Without even thinking, my heart was seized with a nameless terror!" Others drew associations between "black people," "refugees," and "danger," often attaching to particular neighborhoods. For example, Cihui referred to a friend who lived in Melbourne's northern suburbs, "where there are all the refugees and Africans," and as a result was constantly afraid of being attacked or robbed. In June 2017 Shunzi echoed then-current WeChat news articles—themselves echoing the Australian right-wing press—criticizing the extravagant welfare payments that refugees were supposedly receiving from the Australian government.[6] She argued that such payments encouraged indolence and were unfair to the more hardworking and law-abiding Chinese migrants. The same month, when I started a conversation about perceptions of danger in Melbourne in our own WeChat group—without citing race or refugees but in fact trying to find out more about participants' gendered perceptions of risk—the conversation quickly took a familiar turn. Qin said her parents constantly worried about her safety "since the refugees have gotten so numerous." Liangya added that she'd heard that Flemington was particularly lawless (乱 *luan*): "I think there are buildings there where refugees live." When I queried the connection, observing with a laugh-til-you-cry emoji that the majority of criminals in Australia were obviously white people, she replied, "I don't even know—I feel like it just seems like as soon as everyone hears 'refugees,' they sort of don't want to get too close." When discussing this heightened fear in public space and especially its racialized aspect—since within this speech community, "refugees" works fairly directly as code for "African-looking people"—some participants linked it directly back to the events of 2016: from that time on, urban and suburban space in Melbourne increasingly had become, for them, landscapes of racialized fear.

In her analysis of landscapes of fear, based on suburban gated communities in the United States in the 1990s, Setha Low (2001) explains the pervasive discourse of urban fear as a spatial expression of class and race antagonisms by a dominant group—the white middle classes—that feels it has "lost its place" in the city center. My usage of *landscape of fear* differs from Low's, first insofar as it describes not privatized architectural defenses against urban fear but rather student transmigrants' experiences of the "undefended" urban or suburban street as an anxiety-producing environment. Second, and more important, the social positioning of the group in question is very different. Unlike Low's white middle classes, in Melbourne the Chinese student transmigrants are themselves a minority group with credible claim to being marginalized by the city's dominant social and regulatory systems (the police, mainstream English-language media, and so on). They cannot feel displaced from the city in the same way as Low's middle-class Anglos, because their own encounters with anti-Chinese racism and wider social exclusion mean they were never given to feel that they were fully entitled to occupy these spaces in the first place. Nevertheless, this discourse of fear—both in WeChat news stories and in some participants' own accounts—also expresses class and racial antagonisms, as in Low's example. Class is in fact absolutely central to the students' assertion of an encapsulating boundary separating them from "Africans" and "refugees." In opposition to the students' own "good" form of mobility—the middle-class pursuit of transnational education—they, encouraged by WeChat's tabloid news, construct the refugees' "bad" form: arriving in Australia the wrong way, destitute, desperate, and destined to become a drain on state resources. When these two different kinds of migrants encounter each other in the city, the students' mediated self-image as part of a global Chinese middle class comes face to face with a local underclass constructed by that same media as dangerous and criminal. Here, the utopian dream of Melbourne as the site of global middle-class aspiration (chapter 2)—pleasant environment, elite education, tasteful consumption, friendly whiteness, transnational spatial mastery, secure neighborhoods— meets perhaps its sharpest challenge. In the student-transmigrant discourse's persistent questioning of the rights of various Others to occupy urban space— "Africans," "black people," and "refugees"—one senses the energies released by a shattering dream: the intimation that "Melbourne," as a superdiverse city, is coming to mean something very different from the utopian fantasies one had invested in it.

Reflexive Media Engagements

Although, overall, continued exposure to sensationalist reporting on "African gangs" and multiplying dangerous "refugees" by local WeChat news accounts tended to increase participants' mistrust of other groups and erode their sense of security in the public spaces of the city, there is also a more complex story to tell. Many participants revealed a high degree of reflexivity in their consumption of media like MelToday: it is known as a deeply sensationalist platform, and many—as in Niuniu's initial suspicions about the veracity of the "African gangs" stories—approached its stories with skepticism. For example, a couple of months after the main wave of reports on phone thefts, one participant, Jiale, took a calm, pragmatic approach to the issue. She observed that in big cities in China like her hometown, such thefts occur all the time and yet are seldom reported (indeed, several participants returned from trips back to China to relate with no more than passing exasperation that their iPhones had been stolen while they were there). In contrast, Jiale thought, Melbourne's Chinese community was much smaller and so intensely networked that minor incidents quickly became known to everyone, and panic readily set in. Several others echoed this pragmatism, adopting an unpanicked, quasi-fatalistic stance toward the possibility of becoming victims of street crime.

Mingxi was part of the group of participants enrolled in a joint program between a Chinese university and Queens University in Footscray. When I interviewed Mingxi with two of her classmates in Henan predeparture, they expressed some unease about stories they'd heard that social order was lacking in Footscray, connecting the suburb's supposed danger and lawlessness (*luan*) to its being home to "many Africans and Vietnamese people." However, after Mingxi had been living and studying there for several months, and following the wave of reports about phone thefts by "African gangs," I asked Mingxi whether she was now more worried than before about her personal safety. Mingxi replied that she wasn't. "I'm not scared of Africans," she said. "I mean, you see them in the street in Footscray all the time, but they're fine, they don't do any harm." Such a statement is hardly a shining example of deep intercultural exchange and multiethnic harmony. However, as Christina Ho observes, the more modest goal of "respecting the presence of others" or "recognition of the other's legitimate presence in a shared social space" can also be seen as an indicator of workable everyday multiculturalism and may in some cases be a more realistic goal than "harmony" (2011, 614). And two years after the phone-robberies panic, Yueming—now pursuing a postgraduate degree in Sydney—even told me that she had bonded with a young African-Australian Uber driver based on their shared frustration with Anglo-Australians' racism. Like most media consumers, then, the student transmigrants were not dupes: they actively weighed reportage against the accumulating evidence of their own experience and tempered their understanding of and response to social media news accordingly (Hall 1980b). Despite the strong drive toward ethnic encapsulation in some local WeChat news, then, the extension of lines of connection, communication, and respect between different groups within the urban multiculture is never precluded.

The Newness of Ethno-transnational Media

The conflict between "Chinese international students" and "African migrants" represented in the poster in figure 3.1 arises from the structural situation of the communities in question vis-à-vis multiple socioeconomic, micropolitical, and media-related factors pertaining to their specific contexts in Melbourne (Park 1996; Amin 2002a; Mankekar 2015, 93–104). The Chinese students' responses to the phone robberies, while building on a preexisting kernel of modern Chinese Afrophobia, were more decisively shaped by minimally regulated ethno-transnational media driven by a commercial imperative that tends to preclude effective consideration of media ethics (Wanning Sun 2016). These media encouraged student transmigrants to interpret themselves in relation to an essentialist discourse of globally extensive Chinese ethnonational identity (as Zhongguoren/Huaren) and to interpret local sub/urban space along strongly racialized and class-stratified lines.

MelToday is a localized example, but it is part of a broader trend toward commercial Chinese-language social media as a (even *the*) major source of news for Chinese student transmigrants and other diasporic communities worldwide (for a US comparator, see Han Zhang 2019). Today's ethno-transnational media are qualitatively different from what was available just a decade or so ago, and this makes a material difference in the affordances of the media and hence their social effects. First, new social media like WeChat news accounts are even *more transnational* than older media, insofar as they are accessed from a Chinese platform that allows seamless continuity of use when users travel abroad; they provide instantaneous, real-time links to people and social life overseas; and their content is regulated largely from China. Second, thanks to mobile networked technologies, this type of social media is far *more ubiquitous* than older media in everyday life. In the case addressed in this chapter, where ubiquitous social media became host to a racist panic, it seemed at times that for the students involved there was precious little space in everyday life away from the online narrative, where the panic might be avoided. Third, these new types of media operate in the wider global context of *intensified deregulation, commercialization, and digital networking of news media*, with attendant risks for the quality of content vis-à-vis journalism's civic function (Fenton 2010; Taylor 2016). Fourth, as a result of a combination of the preceding factors, this type of media is much more readily able to *evade legal regulation in the host nation,* including evading laws aimed at enhancing shared social life in a culturally diverse society. Finally, therefore, the example I have addressed highlights the capacity for some forms of new ethno-transnational media, paradoxically, to *undercut multiculturalist values* as much as to enhance them.

Miyase Christensen and André Jansson propose that "the concept of communication, literally meaning 'making something common,' provides us with a stepping stone for thinking about the relationship between media and cosmopolitanism" (2015, 8). Yet underregulated, commercially driven WeChat news accounts invite what amounts to the opposite effect: not a cosmopolitan opening up but a hostile turning away from the (African, refugee) Other and a closing in around a "Chinese" identity that is performatively enacted in repeated references to its commonsense ethnonational self-interest (J. Ong 2009). This example, then, reveals the flip side of WeChat's tendency to amplify a sense of in-group identification: in-groups are exclusive as well as inclusive and may be particularly so in transnational and cross-cultural contexts.

Toward Cosmopolitan Connection?

This chapter has considered the plural and contradictory ways in which Chinese student transmigrants' media practices make Melbourne at an everyday experiential level. We have seen how students' emplaced uses of translocal, mobile networked media in the city produce syncretic experiences of place, interweaving digital and physical elements and near and far reference points. We have also considered how city-based leisure-and-lifestyle accounts on platforms including WeChat and Weibo support geographic localization in and extension across the spaces of the city. In contrast, we have seen how some uses of WeChat can also invite an ethnocentric closing in around a mobile, transnational, and exclusive form of "Chinese" identity. I have argued that this operation occurs in three stages: first, through the app's inherent technosocial tendency to produce a mobile sense of in-group affiliation, as theorized by Sun Wei (2015); second, through the amplification of this effect in overseas settings when the newly salient "Chineseness" of the app parallels one's own heightened consciousness of ethnonational identity; and, third (and most powerfully), in the content of some popular tabloid news accounts, which explicitly invite the user to see herself as a "Chinese" person under real and present threat from "Africans" and/or "refugees." In these ways, the chapter has revealed mobile networked media's simultaneous affordances of *spatial syncretization, territorial extension,* and *social-subjective encapsulation.*

I have also tried to underline throughout both the simultaneity and the partiality of these effects. In relation to mediated social encapsulation, in particular, we have seen how some participants resisted this effect through other everyday practices. Individuals sought out cross-cultural social connections and maintained diverse friendship networks, took a critical stance toward social media news, coexisted respectfully with other groups in sub/urban space, and even developed a sense of empathic solidarity with African Australians on the basis of shared experiences of racism. While participants sometimes identified unreflexively with the banal ethnocentrism of WeChat tabloid news, at other times their engagements with the concept of Chinese identity were much more critical and nuanced (see chapter 7). Also, Chinese-language social media are not the *only* forms used by student transmigrants, even if they are the dominant ones. Many participants made parallel use of alternative platforms like Instagram and Facebook, and a couple actively avoided Chinese-language social media in order to nurture a more diverse and localized social network in Australia (S. Chang, Gomes, and Martin 2018).

Nonetheless, the significant place that local WeChat tabloid news occupies within the digital mobile scene that accompanies Chinese students through Australian cities and the negative impacts this type of news may have on students' experiences of urban sociality suggest that these questions are worth further consideration. In fact, the superficially local, place-bound concerns addressed in this chapter connect with much broader questions about human mobility, social diversity, media, and urban life in the world today. In a widely influential popular understanding encountered across Australia, China, and many other contexts, human mobilities in globalization are constructed around a series of oppositions. On one hand, what we might call the neoliberal dream of mobility—the dream of flight that lies at the heart of students' own international education ventures—centers agential movement, striving, a forward orientation, and independent self-advancement. On the other hand, a very different kind of mobile subject is emblematized in the figure of the refugee. This figure is associated, including by the study participants, with forced movement, drifting, backwardness, and welfare dependence. In superdiverse cities like Melbourne, flesh-and-blood avatars of these imagined types find themselves sharing public space. When influential WeChat news accounts reproduce the anti-African, antirefugee racism of the reactionary Australian press while also offering a flattering reflection of their Chinese readers as respectable migrants and innocent victims, then, in the absence of strong alternative narratives, student transmigrants are led to interpret the social space of the city according to this dualistic schema of good versus bad migrants.

Such an outcome is also indirectly supported by the actions of Australia's international education industry. The neoliberal transformation of higher education into an export commodity by Australian universities and governments goes hand in hand with marketing the dream of globally mobile, middle-class subjecthood to Chinese students and actively promoting Australian cities as ideal environments in which to achieve this form of identity (see chapter 2). Popular Chinese media like WeChat news accounts help to naturalize a utopian imaginary of Australian cities, promoting the idea that to allow the "good" migrants, including educational transmigrants, to flourish, such cities *ought to* be kept "safe," orderly, tightly policed, and free from the threat of troublesome Others. Yet, given the complexities of social life in superdiverse cities, with their colocation of multiple forms of human mobility and cultural, ethnic, and class difference, the assumption that a city like Melbourne could unproblematically reflect the soothing dream of a global middle-class lifestyle is bound to be challenged in practice. Moreover, as Julie Matthews and Ravinder Sidhu note, while "international education can and should create conditions of possibility for the formation of globally oriented subjectivities which are informed by a broad-based cosmopolitan virtue," there is nothing about market logic that nurtures a concern for social justice, and "marketized expressions of international education are ultimately disengaged from notions of a global public good" (2005, 62–63; see also Kell and Vogl 2012; G. Li 2016; Astarita, Patience, and Tok 2019). The result is a jagged disjuncture between student transmigrants' imaginations of the Western city as a study destination and their capacity to make sense of its complex social worlds in practice. This is hardly conducive to nurturing cosmopolitan virtue.

It remains to be seen whether new forms of popular media may organically emerge in the Chinese student-transmigrant community that are able to respond more productively to urban life in superdiversity, supporting the small, everyday forms of intergroup connection that punctuate students' experience of the city. Arguably, it might also be seen as a civic responsibility of Australian agencies (including governments, universities, and media industries) to work more proactively and collaboratively toward promoting an equitable and inclusive vision of the public good in the superdiverse city. Against the clickbait caricatures of commercial online news, more communitarian visions of the city could be developed to foster a stronger sense of belonging and cross-group connection for student transmigrants and all urban residents, challenging encapsulation along the lines of ethnicity, nationality, and class in favor of a more truly cosmopolitan vision of urban life in the era of intensified human and media mobilities.[7]

4. WORK
Emplacement, Mobility, and Value

*

I got the job at the pizza place on a classmate's recommendation, and they pay fourteen bucks an hour, but it's in Carnegie, it's pretty far, I live in the city. The return trip takes an hour each time, and the tickets cost eight bucks. When you do the math, you see I'm only taking home a bit over ten bucks an hour, it's a bit low. . . . The problem is the boss makes you work every second of the time, you can't stop. So I couldn't use a camera, I had to use my phone to take pictures secretly, and I had to think about how best to express what I wanted to say. I thought I'd use my hand, so my left hand is working, and my right hand is [taking the photographs]. I took them like this while I was working.

The interesting thing about this one [figure 4.3] is the [sign saying] you should be careful, and my hand is right there like that; this is a machine

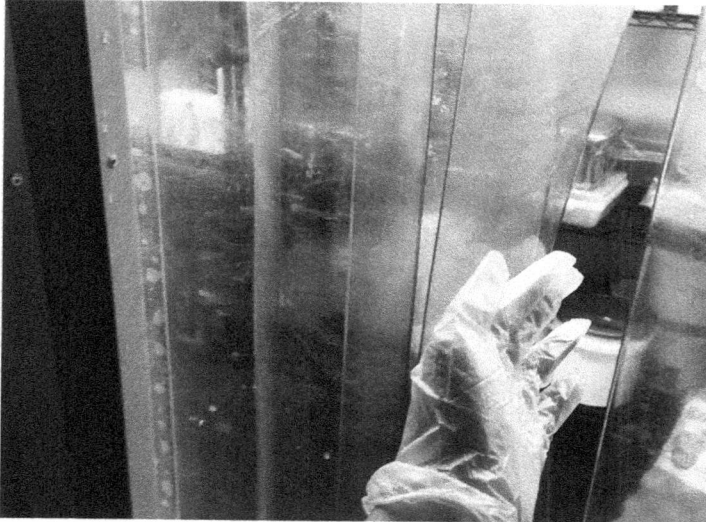

FIGURE 4.1 Shang's pizza restaurant photo series, Melbourne, 2016.

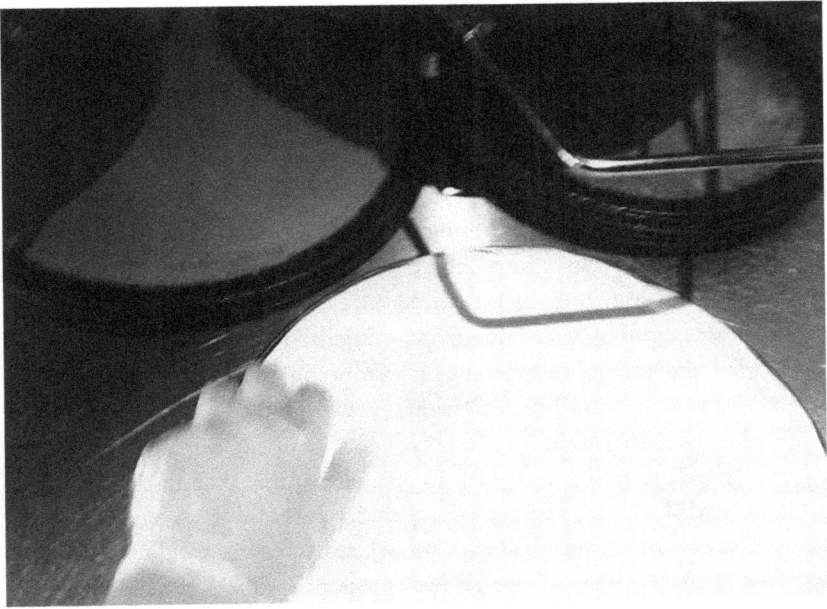

FIGURES 4.2 AND 4.3 Shang's pizza restaurant photo series, Melbourne, 2016.

for making the bases. When I took this one, I was thinking, after working for a long time, I've started to feel it's a bit of a drag, I'm sick of it, and my mind becomes very unclear, and I don't feel like talking to anyone. Then I start to feel as if I'm just a robot. I really hate that feeling, as if I've become a robot, and feeling really bored.

As everyone knows, this type of work is unrelated to our studies, so it really does [*laughs*] get a bit boring. . . . So I'm thinking at the end of this year I might give it up. I mean, there must be some other work opportunities, maybe someone will give me an in, even the opportunity to work in a business run by locals. But my poor English really is a problem, yeah.

I felt like [that job] turned me into a robot. It made me feel as if I was wasting my time. But later I thought, everyone has to work, right? As a pizza maker, as whatever. These kinds of people need to exist. So I can't say that I'm so great, that my time is so precious, or that the value of my life is such that I shouldn't be there doing that. [To think] that is wrong. . . .

That feeling [of turning into a robot], at the time it would just occasionally surface; if I was feeling down emotionally or feeling a bit sad, it'd be exaggerated. I think it's probably a common problem for international students like me, new arrivals, especially if we haven't had any work experience before. . . . You feel you've got no family or friends over here, so you become a bit timid, and you don't know how to integrate into local society, into the new environment. So you keep sort of trying to escape it. . . .

FIGURE 4.4 Shang's pizza restaurant photo series, Melbourne, 2016.

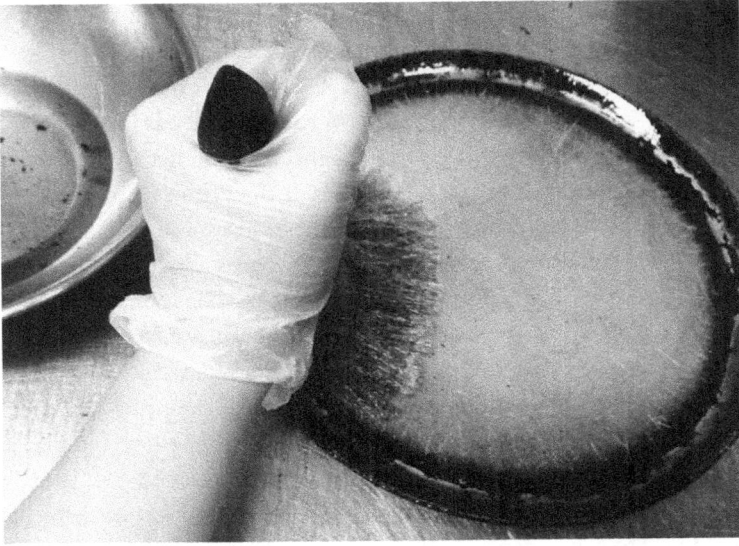

FIGURE 4.5 Shang's pizza restaurant photo series, Melbourne, 2016.

With these photos, you'd asked me to photograph my work environment, and I also wanted to reflect how I was feeling at the time. So I guess I was working and taking photos and thinking, all at once. Why did I have to be working there? What kind of work was it I should be looking for? (Shang, 23)

*

The photographs in figures 4.1–4.5 are part of a series that I asked Shang, a twenty-three-year-old student from Hunan who had previously studied photography, to take as a way of reflecting on her experience working part-time in a suburban pizza franchise in Melbourne. Shang's situation in this job was representative of those of many Chinese student transmigrants working in Australia. She landed the job through a contact in the Chinese community, the restaurant was run by a Chinese boss, the dominant language in her workplace was Mandarin, and the work was low-skilled and low-status, and paid less than minimum wage.

The photographs, together with Shang's commentaries on them, reflect an intertwining of material practice, everyday affect, and reflective cognition. Shang introduces the viewer to the hidden world of the restaurant's backstage (figure 4.1). She inserts herself into the harsh-looking scenes of the commercial kitchen as a gloved hand, its organic life partly concealed but revealing itself in pinpricks of condensed perspiration whose warmth and humidity contrast with the inorganic hardness of the objects in the hand's environment: plastic, metal, machines, implements (figure 4.4). Shang's discussion reveals both the thinking (思考 *sikao*) and the feeling (感觉 *ganjue*) that was intertwined with the process of taking the photos. Her thoughts focus on her (thwarted) desire to find professional work in a "local"-run (as distinct from Chinese-run) business in the area of her studies, her loneliness, her sense of failed integration (融入 *rongru*) into local society, and her worries about her English level. Her affective experience is dominated by a sense of alienation, of having been turned into a robot. This robot has a clouded mind, feels timid and bored, and has a desire to avoid talking to people and a reflex toward escape. The photograph of Shang's hand gripping the mouth of the pizza-base machine (figure 4.3) seems to solicit a metaphorical reading: the yellow-and-black sign in the upper left reads "CAUTION: THIS MACHINE CAN MAIM," and Shang draws an analogy between the machine (机器 *jiqi*) and her sense of having been reduced to robot status (机器人 *jiqiren*). Although, on reflection, Shang expresses humility, morally recoiling from the implication that she thinks she is too good for such work, the energies in figure 4.5—the tension creases in the plastic glove, the force with which the brush's bristles are flattened against the pizza tray, the shape of the fist—nevertheless suggest frustration and perhaps suppressed anger at being stuck in this type of job: "Why did I have to be working there?"

Extending the previous two chapters' focus on quotidian sociospatial practices producing the translocal city, this chapter considers how participants' work practices illuminate complex relationships among mobility, fixity, gender, and value. It shows how their work practices in Melbourne linked them both to relatively fixed, localized, diasporic employment networks in Melbourne's Chinese-run restaurant sector and to relatively mobile, transnational, digitally mediated trading networks in the informal, microentrepreneurial activity of *daigou* (代购), or parallel trading: a type of e-commerce that involved buying local goods on behalf of customers in China to whom they on-sold at a percentage profit. I explore how, in these common types of work, participants encountered zones of disconnection and social exclusion at the local scale (as in Shang's story) and—partly in response—took up practices of hyperconnectivity and network building at the transnational scale involving mobile people, mobile media, mobile technologies, mobile goods, and mobile money. However, I underline that neither of these types of work can be seen as *purely* mobile or *purely* fixed: rather, each combines states of fixity and mobility. Through its central examples of two different types of work, the chapter aims to uncover where value—conceptualized as different forms of capital—may lie vis-à-vis individuals' sociospatial emplacement, geographic mobility, and gender.

Valuing Relationships, Mobility, and Gender

In its attempt to develop a conceptual apparatus adequate to the phenomena at hand, this chapter considers how participants' working experiences illuminate three forms of value that have been analyzed with reference to (post-)Bourdie-usian capitals theory, namely, social capital (Bourdieu 1986), network capital (Urry 2007), and feminine capital (Huppatz 2009). Pierre Bourdieu defines *social capital* as "the aggregate of the actual or potential resources which are linked to possession of a durable network of more or less institutionalized re-lationships of mutual acquaintance and recognition . . . which provides each of its members with the backing of the collectively owned capital, a 'credential' which entitles them to credit, in the various senses of the word" (1986, 249). Social capital, in other words, designates a form of collectively held value aris-ing from complexes of social relationships that bind their members together into groups within a given society.

John Urry advanced the concept of *network capital*, meanwhile, as part of his efforts to capture what is new about social life in the late-modern era, in which, as he and his colleagues argue, human and nonhuman mobilities, not geographically delimited societies, centrally define social life (Sheller and Urry 2006; Urry 2007; Elliott and Urry 2010). For Urry, network capital arises from access to the bureaucratic, economic, social, bodily, infrastructural, and tech-nological affordances that facilitate mobility, and designates "the capacity to engender and sustain social relations with those people who are not necessar-ily proximate . . . which generates emotional, financial and practical benefit" (2007, 197–98; see also Elliott and Urry 2010, 9–11). Urry frames the concept of network capital as an attempt to pinpoint mobility's social consequences, proposing that it should replace the concept of social capital as theorized by Robert Putnam (Urry 2007, 196–203). While Putnam (2000) sees social capital as being fostered through geographic propinquity in small communi-ties, Urry insists that in the era of mobilities, relations of interpersonal trust and copresence are routinely generated and sustained at a distance.[1] In Urry and Anthony Elliott's discussions, the advantageous effects of network capi-tal for those hypermobile groups that possess high levels of it—their paradig-matic example is the new class of ultrarich "globals" (Elliott and Urry 2010, 65–83)—exceed the benefits afforded by these groups' economic and cultural capitals alone (Urry 2007, 197).

Two key points can be drawn out from this discussion. First, in framing the capacity to move and communicate across distance *as* capital, the network capital concept normatively associates mobility with advantage. Only brief mention is made of disadvantaged forms of mobility (Elliott and Urry 2010, 6), so mobility in these accounts appears to be inherently linked with power (Gilbert 1998; Franquesa 2011, 1016). Network capital is framed as paradigmatically a "strong" form of capital, associated with strategic movements by powerful subjects: the elite globals. Second, network capital is distinguished from the older form of capital it purportedly replaces, social capital, by its detachment from specific geographies. I underline these points because, as this chapter will illustrate, they are open to question when considered in light of student transmigrants' experiences of mobility while working overseas; hence, the network capital concept may require rethinking to account for such cases.

Both of the types of work discussed in this chapter—restaurant work and e-trading—are feminized in specific ways. I draw on Kate Huppatz's work on another post-Bourdieusian form of capital—*feminine capital*—to help complicate the network capital concept. Drawing on the earlier work of Beverley Skeggs (1997 and 2004), Huppatz (2009) extends Bourdieu's theory of the capitals to include gendered capitals, specifically, female capital ("the gender advantage that is derived from being perceived to have a female . . . body") and feminine capital ("the gender advantage that is derived from a disposition or skill set learned via socialization, or from simply being hailed as feminine"; 50). Feminine capital, the type of gender capital that most interests me here, is associated with "learned competency": "skills and aptitudes" in particular activities that are culturally associated with femininity (53). In the following analysis, I draw on both Huppatz and Skeggs, as well as on Lin Zhang's (2017) work on the gendered aspects of e-trading, in order to develop a new concept—*feminine network capital*—conceived as a "weak" and tactical form of value.

Based on analysis of participants' work experiences in Melbourne, I develop three main interrelated claims in this chapter, all of which engage but also complicate the network capital concept. First, participants' work experiences show that geographic and social mooring in place, as well as mobility, can generate benefit for individuals and groups, just as both fixity and mobility may generate various types of disadvantage or risk. While Chinese student transmigrants' frequent sense of being stuck in low-status hospitality work in Melbourne's Chinese diasporic economy (as in Shang's story) exemplifies a negative valuation of immobility, certain kinds of relatively geofixed social connections in Melbourne are desirable and beneficial for them, albeit also elusive. Second, and as a corollary, participants' experiences reveal that social capital cannot operate entirely independently of geography, as Urry's proposal of network capital as a replacement for the concept of social capital implies. For most people, social capital does not function in a geographic vacuum but works at local as well as global scales and in tethered as well as mobile forms, when valuable social relationships arise from rootedness in place (Gilbert 1998; Ho 2020, 85). Third, through my development of the feminine network capital concept to name a form of value central to the activity of e-trading, I show how network capital may take "weak" and tactical, rather than "strong" and strategic forms—underlining again the pitfalls of associating mobility and networking unilaterally with power and advantage.

Chinatown Work: Emotional Labor in the Zone of Exception

In predeparture interviews with study participants in China, most spoke of their plans to find work in "local" (当地 dangdi, implying non-Chinese-run) businesses in Melbourne in the area of their major. They hoped this would provide a means of forging local friendships, improving their English, proving their worth in a meritocratic job market where guanxi connections could not be leveraged, and strengthening their CV. However, after arriving in Melbourne, participants generally found that the types of professional work experience they had hoped for were largely out of their reach.

For example, Yining, enrolled in a media studies master's program, had significant experience in the television industry in China and hoped to gain additional experience in her field of study while in Melbourne. But after a few months she concluded that it was virtually impossible to access that type of opportunity and instead accepted an underpaid casual job with a Chinese entrepreneur selling clothing and accessories at a stall in a subway station. She also applied for jobs at McDonald's and KFC, from whom she never heard back after submitting her applications. Yining mused:

> I'm actually not very clear about why. Because I personally think that among Chinese [students], my English is comparatively good. But maybe when a lot of people see you have a Chinese name, they're not willing [to hire you]. . . . It's not [open] prejudice. They just, very politely, reject your résumé.

Such stories were common. Participants wistfully observed the desirable jobs that their Australian-born classmates seemed to access readily—sales assistant at an Apple Store, intern at a major bank, employee at a fast-food franchise paying the legal minimum wage—while, for the most part, gradually relinquishing their own hopes of landing such jobs. Banks and other businesses in the professional sectors for which the students were training routinely demanded certificates of permanent residency or Australian citizenship as a condition for internships (Marginson et al. 2010, 124; see also chapter 8), while non-Chinese-run hospitality businesses almost always rejected students' applications. One participant told of a friend who was a qualified barista and sought work in an Italian-style café, only to be told by the owner that employees with "Asian faces" were not suitable. Such a direct statement of racial discrimination, though, was comparatively rare: more commonly, as Yining describes, non-Chinese employers seemed simply, "very politely," to reject or ignore applicants with Chinese-sounding names. Such anti-Chinese racism in Australian employment markets has been corroborated by statistical studies (Booth, Leigh, and Varganova 2012).[2] Thus, while some participants initially saw the lack of *guanxi* relations in Australia as ethically desirable, in practice a lack of local social capital, combined with racism, frustrated their hopes to benefit from the supposedly free and fair Australian job market.

Many students, like Shang and Yining, were therefore forced to settle for casual unskilled work (打工 *da gong*) in Melbourne's Chinese diasporic economy, where opportunities were facilitated by shared ethnic background and networks. Similarly to other classes of migrants, student workers thus experience contradictory class mobility. While overseas study was intended to help them maintain or improve their (middle-)class status in China, in Melbourne they became "downwardly global" when corralled into precarious work at the bottom end of the labor market (Parreñas 2001, 150–96; M. Johnson 2010; H. Lewis et al. 2015; Amrute 2016; Paret and Gleeson 2016; Ameeriar 2017). The low-status jobs that many participants took in restaurants in Chinatown and related zones of the city were characterized by a number of common features, the most notable being endemic wage theft. At the time of fieldwork, the standard hourly rate of pay in Chinese-run restaurants in Melbourne was $10, with some starting wages of $8 or less: significantly below the legal minimum wage for this type of casual work (then between $14.85 and $24.09); and standard overtime and weekend and holiday pay rates were not applied.[3] Indeed, the many conversations I had with Chinese student workers about their working conditions revealed that most employers made no reference at all to the relevant legal requirements of employment. They enforced unpaid and sometimes lengthy "trial" periods; did not offer written employment contracts; paid cash-in-hand with no pay slips; did not request employees' tax file numbers; and made no reference to the student visas that allowed students to work only twenty hours per week during the semester (Clibborn 2018).[4] Yaqi, a student with several years' waitressing experience, explained that these employers felt licensed to ignore the Australian regulatory frameworks because both sides assumed that this was "black labor" (黑工 *hei gong*): work done outside legal frameworks, so an unstated "don't ask, don't tell" arrangement was implied. The employers knew that they were guilty of wage theft, but the student workers—even when, as was most often the case, they did not breach the twenty-hours-per-week rule—assumed that they were guilty of tax avoidance, so neither side was inclined to report the other to the authorities.[5] As one would expect in such an unregulated environment, petty deception, breaking of verbal contracts, and short-changing by employers were common. Yaqi recalled one employer who demanded a $200 "bond" up-front as a condition of being given the job, which was very difficult to reclaim when she later resigned; others told of employers refusing to pay wages owed or tricking them out of promised payments for specific tasks.

However, despite their knowledge of their own exploitation, no participants, nor anyone else they know, ever initiated legal action against their employers. The reasons they gave included the off-putting difficulty of negotiating Australia's unfamiliar legal system; the risk to future employment prospects in a tight-knit ethnic economy; a sense of loyalty toward employers who in other respects took on a mentoring role toward student workers; reluctance to challenge authority, which they interpreted as culturally specific; the assumption, also interpreted as culturally specific, that it was normal for bosses to treat workers harshly; a "dual frame of reference" suggesting that compared to wages in China, $10 per hour was a reasonable wage (H. Lewis et al. 2015, 583); and transient employees' sense of the futility of embarking on attempts to improve working conditions in Melbourne when, by the time such improvements were realized, they would probably no longer be around to enjoy them. In Australia the regulation of wages and of workers' employment conditions is enforced via a complaints-driven model—meaning, essentially, that in the absence of complaints from workers, wages and working conditions will not be checked by government regulators.[6]

All in all, the situation of participants in these jobs strongly confirms the conclusions of Simon Marginson and colleagues that international student workers occupy a zone of "invisibility" in Australia, segregated into insecure, low-status work in small businesses, often trapped in exploitative or illegal conditions, and "crowded into a narrower range of jobs than those available to locals. They commonly offset their disadvantages by working for less than the legally defined minimum wage. Relatively few students believe these difficulties are a product of racism, partly because many employers who pay illegally low rates have the same ethnicity as those they exploit" (Marginson et al. 2010, 142).

While it is true that the employers who most commonly exploit Chinese international students' labor through underpayment are themselves ethnically Chinese—complicating any romanticized view of urban ethnic economies as inherently supportive (M. Smith 2001, 86–91)—the broader context is nevertheless that students accept such conditions because of their prejudicial exclusion from the higher-status jobs they initially aspired to in non-Chinese-run businesses.

Elsewhere, Marginson (2012) has characterized international students as inhabiting a "gray zone" with regard to their (non)protection by national regulatory regimes based on the norm of citizenship. Taking this idea further with specific reference to international students' working lives in Melbourne, Aihwa Ong's (2006, 97–118) work on zones of exception proves useful. Ong analyzes zoning technologies in China—the creation of Special Economic Zones and Special Administrative Regions—as a state strategy aimed at proliferating cross-border networks with Chinese-dominated economic and political entities abroad (98). These zoning practices create "spatially fixed and distinctive enclaves" through which "sovereign states can create or accommodate islands of distinct governing regimes within the broader landscape of normalized rule" (103). While the example of Chinese student transmigrants working in Australian cities is obviously very different from those that Ong analyzes, nonetheless, the gray zone that these workers inhabit vis-à-vis their (non)protection by national regulatory frameworks has a certain resonance with Ong's concept of the zone of exception. The effect is similar: the urban diasporic economy functions as an "island" within the broader landscape of state regulation, with the student-transmigrant workers in this economy routinely subject to wages and working conditions that are illegal under Australian Commonwealth law. Given the extreme difficulties they faced finding better-paid work elsewhere, student-transmigrant workers found themselves stuck on the fringes of the formal economy as denizens of this zone (Kell and Vogl 2012, 172).[7] In discussing their reasons for agreeing to illegally low rates of pay, expressions of helplessness and lack of choice (无奈 wunai; 没办法 mei banfa) were common: their own collective, systemic underpayment appeared to them like an established, unshakable system that they lacked the power to challenge (Clibborn 2018).[8]

I first meet twenty-one-year-old Zhenghui and her mother at a café in Shanghai in mid-2015; they are passing through from their home city of Chongqing on the way to see Zhenghui off to Melbourne, where she is heading to undertake a master of finance degree. Zhenghui is an earnest, articulate young woman, lean and intense. In our interview, both she and her mother emphasize personal self-development and self-strengthening as key motivations for Zhenghui's journey. By studying abroad and experiencing another culture, she hopes to develop a cosmopolitanized and self-reliant identity that would not simply enhance her career prospects but, more important, enrich and diversify her life experience.

During her first semester in Melbourne, Zhenghui takes on some part-time work in Chinese restaurants for the standard rate of ten dollars per hour. By October, she is working regular shifts in two jobs to help defray her living expenses, which she sees as ethically desirable to ease the financial burden of her overseas study on her parents. Late one Saturday afternoon, as I sit chatting with some other participants in a small restaurant in Chinatown, Zhenghui unexpectedly dashes in and says a quick hello to us before ducking out to the back to change, reappearing shortly in a yellow-and-black uniform dress, ready for her evening shift waiting tables. It's impossible for us to talk that day, but Zhenghui invites me to come and visit her soon at her other job in a small family-run Chinese restaurant in the outer eastern suburb of Chadstone. By the time I visit that restaurant on a weekday evening a week or so later, Zhenghui has already quit her Chinatown job: the boss was too exacting, demanding that workers complete tasks unreasonably fast and insisting that they occupy every spare moment with the frustrating task of peeling ginger with a spoon.

The Chadstone restaurant, located in a quiet suburban shopping strip, consists of a single small room with a plate-glass window onto the street, backed by a counter and a kitchen behind. The four or five pairs of other diners are a mix of Chinese and Caucasian, and Zhenghui moves between tables, chatting amiably with them all, code-switching dexterously between Mandarin and English. She has to work quickly as the restaurant fills up: they are short-staffed that evening, and Zhenghui has to cover the whole restaurant on her own. She runs efficiently from task to task: welcoming customers, taking orders, running them back to kitchen, serving food, totaling bills, taking payment, and clearing and setting tables. Zhenghui tells me that although this work is physically exhausting and underpaid, she likes her current boss a lot more than her former employer in Chinatown and especially enjoys the chance to interact with "local" (non-Chinese) customers.

A week later, Zhenghui sends me a WeChat message saying that she has quit the Chadstone job and relates why over a series of messages stretching from late that night over into the next morning. It had been a busy night, and once again she was the only waitress on duty. A large table ordered multiple dishes, and Zhenghui checked the complex order with them several times. But when the boss arrived, the customers asked him about a scallion pancake they said they'd ordered but not received. The boss took Zhenghui out to the kitchen and yelled at her angrily, *accusing her of having forgotten the table's order. She maintained that she hadn't forgotten any dishes; it was the customers' own mistake. Later, while working in the kitchen, she burst into tears. She felt she had been mistreated and humiliated; her impulse was to quit right away, but she didn't do so, instead staying on to help the boss finish the busy shift. She later regretted this, feeling she had shown weakness in the face of pressure. Having overheard the boss yelling at her, the customers left Zhenghui a large (twenty-dollar) tip, causing her to burst into tears all over again. The moral of this experience, as Zhenghui sees it, is that she must continue to make herself stronger and fight the personal weakness that she feels the experience exposed. Early the following morning, she sends me a short message:*

For my own self-respect, I just couldn't keep working there.

Later she tells me that the boss still owes her a hundred dollars in wages and has tried to trick her by inviting her to drop by to get the money but then saying that he will pay it only if she agrees to work there again. Zhenghui feels that the hundred dollars isn't worth fighting for. She despises the boss's petty trickery and proudly vows,

I will never go back to work for him.

Zhenghui now plans to take a barista course and obtain a license to serve alcohol; she hopes that working in a non-Chinese café or bar will help her integrate into local society, rather than being stuck in the Chinese community, but is apprehensive about whether her plan is realistic. A few months later, she begins to do some small-scale e-trading in the hope that it will be a less exhausting way of earning money, as well as giving her a chance to develop entrepreneurial skills useful for her future career.

Two points in particular in Zhenghui's story typify many Chinese students' experiences of waitressing work in Melbourne. First, the labor of food serving is highly feminized: female students are directed into these customer-facing service tasks, while male students are more likely to get work as kitchen hands or dishwashers, or in other forms of less socially interactive unskilled labor. Waitressing work, while physically demanding, centers around the performance of emotional labor: that array of indicatively feminine tasks connected with caring for the customer that Arlie Hochschild (2003) characterizes as the provision of "commercial love": the performance of "caring" emotion and lightly sexualized self-display through feminized uniforms.

In addition to these performative aspects, emotional labor also encompasses the work of managing other people's emotions: both absorbing the aggression and hostility of disgruntled customers and accepting tirades from angry bosses. Many participants, who generally undertook service work for the first time in Melbourne, felt emotionally bruised by the stream of negative emotions they had to absorb in the course of their work. Zhenghui's self-defensive reaction to the verbal abuse and public humiliation by her boss was to assert her own self-respect and pride, proactively quitting the job and expressing scorn for the boss's petty trickery, which allowed her to claim moral superiority in symbolic compensation for the poor treatment and the money owed. Another participant, Meng, was deeply affected by her frequent encounters with hostile customers. During an unpaid two-day trial at a Subway franchise, some customers were impatient with her slowness in English comprehension. After she asked one customer to repeat part of his order, he rudely snapped, "Bye bye!" and stormed out of the restaurant; another shouted aggressively at her, "You Asians, you come here—don't they give you an English exam?" On another occasion, an elderly woman who had struck up a friendly-seeming conversation with Meng in the bathroom reported her to her manager for not using soap when washing her hands, although she had not used the toilet but only used the cubicle to change into her uniform. The intensity of the negative emotions that these workers were called on to manage testifies to the low status of both their work and their worker identity (Hochschild 2003, 174). This is rooted in a combination of their gender (in common with all female service-sector workers), their race (in encounters with racist customers), their youth (in encounters with older bosses), and sometimes their nationality (in encounters with bosses who shared their Chinese ethnicity but may have looked down on nationals of the People's Republic).

Second, Zhenghui's story illustrates the prominence of states of relative fixity in this type of restaurant work. This fixity operates in two senses. First, in a geographic sense, the availability of these kinds of jobs is to some extent territorially restricted to particular zones of Melbourne's city and suburbs, especially Chinatown (where Zhenghui worked in her earlier job), the surrounding central business district (CBD), and specific areas in the suburbs with a significant Chinese population (like Chadstone, the location of Zhenghui's second job). As face-to-face service work, waitressing is also inherently tied to the worker's embodied presence in the specific geographic territory of the restaurant. The second sense of fixity is connected with student workers' commonly voiced sense of being stuck in this sector of the city's economy. With a deficit of localized social capital beyond the Chinese community compounding their difficulties finding employment in higher-status jobs, service jobs paying a legal wage, or jobs with non-Chinese employers, and hindered from legally challenging their own exploitation, the student workers tended to feel that they lacked other choices and became trapped in the diasporic Chinese restaurant sector. We see this reflected in Zhenghui's anxieties over whether it was realistic to hope for work in a non-Chinese café or bar, even if she obtained the requisite local qualifications (in fact, she never secured such work).

However, although we might describe this type of work as *dominated* by states of social and geographic fixity, it is important to avoid reifying such work as *completely* geofixed. For example, while, from the point of view of recently arrived student transmigrants, the diasporic Chinese economy in Melbourne appears as a restrictive, localized space, in fact the restaurant owners and managers themselves generally had personal or family histories of transnational mobility, having arrived in Australia as part of earlier waves of migration—often from Hong Kong, China's Guangdong province, Taiwan, Malaysia, or Singapore—and maintained ongoing links with those places (M. Smith 2001, 91–97, 119–21). And while from one angle the enclave-like concentrations of Chinese-run businesses in particular geographic pockets of the city can be seen as a type of geofixing, from another angle the territorial dispersion of the various Chinese communities saw student workers becoming quite mobile across urban space, as when Zhenghui worked in both Chinatown and Chadstone while studying at a university at the northern end of the CBD. Further, the personal capacities that Zhenghui hoped to develop as a result of doing this work—especially her desire to become stronger, more resilient, and more self-sufficient—link directly to her stated motivations for undertaking education abroad. In this sense, her work practices can be seen as part of her broader transnational project of self-fashioning.

Despite the commonness of negative stories like Zhenghui's, it would be misleading to characterize student transmigrants' experiences of unskilled work as wholly negative. Other participants found such work satisfying and enjoyable, offering social connections and peer support from other workers; mentorship from employers; the chance to develop a tougher, more resilient character by "eating bitterness" (吃苦 *chi ku*) (as we also see in Zhenghui's own account); and a sense of achievement and independence in earning money to cover daily expenses and ease the burden on parents.[9] Nevertheless, for obvious reasons, many ultimately tired of this type of work and sought alternatives. Zhenghui, like many others, finally decided to try *daigou* as a less exhausting and (she hoped) better-paid alternative.

Feminine Network Capital in E-Trading

When I commenced this research project in mid-2015, I soon noticed the prevalence of DIY ads for Australian health products and milk powder in my contacts' WeChat feeds, evidently targeted to their social networks back in

China. This type of informal e-commerce is known as *daigou* (literally, "proxy purchase"), a term referring both to the activity and to the traders themselves. It involves students buying local products that are unavailable, very expensive, or subject to counterfeiting in China; selling them on to customers via social media at a markup; and then shipping the products to customers or on-selling agents in China via discount courier services (快递 *kuaidi*) run by members of the local Chinese community. Each nation in which Chinese students study has a "brand" in terms of which products are most in demand. For example, in western Europe, high-end luxury fashion and accessories dominate the market (Lin Zhang 2017); students in Korea and Japan tend to sell cosmetics and beauty products; and Australia's national *daigou* brand is defined by certain in-demand lines of health supplements, vitamins, personal healthcare products and pharmaceuticals, cosmetics, infant and toddler milk powder, and sheepskin products, although *daigou* also trade a whole range of basic supermarket items, from breakfast cereal to cookies, cake mix, and chocolate.

The volume of this informal e-commerce is enormous. In late 2015 a single courier business in Melbourne's CBD reported sending six metric tons of goods to China every week (Battersby and Zhou 2015). In mid-2016 I spoke with an employee working in the freight section of a major airline on Australia's west coast who estimated that each of four major Chinese export companies, linked to the Chinese couriers and through them to individual *daigou*, was freighting fifty metric tons of packages to China each week from Perth alone, with volumes from the three big east coast cities each significantly exceeding this. The spike in *daigou* exports led to temporary shortages on the Australian side as supply failed to keep pace with demand, with discount pharmacies frequently sold out of popular items and news media indignantly reporting a "drought" in popular baby formula brands (Irvine 2015).

Australian-made food and health products have risen in popularity among Chinese consumers because multiple food and pharmaceutical safety scandals in China over the past fifteen years have significantly undermined consumer confidence in locally produced goods. These include a series of highly publicized cases uncovered between 2005 and 2011 in which hundreds of small dairies across several provinces were found to have adulterated milk powder with a melamine-like substance derived from industrially processed leather waste (*Wangyi Xinwen* 2011); in 2008 this led to six deaths and fifty-four thousand hospitalizations (Zhongguo Wang 2010). Safety issues have also plagued locally produced pharmaceuticals. Harbin Pharmaceutical Group Holding Company, China's second-largest pharmaceuticals company, was rocked by ten major scandals in 2006–12, including misleading advertising and the illegal addition of restricted drugs to its health supplements (*Time Weekly* 2013). Combined with the commonness of counterfeit products in China, which inclines consumers to distrust locally purchased products that claim to be manufactured overseas, all of this creates an unprecedented market for food and health products that e-traders can guarantee have been purchased outside of China.

When I first meet twenty-year-old Yueming, she is visiting Shanghai with her mother to accompany her father, gravely ill with advanced cancer, for his treatments at a city hospital. Yueming, a tall, sociable young woman with a warm and easy manner, was born in a rural area of Zhejiang province and plans to travel to Melbourne to complete the final two years of her bachelor's degree in accounting as part of a joint program between her university in Shanghai and Fawkner University in Melbourne's northern suburbs. In our first interview late one summer afternoon, Yueming tells me all about her father, with quiet pride and obvious love. He was born into a smallholding farming (or "peasant": 农民 nongmin) family and earned his first money selling cucumbers. Quickly realizing this was a dead-end path, he followed a family connection to a small city nearby, where he began working as a builder's laborer and soon found himself managing small construction projects. Ultimately, he obtained a night-school certificate to practice engineering and developed a professional career as a bridge engineer, raising himself and his family into the middle classes. Yueming emphasized that her father deeply prized his ability to understand the whole job, from bricklaying to conceptual design, as a result of personal experience—"not like these college graduates with all their theories and no hands-on experience at all." In light of her father's serious illness, Yueming is very ambivalent about going to Australia. However, since he wholeheartedly encourages her to make the move, she does so and begins her studies in Melbourne in July 2015.

Soon after her arrival, Yueming takes up e-trading, setting up a dedicated daigou *account on WeChat on which she posts multiple ads almost every day. She is soon the most successful* daigou *in the whole participant group, owing to the boundless energy she pours into the enterprise, her skill in copywriting, and her wide and diverse network of contacts. Participants from larger cities tell me that they feel they wouldn't be successful at* daigou *since most of their contacts in China already know many other people studying abroad, saturating the market, whereas this is less the case for Yueming given her family's rural background. Unlike other participants, who see* daigou *as just an activity on the side to make a little pocket money, Yueming approaches it with entrepreneurial zeal. She picks up tips from her landlady (a young mother who e-trades virtually full-time), trades with bulk-buying agents in China in addition to individual customers, tries to "develop" new*

Australian products she discovers that are as yet unknown to consumers in China, and singlehandedly takes charge of every aspect of her business. Yueming's average profit margin is around 30 percent. With a mixture of astonishment and glee, she tells me she earned over ¥10,000 (more than $2,200) in her first month of trading: nearly three times what she would have made working twenty hours a week in a Chinese restaurant job for the same period.

In September 2015 I visit Yueming at the suburban house where she is living with two classmates and the landlord's family, to accompany her on a daigou trip. Yueming jokingly refers to her bedroom as her "warehouse," indicating the small mountain of flat-packed boxes, bubble wrap, packing tape, and health and food products neatly stacked along one wall (figure 4.6). Awaiting postage are tubes of tinea and hemorrhoid ointments and pawpaw cream; bottles of FemFresh "intimate wash," vitamin and mineral supplements, and BananaBoat sunscreen; packets of herbal laxatives, dried cranberries, Tim Tam chocolate biscuits, and Maltesers; a few tins of S-26 infant formula; and a whole box of German-made Knoppers chocolate wafers (a hot seller and Yueming's favorite: "I sell half and eat half!"). Yueming explains that she chose to specialize mainly in health products because of the excessive capital outlay for luxury branded products and the hassles associated with trading infant formula. Orders for formula typically demand twenty or thirty tins at a time, which, given the limit on purchases per customer (four tins in supermarkets, one in pharmacies), necessitates visits to multiple stores. Milk powder in such quantities is also heavy to carry, and purchasing it in bulk subjects the buyer to disapproving reactions from locals primed on media stories about the Chinese buying up "their" milk. Health products are a comparatively easy-to-buy and portable alternative and are almost equally profitable.

Yueming proudly shows me her meticulously kept handwritten accounts book, with page after page recording products ordered, quantities sold, purchase and sale prices, and postage details (figure 4.7). She also keeps an Excel master spreadsheet listing some 235 products organized by brand, with columns specifying the purchase price in Australian dollars, the sale price in Chinese yuan, the discount price for bulk-buying agents, a bonus discount for bulk purchases, and the weight per unit to calculate postage costs. Yueming's iPhone contains hundreds of photographs of her customers' national ID cards, necessary when mailing parcels to China. In one WeChat post, she uploads a photograph of her neatly clipped stacks of orders and postage receipts, classified into categories with colored tags, captioned: "Suddenly I feel very professional!" (figure 4.8).

Yueming revels in the professionalism of her daigou activities. She tells me she is motivated not only by her enjoyment of the work but, in light of her father's illness, also by her hope to ease her family's financial burden in funding her studies.

In 2015 Yueming usually does her daigou *trips by tram (though she later buys a secondhand car with her profits), carefully mapping out a route that takes her past four or five pharmacies and can be completed within the two hours' travel time covered by a standard ticket. The day I go along with her and her housemate Xiaoyin, I have my car, which makes transporting the purchases and packaging materials a lot easier: Yueming tells me how exhausting it is to lug the heavy bags of goods via public transport and on foot. As we prowl the aisles of various discount pharmacies, Yueming reveals that she knows each shop intimately: the products it typically stocks, the likelihood of their being in stock, its pricing, and the attitude and competency of its checkout staff. Yueming clearly loves shopping: doing the mental arithmetic of price conversions, exercising her specialist knowledge of the various shops and stock lines, sweeping up armfuls of products and buying them with a tap of her Mastercard—and, magically, earning money at the same time (figures 4.9–4.10).*

Later we visit two suburban Chinese courier shops selling boxes and tape, packing and postal services, and some of the more popular daigou *goods, sold at a small markup. These shops have in recent years cropped up all over the CBD and suburbs, transforming Melbourne's urban geography, and today are as usual bustling with international students and other* daigou *packaging up parcels (figures 4.11–4.13). In one of the shops, Yueming and Xiaoyin meet and chat with three classmates from their university program. Our errand completed, we drive through the curving suburban streets back to their house, where I help unpack the goods and boxes from the back of my car, and they distribute some purchases to classmates living next door, for whom they've bought a few items. Yueming tells me that she does at least three of these trips every week.*

Two days later, Yueming announces in a WeChat post that she is planning to reward all her hard daigou *work with a spur-of-the-moment trip back to China for the university break. Her ticket cost ¥7,500: three-quarters of her first month's profits.*

It turns out to be the last time Yueming sees her father, who passes away as a result of his cancer a few weeks after she returns to Melbourne.

For my purposes, Yueming's story reveals four main points about the *daigou* phenomenon. First, like waitressing work, *daigou* is feminized labor, but it is feminized in distinctive ways. Whereas hospitality work centers feminine emotional labor manifested in live bodily and social performance, the digital commerce of *daigou* centers feminine gender capital operationalized through mediated social performance. Among the many female and male participants with whom I discussed the *daigou* phenomenon, in both Australia and China, *daigou* was universally understood as women's work, and it was generally recognized that far more female than male overseas students engaged in it.[10]

FIGURE 4.6 *Daigou* goods awaiting postage in Yueming's bedroom "warehouse." Photo from Yueming's WeChat post, used with permission.

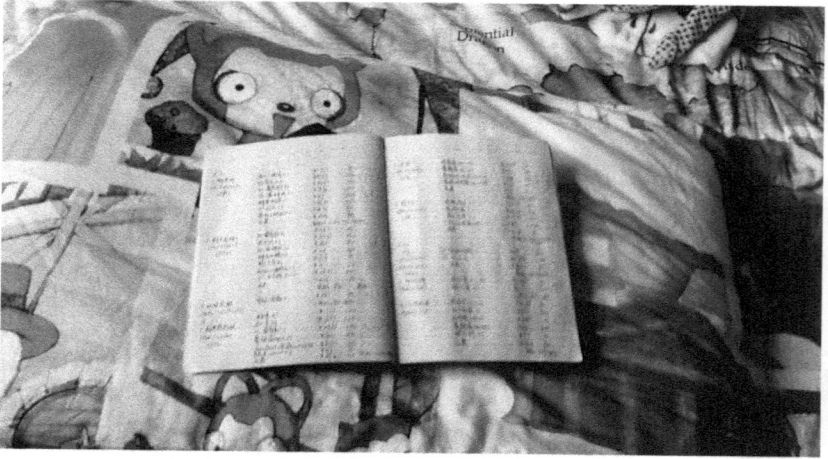

FIGURE 4.7 Yueming's professional record keeping of *daigou* orders.
Photo by the author.

Participants gave three reasons. To begin with, the most popular products traded in *daigou* from Australia are infant milk formula, marketed to mothers of young children, and beauty products and health supplements, whose biggest market is women and of which traders like Yueming, as themselves young women, are assumed to have personal, trustworthy knowledge. Further, several participants told me that young women were suited to doing *daigou* because of their extensive and active social media networks, which they believed were more intense, denser, and more extensive than those of young men. This form of feminine social capital can readily be converted into a customer base for *daigou* products, as we see in Yueming's networks in demographics where studying overseas was relatively uncommon. Finally, participants recognized that much of the art of *daigou* was in the scripting and design of clever and arresting advertisements for the products and tended to think that girls were more skilled than boys in that type of sociorepresentational work. *Daigou* like Yueming wrote witty ad copy and skillfully exploited "life-casted" images of themselves as attractive, cool, or relatable models for the products being sold, creatively reworking the boundaries between private and professional life (figures 4.14–4.15) (X. Zhao 2019b, 136–58). As Lin Zhang writes in her analysis of how young Chinese women fashion their gendered identities through luxury European fashion-and-accessories *daigou*, "Fashioning an 'authentic' self—that is successfully annexing individuals' unique personalities and life experiences to commercial products through visual and discursive narratives—is paramount

FIGURE 4.8 Yueming's professional record keeping of *daigou* orders. Photo from Yueming's WeChat post, used with permission.

FIGURE 4.9 Discount pharmacy in Melbourne's CBD. Photo by the author.

FIGURE 4.10 Discount pharmacy sold out of popular women's vitamins in Melbourne's CBD. Photo by the author.

FIGURE 4.11 Chinese couriers in a Bundoora shopping court that I visited with Yueming and Xiaoyin. Photo by the author.

FIGURE 4.12 Chinese courier in Melbourne's CBD. Photo by the author.

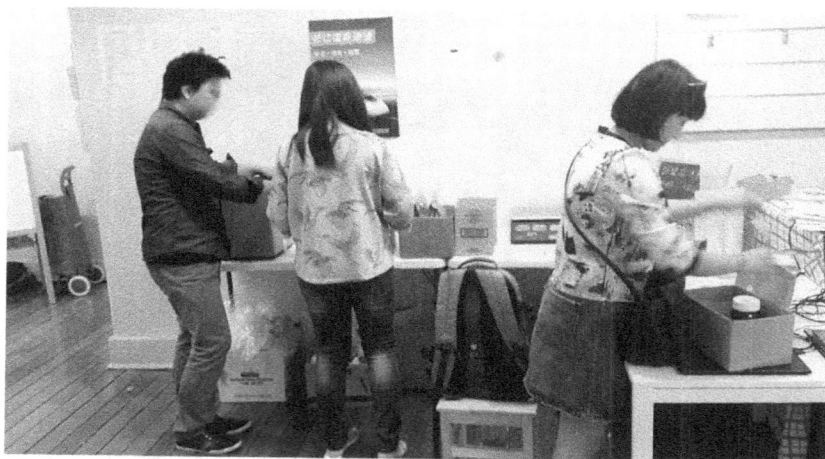

FIGURE 4.13 Customers and a staff member pack up goods at a CBD Chinese courier. Photo by the author.

to attracting customers, enhancing 'stickiness,' and increasing profit margins. To excel amid fierce competition in a risky, mediated informal market, these women must be skilled at communicating their personal and affective appropriation and engagement with . . . [the] brands" (2017, 194).

Each of these three capacities that participants understood as feminine can be interpreted, in Huppatz's terms, as forms of feminine capital: "the gender advantage that is derived from a disposition or skill set learned via socialization" (2009, 50). In making this observation, though, it is important to bear in mind Huppatz's reiteration of Skeggs's Certeauian observation that femininity "can be used socially in tactical rather than strategic ways. . . . Tactics constantly manipulate events to turn them into opportunities; tactical options have more to do with constraints than possibilities. They are determined by the absence of power just as strategy is organized by the postulation of power. Femininity brings with it little social, political and economic worth. It is not a strong asset to trade and capitalize upon" (Skeggs 1997, 10–11). Thus, for Huppatz, feminine capital is inherently a "weak" form of capital: ultimately, it "may only manipulate constraints rather than overturn power" (2009, 59).

The second key point revealed by Yueming's story is that, whereas as I have proposed that restaurant work is dominated by local fixity, *daigou* is dominated by transnational mobility. The activity hinges centrally on access to technologies, services, and networks, including transnational social media, mobile digital payment and transnational electronic funds transfer technologies, transnational courier services, and traders' transnational social networks linking them back to China. Additionally, as with Zhenghui's restaurant work, we see in Yueming's story how undertaking *daigou* linked in her mind with the cultivation of capacities that were central to her wider educational mobility project, especially self-professionalization and the cultivation of entrepreneurial skills. And yet— again echoing the complexity of the earlier example of *da gong*—Yueming's story also shows how *daigou* work, too, is emplaced as well as mobile. Her day-to-day labor of doing *daigou* involved specific places—bedrooms, tram stops, sidewalks, shopping courts—and a tethered sociality peopled by disapproving locals, housemates, landladies, checkout staff, classmates, and couriers. In fact, when Yueming later moved to inner-city Sydney for postgraduate study, although she had originally planned to continue her *daigou* business there (indeed, her choice of Sydney over Canberra as the location for her master's degree study was largely based on *daigou* considerations, especially numbers and costs of supermarkets, pharmacies, and Chinese couriers), she found that, in practice, her new inner-city location presented problems for her business. Supermarkets in Sydney's CBD were too small and were not clustered conveniently

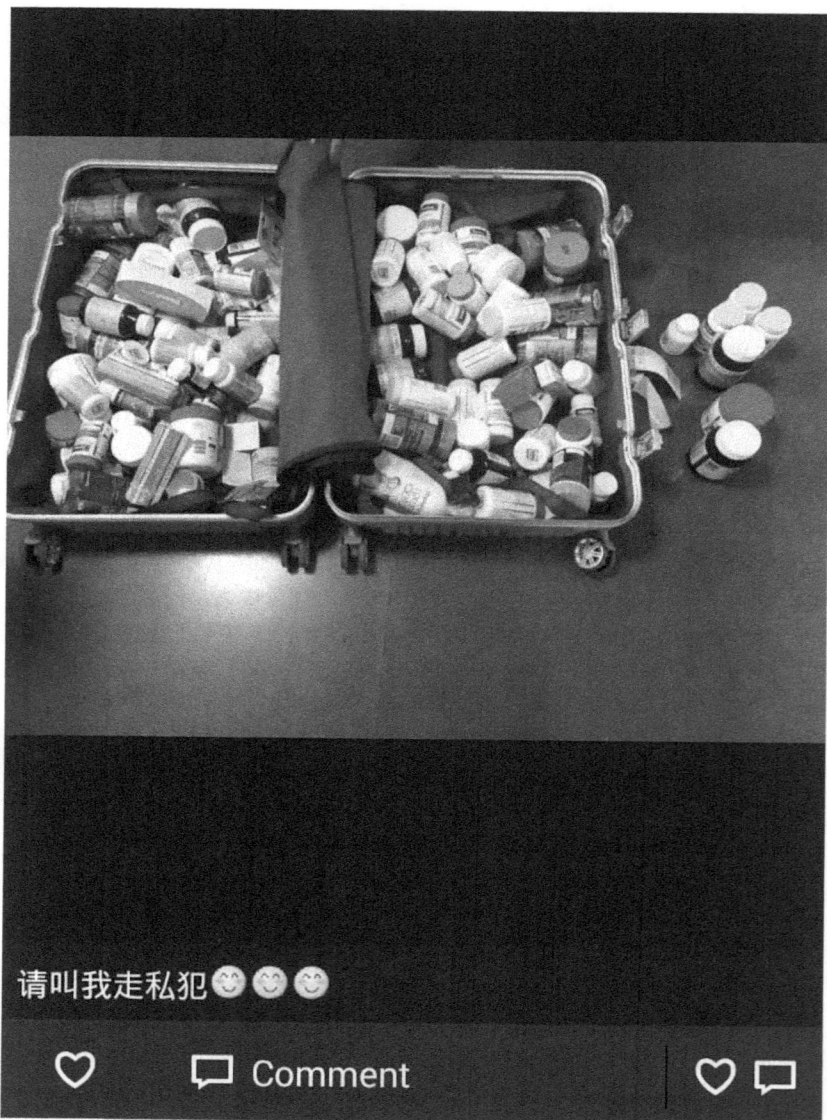

FIGURE 4.14 WeChat posts on Yueming's *daigou* account: "Just call me a 'smuggler' [*three humor emojis*]."

明天要交的商法论文还没开动，而我居然还在打包😂😂😂

FIGURE 4.15 WeChat posts on Yueming's *daigou* account: "I haven't even started the essay on commercial law that's due tomorrow, yet somehow I'm still packaging goods [*three misfortune emojis*]."

in shopping centers, and it was hard to find car parking close to the shops and couriers. To avoid wasting hours on logistics, Yueming ended up paying others a commission to buy and package the goods for her, which ate into her profit margin and made the whole business less worthwhile. In other words, it turned out that Yueming's original suburban location in Bundoora had been key to the viability of her Melbourne *daigou* business. Thus, although this type of e-commerce work may be said to be *dominated* by states of mobility, we should avoid reifying such work as *completely* mobile with no aspects of geographic specificity or emplacement.

The third key point is a related one: that in harnessing capacities linked with their mobility, students' *daigou* ventures draw on most of the constitutive elements of network capital (Urry 2007, 197–98). These include possession of the appropriate documentation that had enabled them to relocate overseas for study, distal personal connections allowing them to develop a customer base, the physical capacity to travel across the city and suburbs to purchase and mail the products, social media apps and smartphones through which to advertise and manage orders, access to mail courier and transportation services, and the time and aptitude to coordinate the whole venture. Thus, the capacity to undertake *daigou* represents a confluence of these young women's combined feminine capital and network capital: both sets of capacities are necessary to maximize the viability of their *daigou* ventures. This assemblage I call *feminine network capital*. However, in characterizing these students' *daigou* activities in this way, I emphasize that the type of network capital the students are able to wield—mirroring their feminine gender capital—is "weak" and tactical. Faced with effective exclusion from secure employment in Melbourne, the Chinese students leverage their relatively small reserves of network capital tactically to negotiate the structural constraints that circumscribe their opportunities.

The fourth and perhaps most notable point, however, is that Yueming's narrative also highlights unquantifiable affective dimensions in her experiences of work and mobility. Yueming's story of coming to Australia to study and undertaking *daigou* is entangled with the parallel story of her father's illness in multiple complex ways: the difficult decision of whether to stay in Zhejiang to care for her father or come to Melbourne to carry out his wish to see her study abroad; her filial desire to decrease the financial burden that her overseas education imposed on him as a motivation for undertaking *daigou*; and the fact that her *daigou* profit ultimately permitted her to go home and see him for the final time.[11] Fancifully, perhaps, I am also tempted to hear a certain resonance between Yueming's tender account of her father's life and values during our first conversation in Shanghai and the way she reveled in her own entrepreneurialism in *daigou* in Bundoora: the meticulously handwritten ledgers, the daily exuberance of her WeChat ads. It was as though in taking on the *daigou* venture, Yueming introjected aspects of her beloved father's character. In her narratives, both father and daughter started their ventures from the ground up and took pride in mastering every aspect of the business, from menial labor (Yueming once joked about a "work-related injury" she had sustained to her wrist from the repetitive action of taping up parcels) to executive planning; both were animated by a similar lively enthusiasm for such entrepreneurial projects. Here, perhaps, we reach the limits of highly generalized macrosociological theories, including capitals theory, in accounting for the singularity of subjective experience. I have in mind the concept of singularity in Dipesh Chakrabarty's sense, drawing on Paul Veyne, as something that "comes into being when we look on things in such a way as not to see them as 'particular' expressions of that which is general . . . [and] which defies the generalizing impulse of the sociological imagination" (Chakrabarty 1997, 43; see also this book's introduction and conclusion). As the poignant specificity of Yueming's story illustrates particularly sharply, people's embodied, affective experiences of intertwined mobility and emplacement, traveling and dwelling, might be seen as singular and nongeneralizable in precisely this sense.

Ambivalent (Im)Mobilities

I have framed individual e-trading as an opportunistic exploitation of gaps in the transnational supply chain, but in closing this chapter, it is worth noting that these opportunities may prove to have been temporary. Over recent years, commercial and state interests far larger and stronger than the students have begun stepping in to fill the gaps and reap the benefits of the formalization of cross-border e-commerce between Australia and China. In retrospect, 2015 turns out to have marked the peak of the individual *daigou*. Between late 2015 and early 2016, both Chemist Warehouse and Woolworths supermarkets, two of Australia's largest retailers of *daigou* products, began to market directly to Chinese consumers via stores on Alibaba's TMall Global e-commerce website (Victorian Government 2015; Woolworths Limited 2016). In April 2016 China imposed tough new measures to extract import duties on cross-border e-commerce (*Caixin* 2016; Haigh 2016), and Australia's free-trade agreement with China, effective as of December 20, 2015, has enabled more and more companies to trade direct, cutting out the work of the individual *daigou* (Battersby and Zhou 2015). Corporate "mega-*daigou*" companies like AuMake, listed on the Australian stock exchange since October 2017, soon began to edge out student microentrepreneurs (K. Anderson et al. 2019, 165; Grigg and Murray 2017). By 2018 a clear downturn in small-scale *daigou* trade was felt both by *daigou*-ing participants in Melbourne and Sydney and by courier business owners, turning many away from the trade; this was compounded by additional regulatory changes in China in 2019 that further formalized and corporatized the industry (Durkin 2019; Yu 2020). It is the nature of tactics to be opportunistic, small-scale, mobile, and temporary (Certeau 1984); student *daigou* proves no exception.

By presenting international student e-traders as operationalizing a tactical form of feminine network capital, I have tried in this chapter to productively complicate the network capital concept. The *daigou* example shows that this form of capital can take weak as well as strong forms and may be wielded tactically from positions of disadvantage as well as strategically to consolidate advantage. Moreover, Chinese students turned to *daigou* in the first place at least partly as a result of their exclusion from secure employment in local businesses in Melbourne, which in turn was due partly to the social capital deficit that they experienced as a result of their move away from their home cities in China. *Contra* Urry's framing of network capital, we thus see how social capital in the Bourdieusian sense remains at least partially tethered to place. Examples like these force us to recognize that for most people, social structure—hence social capital—remains somewhat attached to localized personal and family histories and specific geographies. Geographic and social mooring in place can generate benefit for individuals and groups, and being extracted from one location and relocated in another entails losses that cannot be fully compensated by the placeless machinations of network capital.

The situation of these student transmigrants also demonstrates both opportunities and risks associated with the geomobile and geofixed states that intertwine in their experience. For example, as we saw in chapter 1, the transnational educational journeys of many of the young women in this study were motivated in the first place by their families' sense of the specific disadvantages women face in a gender-discriminatory employment market in China: young women became mobile in response to a risk attached to staying put. Analogously, finding themselves stuck in the relatively fixed zone of exception of Chinese restaurant work, student transmigrants tactically turned to the transnational in undertaking e-commerce. Here again, forms of mobility were taken up to mitigate the disadvantages of fixity. But in other cases, geographic tethering represented opportunity, as in the case of localized social capital, to which participants had access in their communities of long-term residence in China but which they tended to lack, to their detriment, when arriving in Melbourne. Mobility, too, brought dangers as well as opportunities. While study abroad was often framed as a response to the risk of getting stuck in a disadvantaged position in China, conversely, some graduate students and education-industry workers observed that graduates from overseas universities returning to seek work in China may actually face *increased* disadvantage as a result of a *"guanxi* deficit": the social connections on which people must often rely to secure jobs tend to wither during their years away, decreasing their competitiveness against domestic graduates (J. Hao and Welch 2012; see also chapter 8).

Mobilities, then, were wielded tactically against the risks of geographic and existential stuckness (Hage 2009), yet these mobilities themselves entailed *new* risks, because they negated the opportunities as well as the dangers attaching to geofixity. Such examples should caution us against any simple equation of mobility with capital understood as an abstract, general, and placeless form of value. Specific forms of mobility entail specific forms of benefit as well as danger, all of them imbricated with both the materialities of particular places and the singularities of mobile subjects' embodied experience.

~

Chapters 2 to 4 have explored how Melbourne was produced as a translocality through student transmigrants' everyday practices of habitation, communication, and work. Melbourne has emerged as a place connected to multiple points outside itself—both in China and elsewhere—by wide and fast-flowing streams of objects, affects, information, and people moving back and forth: vitamins, movies, money, selfies, milk, songs, smartphones, books, promises, emojis, salty snacks, memories, news, degrees, dreams, video chats, new year's blessings, job applications, recipes, debts, skills, rumors, academic transcripts, medicine, worldviews, flight paths, door curtains, yearnings, grief, and gendered bodies. These flows are not abstract but form a material and shaping part of people's everyday lives. Student transmigrants' engagements with these streams of moving things result in places—a city, a suburb, a street, a country, an apartment, a bedroom, a workplace—coming into being from moment to moment with a specific character: safe or dangerous, boring or interesting, full or empty, rich or meager, promising or hopeless, connected or cut loose. In other words, these streams connecting Melbourne to its various outsides are not separate from participants' experience of locality but *in large part constitutive of it*. The city is not simply "connected to" its elsewheres (as though the two were ontologically separate), but at the experiential level, to a significant degree, the city *is* its connections, so that here and there are interwoven and mutually constitutive.

Maintaining the emphasis on how feminine gender shapes these transmigrants' experiences of educational mobility, the next three chapters shift the primary focus from the external world of participants' sociospatial practices to the internal realm of their affective and subjective experience by exploring participants' engagements with intimate relationships, religion, and national identity. Chapter 5 turns our attention toward temporality, demonstrating how study abroad is a liminal time in which participants reconfigure the meanings of intimacy, sexuality, and the gendered life course.

5. SEXUALITY
Liminal Times

*

The pressure [to marry by a certain age] does decrease, over here [in Australia]. . . . It really does all get delayed by a few years, including settling down in a job, falling in love, and getting married. . . . I feel that in those few years, anything could happen. If your way of thinking changes, then maybe your career will turn out to be the center of your life; maybe the whole system will change [for you]. . . . You may think that you don't have to do things [the standard] way, like quickly get married and settle down when you're twenty-five; there's no need to. I'm actually pretty scared, pretty scared of settling down. Super scared! [*laughs*] . . . Within myself I still sort of reject the expectations society places on adults. . . . Personally, I think that if you're economically independent and make your decisions for yourself, then you are an adult. . . . But there's a contradiction. On one hand, this is how I think, but on the other hand . . . what others expect of me, I also expect of myself. . . . So I'm in a very contradictory period right now. Three years ago when you interviewed me, . . . I thought I could do whatever I wanted. Right now, I'm entering this contradiction. . . . I'm realizing what society expects of people. (Song, 25)

*

At the time of our conversation, Song had graduated with a master's of teaching and was working as a tutor for students prepping for the International English Language Testing System (IELTS) test. She was concurrently studying toward a certificate qualification in her new passion: personal fitness training. Song had a boyfriend, also from China, but no firm plans to get married, preferring to hold on to the sense of personal space she enjoyed in the inner-suburban single-bedroom apartment where she lived alone. Song's reflections touch on the key issue explored in this chapter: the connection between the temporality of transnational education and the temporal regulation of gender through the normative feminine life course. Song's discussion underlines that for young women like herself, the regulation of time is fundamental to the regulation of gender (Lahad 2017).

To be accorded the status of a proper adult woman in contemporary China, one must fulfill certain social expectations. In particular, the chrononormative promptings of both the state and public opinion hold that one should get married and settle down into the role of wife and mother at a quite specific time: one's mid- to late twenties, which Song was entering at the time of our conversation (E. Freeman 2010). The gendered double standard of aging that pushes middle-class women like Song to achieve marriage, reproduction, education, and professional employment in a far shorter time span than their male peers was keenly felt by most participants during this project (England and McClintock 2009; Ji 2015; J. You, Yi, and Chen 2016). Despite being geographically located outside China, these educational transmigrants did not simply escape Chinese regimes of gendered power but instead experienced a transnational form of gendered life-course regulation (Tu and Xie 2020). Although Song was living in Australia at the time we spoke and hoped to stay there permanently, when she talked about her consciousness of gendered life-course expectations, she mainly cited reference points back in China: her mother's hopes for her and the life pathways of similar-aged female friends in her hometown in Jiangsu. While living in Melbourne, Song had for several years felt distanced from those expectations. She made the observation—often repeated by others—that studying abroad tends to delay the standard feminine life course by a few years, and she framed those extra years as a liminal time of nebulous possibility. If being away from China allowed one's thinking to change enough, then "anything could happen," including a decisive shift away from a standard feminine life script hinging on marriage and family. In other words, time spent away pursuing transnational education could interrupt, transform, or even decisively derail the temporal regulation of feminine gender, whether by changing women's priorities ("maybe your career will turn out to be the center of your life"), altering the timing of life transitions ("it really does all get delayed by a few years"), or changing the nature of the intimate relationships that women pursue (as in Song's relishing of her independent, self-contained lifestyle and reluctance to "settle down").

Vis-à-vis the life course, on one hand, Song's generation of young women is affected by the normative, linear life-stage model of the elder generations, which is more compressed for women than for men, leaves them little leeway for deviation between stages, follows fixed chronological markers with regard to proper states for each phase, makes nonmarital sexual activity potentially risky, and directs them toward a family-focused identity by age thirty. On the other hand, women like Song are simultaneously drawn toward a more open and contingent understanding of personal biography, incorporating a greater diversity of possible pathways and a looser and more extended transition to adulthood that may include nonmarital sexual relationships.[1] This chapter explores how time spent abroad affected participants' negotiation of these contradictory models. It focuses on participants' experiences with intimate relationships because the regulation of women's sexuality is at the core of the social organization of gender. As a corollary, women's elaboration of alternative forms of sexuality and intimate relationships—alternative, that is, to the hegemonic definition of proper feminine sexuality in China today: heterosexual, monogamous, and marital or protomarital—has the potential to challenge and rescript dominant models of feminine gender at a basic level, for example, by intervening in the temporal regulation of femininity in the normative life course, altering the dynamics of patriarchal relationships within families, decentering marriage as a primary life goal, or challenging heteronormative gender roles, to name just a few possibilities. Exploring how practices and norms of sexuality and intimate relationships are reconfigured through educational mobility thus enables us to get at the heart of how transnational education affects the ways women are able to understand and practice gender. In addressing these questions, this chapter further develops some central themes that have already surfaced in earlier chapters. These include the rise of neotraditionalist familialism in China's reforms era and the associated "leftover women" discourse that discourages educated, middle-class urban women from delaying marriage beyond their mid- to late twenties (see the introduction) and the way that some young women, in the face of such pressures at home, frame study abroad as a means of postponing or resisting the normative gendered life course (see chapter 1). Those chapters outlined these points as a broad context for this study and as factors that young women and their mothers considered before the commencement of overseas education. This chapter explores how participants negotiated these issues in practice during their time abroad.

The central question addressed in this chapter, then, is this: In the context of the gendered temporal pressures associated with middle-class Chinese women's normative life course, how does educational mobility shape these women's navigation of sexuality and intimate relationships? The answer suggested by participants' experiences is that studying overseas creates a "zone of suspension"—a liminal "'time out' from the life course" (Griffiths, Rogers, and Anderson 2013, 6)—insofar as it temporarily, incompletely distances student transmigrants from certain aspects of sex-gender regulation at home and enables them to develop revised norms (see also Ramdas 2012; Y. Hao 2019; Robertson 2020; S. Zhang and Xu 2020). The chapter considers in detail how participants renegotiated the meanings of feminine gender, the life course, intimate relationships, sexuality, and family during the liminal time of transnational study. In particular, the latter part of the chapter draws on participants' stories to work through three specific potentials of this liminal time: the creation of new forms of intimate isolation, the opening up of queer possibilities, and the scrambling of patriarchal power coordinates within families.

First, however, it is necessary to consider contemporary cultures of sexuality and intimate relationships among middle-class urban youth in China. These contexts were a shaping force for the participants not only in their younger years before leaving China but also day-to-day in the present, given the ubiquitous digital media connectivity they experienced while living abroad, which continually linked them across geographic distance into ongoing exchanges with family, friends, and Chinese public culture (chapter 3).

The Chinese "Sexual Revolution" and Transforming Patriarchy

Based on large-scale qualitative and quantitative studies, researchers on sexual cultures in China, including most notably the sociologists Pan Suiming at Renmin University and Li Yinhe at the Chinese Academy of Social Sciences, have posited that Chinese society in the reforms era—from the early 1990s in particular—has been undergoing a "sexual revolution" (Li Y. 2003; Pan S. et al. 2004; Pan S. 2006).[2] Pan and his research team understand this revolution as constituted by five key "transformations in the primary life cycle" facilitated by structural changes to the regulation of sexuality in China since the late 1970s. These are the separation of sex from reproduction and its intensified association with pleasure (facilitated by the one-child policy and concomitant normalization of contraception), the transformation of understandings of marital sentiment from traditional conceptualizations of "favor and gratitude" toward a valorization of romantic love (linked to the reframing of marriage in the 1980 Marriage Law), an increasing emphasis on sexual pleasure within marriage, a growing detachment of sexual desire from romantic commitment outside marriage, and generational changes in women's sexual attitudes and experiences, especially their increasing awareness of their individual rights in intimate relationships (Pan S. et al. 2004, 404–28; Pan S. 2006). Pan's team demonstrates that these changes occurred first among well-educated youth in cities, with men's behaviors changing more and earlier than women's but, in recent years, women experiencing more rapid change than men (Pan S. et al. 2004; Pan S. 2006). These findings resonate with the work of James Farrer, who has documented transformations in youth sexual cultures in Shanghai (2002) and nationwide (2014a, 2014b) since the 1990s. Farrer shows how the increasing (though by no means total) conceptual separation of sexual relationships from marriage and the normalization of premarital serial sexual relationships have facilitated greater sexual autonomy among youth and led to the emergence of "a 'new normal' of (moderate, romantically linked) premarital sexual experience for young women" (2014b, 154–55, 159). The increasing emphasis on romantic love as a moral value is central; Farrer observes:

> "Love relationships" (*lianai guanxi*) in practice have become increasingly independent of marriage. . . . As marriage in urban China has been delayed, especially for educated men and women . . . , the period of life spent in (or pursuing) such informal love relationships has expanded. Except for the minority who still believe that marriage is the only appropriate context for sex, most young urban Chinese have found a new normative context for sexual intimacy in the dating/love relationship. In sum, by the first decade of the millennium, the "love relationship" has become a new legitimate cultural scenario for sexual intimacy. (2014a, 66)

Along with the normalization of premarital sex and the acceptance of love as a moral basis for a sexual relationship have come the growing appeal of the "pure relationship" anchored in individual affective rather than external structural factors (Giddens 1991; Kajanus 2015, 117–18), the rise of a culture of individualized dating alongside the older familial courtship model (Jankowiak 2013; Farrer 2014a; Jankowiak and Li 2017), growing youth autonomy in the choice of a marriage partner (Harrell and Santos 2017), and increasing—albeit hotly contested—potential for diversified forms of sexual relationship (for example, casual, same-sex, in exchange for money or gifts, multiple, and extramarital; Farrer 2002; Pei 2011; Kam 2012; Deborah Davis and Friedman 2014; Engebretsen 2014; Kajanus 2015, 111–15; Zurndorfer 2016; Bao 2018). Based on such changes, Deborah S. Davis and Sara L. Friedman even argue that marriage itself may be on the way to becoming "deinstitutionalized," in Andrew J. Cherlin's (2004) term: "a process through which previously taken-for-granted assumptions about the propriety of premarital sex, grounds for divorce, or even the necessity of marriage no longer prevail" (Deborah Davis and Friedman 2014, 3; see also Ji and Yeung 2014).

Despite these significant transformations that appear to point broadly toward sexual and relationship liberalization, however, equally salient is the persistence of gendered inequalities owing to the enduring patriarchal currency of female sexual honor, propriety, and shame (I. Fang 2013). Pan Suiming and his coauthors (2004, 105–49), for example, advance a robust critique of the sexual double standard inherent in the ideal of female premarital chastity, which lingers on a symbolic level despite the increasing prevalence of premarital sex. Farrer's research in Shanghai during the 1990s likewise reveals the endurance of female premarital virginity as a cultural value (2002, 224–57), despite challenges to this as a result of the increase in female sexual autonomy in recent decades (2014b; see also Pei 2011; Jankowiak 2013; de Kloet and Fung 2017). All of this suggests, as Stevan Harrell and Gonçalo Santos (2017) argue, that in spite of momentous changes, Chinese patriarchy has transformed rather than disappeared in the late reforms era. Defining classic patriarchy as the power system based on the twin axes of generational hierarchy (the power of elders over the younger generation) and gender hierarchy (the power of men over women), Harrell and Santos discuss the transformed relationship between a still-strong gendered axis and a weakened generational axis whose remnant hierarchy now expresses the elder generations' symbolic prestige more than their actual power: "With the huge changes in the generational axis, male domination has taken on a more basic, unmediated form. If sex and marriage are deinstitutionalized, in the sense that individuals have more freedom to script their lives, men still dominate in the newer, more flexible atmosphere. But men's domination is much less tied to their position in intergenerational patriarchal structures than before" (27). Thus, on one hand, young women today have increasing opportunities for sexual autonomy, while, on the other hand, neopatriarchal logic ensures that their autonomy in this area always remains less than men's. In this sense, in the realm of sexuality as in that of work (chapter 1, chapter 8), the present moment in China is one of deep and thoroughgoing contradiction in both the social framing of feminine gender and women's experiences of it (see the introduction; see also F. Liu 2014; F. Martin 2014; Ji 2015; J. Zheng 2016, 99).

Sex and Relationships Abroad: Diversity and Contradiction

The wide range of often-contradictory social scripts currently available in China on love, marriage, sexual propriety, relationships, and the life course makes for diverse attitudes toward and practices of intimacy in the current generation of middle-class urban youth (Farrer 2002, 224–27; Jeffreys 2015, 67; Kajanus 2015, 112; Zavoretti 2017, 134). This was clearly reflected in participants' discussions of their own intimate relationships. In our initial interviews, the majority said that they expected to get married and that sometime between the ages of twenty-six and thirty would be the best time to do so. But a handful—including a group of five or six committed feminists who were outspokenly critical of sexism in many contexts—expressed more unconventional views and said that there was no ideal age for marriage but rather that one should let relationships take their natural course, or that they hoped to remain unmarried or could accept it, or that they would be just as happy with other alternatives (for example, marriage in middle or old age, de facto relationships, or career taking precedence over marriage). Broadly, the participant group's preference for somewhat "late" marriage tended to solidify and intensify as the years passed. Graduating with an overseas postgraduate degree, which almost all participants ultimately did, tended especially to sharpen their sense that giving up professional development in favor of early marriage and children would be a waste of their own and their parents' educational investments. Participants regularly shared cautionary tales of friends or relatives back home who were finding themselves persuaded into premature, loveless marriages for the sake of keeping the elders happy. However, those participants who remained or became single during the course of the study often felt under pressure as a result of comparison with peers back in China and the looming deadline for marriage. Many experienced direct marriage pressure from their parents: some dutifully submitted to parental matchmaking (at least one met a fiancé in this way); others redoubled their own efforts and found boyfriends independently; others attempted to sidestep the issue by finding ways to stay abroad after graduation; and yet others put up direct resistance, arguing with their mothers and refusing point-blank to meet the candidates suggested.

There was diversity, too, in participants' understandings and practices of dating while abroad. Several never dated anyone during the period of the study, preferring to remain single or wait for true love; others endorsed relationship practices they saw as "Western," such as hookups and friends with benefits. In contrast, a few told me in somewhat judgmental terms about Chinese female flatmates whom they characterized as more sexually "loose" (放荡 fang-dang) than themselves. During their years in Australia, many participants went through a series of monogamous heterosexual relationships, largely with mainland Chinese partners but also with Australians and men of other nationalities.[3] Participants were reflexive about the differences they perceived between Chinese and Australian cultures of sexuality and intimate relationships. Following a kind of popular civilizationalist discourse that posits essential cultural differences between "West" and "East," they noted distinctions in conceptualizations of marriage (in Australia, understood as about two individuals; in China, as about two families), desirable "girlfriend" femininity as judged by straight men (in Australia, assertive and confident; in China, passive and sweet), and dating (in Australia, dating and having sex in order to get to know someone; in China, getting to know someone before beginning to date and have sex). Some participants, both during their time in Australia and after returning to China, described feeling caught between cultures in one or more of these regards: "too westernized" for Chinese men and the Eastern system, yet "too Chinese" for Australian men and the Western system.

Broadly, however, participants' discussions of these questions echo the findings of a 2018 survey of over seven hundred Chinese-speaking international students across Australia (F. Martin et al. 2019), which showed that a large majority of mainland Chinese respondents accepted premarital sex, couples living together, and (more narrowly) men and women having several sexual partners before marriage. Comparison of those results with data from studies of university students in China (e.g., Zhongguo Jihua Shengyu Xiehui 2015) suggests that respondents studying in Australia held significantly more liberal attitudes on these questions than their counterparts in China.[4] This lends weight to the idea that while living abroad, Chinese students may be developing a culture of sexuality and intimate relationships somewhat specific to their own transmigrant world.

Zone of Suspension

Earlier studies have raised the question of how educational mobility affects Chinese university students' negotiations of sexuality and intimacy. Indeed, one factor in the development of the increasingly liberal (开放 *kaifang*) youth sex cultures that Pan, Farrer, and others describe in China's large cities is the commonness of domestic geographic mobility. In the reforms era, youth of all classes have begun to migrate on an unprecedented scale to big cities in search of educational and economic opportunity, leading to the dilution of parental authority (Nyíri 2010; Jankowiak and Moore 2012, 279). In the case of Chinese young people traveling abroad for study, a parallel logic seems probable, such that existing trends in metropolitan China toward youth as a period of sexual exploration may be extended and accelerated by time away (Farrer 2002, 168). Anni Kajanus's study supports this in relation to women students in particular: "It is notable that all female informants who had particularly liberal views on sex and sexuality were returned student migrants. . . . Most of these women claimed that staying abroad had had a significant impact on their views. . . . As the students' immediate living environment is controlled by different social norms, they feel less pressure to follow the Chinese conventions. Even after returning to China, the cosmopolitan orientation allows some student migrants to maintain some distance to the local power systems" (2015, 114–19).

Popular Chinese media focusing on the experiences of students abroad frequently explore related themes in relation to women. For example, in his bestselling book about a previous generation of Chinese students who studied in America from the late 1980s, Qian Ning ([1996] 2003, 245–61) observed that while Chinese husbands experienced a status drop in moving from China to the United States, wives became "liberated" from the yoke of Chinese patriarchal tradition. Today popular accounts on WeChat and Weibo targeting Chinese students abroad regularly run features on international students' sex lives and relationships, often focusing on the increased autonomy and correspondingly heightened reputational risks that overseas study may entail for young women. For example, one 2016 WeChat article, entitled "Can't Accept Getting Married the Moment You've Held Hands but Can't Stand Going to Bed with Nothing to Show for It: International Students Caught between Conservatism and Passion," focuses on Chinese students' confusion at differences in youth sexual norms between China and the United States. The article criticizes what it claims is a common stereotype:

> [People] think that when overseas, students get influenced by local liberal [*kaifang*] sexual culture; that just like in [American] TV dramas, they're always getting together in big groups of boys and girls to *party*, hook up, have promiscuous sex, pass out drunk, etc.; and that, as a consequence, those who study abroad tend to become "easy" [随便 *suibian*], "loose" [*fangdang*], and "untraditional." One netizen even commented that he would never marry a girl who had studied abroad. (Queenie Gu 2016)

Indeed, Yining's mother made regular reference to just such a stereotype of the promiscuous female overseas student during arguments in which she pressured her daughter to find a fiancé, which she felt would mitigate reputational damage at home resulting from Yining studying in a Western country as a single woman.

Another WeChat article the same year, entitled "Ha! That's a Good Question, Why Do Girls Who Study Abroad Tend to Stay Single?," discusses the impacts of overseas study on women's understandings of gender (Moerben Weishenghuo 2016). Referring to the popular idea that "there are many leftover women among those who've studied abroad" (海归多剩女 *haigui duo shengnü*), the article explains this purported phenomenon by citing female international students' intense study focus, the masculinizing effect of increased independence and ambition, women's "value depreciation" in the Chinese marriage market in their late twenties, and contrasts between Chinese feminine beauty aesthetics and views on suitable marriage age (slight and pale; lower) and those in Western countries (toned and tanned; higher). The article ends with a lyrical paean to the independent spirit of women who have studied abroad and remain single by choice (see also *Aozhou Mirror* 2017).

Such stories suggest the circulation of a popular understanding that time spent studying abroad, especially for women, may (for better or worse) distance them from aspects of sex-gender regulation at home and enable the development of revised norms in relation to sexual relationships, marriage, femininity, and life-course management. Indeed, for many study participants, living overseas did seem to bring a certain distancing from the pressures of home and a greater sense of personal autonomy in decision-making, both in relationships and in broader life plans: a liminal "zone of suspension" in relation to time, space, and regulatory structures (Robertson 2013, 7). Like Song, several participants characterized their time away as a time of radical openness, in which future directions that may once have seemed clear grew uncertain. For example, a few months after arriving in Melbourne, twenty-three-year-old Niuniu mused:

> With each life stage—like, for example, [between when] I'm twenty [and] twenty-three, I'm studying . . . ; then maybe after twenty-three you work for a couple of years, your parents start to get ideas; they think, you already have a steady job, you've already pretty much completed that part of your task, so you should start on the road to the next stage of your life. . . . [But] I think that being overseas entails more possibilities. That is, you have only a hazy image of what your future life might be, because you have more choices.

Niuniu's friend Huisheng (also twenty-three years old) agreed:

> If you're working in China, then even if your parents are in Shandong and you're working in Shanghai, they can call you once a day and give you a push [toward marriage], but overseas, it's just too far away. This is a very important reason why everyone [here] does everything late; it's because they can't be controlled, and so their own views can be expressed more.

The two friends' tone in this conversation implied that they saw the "haziness" of their futures and the delay in the standard life progression in a largely positive light: as an expansion of choices in this liminal time of educational mobility (Cwerner 2001, 27–28).

Several participants also commented that living abroad—geographically and psychologically removed from parental authority, social surveillance, and familiar interpersonal networks in China—effectively suspends some of the standard gendered rules around sex and intimacy that would apply if they had remained in China, so that the whole feel of romantic relationships (谈恋爱 tan lianai) was completely different abroad (see also Baas 2012, 140–44; King and Sondhi 2016). For example, Niuniu reflected after a year and a half in Melbourne:

I've always thought that, comparatively speaking, Chinese people are rather conservative in terms of [sexual] matters. But I'm finding that here overseas—well, they're not! There are quite a few matters on which the standards seem to be altered here.... Such as, for example, very quickly, er, taking things to the next level [having sex].... Like, after knowing each other for just a week! It might even be faster than local standards—isn't it? You know each other for just one week, or go out for one week, and then—

While Niuniu underlined altered norms around the pacing of sexual relationships, Mei (twenty-seven years old) reflected on how geographic distance reduced the pressure to follow the normative feminine life course. Comparing her own calm, self-contained life as a single woman in Melbourne with the lives of friends her age in China, she told me:

There, it's like, "Oh, I'm twenty-six, I have to get married; I'm twenty-eight, I have to have a baby." There is a mysterious pressure [莫名的压力 momingde yali] that pervades everything, pushing everyone to do the same thing—yet nobody asks why you have to follow that path. Because actually, there's more than one way to live your life, right? There are many different ways.... [In Australia] it is more individual focused, you could say that. Putting yourself at the center of your own life. More individualist, I guess? I don't know if this way of living should be called selfish, maybe? According to the value system in China, people would call it selfish. Because a lot of people there actually get married for the sake of the elders.

Relatedly, others discussed how traveling back and forth between overseas and their home cities in China created a disorienting kind of "norms lag" between the two places, as Song experienced when she moved between her married peers in Jiangsu and her own contentedly nonmarried life in Melbourne (see P. Ip 2018, 253–93).

Fenfang (twenty-three years old) came to Melbourne to pursue her master's of accounting. She had not had a boyfriend before arriving in Australia, but after a year in Melbourne, she met someone (also an international student from China) through a WeChat singles club: a privately organized weekly chat group where young Chinese men and women could get to know each other for either serious dating or hookups. When I met Fenfang to chat about her new relationship about three weeks later, she said that they both really liked each other and were serious about the relationship, even planning to travel to China during the next university break to meet each other's parents. She felt that her boyfriend had been insinuating that they might move in together, extolling the livability of certain suburbs in "casual" conversation, as though they might soon start considering where to rent. Our conversation turned to the commonness of cohabitation (同居 *tongju*) among Chinese international students in Australia. "It's <u>totally</u> common here!" said Fenfang. "Among the couples I know, not one of them <u>isn't</u> living together!" Back in China, though—especially in smaller cities like her hometown in Hebei—the practice was far less usual. Before she left China, Fenfang said, she'd felt that she would want to be married before moving in with a partner (an attitude that her more liberal-minded flatmate described as "so last century"). But now she saw sense in the idea she'd heard from friends that before you get married, you should "test out" whether you're compatible.

Fenfang did worry, however: What if you move in together only to find you're *not* compatible? She had a friend in that situation, and her friend felt bound to stick with her boyfriend despite their incompatibility, since if she cohabited with him but then broke up with him, she might appear morally "loose." Fenfang thought that in her own case, her parents wouldn't necessarily oppose her moving in with her boyfriend, which echoed the attitude of the parents of other respondents who cohabited with boyfriends in Melbourne: some parents accepted this happening in the overseas setting, on the condition that the relationship was serious and likely headed for marriage. However, Fenfang underlined that if she did move in with her boyfriend, she would need to be "extremely careful" about telling friends back home, because they might judge her morality and spread ugly rumors that could damage her reputation and that of her family. She would therefore tend not to reveal the situation to any but her most deeply trusted friends in China.[5] Indeed, transnational secret keeping was a notable feature of the zone of suspension that participants created around sex-gender norms while overseas, with relationships often kept completely secret from parents when they involved partners of whom parents were unlikely to approve (for example, same-sex partners, men of different races or nationalities, divorced men with children, or short-term partners) (Xi Chen 2018, 18).[6]

Fenfang offered some interesting discussion of the different subjective feeling of sex-gender morality in her hometown versus in Melbourne, which resonates with Mei's remarks quoted earlier:

> There, you are constantly aware of the eyes of others on you, and what they may be thinking: you walk out your front door, and there are the

neighbors—will they start up with "Oh, such a big girl like you, when will you find a fiancé?" "Have you got a boyfriend yet?" You're just aware of that kind of pressure all the time, because your social network is wide, and tight-knit. Whereas here you feel more free of it. What you think or do is what you want to think or do. You feel freer, you don't have that burden so much.

Such observations echo Yingchun Ji's analysis of the dense social networks that continuously pressure parents and daughters alike, especially in China's smaller cities, about daughters' marital status and prospects, creating an anxiety that "seems to permeate the entire Chinese society" (2015, 1064). Fenfang underlined how Chinese students in Melbourne "absorb the atmosphere" of Australian values on intimate relationships but—as in her own story—also have to negotiate their continuing relationships with people back in China, who are immersed in a different moral scheme. With the ubiquitous transnational connectivity of mobile telephony and social media, young women like Fenfang are, in this sense, living, thinking, and planning transnationally, moment to moment, across two very different and in some ways contradictory cultural and moral sex-gender systems (S. Zhang and Xu 2020).

Fenfang's story suggests that studying abroad enables a certain (partial) deinstitutionalization of marriage (Cherlin 2004) and an experimentation with pre- or nonmarital intimate relationships that is possible, in significant part, as a result of the subjective distance from Chinese public opinion (after she graduated and found work in Melbourne, Fenfang did, in fact, move in with her boyfriend). This is not necessarily about a distance from parental authority: pragmatic parents may actually support unconventional intimate practices such as premarital cohabitation, since the effective insulation that geographic distance offers from prying neighbors and extended family means that the young woman abroad runs less risk of reputational damage. Distanced from the dense web of moral surveillance within the wider family and public culture that keeps young women's intimate relationships in line at home, young women like Fenfang may experience a sense of individualized freedom while abroad: "What you think or do is what you want to think or do." In this sense, life in Melbourne appeared to provide a space for remaking the sex-gender rules—or accelerating changes already evident in some youth scenes in larger Chinese urban centers—and in the process elaborating new meanings for feminine youth.

Yet this freedom was far from total. Fenfang's account shows that even while living in Melbourne, she was far from unaffected by conventional Chinese gendered norms; as Saulo B. Cwerner argues, "times"—in this case, the time of the normative middle-class Chinese feminine life course—"*migrate* with people" (2001, 7). At the time of the conversation quoted earlier, Fenfang's short relationship with her new boyfriend was already heading in a marriage-like direction, and parental introductions were made during the couple's visit to China soon afterward. Moreover, the superficial freedom of premarital cohabitation actually seemed to present a minefield of gendered risks, with feminine reputational damage lurking around every corner: the inadvisability of moving in together and then breaking up; the danger of damaging rumors if social networks back in China got wind of the situation.[7] Other participants approaching their mid-twenties told of mothers phoning them almost daily to push them to find a fiancé, causing the daughters significant stress. Yining's mother said extremely harsh things to her on the topic, including quoting the classic Confucian child-shaming line *bu xiao you san, wu hou wei da* (不孝有三 无后为大: "there are three great offenses against filial piety, among which leaving no descendants is the most serious"). Time away from China, then, certainly did not bring definitive immunity from the pull of the normative feminine life script.

Further, given the pervasive gendered double standard for sexual morality, the liminal time of educational mobility may not only broaden the range of sexual and relationship scripts available to women but also create new forms of intimate isolation. As Xi Chen observes in her study of Chinese international students' negotiations of dating practices in Sydney, "Peer pressure casts a scrutinising gaze over sojourners' sexuality.... Within this mechanism ... one's identity is determined by how much he/she conforms to hegemonic norms within the community.... Members who do not conform ... tend to be alienated and pushed to the social fringe by their own people" (2018, 21). Thus, "when it comes to dating and intimacy, sojourners often find themselves unable to turn to ... peers for help due to a fear of judgement, shame or alienation" (37; see also Farrer 2002, 240). Xiaosu's story illustrates this particularly vividly.

First Secret

Xiaosu represents herself to me from the time I first meet her in China predeparture as someone whose worldview and interpersonal ethics are very "Western": she yearns for freedom, wants to put herself at the center of her own life, and hates the idea of following a standard gendered life course that would force her to focus on husband and child. During her time in Melbourne, discussing her current boyfriend, she tells me:

I've never told [my parents] about any of my boyfriends, from the first one until now. If I told them now, there'd be such a long story to tell about all I've done that they don't know about—I'd probably be beaten to death! So it's best not to tell them. I've lived apart from them for years, because of schooling away from home. I basically don't tell them about my life. Every single thing they told me not to do, I've done! They say: The world outside is dangerous, take care out there. But I'm someone who enjoys risk-taking—basically, if they tell me not to do something, then I'll go straight ahead and do it. . . . I want to be someone interesting. I want to try lots of different things, enter society, live a little. I like it here, basically. I like the freedom.

But despite her self-understanding as rebellious and antitraditional, Xiaosu turns out to be far from immune from the effects of conventional gendered sexual morality. She contacts me one night saying she urgently needs to talk as she's just broken up with her boyfriend and is feeling upset. We meet a couple of days later, and over lunch at a Taiwanese restaurant in the city, Xiaosu tells me the full story. In a low voice, wiping away tears, she tells me that she and her Chinese boyfriend had been together only a very short time when she decided to break up with him, having realized she didn't really want to be with him and had only agreed to go out with him out of loneliness. But the night before breaking things off, she slept with him (she couldn't bring herself to say it out loud and instead made a shy hand gesture: "Do you get what I mean?"). Momentarily persuaded at the time by his insistence that having sex was "the Western way of doing romance" (国外谈恋爱 的方式 guowai tan lianaide fangshi), Xiaosu is now covered in shame and regret, on one hand worried that the ex-boyfriend will spread ugly rumors about her and on the other hand so ashamed of her behavior that she feels she "can't face people" (见不得人 jianbude ren) and doesn't dare to see her friends. Xiaosu tells me:

If my parents found out they'd kill me! You're the only one I've told. I daren't tell anyone else. I know for Westerners this sort of thing is common, but in China, if people find out, they'll remember and use it as a weapon against you.

Giving in to pressure to sleep with someone and then not continuing as a couple has left Xiaosu torn between her own sense that she had simply made a mistake, and a sex-gender code that would frame her as an immoral woman.

After a few months, Xiaosu puts this painful experience behind her and again extolls the freedom afforded by nonconventional intimate relationships. She tells me that she can now accept what she sees as a "Western" model of dating in which a woman can spend a lot of time alone with, maybe even have sex with, a male friend without assuming they must become a couple or that the woman "loses" anything in the process. She adds:

> *I think I'm [now] freer. . . . To put it in a negative way, you might say I like playing [爱玩 ai wan]. But I define this "playing" in a positive way, I don't think it's something bad.*

When she tells me this, Xiaosu and I are having a three-way discussion that also includes Fenfang, who maintains discreet (but total) silence about what Xiaosu is saying, while wearing an impassive expression that suggests that she means to distance herself from these ideas. On one or two other occasions, other participants also make ambiguous, jokey asides about Xiaosu's lifestyle that suggest a similar kind of moral distancing.

Later on, however, after a period back in China, Xiaosu starts a serious relationship with a Chinese boyfriend whom she describes as much more conservative and "traditional" than herself. She grows out her short, spiky hairstyle, dyes it from red back to black, and tones down her old street-fashion clothing style, ditching her trendy trucker caps for a more conservative style of feminine self-presentation. Xiaosu tells me her boyfriend doesn't go out at night in Melbourne for fear of crime and asks her to return to their apartment before dark as well. When I point out that this makes a big contrast with her former life, when she'd often stayed out late partying, she says she is pleased to do as her boyfriend asks because she cherishes the sense of security the relationship gives her, and her boyfriend's advice reinforces that of her parents.

Through all of these twists and turns in her intimate life and relationships, Xiaosu seemed to be bouncing between two different sex-gender value systems, oscillating between the "freedom" (and risks) of "Western"-style sexual liberalism and the "security" (and shame) of "traditional" sex-gender conservatism. This sense of a double or split value scheme is a theme that runs strongly through many of the responses discussed thus far. It was sometimes presented as a distinction between one's own, independent beliefs and the values of "society," "other people," "tradition," or "people in China." But as we see in the stories of both Fenfang and Xiaosu, when the values in question were specifically connected with unmarried women's sexual behavior—unmarried cohabitation, multiple sexual partners, sex outside committed relationships—the gendered double standard meant that they might be left to deal with the complexities of their intimate lives alone, owing to fears about their reputation. This was the case despite common assumptions about conational peer groups as a source of support (Xi Chen 2018, 59) and regardless of the fact many in this cohort of young women abroad were likely experiencing quite similar issues. The intimate isolation bred from fears of reputational damage meant that these women's emergent alternative value systems, like the one that Xiaosu periodically gave voice to, could not spread or grow easily among them as a group. Hence, the conventional feminine sexual morality was able to remain hegemonic despite the geographic distance that afforded alternative versions a certain limited space for development.

QUEER POSSIBILITY

As is the case with youth sexual cultures generally, queer sexualities are also shaped significantly by spatiality and mobility. Elisabeth Engebretsen (2017, 179–80) makes this point with regard to lesbian and gay youth in China, noting how the potential for domestic mobility between cities puts queer possibility in much easier reach for well-educated urbanites than for the less educated and those "stuck" by economic or family circumstance in small towns and rural areas. Tingting Liu's (2018, 187–91) research with rural migrant workers establishes a link between domestic labor mobility and working-class women's capacity to make queer lives, while Lucetta Yip Lo Kam (2020) analyzes the growing prominence of *chuguo* (出国: going abroad) as a normative value within the homonormative culture of middle-class lesbian scenes in urban China. With regard to gay Chinese students in Western nations, Anni Kajanus (2015, 114–15) considers how spatial and social distance open up queer possibility, and Haiqing Yu and Hayden Blain (2019, 70) observe a parallel between *chuguo* and "coming to terms with oneself as gay"; however, Xi Chen (2018, 21) emphasizes that homophobia in Chinese international student communities may reproduce some of the social pressures from home.

For some straight-identifying students, though, increased openness to queer sexuality and relationships was one of the most notable changes they observed in themselves while studying in Australia. My own former students, some of whom I have kept in touch with and visited in China over the years since their graduation, made this point spontaneously on a number of occasions. They recalled how seeing LGBTQ pride marches in Melbourne, reading news about the legalization of same-sex marriage in Australia, and meeting openly gay or lesbian friends overseas not only prompted in them a greater acceptance of sexual diversity—and sometimes relaxed the pressure they felt to adhere to a normative heteromarital life course—but also made them more aware of LGBTQ cultures and communities within China. As study participant Shuangshuang observed after two years in Melbourne:

> I have some gay friends. . . . I got to know them, how they try to live . . . and open up to people, and even to their parents. So I find it quite interesting . . . because in China even if you are gay, you try to hide it. . . . But here my four gay friends, they all told me that . . . they were gay. . . . It makes me feel like pay[ing] more attention to their rights . . . like, I'll try to . . . understand them more, like, how their lives are different.

For others, forms of queer relationality observed in Australia became a source of personal inspiration. For example, Niuniu reflected on a housemate she befriended in the share-house where she lived in Melbourne:

> This Spanish housemate of mine was very interesting. He's a guy, right, and he's gay. And he liked to, you know, . . . pick guys up, to have short-term sexual relationships. I just thought he was really smart, really smart about people, especially in that respect. I was curious, so I asked him: How do you do it? Be so happy, and yet so free and easy? Because he'd break things off with them really fast, and yet every time he was with someone, he was totally into it. . . . He threw himself right in. But when they'd break up, he'd be like, Well, even though we broke up, even though it's a pity, that's just the way it is. . . . It seemed he was able to focus on fully enjoying the relationship. When I asked him how he did it, he said: Even though you're in a relationship with a partner, even though there are two people involved—and maybe some people like to be involved with even more than that—anyway, you have to put the pursuit of your own happiness first, that's the most important thing. You shouldn't constantly be wondering whether what you're doing is making them happy, or making them uncomfortable, because if you do, then you'll slowly start to feel tired, or else the other person will start to feel something's off. . . . No matter what kind of relationship you're in, and no matter what stage the relationship is at . . . , if you put your own happiness first, then even if you break up, . . . the relationship will still seem sweet to you, and you'll have good memories. You won't later feel that you hate him, or feel tortured, or whatever. I think what he said really makes sense. . . . You have to put your own feelings first.

When Niuniu related this to me, she was single and had never been in a romantic relationship, nor did she particularly want to be. Her housemate's alternative view of sexual relationships—which queers not only the gender of object choice but also hegemonic romantic ideals of true love, relationship longevity, exclusivity, mutuality, and self-sacrifice—became food for thought. His emphasis on personal pleasure seemed to resonate particularly with Niuniu's reluctance to sacrifice the freedoms of singlehood for a conventional romantic relationship.

Among young women who themselves had same-sex or genderqueer desires, years spent studying in Australia became a time of queer possibility in a number of different ways. In this book's introduction, we met Yiruo, the young tomboy for whom educational mobility, first to Kuala Lumpur and later to Melbourne, meant time away from parental surveillance in which she could more readily develop and express her genderqueer subjectivity. Almost three years after that first meeting, Yiruo came out to me about her sexuality, in conversation with two of her close friends (also participants) over beer and chips one hot Saturday afternoon at a pub in inner-suburban Melbourne. Our meandering conversation about marriage pressure first prompted Yiruo's friend to tell a story about a lesbian friend, also a student from China, who planned to bring her girlfriend out from Beijing to get married, since the Australian parliament had finally passed the same-sex marriage law late the previous year. Excited, Yiruo asked with her trademark boyish enthusiasm if she could attend the two women's wedding as her friend's plus-one. She then began speaking directly and openly for the first time (though she had hinted at it before) about her own queerness and its impacts on her relationship with her parents. During the long conversation that followed about sexuality, family, marriage, coming-out strategies, and life plans, Yiruo told us that when she revealed her same-sex preference to her parents, after a series of difficult discussions in which her parents refused to accept her homosexuality, her father finally told her that if this was really how she felt, then it would be much better for her to stay in Australia after graduation. This became Yiruo's goal, and she later switched her postgraduate major to train in a profession included on the Australian government's Strategic Skills List in order to facilitate her transition to a skilled-migrant visa. "The most important thing for me in all this is freedom. All I want is the freedom to be how I want to be and to be who I am," she told us.

Second Secret

Twenty-two-year-old Jun, pursuing an arts-related major, seems like a free spirit: full of curiosity, humor, and meditative reflection. At our first meeting in Melbourne, she tells me about her parents' liberal approach to child-rearing, her hopes to delay marriage for as long as possible, and her view of herself as a bit boyish or *"gallant"* (豪爽 *haoshuang*), *maybe, she thinks, because her father treats her somewhat like a son, which she connects with a regional form of femininity in central China, in contrast to the hyperfeminine norm on the east coast. Jun's habitual wardrobe speaks the global language of urban cool: Doc Martens, jeans, an Adidas jacket, a unisex black T-shirt.*

One afternoon about nine months after we first meet, I ask Jun if she has any romantic stories to share. She gazes at me across our lunch table for a long moment, with an ambivalent, speculative smile, then says:

> Actually, there's something I've been hesitating whether to tell you—it's that I'm not really certain of my sexual orientation. When boys signal that they're interested in me, I just want to put distance between us. I've never felt anything strong for them. With my close girlfriends, I do feel something. But I'm not sure what it is—

Over the next couple of hours, Jun reflects on her uncertainties and reluctance to speak with her parents about her sexuality and cause them unnecessary worry, since in any case she isn't sure what she is feeling. She says that what she is telling me is explosive information in the Chinese student community and that, so far, I am the only one she's told. Jun feels that even if she does one day become surer of her same-sex desires, she would rather bear the burden of keeping them secret her whole life than put her parents through the pain of finding out they have a queer daughter.

Jun's life plans, meanwhile, continue to focus on geographic mobility. On a trip back to China the following Chinese New Year, she asks her parents to allow her two years after graduation to "float" (漂 *piao*):

> You know, float north, float south, work a bit here and there away from home. . . . Just [ask my parents to] leave me alone, don't push me to get married. . . . Don't keep pushing me to settle down, like to go home and take the civil service exam or work at some local TV station back home. I think I should take the chance to travel around and look at things, try things out first.

Two and a half years after arriving in Melbourne, on the eve of going back to China to look for work, Jun tells me that she is now surer of her same-sex attraction. She links her new understanding of her sexuality with her geographic and social location, mentioning the recently passed Australian marriage equality law and a lesbian classmate who is planning to bring her girlfriend over from China to marry. In Melbourne, Jun feels she is surrounded by a sea of both visible and invisible queer allies:

I might have lots of friends like this around me; some haven't told me, and others are public about it. Actually, there are lots of this type of people around.

I ask her to expand on how she feels living in Australia might have affected her negotiations with her sexuality, and Jun explains:

I actually started thinking about this in junior high school. Because I liked a girl back then, too. . . . I've continuously been reflecting on all this within myself, ever since. After I came here . . . I met this girl, and I guess it was love at first sight. And I kept exploring [these feelings] in darkness, drawing closer to them. . . . After coming overseas, my thinking on this has definitely become more liberal [kaifang]. Over here—well, that law wasn't passed before [now], but everyone's acceptance is pretty high. . . . Over here, I've met many more friends and classmates: if I hadn't come to Australia, I wouldn't have met that girl, and I wouldn't have met those [queer] classmates, those friends, and I wouldn't have met you either, right? So I feel like it's an amazing kind of fate [缘分 yuanfen]. Actually, coming to Melbourne has had a completely different impact on the development of my personal thinking than if I'd stayed in China. I think if I'd stayed in China, I might have just stayed repressed. Whereas over here I've been more able to mold my character in that direction—more liberal, more relaxed, more calm—because the atmosphere is great here. My thinking doesn't continually get suppressed; it's given me the chance to express my nature a bit more, right? . . . If I were in China, I think it might be very hard; that little seed might have just gotten squashed right away [laughs]. . . . I've always been someone who loves freedom, but after coming here, I love it even more and understand its value even more clearly. . . . I want to live my life in my own way. . . . Freedom of choice . . . , freedom of behavior, freedom of thought—all kinds of freedom—I love freedom with a reckless abandon! [laughs].

The last time I see Jun, she is renting a room by herself in the suburbs of Shanghai, eking out a precarious living in a series of entry-level creative-industry jobs. She is still not completely certain about her sexual orientation—but she has met another girl she likes and thinks it might be mutual.

Although Jun decided to go back to China and Yiruo decided to stay in Australia, both of their stories underline the decisive ways that geographic location and mobility intersect with and shape queer possibility. According to her own account, Yiruo was able to develop her queer adult self in significant part as a result of living away from her parents during much of her adolescence and early adulthood, and her decision to stay in Australia resulted from her and her father's shared estimation that a queer life outside China would be easier and better for her (and her parents) than her returning. Like Yiruo, Jun, too, experienced transnational education as an opportunity to explore queer self-making, and her geographic decisions also hinged on her sexual circumstances—specifically, her lack of a partner to keep her in Melbourne. She contrasted this with her friend "who is [staying] for her girlfriend. It makes her more determined: she wants to stay here, get PR [permanent residency], get the right visa status, and then bring her girlfriend over here to get married." The symbolic role of Australia's same-sex marriage legislation is also central here. For both Yiruo and Jun, the prospect (even hypothetical) of being able to be queer and also get married to the person one loves exercised considerable allure, since in China marriage remains the marker of adult personhood, and queerness tends to stand in the way of achieving it (Kam 2012; Engebretsen 2014, 2017).

Another obvious continuity is their shared emphasis on freedom (自由 ziyou) as the most important gain in a queer life lived openly. Neither Yiruo nor Jun proposed, exactly, that Australia was a "land of freedom"; rather, they felt that living there had led them to realize the importance of living freely, wherever they might be located geographically. Jun's proposal to her parents that she be allowed to "float" for a few more years is interesting in this regard. Floating could be seen as the antithesis of striving (see this book's introduction). The emphasis in Jun's account is not so much on *where* one is geographically—in Australia, in China, in the north, in the south—as on the *nature* of one's movement: not pushing relentlessly onward and upward but rather drifting (temporarily at least) untethered, undirected, off to one side of the normative milestones of marriage, civil service exams, a job, and settling down. When she left Australia, Jun certainly envisaged her two years of floating as a time to further explore queer possibility in sexuality and relationships, but in another sense, the very notion of floating denotes, perhaps, a kind of queered time in relation to the normative life course (A. Hansen 2015; see further discussion in chapter 8).

SCRAMBLING PATRIARCHY

Third Secret

When I first meet Jiaying, at a Spanish café in Melbourne's northern suburbs, she brings her boyfriend along: a tall northerner completing his master's degree in a management-related area. Jiaying, then twenty-one, is from a small city in an ethnic-minority prefecture in southwestern China, and she and her boyfriend contrast in almost every way—looks, height, accent, cultural background—but they are obviously a close, established couple, and Jiaying speaks matter-of-factly about their hope to get married within the next four to five years. She is studying early childhood education in the hope of converting to a skilled-migrant visa after graduation. A lot will depend on her: after her boyfriend graduates a few months later, despite his professional qualifications, the best work he can find is as a builder's laborer. The couple's plan is for Jiaying to get her permanent residency first so that her boyfriend can then apply for a spouse visa.

The following summer, when I meet Jiaying for a smoothie during a break in her demanding study and practicum schedule, she tells me that since the Chinese government is now allowing couples to have a second child, her father is pressuring her mother (now in her early forties) to do so, though her mother is reluctant. Jiaying's father is worried about his family name dying out since there is only one remaining male heir, Jiaying's cousin. Jiaying's father, a powerful local official, sometimes even berates Jiaying when she disagrees with his views: "I give you all this money for university fees and still you argue with me—I'd be better off investing in your cousin!" In fact, he does help the cousin's family out financially from time to time.

Early the next year, I start a discussion in our project WeChat group by asking how participants think brides' and grooms' families should handle the provision of property for marriage. Jiaying responds with a series of private messages about her own situation. Her mother doesn't approve of her marrying her boyfriend, she writes, because in his current financial circumstances he can't provide a house. She then forwards me a series of screenshots showing her mother's conversation with a friend comparing their two daughters. Her mother expresses envy of her friend's situation, with a daughter who instead of pursuing postgraduate studies overseas is getting married (to a loser playboy who couldn't previously land a decent girlfriend, Jiaying points out). "Ahh, how I envy you. Xiaoxing is so young and she has everything, but Jiaying is a heavy burden. I don't know how many more years she'll have to struggle before she catches up with Xiaoxing." Jiaying feels her mother's values are all wrong:

> She always brings this up to get at me. When I see it, I feel awful. I study and sit for IELTS and immigrate all by myself, is that some great shame? Is leaning on a man so glorious?

As for marriage:

> I don't consider my mother's opinion. Love [感情 ganqing] and the character of the person [人品 renpin] are number one. . . . Last year when the

marriage topic came up, my mum found someone and asked him for a million in bride price [彩礼 caili] [two facepalm emojis]![18] . . . *By doing that, she deeply wounded the feelings between us.*

Jiaying explains that she is especially motivated to marry for the right reasons because of her mother's own negative example: family gossip has it that her mother married her father not because she loved him but because he agreed to provide a home and schooling for her younger siblings. Jiaying sees this utilitarian motive as the cause of her parents' unhappy marriage.

A few months later, Jiaying posts an emotional message on her WeChat Moments feed:

I didn't wish to be a girl; by being a girl, have I committed some wrong? Because a girl can't continue the clan surname, does her father think she can't be relied on in the future? Can't a girl bring honor to her clan? Should a girl therefore accept humiliation from an outsider and be cursed to hell and back by her own father? But being cursed, all I can do is take it. Afterward I'm supposed to be nice to him, I'm still supposed to be nice to him. For some outsider to the family to curse me to tears, it really is unbearable.

It's the first time I've been so thoroughly humiliated
And by my own father
Without even the chance to reply
Overseas struggling by myself, have I done anything wrong?
When I'm sad, all I can do is hide all alone under my quilt and cry
Even those closest to me can't give me any comfort
What's the point of living, like this

I meet Jiaying the following week. She explains what is behind her post: her parents finally divorced the previous year, and now her father has a new girlfriend: a much younger returned migrant laborer. The couple have known each other only a very short time but are already planning to marry and undergo in vitro fertilization. Jiaying assumes this is to enable sex selection and produce the male heir her father has wanted all along. She describes her hurt when her father told her that he can't rely on her because she is a daughter, and she criticizes his traditional outlook that makes him fear being ridiculed if he doesn't leave a son to continue his family name. In addition to this gendered insult, Jiaying also worries about the material implications of her father's impending remarriage. His fiancée is insisting on moving into a family apartment that was meant to be left to Jiaying, sharing assets equally with her husband, having a say in Jiaying's father's spending, and *revising the size of Jiaying's inheritance if the couple now produce a son. Jiaying worries that the fees for her final year of postgraduate study, which her mother cannot afford and her father had promised to pay, may be in jeopardy. Meanwhile, her father seems to be taking it all out on Jiaying, saying that she is unfilial and ought to respect his wishes. "He says I'm standing in the way of his happiness!" Jiaying fumes. Jiaying tells me her mother has become depressed:*

> *She's dedicated everything she had to her family, and to me. And now she's left with nothing—the divorce settlement completely favored my father. And even the daughter for whom she sacrificed so much might get cut out—by her own father! My mum just feels she's left with nothing.*

Jiaying's paternal grandma, too, is taking Jiaying's father's side. This hurts her mother even more, since they lived under the same roof for decades. Grandma reads fortunes and says that unless Jiaying's father remarries soon, the whole family will suffer misfortune; her father then argues it would be unfilial not to follow the advice of the elders. As we part after our long lunch, Jiaying tells me, with a look of steely determination, that she is going home at Chinese New Year to sort the whole thing out.

The afternoon she tells me all this, Jiaying mentions that something else major has happened for her as well, but she isn't yet ready to tell anyone. Four months later, I get a huge surprise when Jiaying tells me via WeChat message that she gave birth to a baby son the year before! I am among the first to whom she tells her momentous secret. She accidentally became pregnant, and her parents advised her not to keep the baby. But in the Melbourne clinic where she was booked to have the termination, she changed her mind at the last possible moment. She married her boyfriend in a civil ceremony and gave birth to her son in Melbourne, keeping all this secret from her parents and friends, so that the first her family knew of it was when she disembarked from the plane at Chinese New Year carrying her new baby boy. Once they met the baby, her parents were thrilled. Luckily, Jiaying's husband's lack of regular work means that he is available to take care of the baby while she studies. Later, she sends her son back to China for a few months to be cared for by her husband's parents; then her own mother visits Melbourne to look after him while Jiaying completes the final semester of her postgraduate degree.

I meet Jiaying's son when he is just over a year old. He is a strong, serious, and determined little boy. I get the feeling that, like his mother, there will be virtually nothing he can't achieve.

The unfolding of Jiaying's dramatic story illustrates sharply how the liminal time of transnational study can scramble both gendered and generational power coordinates within families. Both of Jiaying's parents, for different reasons and in different ways, tried to interpellate her into the role of filial daughter within a deeply patriarchal, neotraditionalist family context. Attempting to shame Jiaying through comparison with her friend's more "successful" daughter, her mother pressured her to get married and abandon her studies. She disapproved of Jiaying's boyfriend because he could not meet the patriarchal expectation that the groom's family should provide the major capital for marriage in the form of property, then humiliated Jiaying further by proposing to marry her off to a wealthier stranger for a high bride price. Jiaying's father, meanwhile, exercised quite a pure form of old-style patriarchal authority. He stopped at virtually nothing in his drive to procure a male heir: providing financial support to Jiaying's male cousin, pressuring his wife to have another child, and finally divorcing her and marrying a younger woman, seemingly with the express purpose of producing a son via sex selection. Clearly prizing the continuity of his family name over his emotional relationship with his daughter, he insulted Jiaying on the basis of her gender by calling her ungrateful in comparison with her male cousin and unreliable in comparison with his hypothetical future son. Moreover, by virtue of his position as a male government official, economic as well as social power was concentrated in Jiaying's father's hands, which he used to secure his own patriarchal purposes in obtaining an heir. In transferring his affections and resources from his ex-wife to his new fiancée, he threatened to leave Jiaying and her mother with virtually nothing: no property, no security, few assets, and, in Jiaying's case, a uselessly incomplete degree.

However, as a result of both geographic distance and the accrual of new kinds of resources stemming from education abroad—a combination of academic and mobility capitals (Kaufmann, Bergman, and Joye 2004)—Jiaying was ultimately able not only to extract herself from this situation but to some extent to turn the generational and gendered power coordinates around. Her father's initial investment in her overseas education ultimately allowed Jiaying to get herself into a position where her capacity to stay in Australia long-term granted her a new kind of decision-making power in relation to her own life and family. Not only did Jiaying continue her postgraduate studies against her mother's wishes, but her location away from direct family surveillance and favorable position vis-à-vis future earning power and migration also enabled her to marry a man of whom her parents explicitly disapproved and to give birth to her son against their advice. Jiaying's mobility also enabled her to effect an intergenerational transfer of the gendered burden of childcare (Tu and Xie 2020). She turned her situation around to the extent that her mother found herself providing care for the very child whose birth she had advised against and of whose father she disapproved. Within her own conjugal family in Australia, meanwhile, Jiaying was also in a powerful position owing to her qualification in an area on the Strategic Skills List, which would enable her (unlike her husband) to transition to a skilled-migrant visa. Not only did she have higher earning power than her husband, making her likely to become the family's main breadwinner, but he would be reliant on her for his own visa. Furthermore, while Jiaying completed her studies and later began working, her husband became their son's primary caregiver, turning gendered convention on its head: "In China this is extremely rare. The traditional morality is still that looking after children is the mother's job," Jiaying emphasized.

In Jiaying's hands, academic and mobility capitals thus became game-changing resources for negotiating with patriarchal power. This is far from the classic "patriarchal bargain" in which women's "protection [is] exchange[d] for submissiveness and propriety" (Kandiyoti 1988, 283; see also Wolf 1985; Zavoretti 2017). Jiaying's story describes a much more thoroughgoing overturning of patriarchal norms and gendered roles. The old gendered and generational logics of her natal family were scrambled by the new power Jiaying gained by being located overseas, becoming highly educated, developing independent earning power, and becoming eligible for residency rights abroad. While she was initially reliant on her father's financial support to reach this position, once she attained it, she became far less subject to his and his family's power over her.

But this was not without cost. The price Jiaying had to pay was the intense emotional stress of fielding patriarchal pressures within her natal family, which at every turn attempted to shame her for failing to embody proper, neotraditional daughterhood, while forging her own path outside—and in opposition to—her natal family's patriarchal organization.

Liminal Times, Divergent Systems

This chapter has considered how the time of transnational education functions as a zone of suspension in relation to the norms of femininity: a liminal moment when alternative forms of sexuality, intimacy, and gender may be imagined and practiced. In student transmigrants' home contexts, feminine gender is itself regulated temporally, through the chrononormative staging of the heteromarital life course, and transnational educational mobility may trouble this by enabling women to rethink that course and possibly delay it or reroute it altogether. By attending to participants' stories, the chapter has explored how educational mobility may enable dominant models of feminine gender to be rescripted, including in the elaboration of alternative sexual cultures, in the flourishing of queer possibility, and in the rearrangement of gendered and generational power dynamics within families.

Can a young woman exercise sexual autonomy and pursue sexual pleasure as men do and still be a "good girl"? Is a "good daughter" one who follows her parents' wishes or one who strives to optimize her own position? Is a "good woman" defined by the sacrifices she makes for others or by responsibility toward her own desires, interests, and needs? Does a "good mother" shoulder the primary care work for her children as a matter of principle or instead maximize her own and her family's opportunities by pursuing educational and professional advancement? These are some of the ethical questions thrown into relief by participants' experiences during the liminal time of transnational education. With their themes of gendered subjugation versus autonomy, obedience versus independence, self-sacrifice versus self-interest, and conformity versus rebellion, they illustrate how time spent studying and living abroad may sharpen women's desires for female individualization over and against the putative virtue of the "traditional" girl, the obedient daughter, the self-sacrificing woman, and the family-focused mother (Kim 2011). Whatever may happen in the future for the women whose stories have been presented in this chapter, there are signs that, for some of them, educational mobility may have marked the beginning of a rerouting of the normative feminine life course.

Yet while the stories related here reveal multiple points of resistance to the normative regulation of feminine gender, the central theme is not so much the decisive overthrow of neotraditionalist ideals but rather the exhausting emotional work that these mobile women had to perform in mediating between divergent systems of sexual and gendered value. The exercise of sexual autonomy and nonconformity may come at the cost of intimate isolation; pursuing queer possibility may bring the all-but-unbearable prospect of disappointing one's parents and causing them grief; and the capacity to defy patriarchal power may entail the emotional cost of being ruthlessly humiliated by the power one defies. The women in these stories do not escape Chinese oppression to find freedom in the West; rather, they endlessly mediate between divergent systems, personally absorbing the stress generated by the contradictions between them and providing a sharp illustration of the emotionally embodied nature of sexed and gendered migration (Gorman-Murray 2009). Evidently, there is a significant impetus for academically, professionally, and personally ambitious young Chinese women to elaborate alternatives to the neotraditional ideals of respectable femininity and gendered life course that are hegemonic in China today. For some such women, at certain times, educational mobility seems to represent a step toward an alternative: delaying or derailing a standard life course and elaborating new forms of sexual morality, intimate relationships, and gendered selfhood. But the contradictions of both femininity and life script tend to be reconfigured, rather than neatly resolved, in the partial zone of suspension that educational mobility affords.

The next chapter moves on from sexuality to explore a different form of embodied and subjective experience—but one that is, for some, just as intimate: religious belief and practice.

6. FAITH
Spirits of Movement

In the context of religions' increasing transnationalism in late modernity (Csordas 2007; Knowlton 2007; Meyer 2010; Kong 2013), the upsurge in Christian faith among Chinese people both within and outside China over the past thirty-odd years is widely seen as indicative of the ongoing global reconfiguration of Christianity. In China, despite low levels of religious faith by world standards, the number of practicing Christians has grown so significantly since the easing of the state atheism policy at the end of the Maoist era that prominent sociologist of religion Fenggang Yang (2015) describes China as "the leading edge of Christian expansion in the twenty-first century" (see also Wenzel-Teuber 2016). In Western nations, meanwhile, Christian conversion has become a mass phenomenon among Chinese migrants (F. Yang 1998; F. Yang and Tamney 2006; Xuefang Zhang 2006; Han 2011). Significant numbers of Chinese international students are also involved in Christian churches across Europe, the United States, and Australia (Nyíri 2003; Y. Wang and Yang 2006; Roman Williams 2010; Fincher 2011; L. Liu 2016a). Indeed, some Christian churches in the countries where Chinese students study, including Australia, selectively target these students in evangelizing strategies that position mobile students as future "missionaries" expected to spread the gospel and "act as . . . messengers of God" in their homeland (L. Liu 2016a, 136; see also Nyíri 2003; X. Zhang 2006; Y. Wang and Yang 2006).[1]

The attraction of Christian churches for Chinese youth and migrants has been interpreted, broadly, in two ways, each of which resonates to some degree with the experiences of the student transmigrants who participated in this project. First, Fenggang Yang (1998) has influentially proposed that evangelical Christianity appeals to first-generation Chinese immigrants in the United States in the context of their experiences of China's coerced modernization. Pointing to the repudiation of traditional belief systems in the process of socialist modernization and the widespread social turmoil of China's violent twentieth century, Yang argues that Chinese migrants are "both free and bound to seek alternate meaning systems" (253), among which Christianity is a prominent option (see also Y. Wang and Yang 2006). Similarly, young people within China may seek out Christian faith to help them to cope with personal alienation, disorientation, and insecurity resulting from the rise of a market society alongside continuing political repression (F. Yang 2005). In sum, Yang proposes that Christian conversion can be seen as contemporary Chinese people's response to moral and spiritual disenchantment in postsocialist society.

The second explanation for Chinese migrants' involvement in Christian churches emphasizes what we might call, in geographer David Ley's words, the "immigrant church as a service hub" (2010, 216). Along these lines, Huamei Han (2011) proposes that Christian evangelism is effective among Chinese migrants in Canada because it acts as a salve to their experiences of racial othering and settlement difficulties, and Ruth Fincher (2011, 914) makes similar points about Chinese international students' church involvements in Melbourne (see also Ley 2010, 213–17; Ley and Tse 2013). Researchers point to churches' provision of pragmatic help to Chinese students and migrants, from welcome activities to English lessons, furniture donations, and practical advice about life in the local context (X. Zhang 2006; L. Liu 2016a). In these ways, Christian churches in Western nations not only minister to spiritual needs like those that Yang highlights but also take on what is essentially a service-provision role, responding to Chinese students' and migrants' more immediate material needs in acculturation, settlement, and socialization.

Participants in this project encountered a range of religious (largely Christian) organizations while studying in Australia. These ranged from random street encounters with proselytizers from various modern Protestant churches who sought them out as targets for evangelization, to casual attendance at church activities in transactional exchange for social services, to (more rarely) deeply transformative involvement and religious conversion. This chapter provides an overview of the range of these experiences and participants' reflections on them, followed by two more in-depth case studies of student transmigrants'—and my own—engagements with a Mandarin branch of the Church of Jesus Christ of Latter-day Saints (the Mormons) and a Pentecostal megachurch.

The chapter is primarily interested in three questions. One, which carries over to some extent from the sociospatial preoccupations of the first part of this book, is about how student transmigrants' engagements with forms of deterritorialized Christianity in Melbourne demonstrate new and complex imbrications of locality with transnational mobilities, underlining once again the deeply translocal character of these students' experiences.[2] Another question concerns the division of labor among churches, universities, and governments in the provision of settlement and socialization services to international students and the ethical and gendered implications of that division. Rather differently from the analytic (and secularist) bent of these two questions, the chapter's final question concerns religious affect. Given the centrality of noncognitive, embodied, inspirited, and supernatural experience in many forms of religious practice, the ethnographic study of such practices, with its conventions of secular(izing) narration, poses unique challenges (Chakrabarty 1997; Pellegrini 2007; Ley and Tse 2013; J. Johnson 2017; Fernando and Harding 2020; Harding 2020). Accordingly, interwoven with the analytic sections, this chapter includes fieldwork story segments in which I hope to do some faint justice to the ways in which the affective experience of immersion in religious scenes—even in the scholarly guise of ethnographic observation—tends to elude the clinical grasp of academic analysis.

First Encounters

In line with the generally low levels of formal religious affiliation within China (Wenzel-Teuber 2016), only three study participants were practicing adherents of an organized religion when they arrived in Australia, all of them following a family faith. Shuangshuang from Sichuan came from a Catholic family; Liangliang from Henan was ethnically Hui, hence Muslim; and Changying from Anhui, like her mother, was a practicing Buddhist. After their arrival in Melbourne, these three kept up their religious observances to varying degrees. Shuangshuang sporadically attended a local Catholic church as well as a Protestant Bible study group on campus; Liangliang maintained her dietary practice of avoiding pork, though she did not visit a mosque or follow a strictly halal diet except when with her parents; and Changying never visited a Buddhist temple in Australia (since her mother believed it preferable to pray to a specific Buddha who resided at home) but continued to worship back in China during holiday breaks.

Although most participants did not have much experience of organized religion when they arrived, a few said they had had brushes with Christian proselytizing on university campuses in China where Christian students openly evangelized (Fish 2015, 147–60). Fenfang, for example, revealed that at the university in Anhui where she had received her undergraduate degree, Christian students were very active, conducting "dorm sweeps" (扫楼 *sao lou*) at the start of each new semester to find Christian freshmen whom they could invite to join the campus fellowship. Chinese university authorities, however, were not necessarily happy about students' religious activities. Fenfang's roommate in Anhui had been a Christian and was constantly called to special meetings with her *fudaoyuan* (辅导员: party-affiliated guidance counselor): "The more radical *fudaoyuans* will try to get Christian students to deconvert," Fenfang told me. Indeed, within a system where a strictly controlled "red market" of state-sanctioned religious organizations is tolerated but Chinese Communist Party policy endorses and promotes atheism (F. Yang 2006), tension is everywhere evident between the party and religious groups. Participants whose parents were party members and who developed an interest in Christianity while studying abroad were particularly nervous about news of their religious affiliation becoming public back home and causing problems for their families. Predeparture advice from education agents sometimes included warnings against "heterodox cults" (邪教 *xie jiao*)—the party's term for unapproved spiritual movements—and some participants' parents expressly forbade them to take part in religious activities while overseas.

Student transmigrants thus left an environment in China in which organized religion formed a minor and strictly regulated part of everyday life, to find on arriving in Melbourne that they became the target of all manner of churches clamoring for their attention. Traversing the northern end of Melbourne's central business district (CBD) on foot, a neighborhood dominated by two university campuses and a high density of student housing (see chapter 2), participants regularly ran the gauntlet of Mandarin-trained missionaries from the Jehovah's Witnesses and the Mormons, both of which maintained regular beats at the north end of Swanston Street. This was news to me: despite living in Melbourne for most of my life, I had never once been approached by Christian missionaries in the CBD and had not even really been aware of their presence. Evidently, the missionaries were targeting the Chinese students based on an ethnically specific evangelical strategy. Several times when I met up with participants in this area, they arrived clutching bilingual tracts and asking me in bewilderment what type of cults the missionaries represented. Some found the young white American Mormon men particularly unnerving with their vigorous approach, uncanny Mandarin ability, and relentless wreathment in smiles.

University campuses, meanwhile, were the domain of Seventh-Day Adventists and Christian student fellowships. Soon after arriving in Melbourne, Yixin and her friends were approached outside the library at Capital University by Seventh-Day Adventist missionaries, who obtained their phone numbers and then called them daily asking them to attend church activities, which they ultimately did out of embarrassment at being invited so insistently. The event they attended was a tutorial on proper diet at the nearby Adventist Centre in Carlton, which included cooking demonstrations and a free meal. Yixin did not attend again, since she felt guilty about accepting the food with no intention of converting. Others were waylaid by members of campus Christian fellowships. Xiaoxing was attracted by one group's offer of a weekend trip to the seaside city of Geelong and a social get-together. But when the get-together turned out to be a Bible reading, Xiaoxing said:

> To be honest, because I don't believe [in Christianity], I couldn't really accept it. They were singing those hymns, reading bits from the Bible [*makes a gesture of solemn Bible reading with her hands*]. And then they'd pray [*bows head, closes eyes*]. I didn't really understand it, but you have to respect others, so you have to go along with it. I didn't want to go again.

Others had similar stories of attending events advertised as general social activities that turned out to be a cover for Christian proselytizing. Shunqing joined an activity run by another campus Christian fellowship group that targeted international students. She went along with a friend who said she went for the free food and advised Shunqing to say she was already a believer to avoid being hassled. Like Xiaoxing, though, Shunqing found the experience peculiar, especially what she perceived as the forced enthusiasm of the all-Chinese members in their singing, praying, and hand clapping: "Surely if you're going to be a Christian, then it would be to learn about and fit in with local culture. But the Christian group was all Chinese!" Many participants' chance encounters with evangelical church groups turned out similarly, ending in embarrassment, suspicion, or bemusement, with the students professing in-principle tolerance toward religious diversity but little interest in further participation.

Church as Service Hub

However, the church-as-migrant-service-provider model that has been observed in other contexts (Ley 2010) also pertains in Melbourne. Bible study groups run by various Protestant churches in and around the city offered evening English lessons, which several participants attended. In addition to the food, social activities, and English classes provided by churches, participants underlined that church activities were also one of the few places where conversation and friendship with locals were accessible to them. Yixin said of the Seventh-Day Adventists that while she had her suspicions about their teachings, the missionaries she met on campus were simply friendlier than other locals she had met: "They are the only ones who will talk with me like that and hang out." Xiaofen made similar remarks about the leaders of the Anglican-affiliated CrossCultures Bible study fellowship she briefly attended: "You know, we hope to get the chance to get to know people here. Well, unlike some people you meet, who can be a bit distant, you get the sense that [the Christians] are really interested in you, really willing to communicate with you and find out about you."

Meng, studying at Queens University in the inner-west suburb of Footscray, had been approached multiple times in the street there by evangelical Christians—including once by Koreans who addressed her in Korean—but, like most others, she had brushed them off. When she began experiencing academic difficulties and emotional stress, though, she turned to these churches for help:

M: I failed a subject in my first semester. Times were very hard for me . . . and at that time I did go along a bit [to church], though I stopped going later. But really they were all really good people. It's like a safe harbor that can protect you in times of trouble, or when you're emotionally [down]. But I just felt it wasn't a long-term thing. . . . I went once to the church in *Springvale*, the Korean one, and two or three times to one in *Footscray*. . . . I think society really needs something like this. . . . At times when people are very, very fragile, you need a place that lets you . . . vent a bit, or whatever. But it's not a long-term thing. . . .

F: So when you were attending these churches, did you feel as if you might begin to believe?

M: No, no, it was too hard. I tried to force myself, [but] it was too hard. . . . [I needed] to have someone with me, to listen to me, and to have some selfless [无私 *wusi*] friends, that's all. . . . It's a very important role in society. I think those people are pretty selfless. . . . Their beliefs, perhaps we have no way of understanding. But if it makes them that selfless, then I think religion is a good thing.

In each of these instances, churches were providing for participants' social needs: the need for friendship, companionship, and emotional support in difficult times. In Shuangshuang's words, taking part in Christian activities brought feelings of being "loved, warm, not alone." On one hand, churches partly filled the gap left by many Chinese students' "missing friendships" with indifferent local peers (McKenzie and Baldassar 2017): unlike most local classmates, church people would talk to you, hang out with you, invite you home, take an interest in you. On the other hand, churches provided a structurally similar but apparently sometimes more effective form of emotional support than university services were able to offer (Meng had also consulted a professional counselor at her university, on my suggestion, which she found somewhat helpful but not as effective as the church groups). In line with this service-provision role, some participants treated the churches in a more or less utilitarian and instrumental way, turning to them in times of need but drifting away once the need was fulfilled. As Meng said, "It's not a long-term thing."

The Need to Believe

In contrast, other participants' reflections on what attracted them or their friends to deeper religious engagements echo Yang's (1998) theory that religious faith may fill a perceived moral vacuum in contemporary Chinese society. Participants spoke about the "need to believe" in terms that framed religious belief as something that might help them navigate the intense pressures of contemporary social life in China, including the relentless neoliberal-style imperative to be self-reliant (靠自己 *kao ziji*; see this book's introduction). Yining, who (like several other participants) first took part in church activities in Melbourne out of a self-educational desire to learn more about the cultural foundations of Western societies, spoke at length about how she and her friends began to feel that religion might provide a moral compass in Chinese society. Old-style morals had lost their grip, she explained, as evidenced by the dominance of materialism and the deterioration of sexual values, for example, in the prevalence of young women seducing wealthy married men for their money and being popularly applauded for doing so. A Christian value system, she thought, would condemn such behavior. Yining related:

> More and more of my [Chinese] friends [in Melbourne], who weren't originally *Christian*, now they're all sort of thinking, I really do need some belief, because I just can't make it by relying on myself alone. (我觉得我现在真的需要一个信仰，因为我光靠我自己是没有办法 *wo juede wo xianzai zhende xuyao yige xinyang, yinwei wo guang kao wo ziji shi meiyou banfa.*)

Yining was only a casual churchgoer in Melbourne, but after returning to China and finding a job in Shanghai, far from her family, she experienced significant gendered work and emotional pressures (including overwork, sexual harassment at work, and relationship difficulties) and began regularly attending a weekend Bible study group. She felt that it provided a counterbalance to the society around her that cared only about money and lacked a deeper moral foundation. Her grandparents' generation might once have believed in the party and the revolution, she told me, "but that's so long ago now."

Relatedly, Yuli told me how she had joined a Christian church several years earlier, while studying in New Zealand. She felt the experience had helped shape her as a person at a formative stage, especially in conveying the ideal of selflessness and the concept that one should serve the good of the wider society without looking for anything in return. She told me forcefully, "There is <u>nothing</u> like this in China. Nothing that could help you think this way." Rather, she felt that the dominant mode of social interaction there was self-interested exchange. This recalls Meng's reflections on her church experiences in Melbourne, especially how impressed she was with the selflessness of the people she met there. Meng explicitly contrasted this with her impression of life in postsocialist China:

> In China there isn't this concept of comforting you, of helping vulnerable groups. There's no religion there, nothing like that. People will make demands of you—some people will even criticize you: you're not allowed to be weak, you have to be strong, that's what it's like in China. . . . There aren't these groups that are uncompensated and selfless.

As well as contrasting Western religious belief, morality, and compassion for the vulnerable with what they felt was a general lack of these things in postsocialist Chinese society, participants also contrasted Christianity with Chinese folk religion, associating the former with belief/faith (信仰 *xinyang*) and the latter with culture-specific customs (习惯 *xiguan*). Visiting the temple to pray to the Buddha for good luck, as many people did at home, was merely a type of Chinese custom, several participants told me, whereas Christianity was about "real belief." In the terms proposed by Richard P. Madsen (2008, 295, 297), a sociologist of Chinese religions, these young women were attracted to Christianity as a form of rational-ethical religiosity, which is distinguished from parochial, particularistic, habit-driven folk religion by its emphasis on abstract, universalist ethical principles rather than magical ritual; its embodiment in formal, bureaucratic organizations; and its resonances with rationalized, reflexive middle-class aspirations toward cultural and subjective modernization.

Further support for the idea that Christianity may appeal to middle-class urban youth born into postsocialist society who feel a socially and historically conditioned need to believe comes from instances when participants sampled Christian faith alongside a range of other, nonreligious belief systems. For example, Zhenghui at one time expressed interest in attending church activities, but when I asked several months later whether she had done so, she responded that she had found the inspiration she needed in self-improvement books instead. Her WeChat feed was full of the titles she was reading, especially popular American authors emphasizing corporate, neoliberal-style discourses of self-improvement, including Daniel Goleman's *Focus: The Hidden Driver of Excellence* (2014) and *Emotional Intelligence: Why It Can Matter More than IQ* (2005) and Charles Duhigg's *The Power of Habit: Why We Do What We Do in Life and Business* (2013). Comparably, during a conversation with Xiaofen about her experience of the CrossCultures fellowship, she explained,

> I feel that at some point in my life, religious belief may play a role—I may need it: especially when times are hard. But right now I'm just exploring, trying to understand more, so I can get a feel for what kind of spirituality might ultimately be right for me.

Without missing a beat, she went on tell me that she was also interested in the possibility of alien life beyond Earth and the existence of parallel universes: "I can't be sure these things <u>don't</u> exist. I'd like to keep an open mind toward them." In examples like these, exploration of Christianity became one strand in a broader, reflexive search for alternative frameworks for understanding the world (or cosmos) and one's relationship with it. Zhenghui and Xiaofen presented this search as a type of introspective self-cultivation in which personal growth was believed to follow from training oneself in a certain attitude of mind or seeking expert instruction in the entrepreneurial project of (re)making the self (C. Freeman 2014).

The preceding examples have focused on participants whose encounters with religious organizations were more or less brief, superficial, or exploratory. Others made far deeper religious engagements during their time abroad, though these stories, too, reflect some of the themes identified so far.

Transnational Tendrils of the Latter-day Saints

Wenling was a young seventeen-year-old with dental braces when she arrived in Melbourne from her hometown, a small city in Jiangsu. Although she seemed gregarious and always eager to catch up for a chat, I sensed in the way Wenling reached out to me that she was struggling emotionally, both from loneliness—her parents never visited her in Australia, as they were too busy working, and I noticed she did not readily form friendships with other participants in the study group—and from academic difficulties and fear of failing. She also had an unhappy time in her first homestay, where the landlady underfed her so severely that she lost five kilograms in a couple of months. We met up often and Wenling became more and more open and chatty, so I quickly learned a lot about her background. Both of her parents were party members and well-educated professionals; indeed, Wenling was born while her mother was studying toward her PhD. With her mother busy with her studies, as a baby Wenling was left in the care of her elderly grandmother but in practice spent most of her time with a deaf-mute auntie. As a result, she was slow to acquire language. At kindergarten and then school, she struggled academically and was diagnosed as developmentally delayed. Angry at their daughter's academic failures, Wenling's high-achieving parents beat her. They later enrolled her in a high school that taught the Australian curriculum, seeing study abroad as a way to minimize the risks attaching to her lackluster academic performance at home. During the time I knew her in Melbourne, Wenling suffered bouts of severe anxiety attended by insomnia, panic attacks, and, once, thoughts of self-harm.

After several months in Melbourne, I discovered via a Facebook post that Wenling had become a Mormon. She had joined following an encounter with the American missionaries at the north end of Swanston Street and was baptized soon afterward. Soon her whole social life revolved around church activities: temple on Saturday, Mandarin service and Sunday school the next day, missionary training, and lots of socializing with other Mormon youth, including several vacations in Brisbane, where some of them lived (see also chapter 2's discussion of Mormon sociality in the suburban neighborhood where Wenling lived in Melbourne). When I met up with her, Wenling was always bubbling over with the latest gossip from her young American and Chinese Mormon social circle, whose pictures and videos she would show me on her phone: who said what to whom and who misunderstood; who was going to get married; who was angry at whom; which boy had told her he liked her and whether or not she liked him; what the church elders thought about such-and-such a relationship; who had just been transferred back to the United States on completion of his mission. Wenling even visited Salt Lake City several times for vacations and hoped that she might undertake postgraduate studies there. Telling me often how keen she was to find a boyfriend, she envisaged marrying a Mormon man and settling down permanently in America or Australia. Only after changing her citizenship would she be able to reveal her new faith to her party-affiliated family, who might otherwise face trouble as a result, she told me, "because the government can't investigate you if you're not a citizen anymore."

The Church of Jesus Christ of Latter-day Saints (LDS)—colloquially known as the Mormon church—is a modern restorationist Christian movement originating in the United States, where it was founded by Joseph Smith in the early nineteenth century. Following World War II, the church expanded internationally through vigorous missionary activity, including in Australia, where Mormons had first arrived over a century earlier, so that by the late 1990s international members outnumbered those in North America (Phillips 2006, 52; LDS Newsroom, n.d.). The church is highly centralized but growth oriented and globally outward looking. Anthropologist David Clark Knowlton compares its bureaucratic structure with "the modern multinational corporation, where upper management has substantial independent power beyond that of lower levels of the organization" (2007, 402). He also highlights "how strongly the identity of Latter-day Saints now seems translocal and indeed supranational . . . connected with an international, multiethnic, and multiracial people who are the children of God" (404). Underlining that the LDS Church today tends more and more to base its claims to legitimacy and efficacy on its transnational growth, Rick Phillips questions the church's own international membership statistics and draws back from characterizing it as a world religion, preferring to see it, slightly at variance with Knowlton, as "a North American church with tendrils in other continents" (2006, 52). Both authors, though, agree on the church's increasingly transnational focus and ambitions.

The LDS Church has been keen to make inroads into China for many decades. Under Maoism, the church's missionary work was confined to Chinese communities in Hong Kong, Taiwan, Singapore, and Western nations, but since 1976 it has been working hard on establishing formal diplomatic relations (Heaton 1980). It sent an emissary to China for Mao Zedong's funeral in 1976, and performance groups from Brigham Young University throughout the 1980s (Heinerman and Shupe 1985, 219–22). Although, in line with its strategy of working strictly aboveground, the LDS Church respects the governmental ban on proselytizing in China (LDS, n.d.), it trains missionaries in Mandarin and—as is evident from its activities in Melbourne—tasks them with targeting Chinese citizens abroad. As Pierre Vendassi (2014) shows in his detailed study of the LDS Church's China strategy, people converted in Western nations, including Australia, make up a significant proportion of Mormon congregations in China. The seeding of such congregations within China may gradually lead to the spread of the faith despite the state prohibition on proselytization, since converts are legally authorized to share their faith with family members, and their acquaintances may voluntarily visit their meetinghouses to learn more about the LDS. Thus, especially in light of the prohibition on religious contact between foreign and Chinese Mormons within China, returnee converts may appear to the LDS Church as an efficient means of spreading the faith while remaining on the right side of the authorities (Vendassi 2014, 48).

A few months after Wenling is baptized into the Mormon faith, she invites me to attend a Mandarin Mother's Day service at the LDS meetinghouse in Melbourne's CBD. It's a cloudy, drizzling Sunday morning, and as I wait for Wenling outside the Yangtze Couriers shop, the city sidewalks are quiet save for a handful of partygoers reeling home from the night before. In my carefully chosen pleated skirt, stockings, and woolen coat, I feel very respectable. Wenling arrives and leads me up Lonsdale Street to a modern office block where the LDS Church occupies the full second floor, sharing the building with international education provider Navitas. Exiting the elevator, we walk along a short corridor. A map of mainland China hangs on the wall, with colored drawing pins marking various locations, mainly along the east coast. Wenling leads me into an office where young men and women are practicing a contrapuntal hymn about Jesus and little children, reading from sheets of musical notation with the words printed beneath in Chinese characters and pinyin romanization. The singers are a mix of Chinese and Anglo-American young people. The American men wear the trademark dark suits and neat crewcuts, while the women are in pale-colored dresses and skirts and wear their long, mousy hair in braids. Bilingual name tags identify everyone by honorific (Brother, Sister, or Elder) and surname. Wenling strides in beaming, calls out cheery hellos to several of the young American men, and introduces me. Milling about before the service, I am also introduced to several male elders from America and Hong Kong, who grip my hand in a firm shake and fix me with an intense smiling gaze as they establish who I am and why I'm there. Aside from a handful of participants who might be Australian-Chinese, I seem to be the only local-born attendee: everyone else I meet is from the United States, Hong Kong, or mainland China. As we chat in Mandarin, muting my local accent, people assume I'm American or guess another country: France? Germany? The choir keeps practicing; some young men wheel a video screen past in the corridor. Wenling is focused on the social scene, joking with her friends. There's a gentle hustle-and-bustle buzz in the air.

The service, attended by about forty people, is held in a wide space like a seminar room with fluorescent lighting, a low ceiling, gray carpet, blue plastic chairs, and a pinewood pulpit. About half the chairs are empty. Wenling and I sit with a group of young people toward the front, with the older congregants to our right. A table to one side holds trays of holy sacrament (torn-up white bread), little plastic beakers, and a squat Perspex jug of holy water, which is offered during the service. Four elders sit in their dark suits at the front facing us and take various roles in the service. A piano played by a smiley young Chinese woman accompanies the hymns, which are sung in a mixture of English and Mandarin and seem somehow similar to and yet oddly different from those that sank into my bones at the Church of England girls' school I attended as a child.

The service is in Mandarin with occasional translations from some speakers' Cantonese. It is presided over by a thickset middle-aged elder from Hong Kong. His short salt-and-pepper hair grows thick and low over his brow, and his gaze seems direct and sincere. His look reminds me of a good Canadian-Taiwanese friend of mine, and I warm to his southern-accented Mandarin and his air of authority and humility.

The temper of the service is serious yet relaxed, punctuated by occasional giggles and mild humor but pervaded by gravity. Wenling is called to the pulpit to offer a prayer, then a ritual is held for a young Chinese man in a striped polo shirt who was baptized the day before. The elders lay their hands on him while prayers are said, and we are invited to raise our right hands in affirmation (I decline: I am an outsider). A young mainland Chinese woman speaks about what brought her to the church. She had come to Melbourne from Brisbane for study and felt friendless and lost in the new city, utterly alone and at an all-time emotional low. Mormon missionaries approached her three times in the street, and she wondered why they always smiled and seemed so happy and "hai" (嗨: her colloquial term for "high" is met with giggles from the young Chinese congregants and consternation from the American missionary sitting next to us, who shifts in his seat, looking around sharply for an explanation). But now she knows! With a future beyond death bathed in eternal glory, why would you let the trifling hardships of this life get you down?

Other parts of the service take up the Mother's Day theme. Mothers in the congregation are asked to stand to receive a gift of rose and carnation corsages. I am awkward being called on to embody the role of virtuous mother, but when I receive my flowers, the grace with which they're given suffuses me with warmth. Next, all the other young women present are invited to stand to receive flowers as well—in their capacity as future mothers. An elder speaks about the need for women to look inward to the mirror of our immortal souls just as often as we look in the physical mirror to admire our outward beauty (I rankle, resenting this on a number of levels). The importance of parents is stressed repeatedly. "Do you think Jesus found his parents annoying or was too busy to speak with them? No, of course not. Jesus had good filial piety."

The elder with the thick-growing hair gives a sermon in which, with understated tenderness, he tells his mother's and two grandmothers' stories from around the time of World War II in Hong Kong and Indonesia. One grandmother died young for lack of medicine, the other suffered with leprosy for years, and his own mother worked herself ragged at two jobs as a hospital cleaner in Hong Kong. Beside me, Wenling fiddles distractedly with her long pink-painted fingernails, but I listen intently, unexpectedly moved.

After the final hymn—"God Be with You Til We Meet Again"—Wenling and the others I've met say goodbye and see me to the elevator, readying themselves for an afternoon of scriptural study. A tall Chinese girl comes down in the elevator with me. She's been studying in Melbourne for two years, and this has been her first time attending church. She asks if I have children and gives me a hug there on the rainy pavement when I say yes. She's off to call her mum like the elder said she should.

Walking through the city streets to the tram stop, the final hymn plays on in my head. God be with you til we meet again. I feel the presence of a huge, quiet, black-feathered bird—a crow, perhaps—with its wings spread over all of us, enfolding, protecting; its expression stern but steady. We will be safe beneath dark wings. All-powerful. Inviolable.

The Pentecostal Spirit of Mobility

Whereas the LDS Church is structured on a treelike model as a centralized bureaucratic structure with transnational shoots or tendrils (Phillips 2006), the global Pentecostal movement is a wilder, more rhizomatic growth. While its most common origin story traces back to the United States and the Azusa Street Revival led by African American preacher William J. Seymour in Los Angeles in 1906, some argue against framing North America as the definitive origin of the movement, since it also has deep historical roots in a wide range of other locations worldwide (A. Anderson and Tang 2005; E. Miller 2015, 183–85). These include China, where Pentecostal Christianity has survived since the early twentieth century, even through the antireligious Mao years, in noninstitutionalized forms among rural populations, where its practices of miraculous healing, exorcism, and spirit possession resonate with local folk rituals of *ling* (灵: the holy; Madsen 2013). Pentecostalism has revived strongly since economic reform so that today it constitutes the dominant form of Christianity among non-state-endorsed church groups (Oblau 2005; N. Cao 2013).[3]

Pentecostal Christianity is not a formal denomination but a series of interlinked renewal movements within evangelical Protestantism that share a repertoire of key characteristics. These include faith in biblical authority, emphasis on a personal and transformative relationship with Jesus Christ, ritual performance highlighting the presence and power of the Holy Spirit, and prominence accorded to charismata, or "gifts of the Holy Spirit" (divine healing, prophecy, exorcism, speaking in tongues, etc.) (Hefner 2013). The emphasis on a personal relationship with God and the lack of any strong institutional center or formal accreditation for pastors mean that, unlike LDS branches, new Pentecostal churches may be planted relatively easily, if the necessary resources and a leader divinely inspired to adapt the repertoire to the local context are available (Robbins 2004; Knowlton 2007; Meyer 2010). These features lead David Martin, a prominent sociologist of global Pentecostalism, to describe it as a "multi-centred" movement marked by "fissiparous pluralism" (2002, 168–69): "Pentecostalism is a prolific set of burgeoning affinities constituted by recognition of kind. It follows that there is scant chance of some hierarchy of religious . . . power canalizing the flow of energy and controlling it for its own ends. . . . The movement itself simply runs riot in any number of alternative channels" (170).

The fastest-growing religious movement in the world today, Pentecostalism is frequently described as a paradigmatic example of religious globalization (D. Martin 2002; Robbins 2004, 2009; Meyer 2010; Hefner 2013), or, in Elizabeth Miller's apt phrase, as "a new form of de-territorialized Christianity" (2015, 176). Numbers are burgeoning not only among the poor, marginal, and dispossessed in the Global South but also increasingly among middle-class congregants in suburban megachurches worldwide, including in Australia (D. Martin 2002; J. Connell 2005; Hey 2013; Miller 2015). Pentecostalism is marked by its contextual flexibility: global cross-linkages—emphasizing brotherhood in the Holy Spirit over national identities—work alongside strong and effective localization (Robbins 2004). This form of Christianity appeals particularly to displaced populations: Martin describes Pentecostal churches as "way stations punctuating the routes of contemporary migration" (2013, 48). The movement itself is centrally defined by mobility (Hefner 2013, 27; Miller 2015, 194): "a church of flows rather than place" (J. Connell 2005, 330) that is "align[ed] . . . with the culture of global capitalism" (Maddox 2012, 153) and connected by transnational networks circulating media, pastors, believers, and money (Meyer 2010, 120).

In addition to Pentecostalism's "glocalism" and association with mobilities, three other characteristics of the movement are worth highlighting as well, as context for exploring a Pentecostal megachurch's engagement with Chinese student transmigrants in Melbourne. First, since the revivals of the early twentieth century, Pentecostal churches have often (though unevenly) been characterized by multiracialism and a deemphasis on ethnicized identities (Robbins 2004, 125; Miller 2015, 183, 194). Second, Pentecostalism tends to take characteristic forms in relation to gender, with more female than male believers and charismatic practitioners in many places but with pastoral leadership roles reserved for men, based on the gender hierarchy of masculine headship and feminine submission that is central to most Pentecostal belief systems (N. Cao 2013; Maddox 2013; B. Martin 2013; Miller 2015, 129–72). Third, the practice of

Pentecostal worship centers affective, sensory, embodied experience: services are marked by loud music, bright lights, collective movements, repeated rhythmic cadences, shouting, crying, dancing, jumping, hugging. In Birgit Meyer's terms, Pentecostal worship takes "sensational form" insofar as it "appeal[s] to the senses and the body in distinct ways and by forming specific religious subjects" (2010, 122). Similarly, analyzing the operations of the Hillsong Pentecostal megachurch in suburban Sydney, Matthew Wade and Maria Hynes argue that churchgoers may be seen as "affective laborers enrolled into the production of subjectivity" (2013, 176), generating through their affective work in worship a sense of at-home-ness, collective enthusiasm, and loyalty in excess of reason.

Although today Pentecostalism is on the rise in Australia as elsewhere around the world, the history of its growth is shorter than in the United States and the United Kingdom, with congregations beginning to increase significantly only in the 1980s (Hey 2013, 10; Miller 2015, 17–21). Planetshakers is a classical growth-oriented Pentecostal megachurch that was founded in Melbourne in 2004 by Russell Evans, one of the sons of pastor Andrew Evans, who founded Paradise Church in Adelaide in 1970 and later became a cofounder of the Christian conservative political party Family First (Maddox 2012; Hey 2013, 12). Along with Paradise (now Influencers Church) and Hillsong (Australia's biggest Pentecostal megachurch), Planetshakers numbers among the members of Australian Christian Churches, formerly Australian Assemblies of God, the nation's largest Pentecostal denomination. Planetshakers began as a youth conference at Paradise in 1996, before God spoke to Russell Evans in 2002 and told him to plant a new church in Melbourne (R. Evans 2004, 5, 40)—a divine command that coincided with Andrew Evans passing on the leadership of Paradise Church to Russell's brother Ashley (Shand 2013).

Today the Planetshakers megachurch is headed by senior pastors Russell Evans and Sam Evans, his wife, and has four campuses in central and suburban Melbourne and one in the nearby city of Geelong, as well as in Cape Town, Austin, Singapore, and Geneva (Planetshakers, n.d.). At the time of writing, the church claimed a weekly attendance of seventeen thousand. Planetshakers, like Hillsong, is also a Christian rock band. It formerly featured the winner of the first season of the music talent TV show *Australian Idol*, Guy Sebastian, and has released around forty albums and EPs to date. The organization runs a school of creative arts to "develop your skills for involvement in your worship team" (Planetshakers SOCA, n.d.) and offers a series of religious training courses, admitting domestic and international students, run through Alphacrucis College (Miller 2015, 30). It also hosts conferences each year in different cities in Australia and abroad (in 2019 conferences were held in Malaysia, the

Philippines, Melbourne, and Brisbane). These are multiday arena spectaculars of preaching and music, sometimes with translation into a number of languages, including Korean, Mandarin, Spanish, and Tamil (for the 2019 Melbourne conferences), and a simultaneous Planetkids program for child members (Planetshakers, n.d.).

The Evans family's Pentecostal empire has been subject to media scrutiny over its financial operations. In 2013 the family was estimated to turn over $12 million annually, largely tax-free, with weekly income from Sunday collections of around $200,000, while Russell and Sam Evans—dubbed *pastorpreneurs*—each took home annual salaries equivalent to $500,000 including fringe benefits (Shand 2013). Politicians and media have also raised questions about Pentecostal megachurches receiving large government grants to fund social service and aid programs (A. Ferguson 2005). In 2015 Planetshakers signed a $1 million-per-annum lease on a large office and warehouse property in the Southbank district of central Melbourne to serve as the organization's head office. The building incorporates a two-thousand-seat auditorium, recording studio, school, play center, and café (Schlesinger 2015).

I first heard of the Planetshakers through Singaporean and Malaysian Christian students I was teaching in Melbourne around 2005. Ten years later, I notice Chinese students' photos and videos of Planetshakers services appearing in my WeChat feed. Deciding to go along and experience a service for myself, I contact a WeChat acquaintance, Ling, who is a regular attendee. She agrees to meet me at the Southbank center for the six o'clock service one summer evening.

When I arrive at the four-story office block twenty minutes early, hundreds of cheery young people are streaming out into the street after the previous service, the third of four that run every Sunday. As I enter, I am greeted brightly by a phalanx of black-T-shirted twenty-somethings before stationing myself next to a bronze planet sculpture to wait for Ling. The foyer is booming with excited talk and laughter and exploding with youthful energy. It's quite a rush. The crowd is very multiracial, and the interethnic mingling contrasts sharply with the usual scenes on campus and in the streets. An African woman in a bright printed headwrap chats with a Malaysian student; a skinny Anglo guy walks with his arm around a young Chinese man, both of them grinning deliriously; a Polynesian girl and a white hippie stand deep in conversation. A young woman who might be Chinese American approaches me, beaming, with a clipboard and asks have I signed up for the Awakening conference yet, is it my first time, do I know anyone. I tell her I'm waiting for my friend. A stall in the lobby displays racks of Planetshakers merchandise:

CDs, T-shirts, books, videos, backpacks. Ling WeChats me that she's running late and I should go in first.

Inside the black-walled auditorium, I take a place near the back so Ling can find me more easily. The air throbs with anthemic Christian rock from the Planetshakers band, amplified so that the bass rattles your rib cage, while green, ultraviolet, orange, and yellow lights twirl around the room and illuminate the crowd, flashing off the diamond-shaped mirrors at the back of the stage. In the middle of the room is a dais where two techies film the proceedings for an on-line feed, while a crane-mounted camera swoops above the gathering crowd. LCD screens hung from the ceiling show the stage in close-up and scroll song lyrics, KTV style. Everyone is standing, and the crowd up in front is dancing and jumping up and down, hands in the air. Back where I am, people are sparser and less active. Around 40 to 50 percent of the crowd looks East Asian. Onstage, though, almost everyone is Anglo.

Sonically assaulted by the soulless light rock, I'm having trouble taking this seriously. I suppress a giggle at the lyrics on the screens—earnestly horny lines like "I want only Him"; "When I look in His eyes, I see that He wants me"; "I'm moving closer, ever closer"; "There is awe and glory in His embrace." There is certainly no way I'm going to dance to this—although one blonde singer in sprayed-on pants and stiletto sandals (who turns out to be Pastor Sam) does have a great voice: strong, high, and edgy, with professional technique.

Over the next hour and a half, an array of different pastors speak, interspersed with numbers from the band. After Pastor Sam, another pastor—a chunky guy in black jeans and T-shirt who I think at first has damaged eyes, before realizing he just had them ecstatically closed for the first five minutes of his talk—leads a donations drive. Envelopes, forms, and big black buckets are passed along each row as the pastor speaks passionately about the glory of giving and the importance of doing it consistently every week. "There are so many ways to give. Credit card, online—or cash!" He also praises the healing power of God: as a child, Jesus healed his in-turned leg just before the doctors were about to put it in irons. Clapping, shouting, hand raising.

Although some are at least in their forties, all the male pastors wear grungy outfits that accord with a localized Anglo model of youth (non)fashion: checked flannel shirts, ripped jeans, sneakers. Many of the women, though, wear high heels and hyperfeminine tight pants or skirts. All of the speaking parts are performed by Anglos with broad Australian accents and speech peppered with local vernacular.

I check my phone and find a series of WeChats: Ling can't come (she's had a fight with her boyfriend) and is trying to put me in touch with her friends. I duck out of the auditorium, dodging swaying bodies, waving arms, and T-shirted *staff on the doors and manage to find Clara, a young Chinese woman who smiles warmly, grabs my hand, and leads me down to the front where she has a seat. I take a standing place in the aisle among the packed swaying bodies. The energy level is much higher here, and the bass pounds even heavier in your chest. Everyone seems to have their arms raised, possessed by the Holy Spirit. But I can't join in: it feels too much like surrender. Clara dashes off somewhere. Another Chinese student greets me and introduces herself as Sandy, and I sit next to her.*

Now a shaved-headed pastor preaches to us in American evangelical style: call-and-response, with participation elicited performatively at particular moments by a rising tone, repeated phrases, and key words (God, Jesus, glory, revelation, salvation). The video monitors introduce him as Pastor Russell. He picks up fragments of biblical stories, riffs on them, translates them into everyday language, scatters jokes through the material, and brings it all back to the glory of Jesus and how you can come to know him directly. The content and meaning of this relationship, though, are hazy. I'm left with the general impression of a blinding golden light signifying goodness, glory, ecstasy, and unburdening. "Jesus is in the room with us here tonight! In case you're wondering what that funny feeling is: Is it nervousness? Is it the music? No—it's JESUS!"

In between testifying to the divine agency at work among us, Pastor Russell makes repeated references to international students. He mentions the morning prayer services leading up to the annual conference: "I know some of our students from East Asia like to stay up laaate and sleep in laaaate—right? Well, maybe set an alarm clock? Right?" He also offers a homily for a young Chinese man he singles out of the crowd, on how he sees him struggling with a load of heavy books. "Well, Jesus is going to CARRY those heavy books for you! If you say to him, Jesus, I need to do this task, then he will HAND you the book you need!" The pastor also refers to people feeling great pressure to succeed—he's "getting this from the room"—"perfectionism, magnifying your own shortcomings, feeling not good enough." Everyone's heads are bowed as Russell says this, and he asks people to raise their hands without opening their eyes if it applies to them. "Jesus gives us permission not to be perfect: doing our best is good enough. There's only one perfect being, and that's God!" At this, Sandy, standing beside me with hands raised, breaks down and sobs silently, bending forward over the seats in front of us as if in sudden pain.

Now a younger pastor speaks. "In many ways the main point of the service," he says, "is at the end: the salvation." He urges us not to leave but to stand with every head bowed and every eye closed to see if Jesus is calling to us to come forward. The pastor takes at least five full minutes to get people to raise their hands and be led forward. He asks again and again. Of the forty-odd people who volunteer, a vast majority look to be East Asian students, with just four or five Anglos dotted among them. Two young Chinese men seated next to us walk to the front; before they do, I hear one explaining something to the other in Mandarin in a low undertone. The second man leads the first; I notice several pairs like this. The pastors encourage the congregation to keep singing along with the band. Somehow, I am joining in. I am swaying gently, one arm partway raised, and singing along to the lyrics on the screens as the party of the saved is led off in triumph. I am moving closer, ever closer, we sing. The service is over.

On the way out, I chat with Sandy and her friend Ming, both students from China and both saved by Jesus through the Planetshakers since their arrival in Melbourne. Their eyes are shining, and their faces lit by smiles. Our conversation in the velvety night, later continued via WeChat as we make our separate ways home, seems suffused by a kind of radiance. It must be fate, it must be God's will that we've met, they enthuse! Ming writes that meeting me makes Melbourne feel warmer for her. She agrees to an interview one day soon: she's keen to tell me the story of how she came to the church. In her messages Ming shortens my Chinese name to its final character, "Lan." I'm touched by the intimacy of her gesture.

When I met up with Ming a month later, she shared with me the horrific personal story that had led to her involvement with the Planetshakers. After arriving in Melbourne for a postgraduate degree, Ming met her first "real" boyfriend: a Thai classmate in her English language prep class. They soon decided to move in together. Ming's parents were upset about this, worrying about her reputation, but she followed her own wishes and moved into a city apartment with her boyfriend, where they lived together for nearly three years. Because her boyfriend planned to immigrate after his graduation, Ming abandoned her original plan to move to Canada to join her cousin and switched her major to one that would facilitate her transfer to an Australian skilled-migrant visa, adding several years to her study. The year before our conversation, Ming accidentally became pregnant. She wanted to keep the baby, as she was twenty-seven by then and felt her pregnancy was timely. But her boyfriend argued that he wasn't yet in a financial position to raise a child, so she agreed to a termination. The boyfriend traveled back to China with Ming, met her parents and extended family, explained the situation and his reluctance to keep the child, and formally vowed in front of all the elders that he would marry Ming the following year. Soon after Ming had her abortion in China, she and her boyfriend traveled back to Melbourne. She quickly began to suspect he was having an affair with a Thai girl who kept calling him, and she warned him she was going to Google-translate their messages on his iPad. When she did, she found out that the girl was visiting Melbourne and that her boyfriend had even booked a hotel for them both. He readily confessed to the affair, admitted it wasn't the first, and broke up with Ming. After her abortion less than a week earlier and her boyfriend's recent solemn promises to her parents and grandparents, this was too much for Ming. She attempted suicide three times, finally by hanging herself from a tree in a remote area at dawn. Miraculously, on this most serious attempt, Ming was rescued by passersby. She regained consciousness in hospital. Her ex-boyfriend never visited her, and when she was well, he asked her to move out of their apartment. "He said I had mental problems . . . but considered not at all that what he'd done had hurt me."

The nurse who looked after her in hospital was pivotal in Ming's turn to the church:

> That nurse—I tell you—I think she should be counted as someone—pretty important in my life. Because she kept encouraging me, to an extent you wouldn't usually expect. She was just a nurse. She needn't have spoken with me, she only had to keep a record of my condition, say I wasn't crazy, that I wouldn't try to kill myself again, or whatever. But she did speak with me, and later she came to our place to see me a few times . . . and met me for dinner out. . . . And she told me she hoped I'd . . . get well soon. She also advised me to go to a church, said it would give me an outlet. So then I remembered that friend of mine [who had mentioned Planetshakers].

For Ming, the church fulfilled its function of offering psychological comfort (心理安慰 xinli anwei); emphasizing the affective warmth (温暖 wennuan) of the services, she said, "Maybe they don't know anything about me, and I don't know anything about them. But as soon as I go in there and feel the warmth of that atmosphere, I feel very moved." This contrasted with the way she experienced the psychiatrists and social workers she had been assigned at the hospital:

> They were worried I still might do something stupid. . . . They can help you in very practical ways, like tell you if you should attend some sort of *group* or whatever. . . . But when you're truly emotionally wounded, they—they just keep asking you, "How do you feel you're going now? Are you all right? Can you *carry* your problems?"

When she spoke with me, Ming was upbeat and pointed out that being able to tell her story so frankly—even laugh about parts of it—contrasted hugely with her condition just a few months earlier. But for me this interview remains troubling. Again and again, I expressed my shock and deep sympathy while Ming shared her story—but somehow, afterward, I can't help feeling I let her down. Isn't there something more I could have offered her? Did I respond adequately to her pain? Aren't I just like the state-assigned social workers, gathering the data I need from her, then coldly moving on?

Later, I send Ming a long WeChat message expressing these misgivings, but I don't hear from her again.

Sacralized Social Service, Gender, and Translocal Worlds

Among the student transmigrants I met during the course of this project, Wenling and Ming had the deepest church involvement. Both found themselves, through life circumstances, in extremely vulnerable situations with significant and pressing psychological, social, and personal needs that churches seemed to promise to fulfill. Beyond the acute crisis support that Ming sought at Planetshakers, churches also provided these young women with more general social care, especially that sense of home-amid-movement that has been noted as characteristic of Pentecostal churches worldwide (Wade and Hynes 2013; Miller 2015, 173–209). And the real and symbolic human relationships that student-transmigrant churchgoers are able to experience through their involvement—for example, with American missionaries in the LDS Church and with self-consciously "Aussie" preachers and a whole welcoming transethnic mix in the Planetshakers congregations—seem to respond clearly to these students' missing cross-ethnic friendships in other contexts (McKenzie and Baldassar 2017). The ways in which the Planetshakers invite cross-ethnic mixing and symbolic solidarity contrast markedly with participants' mediatized imagination of and (non)engagement with other minority groups as described in chapter 3 (see also Fincher 2011).

But churches' provision of social services to international students raises some questions when considered in relation to "education export" in Australia as the commercial outgrowth of a public education system in a secular state (Hey 2013, 282). This situation resonates with Marion Maddox's (2015, 2016) observations on the sacralization of Australia's public services more broadly. Maddox (2014; 2015, 190) notes that the neoliberal privatization of formerly government services has led to the transfer of welfare services to church-based organizations to the extent that around half of such services are now provided by religious agencies, while there is a concurrent trend toward private schooling at primary and secondary levels, and private schools are subsidized by the government and over 90 percent Christian. Thus, the Australian government outsources "significant chunks of welfare, aged care, health, mental health and education activities to church institutions" (2015, 191). Maddox speculates that this may reflect intentional desecularization by current and recent governments (2015, 191–92) or may simply be motivated by cost cutting, reflecting "a new phase in the neoliberal state's instrumentalization of religion" (2016). Churches' provision of social welfare services to international students—or, putting it more strongly, neoliberal governments' and universities' de facto outsourcing of a significant proportion of these services to churches—could certainly be seen as part of this picture (R. Connell 2014). Based on my fieldwork, churches' service provision to student transmigrants does seem effective to a degree (sometimes more so than the parallel secular agencies), and doubtless for every missionary-expansionist Mormon and Pentecostal pastorpreneur, there are dozens of ordinary priests, ministers, monks, and imams simply serving international students in a nontargeted way as part of their regular duties to the faithful. Nonetheless, in a situation where secular public universities derive such significant economic benefit from international students' fees and are legally responsible for their pastoral care (Ramia, Marginson, and Sawir 2013, 81–84), the outsourcing of support services for these students to religious agencies may be ethically questionable. Effectively, the nation is exporting not only Australian education but also an increasing national tendency to contract out students' pastoral care to church institutions (Maddox 2014). Rather than querying the quality of churches' service provision, it is more pertinent to ask why these student transmigrants are left so urgently in need of settlement, socialization, and mental health services in the first place and whether Australian universities and governments are adequately fulfilling their legal and ethical duty of care in these respects.[4]

The preceding stories also raise a number of gender-related questions. When they first engaged with the churches, Wenling and Ming were both negotiating pressing gendered issues in their own lives, working out their personal orientations toward intimate relationships, sexuality, marriage, and, in Ming's case, pregnancy. Indeed, given their stage of life, many student transmigrants may be motivated to seek churches' support precisely as a result of their struggles with such issues. The fieldwork stories reveal strongly gendered elements in these churches' teachings as well. The LDS Church models and promotes deeply conservative positions on gender identity, (hetero)sexuality, and marriage. It interpellates all young women as "future mothers" and exalts feminine "modesty," sexual abstinence, and early marriage. Pentecostal megachurches like Planetshakers—with their self-conscious embrace of contemporary youth styles in dress, music, and speech—may superficially appear less conservative. But, in fact, both through their direct teachings and through modeling by church authority figures, they actively promote heteronormativity, sexual abstinence outside marriage (symbolically compensated by the sexualization of the believer's relationship with God), and a flagrantly sexist doctrine of submissive wives supporting men's family and church headship (Sparrow 2012; Maddox 2013, 17). If the secular state can be seen as effectively outsourcing international students' welfare services to religious organizations, then it is disquieting that those with the most reactionary teachings on gender and sexuality—antifeminist, gender essentialist, and often homophobic—seem to be the most aggressive and successful in reaching these students.

Consideration of the operations of these "religious multinationals" (Knowlton 2007, 396) also reveals geographic complexities that speak to this book's broader interest in how various forms of mobility shape contemporary social life. Geographic factors in churches' operations are evident across a range of scales. At the local level, it is through geographically directed proselytizing on university campuses and in Melbourne's CBD—where the highest concentrations of international students are found—that some churches signal their intent to target these populations. For example, Wenling told me that the Mormons' Mandarin mission intentionally focused on the northern part of the CBD in order to engage Chinese students, whereas anglophone missionary work was directed several blocks further south. And given that the heartland for Pentecostal megachurches in Australia has traditionally been in the outer suburbs (J. Connell 2005), it seems significant that the Planetshakers chose a central city location for their headquarters when they took out the lease on the Southbank property in 2015. The operations of both the LDS Church and the Pentecostals are today deeply transnational, whether on a centralized or a rhizomatic model of cross-border expansion. We thus witness *deterritorialized* churches providing *local* socialization services to *transmigrant* students, as transnational Christianity positions itself to act as a salve to these mobile students' local-level social exclusion.

While both the LDS Church and the Planetshakers are keen to draw in Chinese students to swell their congregations, the two churches' ambitions are differentiated geographically. Although the Planetshakers are expanding transnationally into the United States, Singapore, Europe, and Africa, there seem to be no indications that they hope to move into China, where it would in any case be difficult for them to operate given the vexed relationship between Pentecostalism and the state. In Melbourne the Planetshakers seem most focused on growing congregations (and donations) at the local level, and they welcome Chinese students in their capacity as a significant and available sector of the local "market" (Maddox 2012; Hey 2013, 279–81). The American LDS Church, in contrast, seems to be pursuing a strategy that positions Chinese students in Australia as a springboard to expansion within China, where direct missionary proselytization is prohibited (F. Yang 2006). Student transmigrants thus become part of the church institution's own transnational expansion strategy.

The geographic complexity of these scenarios strongly challenges any conceptual opposition of local to global or of immobility to mobility, showing instead how the most apparently local of experiences—for example, being approached by missionaries at the north end of Swanston Street—may be shaped by the transnational engagements and ambitions of a range of actors. Once again, then, the geographic and subjective worlds inhabited and produced by these student transmigrants are revealed as *translocal worlds* at the most fundamental level.

~

But are such rational, analytic responses fully adequate to the question of what encounters with the holy do for people? Or—even for the committedly atheist researcher—does the affective element always escape? A rhythm, a cadence. The déjà vu of a hairline or accent. Some inchoate dream of protective black feathers, radiant warmth.

More than a year after Wenling took me to the Mormon meetinghouse, I ask her to an album launch for the old-style country band I play in with my partner. The launch is held at an old, inner-suburban pub. Wenling is keen to come along for the cultural experience but nervous because her faith prohibits her from drinking alcohol. I reassure her that she can order a soft drink, and she shows up on Saturday night excited and bright-eyed amid the beery crowd. I'm keyed up, too: tonight is the culmination of months of work. My hands want to shake; my throat feels tense.

At the start of our set, we try a new song: a four-part-harmony treatment of the nineteenth-century popular hymn "Uncloudy Day," accompanied by a single steel-string guitar. The crowd quiets down, and the simple gospel magic of the one-four-one progression in the first line makes my heart rise up in my chest like always.

*Oh they tell me of a home far beyond the skies
And they tell me of a home far away.
Oh they tell me of a home where no storm clouds rise.
Ohh, they tell me of an uncloudy day.*

It's hot under the stage lights and the foldback returns our blending voices as a wall of sound. For an instant, as we end our final chorus, the air in the bar seems to shimmer and vibrate. What is that? Probably something to do with the harmonies—or is it my nerves? (Maybe it's the shot of Jack Daniels I took to calm them.)
Inspired, I dedicate the song to Wenling.

7. PATRIOTISM
Feeling Global Chineseness

*

Five years ago, as I stepped off the plane from China . . . I was ready to put on one of my five face masks, but when I took my first breath of American air, I put my mask away. The air was so sweet and fresh, and oddly luxurious. . . .

I grew up in a city in China where I had to wear a face mask every time I went outside, otherwise, I might get sick. However, the moment I inhaled and exhaled outside the airport, I felt free. . . .

At the University of Maryland, I would soon feel another kind of fresh air for which I will be forever grateful: the fresh air of free speech. . . .

I have learned the right to freely express oneself is sacred in America. . . .

Democracy and freedom are the fresh air that is worth fighting for. Freedom is oxygen. Freedom is passion. Freedom is love. . . .

My friends, enjoy the fresh air and never let it go. (Graduating student Shuping Yang, University of Maryland commencement speech, May 21, 2017; author's transcription based on H. Liu 2017)

I just want to fly over to America and give her a punch ☺ (Changying, WeChat post, May 22, 2017)

QIN: I think her argument on democracy and freedom was good, but she used the wrong example. That bit about five layers of face masks or whatever in Kunming [Yang's hometown] went too far. . . . In the context of a commencement speech, with students from all nations attending, I find such blind denigration of China unacceptable. . . . On these types of questions, it's OK for you to state your own views [privately]. In private everyone complains about their own country or family and the problems that exist in it, since after all nothing's perfect.

JIAYING: Her family has been doxed. Too scary [forwards screen cap of Weibo messages detailing Yang's family's home address and her father's employment details].

MEI: Even though it doesn't go as far as insulting China [辱华 ruhua], I do feel her speech was very inappropriate for that occasion. Lots of people are saying that she said what she did to conform with foreigners' stereotyped view of China. . . . It makes me pretty angry to watch. With such a good platform, she could have said more proactively positive things to let more people put aside their prejudice and understand her motherland, even just a little. But she didn't.

SHIHONG: On an international platform, you have to maintain face [面子 mianzi].

NIUNIU: Those netizens' attitude is pretty scary. . . . Sometimes it's not the state system that makes you feel shackled. . . . If I'd stumbled on that video by accident, I'd have thought that some aspects of that girl's speech were extremely inappropriate, but it wouldn't really have concerned me that much. But now it looks like everyone thinks the content of her speech is serious enough to be called denigrating the nation. You must understand that this will make a lot of people follow that view and attack her. . . . Since people like to see themselves as the embodiment of righteousness.

SHUYUAN: I think this student and the netizens all have the freedom to say what they want to say, and news media also have the responsibility to maintain their own political standpoint. . . . If she can say that sort of thing on that sort of an occasion, then naturally she should be prepared to accept responsibility for the consequences.

NIUNIU: I agree with you. Faced with certain things, we must maintain our own point of view and standpoint. When the mainstream doesn't allow alternative points of view to exist, it's very dangerous. Even if she's wrong, I think she still has the right to express herself, just as you can raise your objections.

SHUYUAN: The mainstream media also have to shoulder responsibility for fostering ethnic pride and cohesion, right? You can't say that if someone curses China, then the *China Daily* should come out and support them.

NIUNIU: I'd prefer if everyone could stick to the facts and not escalate the situation. Once that happens, everyone becomes afraid to speak.

YULI: Nowadays many media lose their sense of public interest and care only about exposure and attracting readers. That student's speech falls far short of insulting China, and I wonder whether the media that give her that label have considered the effect it will have on a young person.... What I find really frightening is when for commercial profit, the media attach the ills of society to an individual, that's as inhumane as the medieval witch hunts.... So now whenever I see the news, I add a question mark and don't believe everything.

PINGPING: [*thumbs-up emoji*]

SHUYUAN: Today I saw on [question-and-answer forum] Zhihu that someone checked up on the president of the University of Maryland, and he's got a bit of an anticommunist background. And reading over the text of her speech, it's clear that between the lines it's saying that China is not free and not democratic. Netizens' reactions are understandable, I guess, since in that kind of a forum she was not only representing herself but also representing China.

PINGPING: Does representing China mean you can't say anything "bad" ...

MEI: Watching her video makes me feel kind of uncomfortable. If I were a classmate of hers listening from the floor, I'd be pretty embarrassed and ashamed, I guess. I'd feel like my compatriot was embarrassing me.

SHUYUAN: I think that Western countries hold a lot of stereotyped views of China, and they might even do so a bit deliberately. But although China has a lot of faults, it's continually making progress. You can't just spread a negative image, especially when some of it's not even true.

MINGYU: Yup, I agree with that.

XIAOJUAN: I guess what everyone objects to is her attitude of sucking up to America.... From my personal perspective, I don't like it. I heard the first line and couldn't keep listening. So phony.... It's because of people like her that Westerners think China is bad, China is backward.... I just went back and listened to a bit more. It's disgusting, I feel like my whole body's been drenched in oil [*laughing-crying emoji*].

YULI: When will people be able to deal more rationally with voices they don't like? Even if someone's speech differs from what the majority want to hear, that doesn't mean his/her family should be subjected to doxing. Yang's speech just voiced what one group of people want to hear, and another group of people don't want to hear. If we think someone is a problem just because they say something we don't want to hear, then what's the point of the higher education we've received?

(Excerpts from group WeChat discussion, May 23, 2017)

MINISTRY OF FOREIGN AFFAIRS: Young scholars' thinking undergoes development and change, but as long as deep in their hearts they ardently love the motherland, China will still support and welcome them. Students abroad represent their motherland, so they should speak and act even more responsibly. No matter how far you travel, don't forget where you started from. Perhaps the motherland is far from perfect, but all eyes are on her progress. More powerful than denunciations are our joint efforts to build an even better China. (*People's Daily* Weibo account, May 24, 2017, shared in project WeChat group)

*

In 2017 Shuping Yang's notorious commencement speech—popularly referred to as the "Shuping Yang insults China (*ruhua*) incident," for which Yang soon had to post an apology—became the latest catalyst for the public expression of patriotism by Chinese students abroad.[1] In nations where increasing numbers of Chinese students are studying, including the United States, Australia, and the United Kingdom, this has become a significant preoccupation for scholars, governments, and media commentators. And while youth patriotism has been effectively mobilized by various powers over the course of modern Chinese history, there is a generational specificity to these students' affective orientations toward their homeland. Alongside the idealization of mobility, cosmopolitanism, and a transnational imaginary that is so central to the middle-class 1990s generation's sense of themselves, this generation has also been schooled intensively since childhood in the importance of loyalty to the Chinese party-state. This has occurred both through state-regulated media and popular culture and through a nationwide "Patriotic Education Campaign" (爱国主义教育实施纲要 Aiguozhuyi Jiaoyu Shishi Gangyao, colloquially abbreviated to 爱国教育 *aiguo jiaoyu*) that has been shaping secondary-school history and politics curricula since the early 1990s, in the aftermath of the military crackdown on the student-led Tiananmen democratization movement of 1989 (S. Zhao 2005; Z. Wang 2008; Rosen 2009; R. Chen 2017; Woods and Dickson 2017). The campaign has seen school history curricula revised to focus on a narrative about China's hundred-year humiliation at the hands of Western and Japanese imperial powers from the mid-nineteenth to the mid-twentieth centuries (Callahan 2004). As international relations scholar Zheng Wang shows, in the new teaching materials, the old class-struggle narrative has been replaced with a patriotic one, and "the official Maoist 'victor narrative' (China won national independence) . . . superseded by a new 'victimization narrative,' which blames the 'West' for China's suffering." Thus, "Beijing . . . creatively used history education as an instrument for the glorification of the party, for the consolidation of the [People's Republic of China]'s national identity, and for the justification of the political system of the [Chinese Communist Party]'s one party rule" (2008, 784).

Wang proposes that this campaign's propagandistic reinforcement of the patriotic narrative of China's "hundred years of humiliation" has had particular affective resonance for Chinese youth. Scholarly opinion is divided about whether nationalism is, in fact, rising among Chinese youth, as Western media often claim.[2] But the Patriotic Education Campaign does appear to have contributed to the emergence of new *forms* of popular youth nationalism from the 1990s on, including expressions of "long-distance nationalism" by Chinese students abroad (B. Anderson 1992; Z. Wang 2008, 799–800; Rosen 2009). Accordingly, scholars have considered to what extent mobile students may be induced by the Chinese state to "carry the state within themselves" (Nyíri and Zhang 2010, 53), how their patriotism from afar may affect the politics of nationalism within China (S. Zhao 2005; Nyíri and Zhang 2010), and how effective cross-cultural communication may be realized in the context of Chinese students' patriotism abroad (Hail 2015).

Outside China, the question of these mobile students' patriotic attachments to the PRC state has frequently been in the spotlight in recent years. In Australia, Chinese international students have been implicated in an ongoing series of discussions since early 2017 about "Chinese influence" in the life and politics of the nation. Similar questions have since also been raised in the United States (Lloyd-Damjanovic 2018) and the United Kingdom (Dukalskis 2018). In Australia the state broadcaster (the ABC), the federal government, and the national security agency (Australian Security Intelligence Organisation, ASIO) have each raised questions about the implications of Chinese students' loyalty to their homeland, suggesting that they might be working as spies for Beijing or that their allegiance to the party could imperil the exercise of free speech at Australian universities (ABC 2017; Dziedzic 2017; Garnaut 2017; F. Martin 2017b; Astarita, Patience, and Tok 2019). Both for scholars and for students' host communities, then, the question of how we should understand Chinese students' patriotism abroad has become pressing. As we see in participants' responses to the Shuping Yang incident, this question also preoccupies the students themselves. How, then, do the *trans*national ventures of the current generation of students connect with Chinese *national* institutions and discourses? How does national feeling manifest in and through students' physical and digital mobilities beyond China's national territory? These are this chapter's central questions.

The participants in the WeChat discussion quoted earlier were right to point out that at the rhetorical level, Yang's speech references well-worn tropes for the representation of China in Western liberal democracies. It paints China as the locus of repression and the West as the site of freedom, and implies a correspondingly binary model of available subject positions for Chinese people. They may either be victims who are politically and spiritually stifled by China's oppressive regime—metaphorized as toxic air—or courageously rebel against that regime to champion the "Western values" of freedom and democracy. But the complexity and variety of participants' responses to Yang's speech demonstrate the inadequacy of such a crude framework for understanding these mobile students' affective orientations toward their homeland. This chapter unpacks this complex set of relations, exploring national feeling as a third affective domain, following on from the previous two chapters' focus on intimate relationships and religious faith. It begins by teasing out two key cultural logics that underlie the exchanges quoted above and that, I argue, are central to this generation of mobile middle-class students' national structure of feeling—that is, the shared, historically conditioned, affective orientation toward the idea of China-as-homeland that they enact through everyday practice (Raymond Williams 1977; Edensor 2002). I then draw on fieldwork and interviews to analyze this national structure of feeling in detail, especially its gendered dimensions as seen in the dominant metaphor of China as motherland. The final part of the chapter moves on to explore both continuities and changes in aspects of participants' affective and critical orientations toward China that occurred during the years they spent abroad.

~

The discussion quoted above pivots around two key logics. First, participants' responses to Yang's speech illustrate what I call a *performative ethics of national representation*. This refers to the idea that there are situationally appropriate ways of speaking about China that hinge on to whom the representation is addressed, who is making it, in what capacity, and in which forum. According to this ethical code, the perceived correctness or incorrectness of one's representations of China relate as much to contextual propriety as to adherence to deeply held belief or absolute truth. We see this logic reflected in the response from China's Ministry of Foreign Affairs underlining students' duty to speak responsibly when representing the motherland abroad, and in participants' repeated emphasis on the mismatch between the forum (public, international) and the critical content of Yang's speech, which are contrasted with different contexts (private, among close friends) where criticism of aspects of life in China is more acceptable.[3] This logic also underlies Shihong's invocation of "face" (*mianzi*) and the need to maintain national dignity in international settings (Kipnis 1995), and, relatedly, Mei's underscoring of the embarrassment that Yang's co-national classmates would surely feel on hearing her criticize their homeland in front of outsiders. Indeed, the central charge of "insulting China" (*ruhua*) that hovered around the edges of our discussion concerns, precisely, speech acts that gain their power by virtue of a public, international context. Faced with "insults to China," the ethics of national representation demands that one make counterclaims to defend the national honor against hostile outsiders: heightened consciousness of and sensitivity to foreigners' negative views about China are integral to this national structure of feeling (S. Zhao 2005, 136; Hail 2015). The main dispute in our discussion pivots around a tension between the state-supported view of citizens' collective ethical responsibility to represent China positively abroad and a liberal view of the individual's right to represent herself and her independent personal opinions (the central right that Yang tried to claim in her speech).

The debate also underlines the technosocial mediation of national feeling. Shuyuan defends Chinese state media's established self-appointed duty to foster ethnic pride and cohesion; Jiaying condemns the violence of doxing (人肉搜索 *renrou sousuo*, literally "human flesh search") that saw nationalist zealots target Yang's family; and Yuli criticizes commercial online media's use of stories like Yang's as clickbait in a climate where outrage over "insults to China" can be monetized in what Wanning Sun (2018b) has aptly called "market patriotism" (see also Gao 2015). This marks the historical specificity of the forms of national feeling at issue, highlighting how they are shaped by the technological affordances of contemporary media networks as much as by ideological factors (K. Fang and Repnikova 2017; Schneider 2018; H. Liu 2019).

Less obviously but nonetheless clearly, the excerpts also bespeak a second logic: a *developmentalist narrative of nationhood* in which China is imagined as progressing along a path from economically undeveloped to developed. This narrative ties capitalist development to national self-respect. We see it in participants' sensitivity to Yang's criticism of air pollution in China (which associates the nation with industrial and regulatory underdevelopment); in Shuyuan's statement, endorsed by Mingyu, that "although China has a lot of faults, it's continually making progress" (进步 *jinbu*); in Xiaojuan's anxiety that because of people like Yang, Westerners think China is "backward" (落后 *luohou*); and in the Ministry of Foreign Affairs' statement that "all eyes are on [the motherland's] progress." Together, these two key logics exerted a shaping influence on participants' affective engagements with the concept of China during their time living abroad.

Mother's Dress: The Performative Ethics of National Representation

Imagine you're out somewhere with your mother. You meet someone who says to you, "Goodness, what an ugly dress your mother is wearing!" Now, what are you going to say? Of course, you must come to your mother's defense and argue with the stranger—no matter what you may personally think of her dress.

This allegory for Chinese youth nationalism abroad was related to me by Xinyu Zhao, a young Chinese scholar I first met at an academic conference in Melbourne. It is based on a classical set phrase, *zi bu xian mu chou, gou bu xian jia pin* (子不嫌母丑 狗不嫌家贫): "A son never complains that his mother is ugly; a dog never complains that its household is poor," which is popularly invoked to imply the shamelessness of those who criticize their homeland. The maternal allegory, in both vernacular and classical forms, captures two core aspects of the logic I am calling the *performative ethics of national representation*. The first is the use of intimate metaphors for the nation, most commonly the family. The allegory invokes the feminized figure of the nation as a mother whose honor must be defended: an influential modern political trope that is distilled in the common phrase *zuguo muqin* (祖国母亲: homeland-as-mother) to refer to China. Second, the allegory centers representational protocol: the ethical weight attached to expressing the appropriate feeling in the social context.

The metaphor of one's feelings for one's homeland being like one's feelings for one's family was frequently repeated in discussions with participants. For example, in our initial interview in Henan, before her departure for Melbourne, Yuling explained:

This nation has provided a certain environment for us. You see, if our nation had been in chaos, then we wouldn't have had the opportunity to study, to enjoy this kind of life. And even right now our nation is experiencing some [attacks] from Vietnam, the Philippines; it's not very stable. And lots of Western nations look down on us, too. Actually, our development has been very difficult, and we're in a period of transition. I think our generation needs to do more, since we're about to go off and learn things. In future we should repay our motherland; it's time for our generation to do more. In future, we'll become the nation's backbone.

Similarly, in their initial interviews in Shanghai, others spoke of "affection for my motherland ... the place that bore and raised me" (Qiqi), fears of feeling "homeless" (没有家了 *meiyou jia le*) after leaving China's national territory (Liangya), and gratitude that "I have the opportunities I do today, like going abroad to study, and also having studied at such a good college, because my country gave these to me" (Yining), although these opportunities were more directly provided by students' parents. Each of these statements draws a parallel between the nation and the family. Yuling also echoes a state discourse on overseas students' filial-patriotic duty, according to which they owe their still-struggling homeland a debt of gratitude that should be repaid by returning to "make a contribution" (做贡献 *zuo gongxian*) postgraduation, an idea that Yuling also voiced several times subsequently (Fong 2004a, 641; Nyíri 2001; J. Chen 2019). At other times, participants likened their loyalty to their homeland to loyalty to their alma mater (母校 *mu xiao*): a different but related allegory in which the ethical principle of loyalty owed to a benevolent mentor remains consistent, as do the self-positioning of the speaker as a child and the maternal association.

These examples reflect what Vanessa L. Fong (2004a) has theorized as filial nationalism (see also F. Liu 2012, 61). In her fieldwork with school students in Dalian, Fong found that middle-class Chinese students born in the 1980s "retained a strong sense of loyalty to China, based ... on the idea of an imagined family, in which China was identified with a long-suffering parent who, despite her flaws, deserved the filial devotion of her children" (2004a, 632). For Fong, the 1980s generation's nationalism is more reflexive and critical than that expressed by their parent generation, who grew up in a more closed China, lacking the transnational imaginary that has shaped this generation of outward-looking, urban, middle-class youth. The teenagers she worked with "often spoke critically and reflexively about their country, as if they were already the outsiders they hoped to become. At the same time, they believed they had a duty to bring China into the imagined community of wealthier societies to which they felt they belonged" (2004a, 635). In key respects, this analysis also fits the 1990s generation to which my participants belonged, particularly in the centrality of a transnational imaginary coupled with a reflexive form of filial nationalism that hinges on a developmental narrative about China's progress on the world stage.

One aspect of filial nationalism that Fong's analysis does not directly address, however, is its gendering. The gendering of the concept of *the homeland* (祖国 *zuguo*), the most commonly used term to refer to China in the sense of the primordial nation and one's allegiance to it, is not straightforward (Lieberman 1998, 100–102).[4] The term literally means "land of the ancestors," and while ancestors are both male and female, the traditional clan structure and ideology on which the *zu* concept is based are strongly patriarchal in nature. Explicitly masculine iterations of the primordial nation concept also exist, such as the framing of China as "the land of the ancestral patriline" (父祖之国 *fuzu zhi guo*) (Zhong 2000, 16; Chen Yuping 2017). All this would suggest a translation of *zuguo* as *patria*. However, in modern and contemporary usage in the PRC, China as *zuguo* is almost always referred to in the feminine and translated as "motherland." Political communication studies scholar Pan Xianghui (2018) offers a critical discussion of the historical emergence of the homeland-as-mother (*zuguo muqin*) political metaphor in 1920s China as a selective appropriation and cultural indigenization of French and Soviet nationalist tropes, noting the maternal metaphor's further consolidation in state discourse after the 1949 Communist Revolution. Pan underlines the neat fit between the image of nation-as-mother and the Chinese cultural value of filial piety (孝道 *xiaodao*):

> The traditional Chinese culture of "filial piety" enabled the ready acceptance of the "homeland-as-mother" metaphor, and moreover its extension from the literary realm to the realm of politics. . . . Once the foreign "homeland-as-mother" [concept] was linked with the traditional Chinese "filial piety toward one's mother" concept, then the obedience, service, and unidirectional love central to China's "filial piety" culture become an important part of people's understanding of the relationship between citizens and the state [国家 *guojia*]. . . . From the perspective of political communication, "homeland-as-mother" as a metaphorical trope has important cognitive, symbolic, and directive functions. It belongs to the category of "affective politics." . . . This political trope and metaphor sometimes weaves a kind of "witchcraft-like magic." For example, transforming "the homeland" into a mother who is "ravaged by an aggressor" obviously makes it easier to stir up ethnic hatred and resistance and to effect greater political mobilization. (2018, 101–2)

The pervasiveness of the homeland-as-mother metaphor in contemporary mainland Chinese public culture means that there is an inherently gendered dimension to young people's filial nationalism.[5] The feminine gendering of the homeland-as-mother imaginary produces a double set of connotations: like the cultural image of the familial mother, the homeland-as-mother is sometimes the powerful one who protects her citizens/children and at other times the powerless one in need of protection by them (Pan X. 2018, 93–94). This trope's capacity to associate China with both power and victimization draws on a long modern cultural history in which the maternal signifier has been strongly idealized and associated both with strength and dominance and with pathos, self-sacrifice, and suffering (R. Chow 1991, 121–70; Lieberman 1998). The ambivalence of this cluster of gendered meanings resonates particularly strongly with Chinese transnational students' comingled desire for, anxieties over, and pride in China's progress toward technocapitalist development.

In addition to the familial/maternal allegory, speech protocols are also central to the ethics of national representation that this generation understands. A few months after their arrival in Melbourne, Suyin offered a typical account of these during a discussion with her friend Ruomei:

> In terms of this concept of China . . . , even though we might point out this and that fault with it, nevertheless, actually, in our hearts, we love it. We don't want to hear about China's faults from the mouths of others. What this means is that I myself can talk about our China's faults [*Ruomei guffaws*], but I don't want other people to mention them. . . . In terms of talking about China's faults, . . . for example, how China's economy is underperforming in some ways, that's OK to say. . . . Just don't say insulting or abusive things. Actually, it's OK to talk about specific phenomena. Just don't say things that are insulting, don't curse [China], you know, don't abuse it.

Suyin's emphasis on mannerly comportment, the precise limits of appropriate speech, and the positional specificity that dictates which speakers may say what, when, and where echoes the allegory about the rude stranger who publicly insults one's mother's dress. Such accounts also point to a further sense in which this ethics of national representation can be understood as performative: the loyal Chinese subject's objections to negative representations must be publicly enacted in order to be effective. The filial child must take issue with the rude stranger on the spot, in front of any onlookers who may have witnessed the original insult to her mother (see also Hail 2015, 316).

This performative aspect of righteous national(ist) indignation when Chinese students abroad are faced with "insults" to the motherland is underlined in an important article by Pál Nyíri and Juan Zhang (2010) on Chinese international students' protests against pro-Tibetan independence demonstrators during the international torch relay in 2008, ahead of the Beijing Olympics. They argue that for the 1980s generation, nationalism—far from being experienced as antithetical to a cosmopolitan outlook—became "part of a cosmopolitan Chinese youth identity in overseas locations" (25). Furthermore, "the 'hip nationalism' displayed by Chinese youth across the globe is intended largely for the consumption of other Chinese youth.... As much as it offers a cathartic emotional experience of identifying with the nation (and more particularly, with millions of fellow nationalist youth worldwide), it also provides an opportunity for individual demonstrations of middle-class sophistication, creativity, passion, youthful power and cosmopolitanism" (27). According to this logic, which is also observable in the 1990s generation (G. Yang 2019), the public self-performance of Chinese patriotism overseas—whether by attending a pro-China political rally, enjoying a nationalist blockbuster like *The Wandering Earth* (directed by Frant Gwo, 2019), challenging a classmate's criticism of China, or posting patriotic reflections on WeChat—may be experienced as consistent with and reinforcing of these mobile students' cosmopolitanism.[6]

During this study, several participants proactively engaged in patriotic self-presentations, especially on nationally significant occasions. This was done exclusively via social media rather than via participation in live activities like demonstrations, which they tended to avoid, partly out of lack of interest and partly on the advice of some parents who expressly forbade their children to engage in political activity while abroad.[7] Occasions for the performance and exhibition of digital patriotism (Hogan 2010) included the military parade in Beijing commemorating the seventieth anniversary of the defeat of Japan at the end of World War II (September 3, 2015), when my WeChat Moments feed became a sea of red-and-yellow Chinese national flags, patriotic statements, and accounts of the moving experience of watching the televised broadcast of the parade (figure 7.1)—including from participants who described themselves on other occasions as not very patriotic. Another wave occurred in June 2016, when a video of the Chinese foreign minister Wang Yi dressing down a Canadian journalist for her question on human rights abuses in China spread virally, with many approving comments (Chu 2016). The next month, following the United Nations decision in favor of the Philippines on the ownership of the South China Sea and its islands, many students posted comments and memes criticizing the United Nations decision and supporting the idea that

人在澳洲，心系中国🇨🇳 论中国人在澳洲的庆祝反法70周年及大阅兵方式之一：下个厨，舔个盘，三人举勺干胶原😂😂😂 Swisse液体胶原蛋白口服液，家喻户晓。大S推荐💐妮可基德曼代言，美肌护肤神仙水500ml！注意啦！据资料显示，女性从25岁就开始胶原蛋白的流失，你不补回来，它是不会自己回来的🌷做个聪明女人，内调保养才是根本！饭后记得10毫升哦😉 和祖国一样越来越年轻越来越美丽😝

Collapse

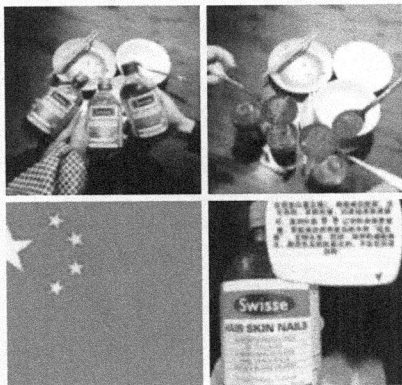

10 minutes ago

FIGURE 7.1 Patriotic exhibition on Yueming's WeChat feed, September 3, 2015: "Body in Australia, heart tied to China [*flag*]. One of Chinese people's ways of commemorating the military parade on the 70th anniversary of the anti-Fascist movement, in Australia: Get in the kitchen, lick some plates, and three of us scoop up some collagen [*three laughing-crying emojis*]. Everyone knows about Swisse liquid collagen protein formulation, recommended by [Taiwanese celebrity] Barbie Hsu [*bouquet emoji*], represented by Nicole Kidman, 500ml skin beautification and protection formula! Take note! Available information tells us that women start to lose collagen from age 25, and unless you supplement it, it's not going to come back on its own [*flower emoji*]. Be a smart woman, internal maintenance is the key! Just gotta remember to take 10ml after eating [*wink emoji*] and you'll be ever younger and ever more beautiful, like the motherland [*tongue-out emoji*]."

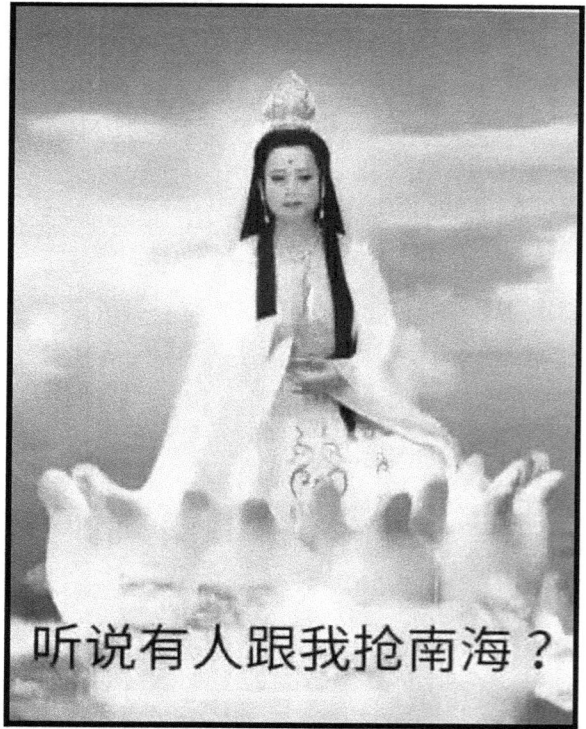

FIGURE 7.2 Anni changed her profile picture to this patriotic meme in July 2016: Goddess Guanyin says, "I hear somebody wants to fight me for the South [China] Sea?"

听说有人跟我抢南海？

the contested islands and waters were an inalienable part of China's national territory (figure 7.2). National flags and other patriotic artifacts again saturated WeChat around October 1, 2019: the seventieth anniversary of the founding of the PRC. I do not question the sincerity of these posts, but the contrast between participants' more ambivalent discussions of their national sentiments in informal exchanges and these situational exhibitions of patriotism on the digital "front stage" of WeChat lends weight to the argument that, for this generation, patriotic self-presentation on social media may serve a performative function connected with impression management (Hogan 2010; Nyíri and Zhang 2010; F. Liu 2012; G. Yang 2019).

The feminized articulations of patriotic sentiment toward the motherland seen in figures 7.1 and 7.2 foreground the creativity, wit, and hipness of this style of digital youth nationalism (Nyíri and Zhang 2010, 27; Schneider 2018). The meme in figure 7.2 depicts the goddess Guanyin, sometimes called "Guanyin of the South [China] Sea" (南海观音 Nanhai Guanyin), who is honored with a massive statue overlooking that sea at Sanya on China's Hainan Island. Known as the Goddess of Mercy, Guanyin is the Chinese version of the Buddhist bodhisattva Avalokitesvara and is usually associated with kindness and compassion. But the text added below her image, with its sly threat, together with the contemporary, anime-like style of the illustration, rescripts the deity's meaning to frame her instead as a formidable guardian of her oceanic territory. Yueming's post, which uses the patriotic occasion of the war anniversary to advertise an Australian beauty supplement as part of her *daigou* (代购: e-trading) business (see chapter 4), is even more playful. Yueming's tone is light and humorous, bordering on tongue-in-cheek as she parallels the Chinese motherland with a savvy and beauty-conscious consumer of products recommended by Taiwanese and Australian celebrities; the post recontextualizes the national flag among cute emojis, product snapshots, and dinner dishes. It is essentially a life-cast advertisement, designed to promote customers' trust by integrating Yueming's *daigou* activities with her performance of overseas-student-in-Australia "realness" (X. Zhao 2019b, 120–61). Such examples illustrate the wide tonal range of the mobile students' patriotic engagements. Rather than dutifully channeling the militant earnestness (and masculinism) of the "red hot patriotic sentiment" solicited by the Chinese state (Garnaut 2017), these young women's exhibitions of popular digital nationalism demonstrate a much cooler, lighter, more reflexive engagement with the motherland trope (G. Yang and Wang 2016).[8] It is also worth noting that, when on an ordinary (not nationally significant) day in late 2018 I asked participants to share other patriotic memes they enjoyed, several responded with veiled horror that young people like themselves simply weren't into those: "They're for middle-aged and old people," as Xiaojuan put it.

From Auntie to Cosmopolitan: The Developmentalist Narrative of Nationhood

The second aspect of the national structure of feeling I am investigating in this chapter is what I call the developmentalist narrative of nationhood. The ongoing preoccupation with development (发展 *fazhan*) in the Chinese narrative of modernity hinges on a binary opposition between the advanced (先进 *xianjin*) and the backward (落后 *luohou*) (Fong 2011). This opposition has been integral to modernization discourse in China since at least the early twentieth century (M. Yang 2004, 724). However, underlining that national feeling does not equate simply with national*ism*, China's perceived position along the path toward development evoked for participants, at different times and in different contexts, a range of contradictory emotional responses. This section unpacks three modalities of the developmentalist narrative as articulated by participants: developmental desire, developmental anxiety, and developmental pride.

Developmental desire—the wish for China to continually "improve" by progressing in economic development—was expressed by many participants in initial interviews, before or shortly after they departed from China. Consider the following reflections:

> I guess I'm pretty conflicted, because I think that China's government really does have some bad points, but it also has its merits. I feel like America, that so-called nation of human rights, sometimes tramples on human rights. . . . Their type of capitalism is actually only about the future of the rich; they ignore the human rights of the poor. Whereas in China we have this anticorruption [campaign], so that's improved a lot. . . . I think China will improve more and more, because nobody can deny China's growing strength. So I think that if this system can lead us to become more powerful, then it does have its advantages. (Qin)

> The way I see it right now is that China has its good side, but it is a newly developing country, it's a country that's in the midst of a development process that's full of unknowns. So I hope that—well, I hope that it can become developed. And then of course right now there are some bad points, too, so to get away from those bad points I've come abroad [*laughs*]. (Pingping)

> We actually really hope that our motherland can gradually become better. Like, for example, when I heard about Tianjin [the major gas explosion in August 2015], in my heart I found it very hard to bear. I found it so scary, and I felt really sorry for those people [who were killed and injured]. So I do hope our motherland can become better, stop having so many disasters and catastrophes. (Suyin)

The emphasis in each of these accounts is slightly different, ranging from Qin's desire for growing international power, to Pingping's vacillation between developmental optimism and emigratory realism, to Suyin's humanistic compassion for the victims of industrialization. But they share a common developmental desire: the hope that China will "improve," "become more powerful," "become developed," and "become better."

These statements also reveal a certain anxiety and ambivalence. Developmental anxieties were even clearer in participants' reflections on what they saw as some Chinese people's low levels of cultural civility (素质 *suzhi*: see this book's introduction) and the bad reputation they felt this brought China and Chinese people in the eyes of Westerners—but also in their own eyes, as self-identifying educated, middle-class youth. Repeatedly, participants described how they felt a burden of representation to embody "good" (polite, law-abiding, well-educated) Chineseness in front of Westerners abroad.[9]

The question of (other) Chinese people's deficit of cultural civility was a serious preoccupation for some. One afternoon, over herbal tea at a café near Capital University, Zhenghui embarked on a long discussion of the issue, which clearly pained her deeply. Zhenghui's boyfriend was Taiwanese, and his mother, who was visiting from Japan, where she and her husband currently lived, had aired the view to Zhenghui that it was Confucian culture that underlay Japanese people's grace, kindness, and consideration for others. In that case, Zhenghui wondered, what had happened in China? Why did ordinary people in towns and small cities behave so badly; why were they untidy, rude, and noisy? Zhenghui earnestly sought my opinion as a scholar of Chinese culture. I offered a relativist take on the divergent behavioral mores of different social classes, suggesting that what was considered normal within one group context might be unacceptable in another, but Zhenghui remained unconvinced. She continued to agonize over the question, citing the clean and neat houses and nice manners she had observed on trips to Australian country towns and contrasting them with the situation in rural China. Perhaps, she suggested, it was just that those people in China didn't understand, had not yet been educated? Perhaps it was the fault of their parents? Zhenghui reached no satisfactory conclusion that afternoon and seemed to continue to nurse a worry that there might be some intrinsic link between ordinary Chinese people and low cultural civility.

Others, too, expressed concern over a sense that, in Mei's sharp turn of phrase, "China just gives people the impression of a peasant who's suddenly struck it rich":

SUYIN: One day, I was having lunch and chatting about [the image of China] with some classmates; that there's really nothing you can do about this. Chinese people are still like that. . . .

F: [*referencing our earlier discussion*] Like what, you mean cutting the queue—?

S: Right.

RUOMEI: Speaking a bit loudly.

S: Screaming at the top of their lungs.

F: Really?

s: Really, I've met lots of them.

. . .

R: Because in earlier times, the people who went abroad for tourism—group tours—were not young people. . . . They were not the younger generation, not people like us, who have received a complete education. There might have been some, like, you know, aunties, old ladies, that kind [laughs].

s: They'd go out traveling.

R: And Chinese people have this kind of mentality, maybe it's because they've been through famine and are traumatized. Like, I want this, I want that, you know. Because my mum and her friends, when they went on a cruise, . . . it had a *buffet*-type thing, and they could choose. My mum and her friends took as much as they wanted to eat. But the [other] Chinese people, lots of them—

s: Took heaps [laughs].

R: And then you feel sort of—

s: Why are they being so wasteful.

R: Right, it's very wasteful, is there a famine on? That time they really did seem like locusts.

s: They were too possessive.

R: This type of mindset, it's not easy to change.

YUEMING: You hear some negative stuff, like about Chinese tourists overseas or whatever, their *suzhi*. And then inside China some people with low *suzhi*, their bad behavior is often exposed. But—but that's just because there are so many of us! [everyone laughs] . . . It's a question of upbringing.

QIQI: Actually, it's also connected to the education system. Over here [in Australia], the level of basic education is pretty good.

. . .

Y: Some of it has to do with *suzhi*, some with upbringing. . . . What I mean is, there are people with low *suzhi*. . . . There are some, . . . for example, Chinese people who spit on the street. . . . There are still a lot of them, they haven't changed their ways at all. . . . When I go out traveling, anywhere at all, not overseas but within China, . . . my uncles will do that, and I feel ashamed within myself, I truly do. Like, once I was like, "I'll cover you, I'll cover you" [laughs] because I was afraid somebody would see.

In these discussions older individuals' everyday bodily practices—queueing, speaking, eating, spitting—come to stand in for a national body that is vulnerable to being shamed when its improper comportment is viewed by non-Chinese people and/or by the young cosmopolitan students themselves. More precisely, shaming takes place when the students witness this unruly national body *in the process of being viewed by* others, since they seem to internalize the censorious gaze of an (imagined) outsider judging such embodiments of Chineseness and finding them wanting. These accounts imply an ideological molecule composed by cross-links among *suzhi*, education, and mobility: they value a cosmopolitan habitus that is about "knowing how to travel"—that is, knowing how one should perform Chinese identity when away from home. There are different degrees of investment in this logic, however. On one hand, Zhenghui expressed real angst over what she perceived as rural Chinese people's uncouth habitus compared with the manners of small-town Australians.[10] On the other hand, Yueming painted a rather humorous picture of herself desperately trying to screen her bevy of hawking uncles from public view, while paralleling their behavior with that of some Chinese tourists overseas. But despite these differences, through all of these examples runs a logic linking domestic class, generational, and rural-urban social distinctions *within* China, framed in terms of *suzhi*, with China's *external* image in international settings. The mobile students' collective anxiety was that the supposed civility deficits of China's culturally "backward" rural, lower-class, and older uneducated populations would come to be associated with China as a whole in the eyes of the developed world. One solution for this, they felt, was for themselves to perform middle-class habitus all the more strenuously while abroad, to ensure that the motherland projected the image of a well-mannered cosmopolitan lady rather than an uncouth peasant auntie, that is, a fast-developing nation at home on the international stage rather than a backward, parochial one.

In the late 1990s and early 2000s when Fong undertook her fieldwork among teenagers in Dalian, she found that while they expressed filial love for China, they strongly disidentified themselves from the "backwardness" they associated with the nation, which conflicted with the image they held of themselves as modern, cosmopolitan individuals (2004a, 644–45). In contrast, nearly twenty years after Fong's study, the participants in the present study—despite their developmental anxieties about cultural civility—tended to feel a growing sense of China's rapid economic and technological development and to express national pride in this progress during the time they spent abroad:

YUEMING: Our feelings for the motherland?

QIQI: Needless to say, very strong.

Y: Stronger and stronger.... Before, we were patriotic. Now, we're <u>sup</u>-er pat-ri-o-tic.... For example, sometimes people say China is bad.... Well, whoever says that, I'll get 'em. For real.

. . .

Q: There are a lot of everyday things, like convenience. In China, actually a lot of things are very convenient.

Y: Super-convenient!

Q: Internet shopping is very convenient, for instance.

Y: I think Australians simply have no way to imagine logistics in China. In their world, it would be unimaginable.

Q: All kinds of things [make you] feel really patriotic, feel that Chinese people are amazing, they've invented lots of things, and it all runs so smoothly and stuff....

Y: And there are some other things that you wouldn't have really noticed back in China, but overseas when you hear whatever kind of good news about China, you're like, "Ha—no shame in China!"

(After two years in Melbourne)

I think that comparatively speaking, Australia is developing too slow and China is developing too fast [*laughs*].... Every time I go back home, [I think,] ahh, this place has changed again, that place has changed again, wow, how can it change so fast? It's just, like, it'll make you really proud, type thing.... I never did think that big cities in China were any [different] from Australia. I think that they are even better than Sydney or Melbourne. (Shunzi, after two years in Melbourne)

Like, for example, I'll say *I'm from China*, and people's first reaction will be to say, "*Oh knee how*" [*mimicking a Westerner attempting Mandarin*].... Or else their reaction will be, "*Oh China. I want to learn Chinese.*" Or else they'll say, "*Today China's economy* has grown very fast." You find that actually your country earns you points.... These are some things that the country gives you, I think it's all very good. In relation to this my view is pretty *positive*. I really do think, maybe when you're in China, you might complain about stuff like air pollution, but once you've been overseas, you really do become proud and gratified on account of your country. (Yining, after two and a half years in Melbourne)

XIAOQING: Your own motherland feels more intimate. I mean, when you've stayed here for a long time and then you go back, you find that the motherland is so convenient, now it's all WeChat and whatever, Alipay, all kinds of stuff to eat and whatever, and the transport system is really convenient.... I noticed that when I hadn't been back for ages, China had developed so fast, whereas I felt that overseas, things had developed—

YALING: —sort of a feeling of stagnation.
(After three years in Melbourne and Canberra)

These discussions highlight the polysemy of the Chinese term *aiguo* (爱国). Since, etymologically, it derives simply from "love (*ai*) [of one's] country (*guo*)," it may be interpreted either in relation to a formal, abstract political stance (nationalism) or in relation to a more concrete affection for aspects of everyday of life at home—or both. The second sense of the term is rather backgrounded in the English term *patriotism* but was often referenced by participants when I asked them about their sense of *aiguo* while abroad. But instead of dismissing comments about the convenience of China's internet shopping, social media, transportation, and electronic payment systems as irrelevant to patriotism in the English sense of the term, we should recognize a connection between this appreciation of new technologies' pervasion of everyday life in urban China and developmentalist national pride. Such pride in fact entails an emergent form of patriotism in the more abstract ideational sense. It also marks a historical and generational distinction between these students and those Fong studied fifteen to twenty years earlier, which is linked to rapid technological developments in urban China over the intervening period that allow the 1990s generation of mobile students to feel that "big cities in China . . . are even better than Sydney or Melbourne" (Shunzi) and that whereas "China ha[s] developed so fast," overseas in Australia, there is "a feeling of stagnation" (Xiaoqing and Yaling). As Yining articulates particularly clearly, all of this leads in turn to a sense of China's rising status abroad: as more and more Westerners recognize China's growing economic strength, far from being an object of disidentification, China "earns you points." Thus, while significant anxiety and ambivalence about ordinary Chinese people's level of *sociocultural* development (or *suzhi*) clearly persists for this generation, their emergent developmental pride in a rising China, especially in relation to *technological* advances in everyday urban life, appears to mark a historical turning point in mobile, middle-class Chinese youth's affective orientation toward the nation (see also L. Yang and Zheng 2012).

We might recall, at this point, the ambivalence student transmigrants expressed about Melbourne and Australia, as captured in the terms Mocun (墨村: Melvillage) and TuAo (土澳: native Oz), discussed in chapter 2. Reconsidering those responses here suggests that the developmentalist dialectic structures their representations of *both* Australia *and* China: each is framed, at different times and in different regards, as front-runner/backwater, sophisticated/parochial, developed/backward. Participants' seesawing back and forth between opposite views of Australia and China—is Australia advanced and China backward, or is China advanced and Australia backward?—and especially their apparent gravitation toward the latter position during their years abroad, suggest that the current time may be a pivot point between two distinct historical moments in these mobile young people's sense of China's place in the world. Spurred constantly to reflect on China's developmental status relative to the Western nations where they study, Chinese students abroad live out the contradictions of this historical pivot point as a central aspect of their experience of educational mobility.

Complicating Chineseness: Transforming National Feeling Abroad

The performative ethics of national representation and the developmentalist narrative of nationhood remained central to participants' expressions of their feelings about China throughout their years of study in Australia. But for some, these feelings were also complicated by time spent abroad. This section explores three instances of this: an increasing tendency to separate the concept of nation from that of government; access to diverse media leading to greater reflexivity in students' views on China; and a growing appreciation of the heterogeneity of Chinese identity.

After a year or more living outside China, many participants told me, when I asked about their feelings for their homeland, that they increasingly understood a distinction between loving the country (*aiguo*) and loving the party or the government (see Hail 2015, 318; Wanning Sun 2018b, 76). Two responses are particularly articulate on this point and worth quoting at length:

I think that these days China . . . in terms of education, mixes up *nationalism* with *patriotism*. In my view, this is something good about the Western education I've received: I can clearly separate the two. What I love is the country, not the party. . . . These days, in order to secure their political power, when they're doing education [in China], what they instill is that loving the country equates to loving the party, loving the party equates to loving the country: the party and the country are one. But actually that's not the case at all. In the broadest possible terms, what I love are the people of that nation. . . . I mean what you hope to see are the people doing well. . . . That is, if everyone's standard of living were adequate, ideally if everyone could at least live a comfortable lifestyle, with enough clothing, food, and warmth. And not be subject to *abuse* by others, a bit freer. . . . I feel that from my Western education, . . . such thoughts have helped clarify my understanding. (Shun, pilot study participant, after eleven years in Australia)

At first, I didn't feel any difference [in feelings for China since coming to Australia]. But slowly I began to realize that culture and government are completely separate, completely different things. It's just like a story I know. You know before the Qing dynasty, there was the Ming dynasty, right? Well, in the final years of the Ming, there was a warrior. He was in charge of a city, and he surrendered it. And lots of people said to him, "That was so wrong of you, why did you surrender?" And so that man had to bear a lot of infamy, because the Qing dynasty was Manchurian—Manchu people, not Han people—and it was a transition to a different political power. But that man said, "What I have done, I have done out of patriotism [*aiguo*]. Because in fact . . . if I didn't surrender, they'd have slaughtered the city's people, nobody would have been left alive. Do you really think that that's the only course that can be seen as patriotic? To sacrifice all of the people? To change to a different government"—he was very honest—"and do more things beneficial to the people, and not have people killed, isn't that better?" So . . . when Chinese people talk about loyal patriotism . . . —the idea that you must be loyal to your sovereign—I don't agree with that. I think that the true good is more important. . . . I think that protecting the people and protecting the culture are completely different from protecting the government. The government is not necessarily the best thing for the people. (Qi, after three years in Australia)

Shun had pursued an undergraduate degree that included subjects on Chinese politics. While at other points in our conversation she expressed strong patriotic sentiment in terms of defending China's honor against critics while overseas, in her comments here she is clear about the role of her Western-style political education in allowing her to understand a distinction between nation and party, which in turn enabled her growing reflexivity on the meaning of *aiguo* for her: pertaining to culture and people, not party and state. Qi, who studied education, describes a related process of disidentification. Significantly, her allegory of the surrendering Ming warrior directly contrasts with the logic of filial nationalism, which assumes the ethical principle that the child/citizen should perform absolute loyalty to the mother/land. By distinguishing between sovereign and people, Qi explicitly rejects that principle, elevating the moral value of the people's good above that of patriotic loyalty and thereby challenging one of the core logics of state-promulgated nationalism. As they begin to discern a distinction between, on one hand, primordialist attachments to people and culture and, on the other hand, political loyalty to a specific state, party, and government, mobile students like Shun and Qi draw closer to what political scientist Suisheng Zhao (2005) calls *liberal nationalism*: a form of nationalism that recognizes a duty to support the nation while disidentifying with the authoritarian state, which Zhao numbers among the main nationalist countercurrents opposing the official line within China.

Another theme that participants raised in connection with their changing understanding of China while abroad concerns access overseas to a greater diversity of media. First, the range of media makes available alternative perspectives on China-related content (Z. Li and Feng 2018); and, second, such media diversity throws into relief, by contrast, the limitations of China's state political reporting. The latter is exacerbated by the renewed emphasis on CCP ideology and intensified regulation of public discussion under President Xi Jinping's regime (Brady 2017) during the years the participants were in Australia. Some participants reflected that being outside China threw into even sharper relief the state's tightening media restrictions within China. For example, Yixin, herself pursuing a media-related degree, reflected after two and a half years in Australia:

> When I was back there for a month recently, watching TV, I was really aware: the political environment has become much more strictly controlled than before. All the news programs are saying how great China is, how it's the strongest country in the world, stronger than any other. People there may not realize [the propaganda] has got worse because

they've been there all along, but for me the change is really obvious. So I was talking a lot about Australia, and how things are different here, and my parents sort of said I was speaking like a traitor to my country, or something.

Having returned to China to work following three years' study in Australia, Qin, who in her initial interview praised aspects of President Xi's leadership, offered related reflections:

When overseas students return to China, it seems we're not too crazy about China's politics. . . . I know that in China some people really praise Xi Jinping, but it seems that when we come back, we really don't. We all think, oh, he's pretty average. I mean, you know that policy, right, the issue of his continuous term? . . . When that [was announced], overseas students raised a storm of protest, both on WeChat and when we got together to discuss it. Everyone was saying, why must you change this policy? It felt like he just wanted to centralize power, that he wanted to concentrate power in the hands of a single person. Actually, we all think Xi Jinping is not too good. But people inside China watch CCTV news every day, and they might think, "Oh, he's pretty good, Chairman Xi," or whatever. . . . [After returning from abroad] I think I have more of my own way of thinking, and, most important, the channels through which we receive information are multiplied: we can see the news overseas, whereas they [in China] can't do so.

Like Yixin, Qin also criticized changes she had noticed in CCTV news content during the period she had been away, such that propagandistic coverage of the president's activities now took up the majority of the broadcast. Her observation about students overseas being critical of President Xi's rewriting of China's constitution in February 2018 to abolish the presidential term limit was borne out in conversations with other participants, several of whom spontaneously raised this as a point of critique, including some who had not voiced any political opinions before then.

Others took advantage of freely available media in Australia to investigate topics more difficult to research at home. These included the Tiananmen Square democratization movement of 1989 and the bloody crackdown that ended it, the treatment of North Korean citizens by that nation's totalitarian government, and behind-the-scenes factional struggles within the CCP, which one participant researched by reading Taiwanese news, even installing a VPN for her mother back home so that she could do the same. During our candid discussions about

Chinese politics, government, history, and media, several participants referred to the Chinese government as "brainwashing" (洗脑 *xi'nao*) the public on certain issues, and a couple said that now that they had access to different information abroad, they felt they had previously "been tricked" (被骗了 *bei pianle*) by the state media and education systems.

Becoming more critical of China's current government did not mean, however, that the students therefore became unpatriotic—as their distinction between loving the country and loving the government underlines. Rather, their critiques of aspects of China's governance tended to coexist with patriotic logics. For example, in one lengthy discussion with Changying and her friend Yuan about China's relationship with North Korea, the two expressed admiration for the Chinese administration for controlling the flow of Korean refugees across the Chinese border effectively and dealing with so many people and such complex social tensions and yet still maintaining a safe and stable society. But Changying also reflected:

> The price for this "safety" is the people not knowing what's really going on. The government won't tell them the true story. The Korean refugees are dealt with, sure—but where do they go? They won't tell you. Are they killed, or what? We don't know. This is the price we pay.

Recalling that Changying stated in her WeChat post, quoted at the beginning of this chapter, that she would like to punch Shuping Yang for her unpatriotic speech underlines the complexity of individuals' orientations toward the nation and state, which commonly encompass patriotism *and* mistrust; affective attachment *and* reflexive critique.

A third way in which students' understanding of Chinese identity was complicated was through some participants' growing appreciation of the internal heterogeneity of Chinese identity as a result of meeting people from Taiwan, Hong Kong, and Macau, where Beijing's line on the cultural and political unity of the motherland is fiercely contested. In a particularly thoughtful reflection early on in her time in Melbourne, Qi summed up how her social experience there had already complicated and even fragmented her former understanding of "China":

> In China you think: China is China. But here we find we need to divide it into China, Hong Kong, Taiwan, and Macau: four places. Some of my mainland Chinese classmates wonder why it gets divided this way and get angry about it. But I can accept dividing it this way. The issue is, I have met some Hong Kong classmates who, when discussing the

mainland, seem not to like it. They think the mainland has put a lot of pressure on Hong Kong, and that's what's forced them to come overseas. So debates arise. But you can't say what's right and what's wrong, since you're not in their position, and you don't understand what it's like for them. When you're in China, your field of vision lets you see the issue a certain way, but you get a more complete picture of things, from other people's point of view, from overseas.

During her fourth year in Melbourne, Shihong began boarding with an elderly Taiwanese landlady at a unit in Melbourne's leafy eastern suburbs. When I visited her there, I commented on the mah-jongg table I noticed folded against a wall in the dining room. Shihong explained that her landlady regularly hosted mah-jongg parties with her Taiwanese-Australian friends, all of whom had been born in mainland China but had emigrated to Taipei during the 1940s along with the Kuomintang's retreat and from there, later on, had moved to Melbourne. Good-humoredly but with veiled exasperation, Shihong described how the landlady liked to make gentle fun of her northern Chinese way of speaking and to imply that mainland China was less economically and technologically developed than Taiwan. The landlady also watched mainland Chinese TV dramas and used the opportunity to rail against their "Communist propaganda" and try to convince Shihong of the inaccuracy of their vilifying depictions of the Kuomintang. But despite these mild everyday tensions, Shihong also revealed that getting to know the landlady and her friends had led her to reflect anew on cross-strait relations. As we sipped our Nescafé lattes by the mah-jongg table, she told me that she now saw that each side had its own view and it was impossible to say which was objectively true. Before, when she had been exposed only to the mainland view, she used to find it incomprehensible that people in Taiwan could claim they were not Chinese (中国人 Zhongguoren). By contrast, she now saw that her landlady and her friends did recognize themselves as ethnically Chinese (华人 Huaren) but conceptually separated cultural identity from the politics of state. Shihong felt that her former view had not been objective because she had only been exposed to the PRC side of the argument. While she still did not agree totally with the views of the Taiwanese ladies, she, like Qi, respected the diversity of opinion and appreciated that each view was formed out of its own context.

Such responses, which were very common, do not entail that the Chinese students had their geopolitical worldview completely transformed by getting to know people from Taiwan, Hong Kong, or Macau while in Australia—although in several cases, as with Shihong, it did lead them to distance themselves from their earlier out-of-hand rejection of certain views counter to the party line. Rather, encounters with alternative iterations of Chinese identity—for example, as a transnational ethnocultural identity (Huaren) rather than one tied to a particular nation-state (Zhongguoren)—enabled the student transmigrants to denaturalize the concept of Chineseness to some degree. From the liminal space of study abroad, they were able to develop increasing reflexivity on fundamental questions of national identity, cultural affinity, and political allegiance and begin unpacking some of the contingent and volatile relationships among these (Chan 2005).

"Leaving the Country Is More Effective than a Hundred Patriotic Education Classes"

In her study of Korean, Japanese, and Chinese young women studying and working in London in the early 2000s, Youna Kim (2011, 93–113) found that these women's experiences of racism and social exclusion in the United Kingdom drove them to disengage socially and emotionally from the host society and reinforced their sense of ethnic and national(ist) allegiance to their home countries (see also Hail 2015, 318–19; cf. G. Li 2016). Despite the several ways that living abroad could complicate and render reflexive students' understandings of Chineseness, the opposite tendency that Kim describes was also evident among participants in the present study. It is encapsulated in the common assertion used as a heading for this section.[11] On one hand, this claim that going abroad tends to increase one's love for China is linked with the developmentalist-pride affective structure, insofar as students contrasted economic and technological development and middle-class perceptions of low crime and social stability in China's large cities favorably with the slower technological development, more visible poverty, and concerns about public safety in Western cities (e.g., Zhang W. 2014; see also chapter 3). On the other hand, the racism and social exclusion that the Chinese student transmigrants experienced in Australia also reinforced their national(ist) identification. Racist abuse, both verbal and physical, was a relatively common experience that tended to interrupt students' nascent local-level sense of (sub)urban belonging, as discussed in chapter 2. Here I focus on how this interruption to local belonging abroad may turn students back toward patriotic identification with China.

In early 2018, on a visit to see Qiqi and Yueming in Sydney, where they were then studying, I had dinner with them and their two male flatmates, also students from China, at their apartment near campus. Over Qiqi's red-braised pork, fried fish, and vegetable dishes and plastic beakers of the Australian shiraz

I had brought, I asked Qiqi and Yueming about their current feelings about China. A discussion ensued among the four flatmates about anti-Chinese racism in Australia. Qiqi recalled often seeing abusive graffiti in the women's bathrooms on campus in Melbourne ("lots of *fucking Chinese*"). Yueming related how a white man had muttered the same thing as he shoved past her while she and some other Chinese women were buying eggs in a supermarket. Qiqi described an even more upsetting incident in which her father, visiting from China, was subjected to a tirade of racist abuse by a young white man when her father mistakenly began to board a Sydney bus before an elderly white woman had had a chance to alight, although the woman had been obscured from Qiqi's father's line of sight and so he hadn't realized she was there. Bringing the discussion back to my original question about their feelings for China, Qiqi reflected:

> I think that sometimes these kinds of [patriotic] emotions can get magnified. Like, for example, we might think, when Westerners go to China, we're so polite to them, we look after them so well and whatever, . . . but yet, over here, we [are poorly treated]—and so these kinds of emotions get magnified. You inwardly feel the imbalance and don't have any sense of belonging, and so you don't like it [here]. . . . Right now in Shanghai you see Westerners everywhere. . . . And you feel like we really are so friendly toward them. . . . So this sense of the difference [in treatment] is really acute, and it's very depressing.

A few months later, I asked Yaling about her feelings about Canberra, where she was studying. She made related observations based on her experience of her and her friends being bullied by an Anglo student who spread lies about their behavior to the dorm administration, to the point that the three Chinese students chose to move out:

> I think that the locals here strongly reject us. . . . [Now] my preference . . . is to live with Chinese people. I felt like [the locals'] rejection of us is much stronger than our rejection of them. . . . We tried, but I feel like they refuse to let you integrate with them. . . . So I guess it's about a sense of belonging. . . . If this place gave you a strong sense of belonging, then maybe your feelings for it would become stronger than your feelings for China. . . . So I think you have to look at the country [Australia] itself, at how tolerant it is.

In light of the concerns expressed so vociferously by Australian politicians and media over the supposed dangers to Australian society posed by Chinese students' nationalism (Bishop 2017; Greene and Dziedzic 2017), Yaling's final observation is very much to the point. Both she and Qiqi underlined that their lack of a sense of belonging in Australia, caused or exacerbated by racism and social exclusion by "locals" (the Anglo-dominated social mainstream), tended to magnify and reinforce their attachment to China, in precisely the type of self-defensive maneuver noted by Kim (2011).

Parallel examples relate to participants' evaluations of Australian media, toward which, interestingly enough, some developed an increasingly critical attitude that echoed similar changes in their understanding of Chinese media. A pointed example is Mingyu's reflections on the effects of Australian media reporting of then foreign affairs minister Julie Bishop's (2017) "blunt warning" to Chinese students regarding their supposed threats to free speech on Australian university campuses. The Australian Broadcasting Corporation's current affairs program *Four Corners* had alleged that students' pro-China political activities on campus were orchestrated by Chinese Students and Scholars Associations (CSSAs) under the guidance of the Chinese embassy and the CCP (ABC 2017). Mingyu, then studying in Canberra, reflected:

> The media was constantly targeting . . . the Canberra CSSA. . . . My friend [in the club] said that . . . people from all the other clubs kept pointing at them and saying, "Isn't what you're doing a bit suspicious, aren't you spies?" and whatever. I actually think that the mainstream media in Australia didn't handle it very [well]; they manipulated the debate just like the media in China do. I think there's also that kind of media here, the kind that are influenced by politicians. They had no evidence, so why did they have to say that stuff? I used to think that in the West there was freedom of speech, but actually . . . I mean, why did they target the CSSAs without reason? . . . It might be that [the media] intentionally wanted to stir things up with them because of something to do with Australia-China relations. . . . I don't think it's really so democratic here.

Mingyu went on to tell me that she had previously considered joining the CSSA herself, since it organized activities for Chinese students who otherwise "have no sense of belonging here." This example underscores that the critical consciousness of media partiality that students may develop as a result of moving between different media systems may lead them to question media's propagandistic function in general—not solely with regard to Chinese media (see also Wanning Sun 2018b). It also highlights once more the vicious circle perpetuated by Australian authorities' public criticisms of Chinese international students' loyalty to the Chinese state, which served as a kind of self-fulfilling prophecy, exacerbating the students' alienation from any sense of identification with their host country.

National Feeling on the Move: Multiplicity,
Mutability, Ambivalence

This chapter has shown that mobile students' affective, political, and imaginative orientations toward the Chinese state and nation were characterized by a number of features. As a generational group, their national feeling was certainly informed by the state narrative taught to them through the Patriotic Education Campaign during their schooling. The state's potent story of a historically humiliated China, victimized by foreign imperial powers and only now able to rise up to defend her honor thanks to sound leadership and rapid economic development, often genuinely resonated for students to the point that, affectively, they experienced the nation's humiliation and honor as their own (Z. Wang 2008, 800). Thus, their identification with the state narrative of nationhood was founded on a deep emotional core. But equally central to their form of patriotism were performative elements: situationally appropriate social behavior and conventional protocols governing acceptable and unacceptable forms of speech about the nation. This patriotism was tied to a gendered metaphor of the homeland-as-motherland that centered the humiliation/honor dialectic, as well as associations with both duty and love that attend the culturally embedded concept of maternal filial piety. The mobile students' national structure of feeling was emotionally multivalent, drawing on a developmentalist narrative that sparked alternating currents of *national desire* for improvements in quality of life and international status, *national anxiety* over perceived cultural civility deficits, and—particularly in more recent years—*national pride* in China's technocapitalist urban development. Participants' national feeling took on a wide range of tonal registers, from "hot," earnest, and solemn to "cool," playful, and reflexive (G. Yang and Wang 2016). Theirs was a national structure of feeling that was imaginatively bound to the national geographic territory and yet most often communicated through—indeed constitutively shaped by—transnational digital media: it was a *digital nationalism* (Schneider 2018). The mobile students' patriotic self-representations were connected concurrently to nationalist and to cosmopolitan identity (Nyíri and Zhang 2010). Theirs was a form of *cosmopolitan nationalism* that was articulated with the imaginary of China's twenty-first-century expansion into the global arena, and which underscored the students' own role, as transnationally connected youth, in projecting positive representations of their homeland on the world stage.

However, although participants' collective orientations toward their homeland may be summarized roughly in these terms, what stands out more than anything is the multiplicity, ambivalence, and in-process character of these mobile students' national feelings. Unsettling totalizing views of both nationhood and nationalism and countering the simplistic assumptions that dominate many public discussions outside China, these young women's orientations toward the concept(s) of China were complex, dynamic, and certainly not uncritical. The experience of studying and living abroad did affect their understandings of, and feelings for, their homeland, but these effects, too, were complex and unpredictable and included either increasing or decreasing (or both increasing and decreasing, in different aspects) their subjective identification with China. Participants' expressions of feeling for the nation over the duration of this study ranged from deep emotional attachment to a primordial sense of people and culture to lighthearted play with national(ist) tropes; from painful anxiety over China's possibly uncultured image in the eyes of the world, to impassioned defenses of its honor in the face of perceived insults, to outspoken pride in the nation's embrace of technological development and its rapid economic, military, and political rise on the international stage; and from support for China's current leadership to indifference toward it to sharp critique of it. Attempting to capture a modicum of this complexity has meant resisting the pull of a cruder narrative that would frame study abroad as enabling the false consciousness of Chinese nationalist indoctrination to be swept aside like so much smog by the "fresh air" of Western democratic liberalism. But that is not these women's story.

Four years after my fieldwork began in mid-2015, those thirty-five core participants who had by then graduated with Australian degrees were scattered across Australia, China, and beyond. Sixteen remained in Australia: seven of these had permanent residency (PR: a five-year renewable visa with a minimum residency requirement of two years), while most of the others were on temporary graduate visas (available to foreign graduates of Australian universities, usually valid for eighteen or twenty-four months). Eleven were in full-time professional work, four were seeking work, and one had dropped out of contact. Eighteen more participants had returned to China, of whom seventeen remained in contact. Of these, one was undertaking further training, and sixteen had found full-time professional work: seven in the state sector, five in foreign firms, and four in Chinese private enterprises. One of the graduates working in China held Australian PR, and another was working there temporarily while waiting for her PR to be granted. The final graduate participant was working for a Chinese company in East Africa. During the course of the study, two participants had married men they met in Australia, and one participant in China had become engaged to someone introduced by her parents.

This summary illustrates some of the defining attributes of the participant group after several years' study in Australia. As well as being highly educated—almost all to master's degree level—these young, middle-class women overwhelmingly remained geographically mobile, professionally oriented, and unmarried into their late twenties. How had international education provided the conditions of emergence for these shared attributes, and how had it shaped participants' understandings of themselves vis-à-vis mobility, work, and their gendered life trajectory? This chapter explores these questions by focusing on participants' postgraduation experiences. It addresses one of the book's central inquiries: how overseas study ultimately impacted on participants' negotiation of the gendered contradiction between competing imperatives pushing them toward career focus and enterprising selfhood, on the one hand, and "timely" marriage and family-focused femininity, on the other. The first part of the chapter discusses graduates' work and work-seeking experiences in Australia and China, while the second part draws on postgraduation interviews to analyze the types of subjectivity that transnational education engendered for participants.

Life in Australia after Graduation: Mobility and Precarity

Most participants who stayed in Australia to work after graduation planned ultimately to apply for PR but (with the exception of two) not Australian citizenship. This was connected with China's nonrecognition of dual citizenship and with some participants' deep sense of loyalty to China (chapter 7). On a practical level, though, graduates tended to prefer the flexibility enabled by Australian PR, and prioritized the ideal of "selective citizenship" (L. Liu 2016b) and potential for ongoing mobility over settling down definitively in either country (Waters 2008; Brooks and Waters 2011, 134; Robertson 2013; Kajanus 2015, 125).

Australia's skilled-migration scheme, under which migrants may apply for PR, operates on a points system that, as Christina Ho (2020, 36–37) observes, reflects a neoliberal approach to immigration policy by hyperselecting for young, middle-class professionals. Points are awarded for applicant attributes including age (twenty-five to thirty-two being the most desirable), English proficiency as measured by standardized testing systems (International English Language Testing System [IELTS], Pearson Test of English [PTE], and others), work experience outside and/or inside Australia in a profession designated on the Strategic Skills List, educational qualifications, history of education or training in Australia, accreditation as a translator or interpreter in a community language, study and/or residency in a regional area, spouse attributes, and sponsorship by an Australian state (Australian Department of Home Affairs 2019). Against this backdrop, many of our conversations around the time of participants' graduation orbited around PR points requirements and the best way of meeting them (Robertson 2013, 88). Graduates enrolled in multiple courses in order to collect points, from certification in translation to IELTS and PTE cram classes; some made radical switches in major to ensure their qualifications would correspond with the Strategic Skills List; others bought internships or job placements from education-and-migration agents. They discussed plans to relocate temporarily to regional areas like Tasmania or Canberra and calculated how to delay applying until after their twenty-fifth birthdays to claim extra age-based points. All this took place in the context of ever-shifting bureaucratic requirements. Not only were certain occupations periodically removed from and added to the Strategic Skills List, but during the period of the study, the points requirements for most occupations on the list trended strongly upward. This resulted in an atmosphere of chronic uncertainty as graduates attempted to second-guess the ever-shifting regulatory system. Jiaying's late-2019 response to my question about whether she had been granted PR yet was typical:

> I haven't, I'm still waiting for an invitation from the immigration department [*sad emoji*]. Once I got four eights [in the IELTS English test], the points [requirement] went up again. Right now, I'm working as a *kinder teacher* in a kindergarten, and after one year this position will give me five points. I hope by then to have enough. . . . At the end of last year, seventy points was enough; then at the start of this year, it went up to seventy-five. Once I turned the right age and had seventy-five, it increased again to eighty-five. If the points keep going up like this, we might consider moving to a regional area. . . . I really have gathered all the points I possibly can: the English test, the interpreter qualification, employment experience—you just have to do everything you can and accept your fate, I guess.

Jiaying also told me that her young son (see chapter 5) was now in full-time kindergarten so that she could work—ironically, as a kindergarten teacher. But since her family's visa status meant that they were not eligible for government subsidies, the kindergarten fees were exorbitantly high and absorbed almost Jiaying's entire salary. In effect, Jiaying was working full-time for zero financial gain, the sole benefit being those five extra PR points. The points-accumulation treadmill is also expensive in other ways, with commercial agents in the expanding education-migration industry targeting aspiring applicants with for-fee services in training, test cramming, and job placement (Baas 2019).[1]

Given the lack of certainty about the ultimate success of one's PR application, some participants prepared two possible routes simultaneously: PR in Australia and job seeking in China. This meant that they might be concurrently scrambling to accumulate PR points while at the same time sending out job applications to companies in China and even flying back to attend the big spring and autumn job fairs and/or interviews. The timing of this could be virtually split-second. Corporate employers in China were understood to give preference to the latest cohort of graduates (应届生 *yingjiesheng*), so that if you spent too long in Australia without finding decent professional work, you could jeopardize your chance of landing a good job in China. A common sentiment was that if you hadn't found professional work locally six months after graduation, you would do better to cut your losses and go back to China while you still had *yingjiesheng* status. The emotional turbulence of this precarious period in participants' lives was compounded by continual flux in their social worlds as friends with whom they had shared their years in Australia seemed constantly to be departing, leaving them feeling emotionally abandoned and questioning their own attempts to stay.[2]

Indeed, participants often expressed ambivalence about PR: Was it really worth the trouble and expense? Did you even want to live in Australia, anyway? Was it becoming so hard to get that you may as well quit trying? Several participants mentioned friends who had been granted PR and subsequently returned to China owing to better job prospects there, so that their PR visas were canceled and all their efforts wasted. Thus, PR was not so much a holy grail (compare Robertson 2013, 88) as part of a wider assemblage of sought-after achievements and statuses connected to multiple possible futures that stretched across complex transnational geographies. Depending on individual circumstances, other parts of this assemblage might include taking up desirable work opportunities in Australia, China, or another country; obtaining internationally recognized professional certifications facilitating future work mobility; gaining party membership and passing the Chinese civil service exam, both prerequisites for a job in China's civil service; and/or acquiring an advantageous 户口 *hukou* (geographically based household registration) in China. Each of these brought with it its own type and level of difficulty and uncertainty, which were amplified by their combination. Thinking and planning across multiple national systems simultaneously, graduates lived amid an atmosphere of pervasive anxiety and risk (F. Martin, Erni, and Yue 2019).

Participants' sense of precarity was often exacerbated by the experience of seeking work in Australia. While one of the selling points touted by Australian governments and universities to prospective students in China is the chance to gain local professional experience after graduation, and commencing students often see this as a significant added value (chapter 1), in reality, many Australian employers simply refuse to accept job applicants—or even interns—on temporary graduate or bridging visas (Robertson 2013, 95). Participants in the accounting and finance fields regularly reported that employers, including some of the Big Four international accounting firms and the four major Australian banks, specified PR or citizenship as a condition of application. Other employers, through a circular logic worthy of Kafka, insisted on local work experience as a prerequisite for being offered local work (Ameeriar 2017, 161–62). Graduates' responses to this exclusion based on visa status (and arguably, more covertly, on race and nationality) were mixed. On one hand, they were frustrated to find themselves summarily locked out of desirable professional opportunities that were open to locals and permanent migrants. On the other hand, some voiced justifications of the employers' preferences, saying that it was "understandable" that bosses required local experience or were reluctant to hire graduates on temporary visas, since they would risk training them and then losing their investment if and when these employees left the country (see also Australian Education International 2010, 16). As we will see later in this chapter, this mixed attitude, aligning simultaneously with the conflicting perspectives of employee and employer, recurred among graduates who returned to China and faced gender-based discrimination in their job searches.

Illustrating the "bamboo ceiling" effect in the business and finance fields in Australia (B. Li 2017, 111–25; Ho 2020, 85–89), Cihui explained that she had chosen to return to China after graduating partly because only one Chinese graduate among all her acquaintances had managed to find professional work in Australia. "Even if you define work as work in a Chinese-run company, unless you want to do stuff like sell real estate or work as a tutor [you can't find work]. . . . There are so many people [i.e., Chinese students] over there, but those who can finally find a job [are so few]." Mingxi concurred:

> My good friend has her heart set on staying [in Australia]. Recently she's been constantly looking for work, and no matter where she looks, it's basically always the same few types available, either in retail sales or in waitressing. She finally found something in real estate, but the agency told her there's no wage, you just have to work for us until you manage to sell a property; and only after that will they pay you a wage. . . . She worked there for half a semester and didn't get paid a cent, just did the work for them. In the end she stopped doing it. It makes me think it's pretty hard for people like us to find work. Now she's found a job in retail sales for UGG [boots], but the pay is just twelve bucks [an hour]. . . . I think it ought to be at least eighteen, that's the minimum wage. These days most jobs are like that [i.e., underpaid]. . . . The people I know—including those who've already immigrated and got PR—are all working either in international education, or in real estate, or as tour guides. I feel like that type of work can't really—I mean, you can't just stay here and do that your whole life.

These observations are supported by figures from the Australian Bureau of Statistics (2016a), which show that among women from China on temporary graduate visas in 2016, a greater proportion were employed in lower-skilled jobs than as professionals or managers, and a sizable proportion were unemployed and seeking work.[3] Another salient point in Mingxi's observations is that graduates may be pulled back into local outgrowths of the transnational China-Australia education industry, for example, as IELTS tutors or education-migration agency workers. Others create microentrepreneurial opportunities on the fringes of this industry, for example, running home-cooked meal delivery services or settling-in services for recently arrived students. Such scenarios illustrate that Chinese graduates who remain in Australia risk becoming "downwardly global" despite their Australian postgraduate degrees (Ameeriar 2017).

The eleven participants who did manage to find professional work in Australia were envied by others and generally understood to possess specific forms of cultural capital, especially very high-level English and outgoing, expressive personalities that enabled them to fit in with local norms of sociability (Blackmore, Gribble, and Rahimi 2017). They worked in a variety of local companies and institutions, including a national bank, various trading companies, accounting firms, a government school, a kindergarten, a superannuation fund, and the Australian arm of a China-based property services group. Most of these workplaces had a majority of Australian-born staff, and the everyday sociality of the office or staff room often represented a turning point in participants' sense of their own "integration into local society" (融入当地社会 rongru dangdi shehui). Participants described companionable intraoffice relations: the novelty of a boss who liked to horse around, the weekly ritual of Friday-evening drinks, and chats among colleagues that seemed to suggest that people's everyday concerns were the same the world over. For those graduates fortunate enough to find professional work in Australia, the workplace often fulfilled a function that the university could not, facilitating a sense of cross-cultural interaction, learning, and subtle self-transformation.

Life in China after Graduation: Inequity and Ambivalence

Although they had returned to their country of citizenship, for many graduate returnees—popularly referred to as haigui (海归), a contraction of "overseas returnees" and a cute pun with the homophone haigui (海龟: sea turtles)—geographic mobility still loomed large both in their work life and in their imagination. In addition to now belonging to a tightly interconnected transnational network of overseas-educated graduates (Waters 2008, 153–87), returnees often remained professionally mobile within China. Many (eight of the seventeen who remained in contact) did not return to their hometowns but found work in larger Chinese cities and, in one case, in an East African branch of a Chinese company. This was sometimes understood as a temporary kind of "floating" (漂 *piao*) or "going out striving" (出去拼 *chuqu pin*) before, some assumed, their parents would expect them to return to their hometowns to marry and settle down. But for others, work-related mobility felt like an ongoing project with no fixed end, and it seemed possible that they could spend most of their adult lives far from their natal family and hometown.[4]

Some conceptualized work-related mobility mainly as short-term, hoping for jobs that would involve international business trips and the chance to take advantage of their knowledge of Australia, for example, in import-export ventures. Others imagined longer-term forms of professional mobility. For example, Shunqing, who landed a job at one of the Big Four accounting firms in Beijing, far from her hometown, reflected:

> Before I studied abroad, I thought I'll just research *Chinese literature*, just research some things about China. . . . Then I studied *finance* and *transferred* overseas, and I thought, "Oh, actually this is not bad, it's pretty good." Maybe in the future I could use English or even go abroad to work; . . . I started to have that idea. . . . If I had the chance, I might go to Europe or America to take a look, find a place that really suits me.

For such graduate returnees, the imagination—if not always the reality—of their lives had a global backdrop: they envisaged themselves in motion among China, Australia, Europe, America, and beyond.

As discussed in this book's introduction, transnational education has become a mass phenomenon among the children of China's urban middle classes. Thus, whereas a decade or two ago a degree from a Western university provided a substantial advantage in the search for professional work in China, today the sheer numbers of returning graduates have saturated labor markets and significantly eroded that competitive advantage (J. Hao, Wen, and Welch 2016; Fan 2017; S. Zhang and Xu 2020). The *haigui* glut and associated foreign-degree inflation were points of concern for most returnees. In this hypercompetitive labor market, job seekers could follow one of two routes: cold-call open application for positions advertised, or application via personal recommendation—the *guanxi* route.

Participants' responses to the idea of using *guanxi* to get a job were complex. They ranged from mild defensiveness, as when Shuyuan lamented the practice but assured me it was surely becoming less common along with rising levels of *suzhi* education in her generation; to proto-anthropological interest, as when Xiaofen compared and contrasted *guanxi* practices with those of Euro-American networking culture; to moral despair, as when Shunqing told me about brilliant colleagues from unconnected rural families who had only been able to secure middling jobs despite impeccable academic qualifications; to resentment, as when Fang told me about a dullard returnee acquaintance who had mysteriously landed a plum job at an investment bank. Many others voiced straightforward pragmatism: you'd be mad *not* to try your luck through *guanxi* connections, if you had them.

In an interview with Qiqi after her graduation, when she was back home looking for work, she offered a frank discussion of *guanxi*-based job seeking among her peers:

> I'm submitting my CV online and stuff, and also going through my parents to see if they can offer any introductions. . . . A lot of [my classmates] are going through internal recommendations; that is, they have relatives or friends working in a certain company, and they get in by recommendation. . . . If you've just graduated, finding a really good job is pretty difficult; it's very competitive in China, especially the finance industry. . . . I've heard that most people rely on *guanxi* and interpersonal networks to get in [*laughs*]. . . . [My parents] do know some people, so I can— but it's not like they know heaps. I can try going through them. I added an employment consultant [on WeChat], and he . . . said it's best if you have *guanxi*, try going through *guanxi* first, give that a go. . . . He said the hardest way is to try searching on your own. . . . Actually, most people who go out to study abroad, their families have a bit of money or else a bit of power, so they know quite a lot of people. So people in that circle, I've heard they mostly try out their *guanxi* first, when looking [for work].

Guanxi-based employment practices rely on established trust relationships between specific individuals, often involving parents and especially fathers. Along with Xiaoqing, Yueming, and others, Qiqi was part of a subgroup of participants who had come to Australia on a joint program between universities in Shanghai and Melbourne, which had low entry requirements but high fees (chapter 1). Qiqi was therefore right that her classmates generally came from well-off families; they also tended to be geographically well located, on China's wealthy eastern seaboard. This is another important prerequisite for effective job-seeking *guanxi*, since one requires connections with people who are powerful and motivated enough to help one and also located in a place where desirable jobs exist. Qiqi and her classmates' situations contrasted with those of other participants whose parents either lacked strong-enough connections or had them, but in the wrong locations (F. Collins et al. 2017).

A couple of years earlier, during a discussion in Melbourne with Qiqi and Yueming, Yueming had patiently explained to me:

Y: If we go back to China, our university majors won't have much of a connection with what we end up doing. . . . Because if you look at the concrete situation . . . [among joint-program graduates] before us—if you look for people who went out and found work that matched their major, . . . there are very few of them.

F: Oh, then how do people find work?

Y: Lean on Dad [拼爹 *pin die*]! [*both guffaw*] . . . For some people, university is a way out: she has to get a good major and then find work in that field, and only then can she have a good life. . . . There are those in remote areas for whom studying is the only way out. . . . But for us, that's not how it is. . . . Just lean on Dad, right. Saying it that way sounds a bit—[bad], but in fact that's the reality.

Qiqi's and Yueming's assumptions that their joint-program classmates would tend to rely on *guanxi* in the job hunt turned out to be accurate. Of the five in their cohort who had returned to China at the time of writing, three had landed professional jobs in the state and private sectors through *guanxi*: two through their father and one through an uncle; one other woman in the wider participant group also secured a job the same way, through her father. Even though a *guanxi* relationship was instrumental in landing these jobs, the graduates' master's degrees remained a prerequisite, since they had to meet the basic criteria to justify their being offered the positions. But sometimes this form of job hunting led to paradoxical results, with graduates "following the *guanxi*" to wind up in jobs far outside the fields of their expertise. As Yueming put it, when following the *guanxi* route, "If you study a certain major and then happen to get a related professional position, that's just good luck." One young woman I met in Shaanxi had a Chinese undergraduate degree in art, an Australian master's degree in media, and a job via paternal *guanxi* as a financial product developer in a state-run loans company.

For graduates who returned to China, the job hunt was also shaped by their understanding of the characteristics of different employment sectors, which related in complex ways to gender. Some parents encouraged their daughters toward civil service (公务员 *gongwuyuan*) positions, which were seen as safe, stable, and low-stress and hence suitable for girls, illustrating how "appropriate employment for women [is] symbolically aligned with the state" (Hoffman 2010, 123). More ambitious graduates, however, resisted this pressure, preferring to pursue opportunities in the private sector, which they saw as more challenging and more promising for professional advancement. State enterprises were often seen as stable but possibly hidebound, with rusted-on senior colleagues unwilling to change with the times and potentially hostile to *haigui* introducing new approaches from overseas. Many participants' first preference was to work in a foreign enterprise. These were understood to have all the advantages of private Chinese companies but with less sexism, better pay, better conditions, and a more global outlook and opportunities: the obvious choice for *haigui* women (W. Zheng 2003; Duthie 2005; A. Ong 2008).

However, foreign companies like the Big Four accounting firms also had a reputation for working new recruits to the bone. As Mingyu told me just before she started working at one of these firms:

> Everyone says it's exhausting at the Big Four. As soon as they hear I'm going there, they're all like, "Oh, you're going there, you better get yourself in shape [赶紧养好身体 *ganjin yanghao shenti*]." . . . But . . . for new graduates, . . . the Big Four are a pretty good springboard.

This view was echoed frequently. The consensus was that if you could stick it out for two years at one of these firms, then you'd be well placed to job-hop (跳槽 *tiaocao*) to a more sustainable position elsewhere.

This image of the Big Four was supported by the experience of Shunqing, who had worked at one of these firms for several months at the time of our final interview. She and other graduates working in foreign enterprises confirmed that the proportion of *haigui* women was high at the entry level and in office-based jobs like finance, marketing, legal, and public relations, although in upper management and "outside" roles like sales, men often predominated. A high achiever but not naturally a driven personality, Shunqing found working at the firm grueling:

> I'm on the *auditing, assurance* track. I knew that I'd be under a lot of pressure [working] over here. . . . I got the job in October last year. Since I began in November, I've been continually doing overtime, every night 'til eleven or twelve o'clock. And then from December to April, I've had to work on Saturdays as well, plus half a day on Sundays. That's how it is. . . . *Super busy*, really so, so exhausting. . . . I feel like when I'm so, so busy, my nerves are on the point of breaking, I'm scared I'm going to get sick. At the end of April, the *annual audit* was finished. . . . Once it was over, there was a holiday, Labor Day on May first. On the holiday I did get sick; I suddenly got a cold and a fever, because my system was so weakened. . . . In China today, work in Beijing and Shanghai is a lot like America's *Wall Street*. If you don't do it, you'll just be fired, and they'll hire someone else, so there's nothing you can do about it; all you can

do is keep pushing on. Because of that, everyone's exhausted, but there's nothing you can do. Nobody will say, "I'm not doing this, *I quit.*"

Unsurprisingly, the employee turnover rate at entry level in the Big Four accounting firms was understood to be extremely high. They churned rapidly through young finance and accounting graduates like some middle-class, professional version of the Pearl Delta's factories with their voracious appetite for migrant laborers (L. Chang 2009; H. Yan 2008; Gaetano 2015; T. Liu 2018).[5]

The returnees' job hunt was directly shaped by gendered pressures and restrictions. Chapter 1 explored participants' predeparture hopes that increasing one's competitiveness by means of a Western degree might compensate for gendered bias in China's professional labor market. But returning with Australian master's degrees in hand a few years later, many found that employers' gender bias still obstructed their path and was sometimes actually exacerbated after overseas study because the graduates were now a few years older. Cihui, for example, described her disillusionment on attending a seminar about the finance industry in which the main presenter, himself an employer in a brokerage firm, directly stated that his firm would hire women as unpaid three-month interns for minor clerical tasks but strongly preferred men as full-time employees. He justified this gendered division of labor and opportunity by asserting that while women didn't mind doing fiddly jobs around the office for which men lacked patience, men were better suited to auditing, which involved work outside the office, including visits to farms and factories in rural areas (Hoffman 2010, 121–41): "He thought this kind of thing wasn't suitable for girls; it's hard work. They like boys to do it, because with boys, no matter how hard you push them, even if they only get three hours' sleep, it doesn't matter." This employer seemed determined to maximize the exploitation of his workforce along gendered lines: unpaid young women inside the office, salaried young men worked to the bone outside. "When I heard that, I felt so disappointed about this industry," said Cihui, "because I'd [unsuccessfully] applied to some of those firms myself and not got any feedback."

Other graduate returnees discussed the toxic combination of gender and age bias that affects unmarried or married but childless female applicants in their late twenties and over:

> I used [before studying abroad] to work as an *auditor* in an accountancy firm, and one of the things I did there was connected with the brokerage line, sort of front-to-middle-office level. But in [my Zhejiang hometown], truly at the age I am now [twenty-seven], a woman who is unmarried and without children can hardly even get an interview. I've even heard of cases

where . . . colleagues got to the final round of interviews, and then they said, "Oh, you're already married—," and then "Let's just leave it here for today then." It's a pretty serious situation. Anyway, the process of my finding a job wasn't very smooth at all. And for those that I did find, the salary was far below the figure I'd hoped for. (Xiaofen)

Here in China, when you're looking for work, age discrimination is still very serious. They think that you'll soon be over the suitable age for marriage and children, so you might be just about to get married and have a baby. That'll be a loss from the company's point of view, so they tend not to hire people of our age [thirty-two]. . . . I think if I were five years younger, I might have more work opportunities. . . . Looking at job ads, I can completely meet their requirements, but in fact one reason why they won't tend to pick me is probably the age issue. (Fang)

Thus, while overseas study may have been intended to counter gender bias in the job market, such bias may paradoxically be exacerbated for graduate returnees given the years needed to earn the extra qualification.

While many participants criticized this situation, a countercurrent also ran through our discussions, with some returnees oscillating between resentment and a degree of sympathy for the employers who discriminated against them. For example:

Y: In looking for work, we really have felt there's a bit of gender discrimination.

W: Yes. I came back previously to do an internship in an insurance company. And my . . . section chief asked if I wanted to . . . go back and work there after graduation. . . . One of the directors and that manager both asked me to stay. Then our dad asked the big boss, the financial manager, and he said they only wanted boys and not girls. . . . Also, this last time I came back, at one of the companies [where I sought work], the same thing happened, a state enterprise. . . . The financial manager also said they wanted boys and didn't want girls. . . .

Y: I made [an application] in *assurance*, auditing. My dad asked—because I was on the waiting list. . . . But then, when my dad's friend went to put in a word for me with the *assurance* [section] boss, it turned out that he said—

W: "We want boys, not girls." . . . With us, it's because our dad knows them that they might tell you straight up. But if you're just directly rejected, there's no way that HR [would tell you]—

Y: Right. If they drop you, you wouldn't even know why you're dropped.

w: But actually if you think about it, it makes sense. . . . Before, when I had an interview, they asked me, "Do you have a boyfriend?" or whatever. They're most worried that you'll get married as soon as you start [work], then have a baby, and they'll have to support [养 *yang*] you. . . . You haven't even learned anything, and he still has to support you. The cost is too high.

. . .

Y: If you stand in the shoes of the employer, actually you can [understand their position].

(Mingwen [W] and her sister Mingyu [Y])

You might have a second baby. If you go looking for work [after your first baby], HR will definitely ask, "Do you have any plans for children in the future?" Or if you're recently married, they'll ask you, "Do you want a baby?" . . . These days the vast majority will all ask that. Because this [connects with] willingness to work. . . . If you start there and straightaway have a baby—the company isn't a charity, after all. Why would I want to bring someone in, act like a charity, right? Once the proportion of that type [of cases] increases, HR will definitely say I'm definitely hiring boys, I'm not hiring girls. . . . When I think about it, I can understand it. You go in, then whoosh you're gone, but you're still drawing your salary. The company won't be willing to hire an extra person, pay double the salary for one share of work. . . . Also, during a woman's pregnancy, the company can't dismiss her, that's against labor law. . . . In China the employment environment is very tough for women. In terms of discrimination, you could say it's inherent, nothing you can do about it, it's just there. (Cihui)

What stands out in these accounts is the split self-positioning of the speakers, vacillating between resentment of their own gendered disadvantage and sympathy for the employers who exclude them. Rather than being inspired to solidarity with other disadvantaged workers or further structural analysis of the gendered costs of reproduction in a market society with limited state funding for parental leave, they tend to view the issue from two contradictory perspectives simultaneously. This echoes the ambivalent attitude of the graduate job seekers in Australia discussed earlier, who resented but also "could understand" employers' discrimination against them based on their status as temporary visa holders. This attitudinal alignment across two different situations suggests a general tendency in the group to identify, against one's own immediate interests as an employee, with the point of view of a business owner or manager viewing her workforce in terms of cost-benefit analysis and profit maximization. This is congruent with most participants' position as daughters of middle-class entrepreneurs, managers, and upper-level professionals. Thus, while, on the one hand, the graduate returnees experienced multiple disadvantages in their job searches related to gender, age, qualifications, family connections, and marital and parental statuses, which sometimes left them feeling helpless and despairing, on the other hand, they tended to put up with the inequitable present while clinging to the dream that things might improve in the future if they could only climb higher up the professional hierarchy.

Haigui *Subjectivity: The Mobile Enterprising Individual*

Xiaofen, the daughter of a university-educated entrepreneur and an administrative worker in a state enterprise, is twenty-four when I first meet her a couple of weeks after she arrives in Australia. She has traveled to the prestigious Capital University in Melbourne to pursue a two-year master's degree in accounting. Following her bachelor's degree from a top-ranked Chinese university, she has already worked for nearly three years in one of the Big Four accounting firms in her hometown: a wealthy medium-sized city on China's east coast. Xiaofen has a steady boyfriend of seven years, and although the couple has no immediate plans to marry, she expects that she will most likely bow to social pressure to get married and have a child before she turns thirty. At our first meeting, Xiaofen tells me she feels she was a bit headstrong (任性 renxing) in deciding to study abroad at this point in her life. In doing so, she is flouting the traditional view that girls her age should settle down into marriage: she feels this is her last chance to realize her dream of overseas study.

Xiaofen does well in her studies in Melbourne and wins a competitive application for an internship in Singapore. During her second year in Australia, she is already working toward a PR application and hopes to gain some local professional experience after graduation.

But during Xiaofen's second year in Melbourne, her plans are interrupted by heartbreak. Out of the blue, her boyfriend back in China breaks off their relationship, saying that his parents are pushing him to get married and implying that she has been unreasonable in leaving him in order to study abroad. Having picked a fight on the issue and forced a breakup over the phone, the ex-boyfriend refuses to communicate with Xiaofen at all, leaving her angry and confused. She redoubles her resolve to stay on in Australia and find professional work after graduation.

But eight months later, Xiaofen is still in emotional turmoil—all the more so after she sees her ex with a new girlfriend during a trip home. As she updates me on her situation, her eyes fill with tears:

I thought I was totally calm and over this, but it seems not—

Xiaofen is at the lowest point in her life so far. She begins to regret her decision to study abroad since it has cost her not only an enviable and well-paid job but also her relationship with her first love. At her age, Xiaofen worries that both will be difficult to replace. She is finding it hard to cope in Australia without close friends and family to support her and recently made a trip back to see her parents:

As soon as I stepped off the plane, everything—from how [my hometown] smelled, to how it looked and sounded, to the knowledge that my parents were there to look after me—it all just drew me back. And I realized I need to spend some time there, to recover, before taking my next step.

Xiaofen goes back to her hometown straight after graduation. After a demoralizing job search in which, as a childless woman of twenty-seven, she is passed over for many positions far more junior than the one she had previously held, she finally finds work at an internet company in Shanghai.

I meet her there shortly after she begins her job. Now feeling emotionally stronger, Xiaofen reflects that studying abroad has consolidated in her a mobile life outlook. She has by now obtained Australian pr and imagines her own future and that of her hypothetical future child unfolding in a global context and involving ongoing potentials for transnational movement.

I would definitely consider [working in Australia], . . . so at least the baby could have a choice. Because I guess I'll probably have a child in the next five years, so later on, even if I don't go over myself, I will be able to choose a [citizenship] status for the baby, right? . . . All [places] are alike, including, for example, going abroad—I think it's just the same [as going to another city]. It's something I could do if I have the opportunity.

I see Xiaofen in Shanghai again the following year. By chance, we meet the day after she returns from a quick trip to Australia to activate her PR visa. She returns again to the same point:

[Studying abroad,] you have to rely on yourself to deal with everything. I remember the first time I arrived in Australia, when I first set foot on that *land, I was so scared. . . . I didn't really understand the street signs; I didn't even know how to get anything to eat. . . . I felt very scared then. But this last time I went back completely alone, and I didn't feel anything at all. . . . So now, actually, if you put me into a new and strange environment—oh, the change [in me] is very great. . . . Today, from making a plan to going there—Where am I going? How do I get there? [I can manage it all]. . . . I really am not afraid of a strange environment. . . . In terms of self-confidence, this experience . . . has really been a big help. . . .*

I feel that having completed this [study abroad], I have more choices for the future. I feel my mind has been broadened. I feel that if the job I have right now doesn't work out, then I could work toward living overseas. That might be easy to say, but it's actually not simple to do. Both physically and mentally, it's a more solitary [孤独 gudu] condition. . . . It seems I have an extra option compared with other people. . . . If I wanted to change my environment and my life, I'd be able to do so right away.

Xiaofen also reflects on having learned from observing what she calls other people's "tough," independent way of handling life problems:

In life, if you run into difficulties or find yourself in a bad situation, you'll certainly have more self-confidence and be able to resolve things more calmly. I really do think this truly is due to having studied abroad. Because if I look at examples around me, like colleagues who've had two children, or classmates who got married and had babies pretty soon after graduating, . . . what I mean is if people around you are all living that way, then you might not realize, oh, there's another, tougher way to live. . . . That when you run into a problem, you can actually look within yourself to find strength and support.

~

Twenty-year-old Xiaoxing is the first among her family and friends to study abroad. The daughter of middle-school-educated small-business owners in an industrial town in Guangdong, she traveled north to Henan for university. There, she enrolled in a joint program in international economics that linked her Chinese university with Queens University in Melbourne: both midranked institutions. Xiaoxing's first language is Cantonese, and while introducing herself at our first full-group activity, she apologizes to everyone for her accented Mandarin. Xiaoxing describes her parents as "feudal" (封建 fengjian) in that they do not permit her to have boyfriends while she is still studying. But she follows their rules.

During her two years at Queens University and subsequent one-year master's course at New Holland University in Sydney, Xiaoxing seeks out every opportunity for volunteering and work-related training, consulting me about what to wear to professional appointments and where to buy such clothes. She speaks with her parents via video call several times a week and during university breaks usually goes back home to help out at the printing shop they run in a neighborhood market. She hopes one day to earn enough money to let them stop working such a physically demanding job.

Although Xiaoxing likes the idea of staying on in Australia to gain local professional experience, in the event, she goes home straight after graduation in order to complete her application for party membership. Xiaoxing started her membership application during her first year of undergraduate studies in Henan, and before she can be admitted as a full member, she still has to be "investigated" by party authorities at home for six months to a year. She explains that her father is encouraging her to join the party as a matter of family pride:

> *For him, it might be sort of a spiritual comfort. . . . Kind of like our family had no one who'd been to university. . . . I'm pretty much the first real university graduate in our family. . . . My dad looks at it sort of like that. He feels it'd be . . . something like an honor for me to join the Chinese Communist Party.*

When I interview her again a couple of months after her return home, Xiaoxing gives the following account of her job search:

> *As soon as I got home, my parents started suggesting pretty strongly that I stay in my hometown to work. . . . A couple of weeks after I got back, I got an invitation for a job interview. The company was in a district of Shenzhen pretty far from the central city area. . . . When my dad found out, he wouldn't agree to let me go. But the way I saw it, if you go to an interview, it doesn't mean they're necessarily going to hire you. I wanted to . . . increase my interview experience to help me in the future. But he wouldn't even let me go there. . . . I had to say, OK, I guess I'll give up this interview opportunity. After that, my parents had a talk with me. They asked me not to put myself under pressure to find work immediately. . . . And then they raised another point, which was that they don't . . . really want to allow me to go even to [nearby] Guangzhou to work. But actually I . . . myself, I have this wish, I really do want to go out and experience the outside world, to grow up a bit. So right now I guess I should work on discussing this further with them. I've mentioned it to you before: their thinking is fairly tradi-*

tional. . . . [But] if my parents don't agree, I . . . can't just insist on going away to work. . . . The place where I live, if I want to find work in the finance field, opportunities will be very, very few. . . . There are probably no positions in the type of work I want to do around this area. Lately [the opportunities] are all in Guangzhou, or in certain other areas, because my hometown has more of a concentration of manufacturing, and lately logistics. . . . It doesn't really fit with my professional direction, so I really need to go to Guangzhou or Shenzhen or another city. . . . Right now, near our home, in a residential area . . . , there is a public institution [事业单位 shiye danwei] seeking staff. I mean, my parents want me to take the civil service exam. But I haven't registered to do it, because I feel that asking me to suddenly change my professional direction like that is a bit much. So right now I'm preparing for the entry test for this job near home, to give it a try, and I'm also still having a go at finding work according to my own career plan, in the finance field. . . . If I can find it, my first preference would be [a job in] a foreign enterprise.

Xiaoxing points to some of the ways she feels study abroad has changed her:

Before, at my old university in China, [my life] was more traditional, really like "three-points-one-line" [i.e., shuttling among dormitory, classroom, and canteen]. . . . Going out [abroad], you have to do everything by yourself, and you need to understand how to manage your own time; you might even need to find a part-time job—you have to organize everything yourself and plan it all—so I feel that I've had this kind of experience a bit earlier [than others]. . . . It's changed my attitude. . . . If I'd stayed at home, I might find going out to seek a part-time job or other work a bit embarrassing, that's how I felt at the time. But since I went out, it just feels like a very natural thing; . . . it even makes me happy to rely on my own efforts to find a job.

But when I next hear from her a few months later, Xiaoxing has taken the job her parents preferred, unrelated to her studies, in the local government organization. In a WeChat message, she describes her work in glowing party-speak:

I've learned lots of new knowledge, especially work connected with party affairs. It's been very good lately; I've had more responsibilities in work connected with building the party, so life has been very fulfilling [grinning emoji]. My work responsibilities are connected with themed activities organized by the work unit to serve the masses of the people and the in-

dustrial park enterprises, for example, a free clinic to promote workplace health, a flower-arranging activity to express care for women, et cetera. It's increased my abilities in event management and my capacity to communicate proactively with others, and brought me closer to the masses of the people and corporate representatives, which assists with advancing my daily work.

~

Xiaofen and Xiaoxing, two young women returning with Australian master's degrees hoping to find work in the Chinese segment of the global financial sector, told stories that mirror each other in some respects but diverge importantly in others. Both expressed desires for ongoing geographic mobility: Xiaofen at the transnational level, as a form of selective citizenship enabled by her Australian PR (L. Liu 2016b); Xiaoxing at the domestic level, as intercity professional mobility. Each woman also embodied a certain amount of mobility capital (Kaufmann, Bergman, and Joye 2004; Brooks and Waters 2011, 155), though the levels were distinguished by class differentials, as were their capacities to convert it. With her comfortable family background, prestigious Chinese and Australian degrees, high-level professional work experience, English language capacity, and Australian PR, Xiaofen was quite conscious of her own mobility capital and understood it through the rubric of multiplied choices. It afforded her a way of experiencing the world such that, with the exception of the affective resonance of her own hometown, "all places are alike." Xiaoxing was also aware of the potential for mobility that her qualifications gave her—they could be a ticket to a professional career in a large city, possibly even a job in a foreign firm: a far cry from the sociospatial restriction of her former "three-points-one-line" undergraduate days. But in the face of parental opposition to her leaving her hometown, she struggled to realize that potential. Xiaoxing's corralling into the state sector in the neighborhood government organization sharply illustrates Lisa Hoffman's (2010, 123) observation about the alignment between neotraditionalist gender regulation and the socialist state apparatus; it also brings into focus a gendered geography of feminine spatial restriction activated through Xiaoxing's parents' class-bound traditionalism (Massey 1994; Hanson 2010).

Feminine gender restricted each woman's potentials, but differently. In Xiaofen's case, such restriction took effect largely in the realms of work and marriage. The combination of her gender and her "advancing" age on the one hand limited her professional opportunities, thanks to employer bias, and on the other hand damaged her chances on the marriage market, demonstrated when her boyfriend and his family decided that her educational mobility made her too big a risk as a potential bride. For Xiaoxing, conversely, it was her own family that enforced gendered restrictions that limited her career options as well as her mobility. For Xiaofen, home and parents played the role of emotional support and sanctuary: a welcome retreat when life on her own became hard to bear. For Xiaoxing, in contrast, family was the locus of both restriction and responsibility: the duty to provide future financial care for her parents was at the forefront of her considerations. Both women voiced an individualized self-view, underlining values of self-confidence, toughness, and self-reliance (靠自己 *kao ziji*), and both tried to place their own desires, plans, and interests at their life's center. But Xiaofen, identifying with a geographically and socially disembedded "solitary condition" of ongoing transnational mobility, was able to voice a stronger version of this discourse than Xiaoxing, who knew that if her "parents [didn't] agree, [she couldn't] just insist on going away to work."

Despite these class-bound contrasts, Xiaofen's and Xiaoxing's accounts of returning to China and reflections on how their journeys had changed them share key elements, which were reflected and extended in the narratives of many others. These elements, which I propose delineate a specific form of *haigui* subjectivity, include a mobile imaginary (see this chapter's first section), ideological individualization, ambition, reflexivity, consumerism, professional orientation, and gender detraditionalization. I return to the final point in the last part of this chapter; the following section elaborates on the middle five points with reference to other returnees' interview responses.

INDIVIDUALIZATION

A central theme in graduate participants' responses about how study abroad had changed them was that the experience had strengthened their resolution to "claim [their] ownness" (Tadiar 2009, 60). They dwelled on the value of "living life in your own way" (按自己的方式生活 *an zijide fangshi shenghuo*: Shang), "living out my own self" (活出我自己 *huochu wo ziji*: Yining), "living for yourself" (为自己而活 *wei ziji er huo*: Ruomei), "living more self-centeredly" (活得更自我 *huode geng ziwo*: Shuyuan), and "living to become yourself" (活成你自己 *huo cheng ni ziji*: Mei) instead of deferring to or relying on others. This equates to the conviction that one's own desires, happiness, and interests ought to constitute the core concerns in one's life and that one should become self-reliant (靠自己 *kao ziji*), independent (独立 *duli*), and autonomous (自主 *zizhu*). Returnees, it was felt, tended to "care more about what they themselves care about and pay less attention to other things" (Shang); they "had more of [their] own ideas" (Yining) and could "make any kind of decision and completely and utterly shoulder the consequences" (Fang). This valuing of gendered sovereignty marks a form of ideological individualization: the aspiration to live for oneself rather than for others (Beck and Beck-Gernsheim 2002; Y. Yan 2009; Kim 2011). Such an orientation is particularly clear in Shuyuan's account of her discussion with a colleague who asked her advice on *haigui* psychology to help him understand his son, a graduate returnee from Sydney:

> I find that [those who have studied abroad] first of all want to ensure that we're not compromised [委屈 *weiqu*]; that is, we want to let ourselves live happily [让自己活得开心 *rang ziji huode kaixin*]. But [my colleague]'s opinion is that letting yourself live happily occupies a position of secondary importance; you should put thinking of your family—thinking of your elders or thinking of your children—in the position of primary importance. My opinion on this only changed after studying abroad. I mean to say, people only live for a few decades, so why should you compromise yourself in order to fulfill others? Even if it's the others in your family—they ought to have their own lives, too. Nobody should live for the sake of others; it ought to be for their own sake.

Many felt that the experience of living abroad without family support fostered temperamental independence and hence self-focus. The change began with learning practical life skills—assembling flatpack furniture, managing housework, finding casual work, negotiating rental leases—and extended into a more fundamental reorientation of one's priorities. The emergent, more individualized identity was then expressed in everyday activities undertaken solo. For example, sisters Mingwen and Mingyu discussed how three years living in Melbourne and Canberra, away from family and collective dorm life in China, had made them much more comfortable eating, window-shopping, and going to class alone. Mingyu also linked this with her imagined future professional habitus:

> I think it's really useful [for work]. Like last time I did an internship—and I'm guessing this is how it will be in future, too—I went on a business trip with my colleagues. We went to Beijing by high-speed rail, but we didn't sit together; I just sat by myself. Before, in China, that would have seemed a bit weird. But now I feel it's pretty good; you feel like you have some personal space. We were on the same train, but we didn't see each other until we alighted in Beijing four and a half hours later. Things like that seem really normal now.

AMBITION

The type of subjectivity that participants felt was fostered by study abroad was not only individualized but also ambitious, proactive (主动 *zhudong*), and self-confident (自信 *zixin*) in its pursuit of goals (目标 *mubiao*). The ideal *haigui* subject embodies a refusal to rely on support from either family or state, striving instead to grasp every opportunity and improve her human capital by her own efforts (Y. Yan 2013). All graduate participants felt a level of compulsion to embody such a drive, even those who were ambivalent about whether a life of relentless striving would be truly satisfying. This attitude was summarized neatly by Shang when I spoke with her several months after her return to China, when she was eking out a precarious living far from home in Shanghai:[6]

> Students who have had this experience of overseas education might be a bit more self-confident; they'll know what they want. They won't be like . . . , I've got a job, I'm going to cling to it for grim death. . . . [If I hadn't studied abroad], I might still not know what I wanted. . . . I've really learned something from [study abroad]; that is, . . . unless you're proactive, you might not get an opportunity. Like, for example, I sent out my CV everywhere. I went around saying, "Could I send you my CV to take a look at?" And I even proactively made contact with HR departments and said, "Could I get an opportunity here?" I made myself more and more into a proactive person. Because I think that opportunities are very limited in the first place, so if you're not proactive, if you're passive, you might not get any opportunities. . . . Through this self-training overseas, I've been able to make myself more independent; I've gone more in this direction, proactively developed myself. . . . All of those who went abroad and came back—unless they prefer something safe and stable, like being a civil servant or a teacher—all of them have certain hopes for their future. They hope to do something.

Shang's focus on self-confidence, a proactive attitude, self-development, and ambition (the "hope to do something") encapsulates the drive toward autonomous self-advancement that is central to the postsocialist *haigui* subjectivity articulated by the graduate group as a whole.

REFLEXIVITY

Shang's emphasis on self-knowledge—the importance of knowing what one wants—also points toward another central feature of self-perceived *haigui* subjectivity: its reflexivity (Qing Gu 2015). The *haigui* subject is a subject who knows herself. She looks out on broad horizons; conscious of the relativity of cultures and systems, she is inspired to reflect on the limits of the local and feels herself to be at home in diversity. Along these lines, Yining reflected during a return visit to Melbourne after a year working in Shanghai:

> Maybe because of having studied abroad, I . . . expect more in terms of tolerance [包容 *baorong*]. People with a narrower worldview, their level of tolerance won't be as high as those with a broader worldview. People with a narrower worldview will only be able to see this little circle, and they'll think the things people outside this little circle do are all wrong. People with a higher level of tolerance will find all of these things *acceptable*, that everyone has their own way of living, and you shouldn't *judge* other people.

This self-ascription of increased tolerance following study abroad was repeated by many. It was typically accompanied by the idea, also seen in Yining's statement, that knowledge of the plurality of cultural systems tended to relativize one's own understanding of oneself and one's beliefs and values. Educational mobility was thought to foster a new level of reflexivity by broadening the *haigui*'s field of vision beyond the "little circle" of local life that previously constituted her world, by which her non-*haigui* peers were understood to remain constricted (S. Zhang and Xu 2020).

CONSUMERISM

Some *haigui* also described a change in their attitude toward consumption as a result of having studied abroad. In Australia the students commonly lived amid the affluent consumer culture in the downtown districts of the large east coast cities, devoting their leisure time to coffee and brunches in trendy cafés and tourist trips to picturesque country attractions, all of which they photographed and circulated via their WeChat and Instagram feeds (chapter 2). Most were also in daily contact with friends, classmates, or flatmates engaged in e-trading (代购 *daigou*), in which the act of consumption itself—of foods, health products, clothing, jewelry, cosmetics, and luxury goods—is monetized for the reseller's profit, once again with images of the commodities circulated endlessly via social media. In this context, returnee Qiqi (flatmate and confidante of Yueming, the "*daigou* queen"; see chapter 4) observed:

> You get a certain understanding of luxury goods and name brands. Before I went overseas, I didn't really know about these. When I was in China before, I thought these were too luxurious to buy. Now that I'm

back from abroad, I think nothing of it.... You're not so wary of this type of high-end consumption.

Shuyuan, too, felt her attitude toward luxury consumption had changed. She attributed this to the generally wealthy background ("kind of a step above middle class") of Chinese students in Australia and the high-end beauty and fashion culture among her Chinese female friends there. Shuyuan contrasted her new openness to luxury clothing, cosmetics, and accessories with her family's consumption habitus at home:

> Previously, I had a very thrifty view on consumption; that's the influence of my family.... My maternal grandma and grandpa lived in very poor conditions when they were young. After they began working, conditions at home improved, but their consumption habits stayed at a very low level; ... they were very thrifty. My mum's like that, too. She thinks that you shouldn't buy things you don't need.... When I first went overseas, I was that way, too.... But later, living in that environment, I integrated with [the wealthy students], and I started to buy [luxury goods]. And once I started, I felt that once you've earned that money, ... if you have nowhere to spend it, then ... it's no use whatsoever to my life. So then I started spending a bit more money to buy a few things that weren't very useful but made me happy.

Shuyuan's narrative illustrates a conceptual connection between discretionary consumption and the broader *haigui* valorization of self-focus and individual happiness.

PROFESSIONALISM

In an earlier quotation, Mingyu reflected that the individualization of everyday practices she had learned while studying abroad might be useful for her future professional life. Others, too, explicitly linked the characteristics of their emergent *haigui* subjectivity to the requirements of the professional workplace. For example, Fang, a graduate returnee from Yunnan living and working in Shanghai, reflected:

> [If I hadn't studied abroad,] my life goals wouldn't be so lofty; you wouldn't look at your career as a very important part of your life; it would be about the same level of importance as your marriage. You might be more inclined to go along with traditional thinking, that is, that girls should just find a safe, steady job and then get married and have children. I also think that my achievements wouldn't be so good.... I think that

study abroad has helped broaden my horizons, so you can see different issues and perspectives, and that could influence your own future [professional] development [发展 *fazhan*]. I think, previously, my worldview wasn't so broad, and I didn't think so much about issues, and my personality wasn't so independent—the limitations in terms of future work are fairly obvious.

After graduation, all participants in this study—regardless of their level of professional ambition, the strength of their drive for self-advancement, their geographic location, their marital status, or their plans for marriage—hoped to work professionally at least for a few years, and most, like Fang, said they prioritized professional development over marriage and childbearing. This is partly connected with their increased subjective investment in a career as a result of the time and money spent on Australian degrees. It also articulates clearly with the *haiguis'* tendency to be increasingly critical of adult women's ascribed social role in the neotraditionalist, family-centric model.

All of these reported changes suggest that the graduate returnees developed an understanding of themselves as mobile, enterprising, self-fashioning individuals, which would fit them well for middle-class urban life and professional private-sector labor. Overseas study seemed to strengthen their identification with exactly the type of desiring, consuming, "self-animating, self-staging subject" (A. Ong and Zhang 2008, 1) that is so ideologically central to China's globally connected market economy and society in the late reforms era (see this book's introduction). The understanding of oneself as a mobile, self-motivating, self-managing, reflexive individual somewhat disembedded from ties to locality and family aligns *haigui* subjectivity neatly with the demands of a neoliberalized professional workforce, whether in China's large metropolitan cities or globally.

Haigui *Subjectivity: Gender Detraditionalization*

QIN: I think that [studying abroad] has made me care a bit more about myself. Students in China might get to the age I am now and, with the "well-meaning" encouragement of their parents, tend to follow the standard steps of getting married and having children. . . . This year I've received so many wedding invitations! . . . But as for me, even though my [relationship with my] boyfriend is very stable, I just don't want to get married. I want to wait until I've realized my self-value through work before I consider this matter. But in China that might not be OK. . . . [If I hadn't gone overseas,] I might have got married very early, I don't know. . . . Back then I tended to see family as my main focus, whereas now I think work is more important. . . . When you go overseas, you have to rely on yourself for everything. So now, when you come back, you still want to rely on yourself. Like, when I was looking for work, I wanted to rent an apartment myself and go out to live. I'm not living at home right now; I'm renting my own place. All this has been my own decision, and I found [the apartment] myself. My mum and dad have been really supportive, but they do hope I'll get married soon. Though I take no notice of them.

. . .

Q: I want my own life plan, but others' life plan is probably to have a baby and be filial toward their parents.

F: So what's your life plan, right now?

Q: Right now? I'm thinking that before I'm thirty I want to achieve "bag-buying freedom." . . . Girls have several stages; one is "milk-tea-buying freedom," and then it's "hotel-staying freedom," where you can stay in whatever hotel you want to. And then it's "bag-buying freedom."

F: Does that refer to the more expensive kind of bag?

Q: Yes, the kind that would cost ten or twenty or thirty or forty thousand [RMB: up to $8,000]. And then it's "car-buying freedom" and then "apartment-buying freedom."

F: I see. So bag-buying freedom by thirty, does that mean you have a particular income level in your sights?

Q: Pretty much. [It means] if you want to buy a certain bag, you needn't hesitate about it too long. . . . Actually, when I said this, my mum and dad couldn't really understand it. Because I told them that until I achieve bag-buying freedom, I won't consider marriage. . . . It won't work, I just won't agree to it. . . . I've deleted "get married" and "have baby" from my to-do list.

F: So, after thirty then?

Q: Not necessarily; I'll just go with the flow. What if I suddenly strike it rich? [*both laugh*] Right? I want to first feel that I can take care of myself, take responsibility for myself, before I think about what comes next. . . . Nowadays I don't have that feeling of being a "leftover woman." I feel I'm constantly living under my own self-enrichment, so I'm always young; I don't [feel as if] I will be eliminated in the social struggle [for a mate] or whatever, I don't at all. . . . I don't have any sense of crisis, perhaps. My [female] cousins all want to find boyfriends early, quickly get married, quickly have children. But I don't have that feeling at all.

F: So you think this is connected with having studied abroad?

Q: It's somewhat connected.... I feel it's connected with having seen more, having learned more.

Although Qin occupied a particularly privileged social position—she was the daughter of an educated, well-off couple (a government official and a high-level professional) and was herself working for an international company in central Shanghai, which was also her hometown—her reflections crystallize many of the key aspects of *haigui* subjectivity as a gendered formation that was generally understood by the wider participant group. Qin reinforces many of the points highlighted in the preceding analysis of the *haigui* self-image—self-focus, self-reliance, and independence; self-fulfillment through professional work; individualized life practices; and discretionary consumption seen as a self-validating freedom. Her striking reconceptualization of women's maturation as a step-by-step progression through income levels and the corresponding types of commodities that they become "free" to consume—which draws on a 2017 internet meme (Tutou Mama Shuo Yu'er 2018)—also highlights another key aspect of *haigui* women's subjectivity: rejection of a gendered life course defined by the milestones of "timely" marriage and childbearing. As a result of study abroad, despite having a steady boyfriend, Qin felt she had shifted her focus toward a professional career, consumption, and a life lived relatively independent from others.

For some women, overseas study from the outset formed part of a strategy to distance themselves from social pressures within China to adhere to a standard feminine life course (chapter 1). Four years later, this disidentification with the normative gendered life script had clearly and consistently intensified. Time and again, when I asked how they felt study abroad had impacted on their view of themselves and their future lives, participants—both those in China and those in Australia—pointed to such a change. Many statements like the following were made during postgraduation interviews:

Before I came overseas, I used to think that [my dad's] statements based on classical sayings were applicable under any circumstances. But after I arrived here, I started to feel that that's not the way things are, that those classical sayings are context dependent.... The first saying is, "... At each stage in life, people should do the things appropriate to that stage." ... When it's the right time for studying, you should study; when it's the right time for marriage, you have to get married; when it's about time to have children, you should have children. You should do what you have to do; one's life should proceed by set stages. But after coming here, I realized that actually this can't be applied to all people. . . . Because I saw lots of different ways of living among the people around me. (Fenfang)

Since living abroad, I feel that the traditional style of marriage has become less important. Perhaps before it would have seemed like a matter of course, but . . . now I feel at least 50 percent that I don't want to be bound by the rule that you have to get married at twenty-five or twenty-six. I feel that it's about meeting the right person and that only after attaining the achievements I want myself in professional life would I consider this question. (Xiaoxing)

When you go back, you feel like your way of thinking is not really the same as others'. My friends have that view that when you get to a certain age, you [should get married]. We ask them, "Why are you getting married?" And they'll say, "Well, I've reached this age, and this person is fine, so let's get married." But I feel like, surely you can't get married just because someone is "fine"?! They think that once you reach that age, it means [you should get married]. . . . We [overseas graduates] are not like that. (Shunzi)

When considering why studying abroad should reorient one's attitude toward the gendered life course in this way, some, like Fenfang, linked it with a vague sense—gleaned from American media, occasional conversations with local acquaintances, and observation of women in the public spaces of Australian cities—that Western women were freer from pressures to marry and have children on a fixed schedule (Y. Hao 2019). Others connected the change, again, with their experience of independent living while studying abroad. As Mingyu said, "It might . . . be because of . . . just being alone by yourself. You tend to feel it's fine to be without a boyfriend; life goes along pretty smoothly, you can go out with friends, you have more freedom." Several *haigui* participants, like Qin, found that the pleasures and freedoms of independent living were difficult to give up on return, which spurred them to move out on their own from the parental apartment or to aspire to do so when finances allowed.

Mobility, Containment, Excess

A value-laden understanding of *haigui* women's identity thus emerges from participants' reflections. In their collective experience, women like themselves who had studied abroad seemed likely to be unmarried, independent, focused on their professional career, following a flexible life course, and geographically mobile. They aspired to individualized identity expressed through everyday practices: activities undertaken alone and lives lived separately from family. They valued professional ambition, cultural reflexivity, and leisure consumption. These features associated overseas graduates, in their own minds, with the positive values of freedom and modernity. By contrast, these graduates understood Chinese women who had not studied abroad as more likely to be married, reliant on others, family focused, adherent to predetermined gendered life stages, and fixed in geographic place. The overseas graduates also associated their China-graduate peers with group orientation, less sophisticated consumption habits, and prioritization of safe-and-stable work over professional ambition. Such attributions linked China graduates with the negative values of constraint and tradition. Thus, overseas study appeared to strengthen women's identification with the globally extensive, neoliberal-style ideal of the mobile enterprising individual and, correspondingly, to weaken their attachment to the neotraditionalist model of femininity promoted in China's postsocialist public culture. That is, transnational education seemed to advance women's *dis*embedding from *national* systems of *gender* ideology and their *re*embedding in more *transnational* systems of *neoliberal* ideology.

However, regardless of how strongly these women identified with mobility as a form of value, at every turn their experiences of mobility and aspirations toward it were met with multiple forms of immobilization and containment (Shamir 2005; F. Martin and Dragojlovic 2019). Graduates' visa- and race-based exclusion from many desirable jobs in Australia was paralleled by their gender- and age-based exclusion from professional opportunities in China. The unequal distribution of power, resources, and cultural capital across the microstrata within China's middle classes is also very apparent. Xiaoxing's story, for example, illustrates gender-based restrictions on professional mobility conditioned by a family's lower-middle-class habitus and concomitant "traditional" preference for keeping daughters close to home. Conversely, Xiaofen's narrative illustrates how in more privileged circumstances, women may leverage academic and mobility capitals to compensate for gender disadvantage in the domestic job market. Meanwhile, the emotional and existential precarity experienced by graduates who remained in Australia navigating the state immigration regime sharply demonstrates both the costs and the limits of this form of mobility (Robertson 2013, 159–68). Yet despite the multiple forms of disadvantage they experienced in labor markets in Australia and China, these graduates tended to project themselves into the position of the employer and thus depoliticize the labor issues at hand, which suggests that the transnational education assemblage may be complicit in reproducing neoliberal subjectivities linked with the demands of a wider global economy and the production of a transnational capitalist class (Sklair 2001; Rizvi 2005; Waters 2007; Astarita, Patience, and Tok 2019; Courtois 2020).

And yet, crucially, these women's stories also demonstrate that the complexity of their experiences of educational mobility resists reduction to any single effect. If in one sense their experiences tend broadly to consolidate ways of understanding the self and the world that we might call *neoliberal*, this is nonetheless not *all of* or *always* what they do. The stories in this chapter have illustrated strong comingling countercurrents in the form of alternative systems, for example, in the tension between meritocracy and *guanxi*—that is, between a neoliberal-style ideological imperative toward self-reliance (*kao ziji*) and the more pragmatic patriarchal principle of leaning on Dad (*pin die*)—as logics structuring job seeking (A. Ong 2008).[7] We have also seen how locally embedded gender traditionalism within the family forges a perverse alliance with the modern apparatus of the socialist state to encourage a highly educated young woman like Xiaoxing *away* from work in the global financial sector and back toward a safe-and-stable government job in her family's local neighborhood. In all their experiential complexity, plurality, and unpredictability, these women's experiences overflow and resist any neat conclusion on subjective neoliberalization—or any other singular effect.

~

    N: I don't have any dream. . . . Actually, before, this sentence, "I have no dream"—I couldn't bring myself to say it. I felt that probably everyone ought to have a dream. And when other people asked me, I'd just make something up on the spot, so it was always changing. Then later I started to think that not having a dream is no big deal. . . . It seems like it really doesn't matter; I guess not everyone can find one. I think if you do, then you're lucky, but if you don't, it's no loss.

    F: But don't you think that wanting to go to Spain and travel around overseas is a kind of dream?

    N: I don't think that counts. It's only short-term. It's just knowing that you want to go somewhere, but you don't know what you want to do there. . . . To me, a dream has to be long-term; you have to continuously work toward it and make sacrifices. . . . You have to sacrifice a lot for it, like you might be willing to work without reward for it or whatever; I think only that is worthy of—

    F: —the name "dream."

    N: Right.

                 (Niuniu, after three and a half years in Australia)

My final interview with Niuniu was over dinner at a gastropub near her share-house in inner Melbourne. We spoke for two and a half hours over fish and artistic salads, struggling at times to make ourselves heard above the raucous conversation of three tipsy blokes in business suits at the next table. The pub was an island of middle-aged Anglos in what Niuniu described as a student-dominated part of the city where "there are too many foreigners, too many Asians." Paradoxically, the "Asianness" of her lifeworld in Melbourne was one factor motivating Niuniu's half-formed plans to go overseas—perhaps to Spain or Mexico, where some of her former housemates came from—to support herself with semiskilled work while immersing herself in new cultures. Niuniu had been on a temporary graduate visa for the past year, working daily ten-hour shifts for below minimum wage at a café on the campus of nearby Capital University. She had given up hope of applying for PR earlier that year when the required points for accounting graduates shot up to eighty-five, and was now saving up to fund further overseas travels when her visa ran out. Niuniu had no boyfriend currently and indeed had never had one, though she had once invented an imaginary beau to quell her mother's nagging. She felt less and less inclined ever to get married or even seek a partner, feeling she was probably more cut out for a single, independent life. She had not told her parents about her current situation or future plans, since she knew they would disapprove of her lack of direction in terms of career, marriage, and travels. Niuniu felt herself adrift both geographically and in terms of life plan. But she embraced her own deviation from the normative life script, having begun to understand her experiences in a different way. She had exchanged the standard dream of competitive self-advancement and linear progress toward sequential life goals for yoga, swimming lessons, a ukulele, and a desire for relatively undirected "lifestyle mobility" (Chisholm 2014; Cohen, Duncan, and Thulemark 2015).

This chapter has explored the tendency for overseas study to strengthen young women's identification with the neoliberal ideal of enterprising self-hood while weakening their attachment to neotraditional femininity. Niuniu's story suggests, however, that sometimes educational mobility may erode young women's faith not only in the latter but in *both* of these models. The increased choices, uncertainties, and risks afforded by this form of transnational movement prompted participants like Niuniu to develop a heightened awareness of the limits of the dream of ceaseless striving (Y. Yan 2013), critique the ideal of linear progression toward predefined goals, and work toward living out alternatives to this fixed life pattern (Robertson, Harris, and Baldassar 2018).[8] Paradoxically, then, overseas study might be seen as both *part* of the postsocialist dream of neoliberal-style self-making and potentially *disruptive* of that dream

(A. Hansen 2015). When experienced agentially, such disengagement from the standard sequential self-advancement script could feel positive, as it ultimately did for Niuniu.

In other cases, however, the impossibility of living up to what some called the "life winner" (人生赢家 *rensheng yingjia*) ideal was experienced negatively as a lack of agency, frustrated ambition, or a sense of stuckness (Hage 2009). As Yueming eloquently put it, lingering on in Sydney after graduation with no clear plans beyond the need to stay put for now to allow her boyfriend to maintain his visa, "There's a Chinese saying, 'Tread upon a melon peel / Land wherever slides your heel' [*laughs*]. . . . I just feel a bit as if I'm wasting time." Other participants passionately wanted to have and adhere to goals—but, paradoxically, that desire seemed at times in itself to *constitute* their clearest goal, while concrete plans remained vague. The structural conditions in which student transmigrants found themselves in Australia were often radically changeable, which made it difficult to stick unwaveringly to any specific plan. The disconnect between the imperative to know where one was going and material conditions of structural uncertainty during this liminal time thus generated an existential anxiety for these mobile young people (Cwerner 2001). Movement through life and the world felt at such times haphazard rather than agential: more like the precarious skid of someone who treads on a fruit peel than the purposeful upward trajectory of the goal-driven dreamer.

But notwithstanding Niuniu's and Yueming's (respectively willing and unwilling) deviations from the self-advancement script, what remain constant across their accounts and those of many of the other graduates are their *disidentification with neotraditional femininity* and their *attachment to a mobile imaginary*. Both were actively resisting family pressures to marry and settle down: Niuniu imagined herself as single for life and traveling for personal enrichment, while Yueming prolonged her undirected time in Sydney largely to distance herself from a coalition of elder female relatives eager to see her home, married, and pregnant as soon as possible. For them, as for many others, settlement in place was associated with retraditionalized femininity, while mobility was linked with alternative, more individualized forms of gendered selfhood to which they aspired. This book's conclusion returns to these imbrications of gender and mobility to further develop some of their broader conceptual implications.

CONCLUSION
Unsettled Dreams

*

When I went home, back to my grandparents' place, I suddenly realized: the
people on that street, from the time I was born until now, they're still there,
there's been no change!... My grandparents have lived their whole life in
that building—don't you think it would be boring?... Nowadays we have
choices.... You can leave—that's something you wouldn't have dared even
think about before, you'd just stay put your whole life. There's an old lady
about the same age as my grandpa who runs a little stall, an odds-and-ends
shop. She's been running that shop her whole life. I mean to say, how can
she live? [*all laugh*]. (Xiaojuan, in conversation with Cihui and Xiaofen)

*

Xiaojuan told this story during a get-together at an upscale Shanghai teahouse
in late 2017. Cihui and Xiaofen's laughter at her comic overstatement of the un-
livability of such a static life suggested that they concurred. Recently returned
with master's degrees from Australia and, in two cases, pursuing professional
careers in a city far from their hometowns, the three saw themselves as the antithesis of the old lady whose life had been restricted to the confines of her little
shop, in the same town and the same street and among the same people she had
lived with all her life. They understood themselves as a new generation and a
new kind of women: women whose multiplied potentials for mobility—their
capacity for dreams of flight—were at the very core of what it meant to live.

One of the central questions posed at the beginning of this book was how
time studying abroad would affect young middle-class women's negotiation
of the contradiction between two competing models of identity available to
them in postsocialist Chinese society: neoliberal-style enterprising selfhood
and neotraditionalist familial femininity. The foregoing chapters have demonstrated that, broadly speaking, according to participants' own accounts, the
experience of transnational educational mobility tended to decrease their identification with neotraditionalist femininity while correspondingly increasing their

attachment to mobile enterprising selfhood. Some were motivated to study abroad partly by their emerging critique of social pressures pushing women in their twenties toward marriage and family (chapter 1), and participants' negotiations with sexuality and intimate relationships during their years in Australia involved elaborating alternative understandings of gendered time that directly contested key aspects of chrononormative femininity in China (chapter 5). Finally, participants agreed, postgraduation, that their experiences of overseas education had opened up a gulf between the gender neotraditionalism that they saw as constricting the lives of female peers who remained in China, and their own developing understandings of themselves as more independent, self-focused, ambitious, consumerist, career driven, reflexive, and mobility oriented. Even those who rejected or felt disqualified from the upward-striving dream of enterprising selfhood found that overseas study had strengthened their disidentification with neotraditional femininity and their mobile aspirations (chapter 8) (Robertson, Cheng, and Yeoh 2018).

The previous chapter concluded by observing participants' conceptual association of geographic settlement with "traditional" femininity and their linking of mobility with the more individualized patterns of life and gendered identity toward which they aspired. The same logic underpins Xiaojuan's story about the old lady trapped in her little store. Tropes of settlement—as *ding xialai* (定下来), *anding xialai* (安定下来), *wending xialai* (稳定下来: all meaning settling down), and *huijia* (回家: going home)—recurred in participants' reflections throughout this study with similar associations, connected especially with some parents' hopes (and directives) that their daughters should return home to marry. *Settling down* in marriage in this sense also implied *geographic settling*, in place: the inverse of that gendered sense of temporal suspension that participants experienced in the liminal space-time of overseas study (chapter 5; Robertson 2020). The English term *settling* also carries a third meaning: *settling for*, in compromise—bringing to mind the stories some participants told about acquaintances back home who seemed to have given in to social and familial pressures to settle for a less-than-ideal job, husband, or life plan. In all three senses, the majority of the women who participated in this study felt that their experiences of transnational educational mobility had made them less likely to settle anytime soon. Against territorializing pressures in the realms of both geography and gender, they felt less inclined than before to *settle down* in place or into a family-centric role and less willing to *settle for* life decisions that would compromise their personal desires.

Unsettling the identification with gender neotraditionalism is the clearest way in which educational mobility shaped these women's understandings and practices of gender (Hanson 2010). Concomitantly, their feminine gender also shaped their experiences of mobility at every stage of their journeys in numerous intricate ways. It motivated their decisions to study abroad in the first place (negatively, as a response to gendered labor market bias and life-course restriction), impacted their experiences of cities overseas (exacerbating fears about personal safety in public space), opened up opportunities in some types of work and closed the door on others (both before and after graduation and both in and outside China), permeated their experiences of sexuality and intimate relationships while abroad (especially through the lingering effects of gendered sexual shame and gendered intergenerational power machinations within families), conditioned their experiences of organized religion (both in the patriarchal worldviews of the conservative churches some became involved with and in the gender-specific vulnerabilities that pushed them to seek support from these churches), and provided the central metaphor for a pervasive structure of national feeling (China as motherland). This book has thus illustrated how, for the 1990s generation of middle-class urban Chinese women, study abroad was constitutively entangled with gendered power relations in ways that decisively shaped these women's experiences of both transnational education and their own femininity.

Gender, Class, and Neoliberal Subjects

If educational mobility tended to increase participants' attachments to a neoliberal-style ideal of the individualized, self-reliant, mobile self while distancing them from neotraditionalist understandings of women's roles, then an important question arises about the relationship between subjective neoliberalization and gender detraditionalization. How should we understand their correlation and combination? How should we interpret the apparently progressive gender effects of subjective neoliberalization in this case?

As the foregoing chapters have shown, even before we consider the impacts of middle-class women's increasing opportunities for transnational mobility, China's market society already generates contradictory gender effects for this group. On one hand, in collusion with the postsocialist (re)essentialization of feminine and masculine "natures," the partial privatization of the economy allows gender discrimination to flourish in employment markets, while the rollback of state welfare provision leaves women shouldering a greater care burden in families. Thus, contemporary practices of neoliberalization need not stand in opposition to "traditional" forms of patriarchy but may draw on and selectively reinforce existing patriarchal power relationships and social norms

(Cornwall, Gideon, and Wilson 2008, 3). On the other hand, the postsocialist discourse of the striving, self-animating subject simultaneously provides unmarried, middle-class singleton women with an ideological tool with which to resist neotraditional patriarchal power in the realm of the family. That is, in the hands of private enterprise and the state, neoliberalism, as both ideology and practice, tends to *promote* gender neotraditionalism, whereas in the hands of young middle-class women, neoliberalism tends to *contest* gender neotraditionalism through individualist ideology and negotiated practices of female independence.

Study abroad exacerbates these contradictions by strengthening women's identification with the ideal of mobile enterprising selfhood. Vis-à-vis the global political economy, by encouraging young Chinese women's individualism and self-investing entrepreneurialism, the transnational education industry doubtless provides a service to contemporary capitalism (McRobbie 2020, 47–51). But vis-à-vis these women's gendered situation in families and the nation, their identification with mobile enterprising selfhood may support some progressive effects. It may, for example, inspire them to remain unmarried for longer than either elder relatives or the state would prefer; to choose to live single, economically independent lives; or to otherwise resist patriarchal authority in decisions about marriage, reproduction, sexuality, and life script—even as this same identification also aligns their worldview with neoliberal capitalist precepts of individualism, flexibility, responsibilization, and conversion of the subject into self-investing human capital (Rottenberg 2017). In other words, study abroad helps these women to take tactical advantage of disjunctures in space and power between the regimes of family, state, and capitalist workplace, as they elude localization (being put "in their place") in the state-endorsed neotraditionalist family by means of transnational mobility, professional self-development, and the shifts in worldview and self-view that these afford (Nonini and Ong 1997, 23–24). All of this suggests that in this case, neoliberal logics—especially their emphasis on choice, "freedom," and individual self-determination—may afford certain gendered benefits.

This situation, however, is thoroughly class bound. Study abroad entrenches middle-class privilege not only generally, by differentially expanding educational and professional opportunities, but also specifically in terms of gender, by contributing to the uneven distribution of cultural and symbolic resources that women can use to negotiate personal relationships (Wanning Sun 2018c, 72). Educational mobility's enabling of young women to partially evade neotraditional gendered power relations within families by exercising a greater degree of individual autonomy means that the middle-class women whose families can afford to send them abroad to study gain an extra advantage in negotiating with patriarchal power compared with their less privileged peers. Reflecting on the connection between neoliberal governance and social conservatism, including in the domains of gender and feminism, Raewyn Connell observes that "neoliberalism shifts the balance between dominant groups and lets in new energy and new claimants to power and privilege, without much disturbing the overall systems of inequality or the ideologies that sustain them" (2014, 35; see also Rottenberg 2018; McRobbie 2020). This rings particularly true in this case. Here young, urban middle-class women become new claimants to (a certain, limited) power, while the overall class-based system of inequality remains intact, including the compounded, intersectional liabilities of gender and class that differentially affect less privileged groups of women, for example, rural, migrant-laborer, and working-class women (Wanning Sun 2018c). Moreover, *the very same* ideological system that provides gendered benefits for middle-class women—a neoliberal-style system that values individual striving over collective struggle, and self-reliance over state protections—*also* provides ideological justification for the continuing exploitation of their less privileged sisters (and indeed, to a lesser degree, themselves) in the postsocialist labor regime (Pun 2005; H. Yan 2008). Thus, while a neoliberal worldview and self-view may offer a degree of gendered benefit for some women in some situations, such a view is thoroughly and contradictorily entangled with more regressive implications in the domain of class.

Unsettling Theory: Gendering Globalization, Grounding Transnationalism

This book has presented a study of microscale experiences of macroscale processes: the intensifying transnational mobilization of tertiary students as an aspect of globalization. I have interpreted the mobile young women's human experiences with reference to a number of concepts drawn from macrosociological theories of late modernity, including capitals theory, individualization, and neoliberal subject formation. But, while finding it useful up to a point, I have also wanted to unsettle this style of theorization in several ways.

First, in foregrounding how gender makes a difference in people's experiences, I have sought to align my perspective with those feminist critics who point out how influential macroscale theories of late modernity tend to elide women's lived experiences by painting an overly optimistic picture of patriarchy and gender inequality as relics of a vanishing past (Mulinari and Sandell 2009; Belliappa 2013, 35–39; Harrell and Santos 2017, 33–34). Indeed, in the case of postsocialist China as in other postsocialist contexts (Daskalova et al.

2012), the myth of some intrinsic link between capitalist modernization and gender detraditionalization is refuted in short measure by the evident gender *re*traditionalization, both structural and ideological, that has occurred along with the end of high socialism and the rise of the market society (see the book's introduction and chapter 1). Even as China's middle-class women increasingly aspire toward individualized identity and develop reflexive orientations toward self-fashioning projects, they face at every turn instances of stubbornly unvanished gender inequality: brazen sexism in professional employment markets, restricted opportunities based on their supposedly natural propensity toward family care work, and tenaciously patriarchal thinking and practices in some families, to name obvious examples. The foregoing chapters have paid close attention to how culturally conditioned gendered power relations, far from withering away or becoming a merely peripheral concern, are intrinsic not only to social life in China today but also to late-modern global-scale processes, including the transnationalization of higher education. Furthermore, in placing front and center the subjective experiences of the student transmigrants themselves, the book has sought to understand small-scale actors at the local level, including women, as not simply "impacted by" macroscale global processes but rather as themselves *agents of globalization* (C. Freeman 2001). This is to work with a gendered understanding of globalization that is "not one in which women's stories . . . can be tacked into . . . the macropicture; rather, it challenges the very constitution of that macropicture such that . . . [women's stories] are situated within social and economic processes and cultural meanings that are central to globalization itself" (1010). The book has thus attempted to further the feminist project of unsettling the masculinism of macrosociological theories of late modernity and globalization by demonstrating the fundamental centrality both of women's actions and experiences and of gendered power relations more generally to transnational processes, including the global commodification of education and the production of human resources for global finance capitalism, among others.

Second, by focusing closely on the minor(itized) and small-scale mobilities of the student transmigrants' everyday lives and their elaboration of translocal networks and subjectivities in place, this study has sought to advance the project of grounding transnational theory by recognizing the embodied, material, affective, and geographically situated character of transnational practices and processes. Chapters 2 to 4, in particular, dwelled on fieldwork stories that demonstrate how human experiences of mobility intertwine with states of fixity and immobilization, as mobility itself unmakes and remakes relations of power in context. This is particularly clear in the case of Chinese educational transmigrants, who, like the Indian information technology workers in Germany studied by Sareeta Amrute (2016), constitute *both* a rising middle-class elite *and* a racialized migrant minority group. On one hand, they are the privileged subjects of transnational education, while, on the other hand, they are subject to racism and social exclusion and tend to be corralled into low-status, low-skilled, and underpaid work in Australian cities (chapters 4 and 8). These women's experiences of educational mobility are always attended by simultaneous pressures toward gendered, racialized, and sociospatial containment and immobilization. Their example illustrates particularly clearly how geographic context matters for identity, since social status shifts and transforms with mobility. While this book has focused most consistently on power relations attaching to gender, it has also shown how educational mobility generates power differentials vis-à-vis both race (the racialization as "Chinese" that happens to the student transmigrants on arrival in Australia) and labor status (their consequent downward mobility in terms of available work). It has also brought to light other complex imbrications of mobility, racialization, and class. While student transmigrants themselves became racialized as a consequence of their mobility, the expatriate culture they cocreated in turn collaborated with a dominant strand in Australian culture in (re)racializing classed Others in Australian cities, including "Africans" and "refugees" (chapter 3). Mobility has been shown not to always or simply be linked with power and advantage, since in many important respects social power remains tethered to geoparticular racial regimes and social networks. Conversely, "minor" mobilities may be wielded against the risks of gendered or racialized containment, as when Chinese women take up transnational education in response to gendered restrictions in the domestic labor market (chapter 1) or when they engage in e-trading in response to race- and visa-based exclusion from professional labor markets in Australia (chapter 4).

This book has framed the student transmigrants as urban agents, actively producing the city they inhabited as a place characterized by alternating currents of sociospatial encapsulation and extension at the local level. Concurrently, they (re)made Melbourne as a translocality: a place constituted experientially by its connections to multiple points beyond itself through fluid tides of mobile things, feelings, media, bodies, and institutions. Underlining how the specificity of these mobile entities *matters*—the heaviness of cans of powdered milk, the transcendence evoked by a song, cramped muscles on a long-haul flight, fear ignited by a headline—undercuts the conceptualization of globalization as a series of weightless flows, showing instead how the countless microvectors out of which the macroprocess we call *globalization* is actually constituted push against and shape human bodies, affects, and lives (Bude and Dürrschmidt 2010).

Subject Formation and Ethnographic Overflow

One of this book's central findings is that transnational education tends not only to consolidate middle-class Chinese women's critiques of neotraditional femininity but also to strengthen their identification with an alternative form of self-understanding, which I have been calling *mobile enterprising selfhood*. In a very broad sense, this study might thus be said to be about educational mobility's propensity to engender forms of neoliberal subjectivity: ways of being that value and aspire toward individualization, self-reliance, self-direction, and personal choice. It has shown, in particular, how experiences of independent living abroad during transnational education may become an important factor in the making of market subjects: a mobile labor force suited in terms of ideological orientation and self-understanding, as well as concrete skills, to work in the engine rooms of global capitalism as financiers, professionals, and high-level technicians.

Although educational settings often present a fertile context for studying processes of subject formation (e.g., Petersen and O'Flynn 2007), in the view that emerges from the foregoing analyses, Chinese students' strengthening identification with enterprising selfhood is less a result of specific educational content learned in Australian universities than a product of the experience of mobility itself. The form of subjectivity toward which transnational education bends its subjects is, moreover, defined by its orientation toward mobility. Through studying abroad, students develop and consolidate *movement capacities* (Urry 2007, 197–98). These include not only the technical skills and practical knowledges that enable them to manage travel timetables, itineraries, visas, connections, and transnational communication, as well as coping with everyday life far from home in unfamiliar surroundings, but also a subjective orientation toward feeling at home in movement—lucidly illustrated in Xiaojuan's suggestion, above, that to live is to have the potential to move. The type of self-understanding we have seen emerging in the foregoing chapters might be seen as a variety of what Anthony Elliott and John Urry have called "portable personhood": an identity that has been "fundamentally recast in terms of capacities for movement," one that involves "the *stretching of self* in both psychological and social terms . . . based upon plasticity, portability, contingency" (2010, 3, 97). In this way, the study illustrates educational mobility's role in producing Chinese students and graduates as "middling" transnationals, a segment of the vast numbers of mobile people worldwide who inhabit the wide middle ground between the elite "globals" and the impoverished migrants who have been the focus of much previous research in migration studies (Conradson and Latham 2005b, 229; Robertson 2013, 160). This is also, perhaps, a story about the making of a transnationally mobile and expansive Chinese self to correspond with the economic and geopolitical expansion of the Chinese nation in this century (chapter 7).

But in telling the story of the formation of such mobile subjects and subjectivities, I hope that through the detail of participants' narratives, this book has gone some way toward illustrating the complexity, nuance, and incompleteness in how such processes unfold in practice. Underscoring the inherent limitations of any abstract, universalizing theory of subject formation—neoliberal or otherwise—is the third way in which this book has sought to unsettle macro theory. *Subject formation*, a term we bandy about so blandly in our theoretical discussions, refers, after all, to *the very shaping of people's core understandings of themselves*—how could such an intimate, contingent, and everyday process be adequately apprehended top-down, in purely general and abstract terms (Barnett 2005)?[1] As Stuart Hall pithily observed in his related reflections on the problem of conceptualizing how *exactly* political ideologies manage to remake already-formed subjectivities, "the level of abstraction at which the theory is operating... is largely incommensurable with the nature of the object it is being wheeled in to explain" (1988, 50–51). And while this study arguably does point very broadly toward a variety of "neoliberal subject formation," the unruly profusion and heterogeneity of participants' stories—much of which, of course, had to be pruned away in the interests of producing a coherent academic analysis—underlines that simply observing this effect could never be enough. People's experience always overflows the interpretive structures with which we try to contain it, and humans are not reducible to ideological ciphers.

By dwelling on this point, I aim to work toward doing justice to the complexity of research participants' experiences as revealed during fieldwork. Keeping in view the wild propensity for people's experiences of themselves and their world to overflow any single principle or disciplinary imperative also challenges a tendency in some studies of contemporary Chinese society, based on a Foucauldian governmentality model, to see ordinary people's subjective experience as merely symptomatic of a single, highly abstract, and generalized symbolic logic, usually thought to be promulgated top-down by the state, global capitalism, or the two acting in concert.[2] In this regard I sympathize, for example, with Carolyn L. Hsu's critique of the scholarly tendency to represent the *suzhi* (素质, "quality" or cultural civility) discourse as simply a tool of governmentality that enables the Chinese state effectively to align the worldview of the citizenry with the interests of neoliberal capitalism (e.g., H. Yan 2003; Anagnost 2004). Hsu (2007, 184–88) rightly points out that the baldness of such a conclusion renders ordinary Chinese people the passive victims of false consciousness, because it fails to tune in to the microfrequencies of everyday speech where the myriad contradictory ways that people actually make use of the *suzhi* discourse become audible (see also D. Lin 2017). The problems that Hsu identifies are largely problems of approach. If one begins with the presumption of a single abstract principle (say, neoliberal subject formation, portable personhood, or *suzhi* as a protocapitalist coding of human value) and ends one's analysis at the point where one discovers this principle reflected in people's thinking, then one's conclusions are bound to be somewhat predictable.[3] Tracing the workings of a given discourse in an individual's consciousness may help us tell the story of the discourse, but it cannot tell us the whole story of the person. Single-minded searches for preconceived metanarratives risk blinding us to the unpredictability and richness of social experience. Instead, by starting inductively from participants' subjective and affective experiences and trying to remain alive to fickle interactions among the plural frameworks they drew on in making meaning from these—including not only varieties of enterprising selfhood and portable personhood but also neotraditional femininity, filiality, and *guanxi* ethics—I hope to have avoided the determinism of an approach that would privilege any single, preconceived symbolic structure. Rather than interpret affective life as merely an epiphenomenon of social theory's "bloodless categories," this study has wanted to remain open to ethnography's capacity to challenge preformulated understandings about what selfhood—or gender, class, place, sexuality, race, religion, work, nation, or any other aspect of social life—will mean for people in practice (Raymond Williams 1977, 128–35; Gordon 2008, 21; García Canclini 2014, 35). As Avery F. Gordon compellingly argues, "We do not usually experience things, nor are affects produced, in the rational and objective ways our terms tend to portray them," and apprehending the complexity of subjectivity and social life hinges on our willingness to be surprised, to grapple "with the difficulty of imagining beyond the limits of what is already *understandable*" (2008, 22, 24, 195).

Neoliberalism, individualization, capitals, networks, globalization—a darkened room, a snatch of melody, the taste of a loquat, an emoji, a tear wiped away. How do these two sets of terms relate, what mediates between them, and how shall we make sense of it? Are the latter merely trivial traces that ultimately point, through some shadowy logic, toward the "big picture" contexts referenced in the masterful language of the former (Foster 2002, 238)? Or could the second group of terms instead challenge the very basis of the former's totalizing claims to comprehend social reality through theoretical abstraction? This book's project has been split by a tension between the analytic imperative to translate people's experiences into abstract contentions about macroscale patterns and ethnography's tendency to undercut such structures of generality by foregrounding the irreducible singularities of subjective and intersubjective experience at the phenomenological level (Chakrabarty 1997; Massumi 2015, 52).[4] I see no simple way to either reconcile or synthesize the universalizing drive of macrostructural theory with the microscopic singularities of affective experience.[5] The incommensurabilities between micro and macro, singular and general, concrete and abstract, practice and ideology, phenomenological and sociological, must remain as dialectical tensions in the analysis.[6] More modestly, I simply hope that such tensions within the ethnographically grounded abstractions this book has developed about gender, educational mobility, and subject formation have been generative ones (Comaroff and Comaroff 2003, 171).

Who Are "Chinese International Students"?

Over the main years of this research project, international student numbers in Australia continued to grow steadily across all nationalities and sectors, rising from some 497,000 in 2015 to over 758,000 by the end of 2019 (Australian Department of Education, Skills and Employment 2020). Students from China remained the largest proportion of these, with numbers increasing from 135,800 in 2015 to over 212,000 by December 2019 (Australian Department of Education and Training 2019). By late 2019, in Australia as in the United States and other Western host nations, increasing tensions were apparent in public responses to the presence of these students, especially in relation to purported political, academic, and financial risks (J. Lee 2019). While during 2019 street battles raged in Hong Kong between pro-democracy protesters and increasingly reckless police, in Australia pundits interpreted campus conflicts between supporters of the Hong Kong movement and patriotic mainland Chinese students as evidence that the Chinese Communist Party was gagging free speech in Australian universities (Lesh 2019). An influential report from the conservative Centre for Independent Studies framed the ongoing "China student boom" as a problem for the nation's higher education sector, finding universities excessively reliant on Chinese student income and alleging compromised admission standards and unacceptable financial risks (Babones 2019). The national broadcaster aired feature investigations about universities profiteering from Chinese student "cash cows" (ABC 2019a) and about the CCP's purported infiltration of Australian campuses through Chinese student groups and research collaborations (ABC 2019b). In August the federal Department of Education announced the establishment of a University Foreign Interference Taskforce aimed at combating Chinese influence in Australian higher education (Tehan 2019). A research topic that may have appeared, five years earlier, a somewhat specialist concern was suddenly catapulted to a central position in national and international consciousness. Ordinary Chinese students had become a symbolic linchpin in Western liberal democracies' broader geopolitical panic over China's global "rise."

The risks that "exporting" education to China may pose to Western nations' universities, political systems, and security have not, however, been this study's main focus.[7] It set out, instead, to ask how transnational education feels for the young Chinese women who undertake it in Australia and has sought to center their own perspectives. Starting from the ground up—again, rather than setting out to hunt for some predetermined principle (for example, CCP allegiance or antiliberalism)—has revealed that questions of geopolitics, the state, and desires to influence their host society politically were barely present, if at all, in the majority of participants' consciousness. We have seen how these young women's plural, in-process feelings about the Chinese state, nation, leadership, people, culture, and identit(ies) while living abroad vastly exceeded the crudely Manichaean framework of Western democratic "freedom" versus CCP brainwashing. We have also seen how these mobile students became conscious of occupying a historical pivot point in China's relationship with the world, as Australian cities began to feel like remote outposts of a rising transnational technocapitalist empire whose centers were in Shanghai, Beijing, Guangzhou, and Shenzhen (chapter 7). But most of the time, students' everyday preoccupations could hardly have been further from international geopolitics. Instead, participants dwelled on their capacities to achieve personal goals (good grades, decent work, opportunities for flexible residency), maintain relationships (with parents, grandparents, friends, teachers, mentors, and romantic partners), and pursue everyday pleasures (shopping, traveling, eating, fashion, creative projects). From their own perspective, the powers shaping most participants' longer-range planning were the market and the family, far more directly and obviously than the Chinese state.[8]

The sheer variety of participants' experiences and outlooks, too, challenges any attempt to draw conclusions about "Chinese international students" as a monolithic group. While Qin's most pressing goal, as stated in her last interview, was to reach the salary threshold that would allow her to buy luxury handbags at will, Yixin had become a committed ecofeminist and vegan activist. Some, like Liangya with her PhD scholarship and Xixi with her array of top student prizes, achieved academic brilliance; others, like Yaling and Honghong, struggled and ultimately failed to realize their academic goals. Niuniu was last seen working as a sandwich hand for below minimum wage in Melbourne, while Xiaofen was earning a five-figure monthly corporate salary in Shanghai. At the time of writing, Qiqi was recently married to a man with whom she fell in love after matchmaking by her parents; many others continued to live unpartnered lives by choice or circumstance; yet others pursued queer possibilities. We have seen participants' wide range of responses to parental directives (how readily to obey, how far to resist), to the party and the state (from moments of identification, to ironic distancing, to sharp critiques), and to future planning (from clear goals and aspirations, to hazier desires, to existential drifting).

In both the variety of their experiences and the commonness of their everyday preoccupations, these students were perhaps, in a broad sense, much like university students anywhere. But what is sorely lacking in the broader public culture in Australia and other host nations is precisely recognition of and respect for Chinese students' human ordinariness (C. Qin 2012, 191). What I have learned from sharing in research participants' lives over the past five years is hardly surprising: each person inhabits a subjective world that is familiar in some respects—with its habits, resentments, attachments, anxieties, compromises, and dreams—and in other respects suffused with the piercing bouquet of the individual's singularity (Sedgwick 1990, 23). But it is my hope that in the face of the Anglosphere's extraordinarily impoverished view of this group of mobile young people, such a simple recognition of their complex personhood and the fullness of their ordinary lifeworlds may hold a certain power (Gordon 2008, 4–5; McCarthy 2008).

Coda: Viral Micromobility

This book began by observing the effects of a transnational assemblage produced by the neoliberal commodification of higher education and organized around a vigorous and ever-strengthening vector linking China with Australia through intensifying flows of bodies, money, knowledge, technologies, and media. As I complete this conclusion in early 2021, elements at every scale within that assemblage are convulsed by new mobilities that are ultramicro in their physical dimensions yet planetary in their effect: those connected with the novel coronavirus that originated in Wuhan in December 2019 and that causes a highly contagious flu-like illness, COVID-19. Following the World Health Organization's declaration of a global health emergency at the end of January 2020, the COVID-19 virus has at the time of writing resulted in over three million deaths and more than 155 million diagnosed infections, first in China and then globally. Entire cities, regions, and countries have been locked down to curb the pathogen's spread, subjecting billions of people to movement restrictions, closing businesses, and massively disrupting the global economy. This still-unfolding scenario marks a number of rapid and radical shifts: from dreams of flight to enforced immobilization, containment, and exclusion; from mobile humans to a mobile microorganism; from face-to-face to virtual education delivery; from business as usual in late capitalism to a state of global crisis. The contingency and fragility of what so recently appeared to be a robust macroscale assemblage within a more or less predictable global system have been exposed by the most microscopic of mobile agents (Yi'En Cheng, Yang, and Xu 2020).

Early on, the Australian government responded to COVID-19 by implementing an entry ban on noncitizen, nonpermanent resident travelers who had been in China within the preceding fourteen days. Put in place just weeks before the beginning of the first university semester in 2020, the ban threw the plans of some 100,000 Chinese students into confusion, since many had traveled home for Chinese New Year and now found themselves stuck in limbo. Itineraries were everywhere in disarray: should one travel to a third country like Thailand to wait out the fourteen-day travel ban, then travel directly from there to Australia? But what if the regulations changed again and one found oneself stranded? Revising one's plans altogether and studying in Canada, the United Kingdom, or another country without a travel ban instead seemed to present another alternative until national borders everywhere began shutting down and international flights dried up during March.

Australian universities initially scrambled to manage the implications of the travel restrictions for enrollments while flipping into damage-control mode in communications with Chinese students. In late January the federal minister for education established the Global Reputation Taskforce (Australian Department of Education, Skills and Employment 2020). Initially conceived to manage reputational risk to Australia as a study destination resulting from the catastrophic bushfires of the summer of 2019–20, the focus quickly shifted to dealing with the public relations fallout from COVID-19. But the Chinese student community did not miss the bald economic logic underlying universities' protestations of enduring friendship, standing as they did in such stark contrast to the government's unusual country-specific travel ban. A promotional video circulated by the higher education sector's peak body, Universities Australia

(2020), to wish students well and express the hope to see them back on Australian campuses soon was promptly satirized on Chinese social media. Brutally superimposed over the reassuring sentiments and beaming vice-chancellors appeared giant Chinese characters laying bare the video's subtext: "Come back quick and pay your tuition fees." Meanwhile, for those Chinese students who had remained in Australia, COVID-19 resulted in a massive upsurge in racism, as also happened in Europe and the United States (Berg and Farbenblum 2020; Pomfret 2020). During those early months of the pandemic, "Asian-looking" people in Australian cities became openly feared and reviled by some businesses, media, and members of the general public as harbingers of the new plague, prompting China's Ministry of Education to issue an official warning that Australia was now considered a risky study destination (Borys 2020). Thanks to the hypermobile microbe, the deep ambivalence of Australian society toward Chinese students thus became ever more nakedly displayed, and the students grew more intensely aware and explicitly critical of the myriad racial, social, and political antipathies arrayed against them.

At the time of writing, the likely longer-term impacts of the COVID-19 pandemic on higher education are gradually becoming clearer. In Australia, international student visa applications have "dropped off a cliff." Analysts forecast a $19 billion loss in revenue to Australian universities over the coming three years if international borders remain closed until the end of 2021 (Morris 2020) and predict that universities will shed twenty-one thousand jobs in 2020 alone as a result of the disruption to international enrollments (Duffy 2020). The Labor Party warns that some universities—including among the prestigious Group of Eight, some of which derive an especially high percentage of their income from international students—are at risk of collapse (Davies and Karp 2020). As I write, my own university, whose student body in 2019 comprised 40 percent international enrollees, is finalizing plans to shed 450 full-time academic and professional positions. The completion of this book about international students' experiences of mobility thus ironically coincides with Australian university staff's collective efforts to save our own jobs, imperiled as a result of these same students' sudden immobilization.

In response to this crisis, while universities attempt to replace physical mobilities with virtual ones by shifting teaching online, the federal government has taken a sharp turn toward domestic priorities. In April 2020, the minister for education delivered a relief package touted as "unashamedly" focused on domestic students, to "help universities pivot towards a closer alignment of domestic industry and student demands" (Tehan and Cash 2020). And in a statement widely perceived by students as heartless, Prime Minister Scott

Morrison baldly stated that it was time for international students who could no longer meet their basic living needs owing to the disappearance of casual work and their exclusion from national support schemes to "make your way home" and allow the government to focus on its own citizens (Berg and Farbenblum 2020; Duffy 2020; Xiao, Zhou, and Zhao 2020). As a result of such treatment, a majority of Chinese students now report being disillusioned with Australia and less likely than before to recommend it as a study destination (Morris 2020).

The Australian government's abrupt pivot from encouraging education "export" to decrease universities' reliance on public funding (Harman 2005) toward a renewed focus on the needs of domestic students is symptomatic of a series of broader shifts precipitated by the COVID-19 health emergency. Responses to the pandemic across multiple national contexts appear to mark a crisis of legitimation for many aspects of neoliberal globalization itself (Grant 2020; Isaković 2020; Verrender 2020). In the face of the existential threat posed by the virus, both media discourse and government responses show a renewed emphasis on the public interest, national sovereignty, and state control. Neoliberal championing of private interests and small government is giving way in some places to a new emphasis on the collective good and public investment, while governments raise public debt to increase welfare provision (Denniss 2020). In Australia this has included doubling basic welfare payments, paying laid-off workers' wages, supporting free childcare, and strengthening anti-eviction protections for rental tenants, among other provisions. The value of nationalized, publicly regulated healthcare systems in supporting population-level well-being, too, could hardly be clearer. Furthermore, the shared community risk burden attaching to widespread casualized and precarious work—the material reality of neoliberalism's "flexible" labor ideology—has been brought forcefully to the fore as the highly contagious virus spreads among workers in health care, aged and disability care, security, meat-processing plants, and cleaning, as well as other temporary, insecure, and poorly paid workers, who have significant economic disincentives to taking time off work when ill (Schneiders and Millar 2020). At a more macro scale, neoliberal support for global trade liberalization and deregulation is challenged by renewed recognition of the value of national industries less susceptible to supply-chain disruption. In a move that would have seemed unlikely just a few months ago, Prime Minister Morrison recently announced the launch of "a new era of Australian manufacturing" supported by $1.5 billion in extra funding. Determined to revive a sector of the national economy that was decimated decades ago by global trade deregulation, the prime minister exhorted, "We need to keep making things in Australia" (Simons 2020; Prime Minister of Australia 2020). The old rhetoric of the coming borderless world seems ever less credible in these times of unprecedented restriction of human and commodity movement. Likewise, a cosmopolitan imaginary valuing mobility, migration, and multiculturalism is everywhere meeting increasing challenges from rising racism, xenophobia, and cultural insularity (Verrender 2020; Xiao, Zhou, and Zhao 2020).

This book has tried to illustrate some of the human effects of a regime of educational mobility produced by a specific set of transnational systems dominant in the opening decades of the twenty-first century. It has sought to trace the processes through which particular forms of gendered subjectivity emerge in complex response to the prevalent ideological, social, institutional, and economic systems of their times. It is impossible to know, at the current juncture, whether these systems and the world to which they belong are now changing irrevocably. What new regimes of (im)mobility will emerge? What kinds of subjectivity will they enable and compel? Such are the questions that remain as our familiar world seems to disperse around us like an interrupted dream.

Notes

1. Following standard ethical practice, all participant names are pseudonyms. Occasionally personal details have been slightly altered or omitted to protect participants' privacy. All participant quotes are translated from Mandarin by the author, unless noted otherwise. The names of participants' hometowns are not specified in cases where these are smaller towns and cities; in these cases only the province is specified, where relevant, the first time they are mentioned. Hometowns that are very large (population over twelve million) and send many students to Australia are sometimes named, given the far lower risk of participants being identifiable based on this information.

2. These apparently generational differences between parents and daughter may reflect relative life stage as much as or more than they do absolute generational distinctions in attitude. Both the parent generation and the daughter generation came of age in eras when posttraditional understandings of gender and the life course were circulating widely in public culture, and some parents voiced such understandings (F. Martin 2014).

3. There are 114–120 males to 100 females at birth for the main birth years of my participants, 1990–98 (World Bank 2006, 4).

4. The definition, significance, and even existence of the middle class in China are hotly contested. First, some point out that the entrepreneurs, managers, professionals, and government officials to whom the term is usually understood to refer represent not the middle-income section of the population but more elite strata (Goodman 2008b, 36; Osburg 2013, 12). Others underline that there is not a single middle class but multiple, fragmented strata that lack the unitary class interest that the term *middle class* may imply (Cheng Li 2010; Chunling Li 2010; J. Wang and Davis 2010; M. Chen and Goodman 2013). Third, the intimate symbiosis between the emerging wealthy classes and the party-state, and relatedly the fact that these classes seem unlikely to act as a politically liberalizing force, makes the Chinese case distinct from that of Europe in the nineteenth century, on which normative ideals of the middle class are based (Goodman 2008b; M. Chen and Goodman 2013).

5. Three additional points are worth noting about Goodman's studies of the entrepreneurial classes. First, Goodman only ambivalently characterizes these as part of a middle class, preferring to frame them as the elite or new rich (Goodman 2008a). Second, Goodman emphasizes the symbiotic rather than oppositional relationship between these entrepreneurs and the party-state (M. Chen and Goodman 2013). His definition of *entrepreneur* is in fact very broad, including owners of collective, private, and foreign-owned enterprises and managers of enterprises, including state-owned enterprises (Goodman

2008b, 31). Third, Goodman emphasizes that 1979 was not year zero for China's modernization and that a type of professional and managerial middle class had existed within the state bureaucracy since the 1950s (2008b, 26–27); the skills, knowledge, experience, and social capital of these government-affiliated managers and professionals were then drawn on in entrepreneurial activities postreform.

6. Based on Jianying Wang and Deborah Davis's (2010) schema, participants' fathers (usually the higher earners within couples) clustered in the upper-professional, self-employed, and cadre subclasses, but significant numbers also belonged to the lower-professional and upper-management subclasses, as well as a handful in lower management.

7. The foreign-study movement in modern China began with the Qing government's sponsorship of overseas educational missions to Western nations, including the United States, in the late nineteenth and early twentieth centuries, with the aim of drawing on Western knowledge to contribute to social reform and nation-building efforts. In the early decades of the twentieth century, many Chinese youth also studied in Japan, which served in some ways as a translator and mediator of Western intellectual culture (Liu-Farrer 2011). Supported by private funds or scholarships, thousands of others studied in European countries including France, England, Germany, and Belgium. Those who studied abroad in the early decades of the twentieth century went on to become some of China's foremost modernizing intellectuals (Ye 2001, 8–11; C. Wang 2013, 5–9). Following the 1949 revolution, the focus of foreign study shifted to the Soviet Union and allied eastern European nations, with the first group of Chinese students sent to the Soviet Union as early as 1951 and exchanges continuing through the 1960s (L. You, n.d.). Following the 1978 political and social reforms, Chinese student migration to Western nations, including the United States and Australia, commenced afresh, proceeding in several waves, first with relatively small numbers of government-funded scholarship students and later, after the gradual relaxation of bureaucratic and financial constraints, with much larger numbers of privately funded students (L. Liu 2016b, 15–40). The brutal military response to the Tiananmen Square student movement in 1989 served as an impetus for tens of thousands of then-overseas students to remain abroad, including some twenty thousand in Australia.

8. The academic and socioeconomic background of participants in this study to some extent marks the particularity of Australia as a study destination. In China even the most prestigious Australian universities are generally considered inferior both to China's top-ranked institutions and to America's Ivy League colleges. Thus, in contrast with the situation in the United States, it is relatively unlikely that the top level of China's academic elite will come to Australia for undergraduate or master's study. The mid-middle-class to elite socioeconomic background of Chinese students in Australia, meanwhile, although broadly similar to that of the cohorts who study in the United States and Europe, may differ from that of those who choose Japan as a study destination. There, as detailed studies by Gracia Liu-Farrer (2011) and Jamie Coates (2015) have shown, a combination of geographic proximity, lower tuition fees, and a flexible student-visa system that not only allows but encourages students to work while studying tends to attract students from a more diverse range of socioeconomic backgrounds, including a larger proportion

from the lower strata of China's middle classes. The gender balance in these student cohorts, however, appears roughly similar, although robust statistical comparisons among multiple destination countries are difficult (Liu-Farrer 2011, 13). For further discussion of factors affecting participants' choice of Australia as a study destination, see chapter 1.

9. I characterize this discursive framework as a structure of feeling in Raymond Williams's (1977, 128–35) sense rather than, say, as an ideology in order to keep in view the fact that this way of understanding the human, while historically conditioned and widely represented in public culture, is also always subjectively lived and affectively "alive" and hence is not fully reducible to a predictably fixed formal symbolic or disciplinary system.

10. Few understand this as simply an instance of a universal neoliberal logic radiating out to China via cultural diffusion from the centers of global capitalism. Rather, China's ideal neoliberal subject is often seen as a split or doubled one: to some extent individualistic and self-authoring but simultaneously also loyal to the authoritarian party-state and its collectivist values (F. Liu 2008; A. Ong and Zhang 2008; Hoffman 2010; Li Zhang 2010; Y. Yan 2013; F. Martin and Lewis 2016).

11. While the striving individual is "industrious, self-disciplined, calculating and pragmatic" (Y. Yan 2013, 282), Yan distinguishes this personage from Nikolas Rose's "enterprising individual" in the western European context based on the impossibility of political or civic engagement in the Chinese context given the absence of classic liberalism, individual rights and freedoms, and a democratic state (Rose 1998).

12. This suggests an interesting potential resonance with the neoliberal rationality discerned by Catherine Rottenberg (2017, 336–37) as guiding the life planning of middle-class undergraduate women in elite universities in the United States, who increasingly see their twenties as a time of striving and self-investment unencumbered by serious romantic relationships.

13. This echoes the experience of some other postsocialist societies in central, eastern, and southeastern Europe; see Daskalova et al. 2012.

14. The reduction of state care services has seen the care burden increasingly shift onto families in the postreforms era (Connelly et al. 2018). Within families, a strong social expectation that wives will perform a greater proportion of care work than husbands remains in place notwithstanding some young women's stated hopes that when the time comes, the work could be divided evenly, and also notwithstanding notable shifts toward conceptualizing marriage as centered on conjugal affection rather than duty and role performance (Jankowiak and Li 2017).

15. Stevan Harrell and Gonçalo Santos (2017) note that transgenerational relationships are growing less hierarchical vis-à-vis material power; however, the hierarchical structure remains in place in terms of symbolic prestige.

16. In his study of female entrepreneurs, Osburg (2013, 26) found that owing to their exclusion from the masculine *guanxi* networks on which businessmen rely, such women tended to be more invested in an individualized meritocratic discourse than their male counterparts, taking pride in the idea that they relied on pure ability and hard work rather than *guanxi* to succeed. Some female students gave voice to a related discourse, hoping that the experience of seeking work overseas would allow them to shine based on personal merits rather than social connections. However, since female graduates entering

the workforce are far more likely to take a first job as an employee rather than attempting to become an entrepreneur without prior professional experience, for those who sought work in China, the *guanxi* route was still open (often via their fathers), unlike the situation of the established female entrepreneurs studied by Osburg.

17. As Maria Elena Indelicato (2018) demonstrates, the rise in international student numbers in Australia over recent decades has occasioned the production of a series of affectively saturated representational strategies in media and public culture. Such strategies, argues Indelicato, press international students into service to express a variety of national anxieties including those surrounding the nation's relationship with the Asia-Pacific region.

18. All dollar amounts quoted in this book are in Australian dollars.

19. I intend *assemblage* in a broadly Deleuzian sense, as developed by Manuel DeLanda (2006); that is, it refers to a system defined by relations of exteriority (detachability and replaceability) and contingency among its component parts, and whose existence affects (enables and/or limits) its component parts.

20. My average number of interactions with the fifty core participants over the life of the project was twelve (lowest number five, highest number twenty-five).

1. BEFORE STUDY

Some material from chapter 1 appeared in an earlier version in Fran Martin, "Mobile Self-Fashioning and Gendered Risk: Rethinking Chinese Students' Motivations for Overseas Education," *Globalisation, Societies and Education* 15, no. 5 (2017): 706–20.

1. Recognizing the social centrality of the awareness and management of such risks, some scholars have put forward the view that postsocialist China, and especially its middle classes, might be seen as transitioning toward risk society: that period in modernization processes when, material need having been objectively reduced, managing the risks generated by modernization itself becomes a central project (Giddens 1991, 1999; Beck 1992; Kohrman 2004; A. Ong and Zhang 2008; Beck and Beck-Gernsheim 2010; M. Hansen and Pang 2010; Hoffman 2010; Y. Yan 2010; Ren 2013; T. Lewis, Martin, and Sun 2016; K.-S. Chang 2017). I have engaged with these arguments from a gender perspective elsewhere (F. Martin 2017a). Here, rather than dwell on the generalizing claims of this macrosociological theory, I focus instead on more specific risks connected with the participants' overseas study projects, especially gendered risks.

2. All translations from Chinese-language written sources are my own unless otherwise noted.

3. While the regulation of gender by means of such a sociotemporal template is by no means exclusive to China (see, for example, Kinneret Lahad's [2017] study of related patterns in Israel and beyond), the precise forms that this regulation takes are, to a degree, historically and culturally specific. See also Lahad's excellent critique of the normative force of the concept of "life course" itself (26–39).

4. Here and throughout, italicized words in translated quotes indicate words spoken in English; underlined words in translated quotes indicate the speaker's emphasis.

5. The *fudaoyuan* performs a student-support role for which there is no real equivalent in Western universities. *Fudaoyuans*—often junior members of staff, sometimes

postgraduate students, and always party members—are tasked with looking after the academic and spiritual/emotional well-being of the students in their care. Each *fudaoyuan* looks after one hundred to two hundred students per semester and is supposed to be their first port of call when things go wrong, from a broken air conditioner in the dorm, to family problems, to academic difficulties. The *fudaoyuan*s I met emphasized the grueling nature of their task: one told me she was required to leave her mobile phone switched on twenty-four hours a day, seven days a week, to cope with the never-ending incoming tide of student help requests. Administrators and academics in joint programs worried that students traveling to study in Australia would be lost without a *fudaoyuan* to look after them. Participants, in contrast, told me they were often annoyed by the *fudaoyuan*s' interference in their lives and tried to avoid them when possible.

2. PLACE

1. In deference to universities' concerns about brand management, all educational institutions in this book are referred to with pseudonyms.

2. The disparagement of Melbourne as a dull, parochial outpost possibly also bespeaks a defensive maneuver in response to Chinese students' effective exclusion from the city's social life. Like the second-generation Wenzhounese youth in Prato, Italy, studied by Anita Harris, Loretta Baldassar, and Roberta Raffaeta (2015), Chinese students in Melbourne may disparage the city as a boring backwater compared to Chinese cities in symbolic response to being socially marginalized there. The pervasive dialectic underlying the contrasting representations of Melbourne—front-runner/backwater, developed/backward—points to a deeper preoccupation in the Chinese narrative of modernity: the binary opposition between the advanced (先进 *xianjin*) and the backward (落后 *luohou*) (Fong 2011). This opposition remains deeply entrenched in comparative understandings of nations among the students and parents I met over the course of this study (see chapter 7).

3. I take the term *microworld* from Amin (2004). I choose the term *expatriate*—perhaps polemically—in recognition of the student transmigrants' relatively privileged position in global hierarchies, even though their Chinese identity unsettles the term's historical associations with whiteness and Western colonial histories. My framing of these students as expatriates in the context of their participation in the microworld also recognizes how their social practices in this context—their self-consciousness and self-enactment as a delimited group, their ambivalent framings of the location of their sojourn, and their class-based self-differentiation from other migrant groups who share these spaces (chapter 3)—echo those of other members of the globally mobile professional middle class who understand themselves as expatriates (Kunz 2016; Polson 2016). Participants' critical reflections on the Chinese international student "bubble" in Melbourne resonate somewhat with Christina Ho's (2020, 119–22) findings on the Asian Australian "bubble effect" in selective high schools in Sydney.

4. Inadequate natural light and ventilation in these developments were subsequently targeted in revised planning guidelines introduced in 2016 (*ABC News* 2016).

5. I also met a few students pursuing property- and construction-related degrees with half an eye on developing a real estate career between Australia and China. This was

the case with Yanyu, studying construction management at the Imperial University of Technology (IUT), whose father ran a property development business in Jiangsu that he hoped to expand transnationally; his business partner's son was also studying property development at IUT. And Qin told me about a Chinese classmate in her master of construction class at Capital University who started a small property development company in Melbourne during her studies, focusing on suburban townhouse developments. For further critical analysis of the geopolitics of Chinese real estate investment in Australian cities, see Rogers (2017, 117–30) and Robertson and Rogers (2017).

6. The term is commonly used to refer to migrant rural laborers in China.

7. For an excellent, in-depth consideration of Sydney's Chinatown as an "extroverted" and translocally connected place-in-process, including the placemaking role of Chinese international (and other) students, see K. Anderson et al. (2019). There are many resonances between Kay Anderson and colleagues' study of Sydney's Chinatown area and the present study of Melbourne's CBD. The key distinction is that because this chapter focuses solely on the perspective of the Chinese students rather than on a wider range of CBD inhabitants, the encapsulating effects of Melbourne's CBD microworld are highlighted, in the context of these students' broader social and spatial exclusion. Anderson and colleagues' wider perspective allows them to emphasize instead Chinatown's capacity to redefine, on an outward-looking, anti-identitarian model, how the city works in a cosmopolitan way to normalize diversity.

8. Linling Gao-Miles (2017) objects to the ethnoburb label for Box Hill on the basis that it performs a protoracist ethnic homogenization and overlooks multiethnic living and everyday multicultural hybridity. Her point is well taken. However, I would underline two points. First, Li's original definition of the ethnoburb does not marginalize but centers the ethnoburb's multiethnic character, hence need not preclude considerations of transethnic encounter and hybridization, even while it recognizes the statistical concentration of a particular ethnicity. Second, I focus here on how my research participants—themselves self-identifying as Chinese—understood and experienced this suburb. For them, Box Hill was understood clearly as a "Chinese area" (e.g., figure 2.17). In participants' usage, to recognize Box Hill's Chineseness is far from an exoticist observation.

9. Across Melbourne, crimes against the person rose between 8.7 percent and 7.5 percent annually between 2015 and 2017 (Crime Statistics Agency Victoria 2017).

10. See chapter 3 for a detailed discussion of the racialization of street crime.

3. MEDIA

Some material from chapter 3 appeared in an earlier version in Fran Martin, "iPhones and 'African Gangs': Everyday Racism and Ethno-transnational Media in Melbourne's Chinese Student World," *Journal of Ethnic and Racial Studies* 43, no. 5 (2020): 892–910.

1. It is certainly possible that such accounts could exceed this effect in practice: users could and sometimes do follow their advice to explore local events (volunteering opportunities, for example) where they make diverse social connections. However, in general,

the city-based leisure-and-lifestyle accounts emphasize consumption over cross-cultural community engagement.

2. A rumor circulated in mid-2016 that MelToday was reported to the race discrimination commissioner for one of its stories; however, I am unaware of any subsequent change in its reporting style. In 2017 the Victorian government education export division, Study Melbourne, began running a monthly "fake news" rundown via its own WeChat public account to warn students about unreliable WeChat news. The young woman I spoke to who was working on that project, however, worried about this service's low levels of reach and influence compared to the popular news accounts.

3. The term *Zhongguoren*, too, is sometimes used more loosely to refer to someone of Chinese ethnicity even though it literally references the People's Republic of China as a specific nation-state.

4. I am grateful to Professor Lu Ye, Professor Sun Wei, and others at Fudan University's School of Journalism for their discussions with me on this point at the forum Communicative Cities and Urban Space in 2017.

5. The panics over African gangs, refugees, and so on also appear to reflect a broader trend for politically reactionary voices to dominate in commercial WeChat news accounts abroad. This was seen, for example, in the leadup to the Australian federal election in 2019 (Karp 2019; Fan Yang and Martin 2020); similar patterns have also been observed in the United States (Jingsi Wu 2019).

6. The payments in question were in fact compensation to a group of asylum seekers for years of mistreatment in government detention on Manus Island, following a class-action lawsuit against the Department of Immigration (Whyte, Tlozek, and Evlin 2017).

7. Such a project is already being tackled, to some extent, by media producers, including the national multicultural broadcaster SBS's Mandarin service (https://www.sbs.com.au/language/mandarin). However, such services currently have a far smaller audience share among Chinese student transmigrants than the tabloid services do.

4. WORK

Some material from chapter 4 appeared in an earlier version in Fran Martin, "Rethinking Network Capital: Hospitality Work and Parallel Trading among Chinese Students in Melbourne," *Mobilities* 12, no. 6 (2017): 890–907.

1. Urry neglects to consider the alternative accounts of social capital from Bourdieu and other scholars. I treat network capital as a variety of, rather than a replacement for, social capital.

2. Alison L. Booth, Andrew Leigh, and Elena Varganova (2012, 558) showed that a person with a Chinese name would need to submit 68 percent more applications than someone with an Anglo name in order to get the same number of responses, making Chinese applicants the most discriminated against of all ethnic groups studied.

3. In mid-2016 two prominent Chinese restaurant chains began paying $18 per hour; rumor has it this was in response to being reported for underpaying.

4. These findings are corroborated by a large-scale survey of wage theft from temporary migrant workers in Australia conducted by Laurie Berg and Bassina Farbenblum

in 2016. The survey revealed that underpayment was the norm for international student employees, especially prevalent in food services and especially severe among Asian employees (those from China, Taiwan, and Vietnam) (Berg and Farbenblum 2017).

5. In fact, the students' incomes almost certainly fell below Australia's tax-free threshold.

6. My discussion is based on email and telephone conversations with representatives of both Fair Work Australia (the governmental regulatory body) and the JobWatch legal advice center, in October–November 2015. Fair Work concentrates on developing a handful of high-profile prosecutions each year to act as a deterrent to the industries in question. In July 2017 the Fair Work ombudsman finally laid charges against a large Chinese restaurant chain and major employer of international students, Dainty Sichuan restaurant group, for underpayment of staff; denial of overtime, weekend, and holiday pay rates; and overlong shifts (Buckley 2017).

7. This to some extent mirrors Gracia Liu-Farrer's (2011) findings on Chinese international students in Japan, who she argues may be used as low-wage service workers to fill local secondary labor market demand.

8. More recent developments suggest the beginnings of an organized response to this situation by Australian agencies, for example, in the establishment of the International Students Work Rights Legal Service in Melbourne (http://jobwatch.org.au/home /international-students-work-rights-legal-centre/) and the International Student Legal Service in Sydney (https://rlc.org.au/our-services/international-students).

9. The emphasis on the value of eating bitterness resonates interestingly with Angela McRobbie's (2020) study of the valorization of resilience in popular neoliberal feminisms in the United Kingdom, suggesting a certain parallel in the social production of gender and youth subjectivity across British postwelfare and Chinese postsocialist contexts.

10. For a discussion of the feminization of e-commerce in China more broadly, see Yu and Cui (2019).

11. The latter two could be seen as examples of transnational money as a currency of care (Singh 2013, 176).

5. SEXUALITY

Some material from chapter 5 appeared in an earlier version in Fran Martin, "Overseas Study as Zone of Suspension: Chinese Students Re-negotiating Youth, Gender, and Intimacy," *Journal of Intercultural Studies* 39, no. 6 (2018): 688–703.

1. The latter model reflects a widely recognized international trend (see Chisholm 2014; Robertson, Harris and Baldassar 2018). For a discussion of how these women's renegotiations of the meanings of feminine youth could be related to Jeffrey Arnett's (2000) influential concept of "emerging adulthood," see Martin 2018.

2. On transforming sexual cultures in postreforms China—a field of study in itself— see also Jeffreys (2006), Liu W. (2010), Pei (2011), Jankowiak and Moore (2012), de Kloet and Fung (2017), and Jankowiak and Li (2017).

3. Although sexual racism and so-called yellow fever are surely a feature of some intimate relationships between Caucasian Australian men and Chinese women (Xi Chen

2018), this topic came up in conversations in this study mainly in relation to propositions from strangers (see chapter 2) rather than the handful of relationships between participants and white men. While some participants shuddered to think of white men objectifying them in an Orientalist fantasy of passive, obedient "Asian" girlfriends, conversely, a few participants who had had Australian boyfriends contrasted Western and Chinese forms of masculinity, associating the former with lower levels of male chauvinism.

4. A partial explanation may be that elite and middle-class urban youth appear to be the most liberal group in China vis-à-vis sexual attitudes and behaviors, and this group becomes concentrated in populations studying abroad (Pan S. 2006; Farrer 2014a). Possibly, too, students completing such a survey at their home universities in China, where student privacy protections are popularly understood to be weak, might be more anxious about confidentiality, hence more likely to give "safer" (more conservative) answers than students responding to an anonymous study conducted outside the Chinese system.

5. This preference was also reflected in survey results, with female respondents most likely to tell close friends in Australia, then parents, then close friends at home if they lived together with a partner and less likely to tell extended family members than any other group (F. Martin et al. 2019, 11).

6. This resonates with the situation that Penn Tsz Ting Ip observes among female rural-to-urban labor migrants in Shanghai, who similarly must negotiate between geoculturally distinct regimes of sex-gender norms and may do so (following Erving Goffman's [1959] terminology) through "audience separation and the creation of a double biography" (P. Ip 2018, 286).

7. This is supported by our survey findings: female respondents were less likely than male respondents to tell acquaintances and family members other than their parents if they lived with a partner before marriage, while women were more likely than men to tell close friends, especially those in Australia. This likely reflects women's gendered vulnerability to reputational damage by gossip back home (F. Martin et al. 2019, 11).

8. On bride-price practices in contemporary China, see Jiang and Sánchez-Barricarte (2012).

6. FAITH

1. However, despite significant numbers of Chinese students who engage with Christian churches while abroad, conversion rates may be significantly lower; see L. Liu (2016a).

2. The term *deterritorialized Christianity* is used in the literature on evangelical Christianity in the era of globalization to refer not to a form of Christianity somehow divorced from geography but rather to the acceleration and intensification of this religion's outward spread from those geographic areas where it has historically been embedded the longest and deepest (e.g., Miller 2015).

3. Unlike the case of the LDS Church, Pentecostalism's spread in the reforms era has been aided in part by the actions of undercover foreign missionaries (N. Cao 2013, 151).

4. See also Honghong's story in chapter 2. In that case, when a student suffered a psychotic breakdown, the gap in university services became extremely apparent. Honghong

got the medical care she needed only as a result of my happenstance intervention, and no one from her university visited her at the hospital, contacted her in relation to her condition, or liaised with her state-assigned psychiatrist and social worker.

7. PATRIOTISM

1. Other examples include the US bombing of the Chinese embassy in Belgrade in 1999, the 2005 controversy over new Japanese history textbooks denying Japanese war crimes in China, CNN's coverage of pro-Tibetan protests of the passage of the Olympic torch for the 2008 Beijing Olympics (Nyíri and Zhang 2010; Gries et al. 2011; F. Liu 2012), and the 2016 Taiwanese election (K. Fang and Repnikova 2017). While the definitional distinctions between patriotism and nationalism are often ambiguous, in this chapter I focus largely on patriotism in the sense of individuals' attachment to their homeland, as distinct from nationalism understood as individuals' hostile political views about other nations. For an overview of the international relations scholarship on this question with regard to China, see Woods and Dickson (2017).

2. For example, Alastair Iain Johnston's (2017) generational analysis of ordinary people's levels of nationalism in the Beijing area shows that on multiple measures, the generations affected by the Patriotic Education Campaign may in fact be *less* nationalistic than older Chinese citizens (see also L. Qian, Xu, and Chen 2017; Woods and Dickson 2017).

3. See also Min Dahong's (2004) related discussion of two parallel tendencies in Chinese cyberspace: growing nationalism vis-à-vis external affairs alongside critical realism vis-à-vis internal affairs.

4. Thanks to the friends who have helped me think through some of these complexities, especially Fan Yang, Jamie J. Zhao, Meng Xu, and Ka Weibo.

5. Patriotism is also gendered feminine in another pervasive trope: the ubiquitous figure of the "Chinese dream doll" (中国梦娃 *Zhongguo meng wa*), a sweet, chubby, animated little girl based on a traditional clay figurine who accompanies Chinese dream propaganda on public service broadcasts and posters throughout the nation (see Central Propaganda Department 2015).

6. The capacity of such popular Chinese media to arouse patriotic sentiment was noted by several participants.

7. Parents often also forbade participation in religious activities (see chapter 6).

8. This resonates somewhat with the "soft" tone observed in the cross-strait meme war over the results of Taiwan's 2016 election, when the term *little pinks* (小粉红 *xiao fenhong*) was co-opted by liberal intellectuals from the name of a Boys' Love fan forum as a derogatory term to designate a new, supposedly female generation of Chinese cybernationalists. However, Kecheng Fang and Maria Repnikova's (2017) research shows that while a majority of traceable participants were overseas students, only a minority appear to have been female; in their analysis, the 2016 wave of cybernationalism remains as relentlessly masculine as most other forms of Chinese nationalism. See also *Economist* (2016); and H. Liu (2019).

9. On the deep entanglement of the *suzhi* concept with the patriotic political discourse on China's cultural revival, see D. Lin (2017); on perceptions of Westerners' "high *suzhi*" by Chinese students abroad, see J. Chen (2019).

10. This was perhaps exacerbated by the context of the conversation Zhenghui related to me, which took place between her (a Chinese mainlander) and her boyfriend's Taiwanese mother, given Taiwan's earlier history of capitalist development, the foundations of which were laid during the Japanese colonial period, and the historically entrenched understanding in Taiwan that mainland China is developmentally backward compared to both Japan and Taiwan itself.

11. The idea that studying or living abroad tends to increase one's love for China is commonly circulated in China's public culture; see, for example, the influential political scientist Zhang Weiwei's (2014) discussion on the topic.

8. AFTER STUDY

1. Such services at times occupy a legal gray area. Several participants quoted the figure of $2,000 as the going rate for a three-month unwaged internship, and Qin reported that an employment consultancy used by a friend charged $20,000 for a job placement (she considered it a reasonable investment: "After all, it's just half a year's university fees"). Pingping had seen blatantly illegal sham schemes operating around 2017 that charged between $70,000 and $100,000 for direct employer nomination (separate from the points system), in which the "employee" being sponsored was not expected to work at all (these subsequently became rarer when policing was tightened). Comparable fee-for-internship services are available from employment consultancies in China.

2. On human mobility as an aspect of experiences of precarity, see Banki (2013); Bélanger and Tran Giang (2013); Castillo (2015); Paret and Gleeson (2016); Piper and Lee (2016); Schierup and Jørgensen (2017); Dutta and Kaur-Gill (2018); and Deshingkar (2019).

3. Lower-skilled jobs include work as laborers, sales workers, clerical and administrative workers, community and personal service workers, and technicians and trade workers. These categories combined accounted for about 52 percent of the total population of employed Chinese women on temporary visas (full-time and part-time). Sixteen percent of the total were unemployed and seeking work. Figures derived from Australian Bureau of Statistics (2016a). On Australian employers' reluctance to hire international student graduates, see also Hobsons Australia (2016) and Chew (2019).

4. For a detailed discussion on the extent to which overseas study fosters transnational or mobile lives poststudy, see Brooks and Waters (2011, 55–60).

5. Since participants in this study were recent graduates, those working for foreign companies had not yet had time to rise up the corporate ladder, like the women that Laurie Duthie (2005) studied, who demonstrated increased opportunities for women in foreign as compared with Chinese enterprises. But participants' experiences as new recruits in some of these firms suggest that the demands of the job may be so great that many may not stay long enough to attain more senior levels.

6. For a detailed and sensitive study on experiences of precarity among single women like Shang working in China's creative industries, see Y. Chow (2019).

7. On the hybridization of neotraditional patriarchal familialism with neoliberal individualism in the context of the state's withdrawal of safety nets and the consequent imperative for families to act as their members' social security system, see Ji (2017).

8. These mobile students' reorientation away from dreams and ambitions and toward a more chilled-out, "let it be" kind of outlook resonates with the attitude of a group within China dubbed "Buddha-style youth" (佛系青年 *Foxi qingnian*). This moniker—an internet slang term that took off in late 2017, derived from Japanese—does not refer to actual Buddhists but rather to members of the post-1990 generation who have become exhausted by and critical of the dominant culture's idealization of personal ambition, market competition, and the relentless pursuit of standard dreams. Rather than being inspired by aspirations toward self-advancement, so-called Buddha-style youth stage a kind of passive resistance, professing themselves content to relinquish desire and striving and instead embody averageness, passivity, and noncompetition (Bu, Meng, and Zhang 2018).

CONCLUSION

1. For work that does ground its claims about neoliberal subject formation in empirical human research, see, for example, Bondi (2005) and Petersen and O'Flynn (2007).

2. For a governmentality approach that avoids this trap by recognizing the multiplicity of technologies of governing, the hybridization of emergent neoliberal with residual Maoist imperatives, and the irreducible complexity of people's everyday engagements with these, see Hoffman (2010).

3. In another example, in her study of migrant women workers' mobile phone use, which is at other moments subtle and persuasive, Cara Wallis follows a top-down governmentality paradigm to conclude that "migrant women have internalized the discourse of *suzhi* (quality), in which compliance with urban norms of feminine conduct and demeanor is supposed to be the manifestation of a corresponding inner self-awareness, knowledge, and worth. Thus, the phone once again is shown to be a literal and figurative technology of the self, as the ideology of *suzhi* found its expression in the representation of the rural, female worker's body, which desired modern subjectivity" (2013, 133). The point here is not whether Wallis's conclusion is correct or not but rather whether facilitating interpellation by state modernization objectives is necessarily *the most important thing* that mobile phones do for migrant women workers, from the perspective of the women themselves, as this passage seems to imply.

4. I hope it is clear that by *singularity* I do not mean cultural particularity in the classical anthropological sense of presumptively discrete, bounded, and incommensurable "cultures"; rather, I refer to a certain ineffability in individuals' subjective experiences of themselves and their world, albeit a world ever more hybrid and interconnected (Comaroff and Comaroff 2003).

5. Eve Kosofsky Sedgwick and Adam Frank's (2003, 108–12) caution about the limitations of conceptualizing "Affect" itself in the generalized terms of high theory is also relevant here.

6. For a range of responses to related methodological questions concerning how to approach multiscaled social and cultural phenomena, see Hall (1980a); DeLanda (2006); and McCarthy (2008).

7. For an excellent critique of this risk discourse, see Kell and Vogl (2012).

8. This is despite the fact that, as Aihwa Ong neatly summarizes, "new practices of market-savvy personhood are not independent of the state but are an expression of self-will that reflects a socialist transformation of the neoliberal practice of 'governing at a distance'" (2008, 185; see also Wu X. 2009, 2010; Connelly et al. 2018). In fact, for some of these would-be "selective citizens," the powers of the Australian state were much more routinely in the foreground of consciousness than those of the Chinese state (L. Liu 2016b).

References

ABC (Australian Broadcasting Corporation). 2017. "Power and Influence: The Hard Edge of China's Soft Power." *Four Corners*, June 5, 2017. Video expired. Accessed June 8, 2017. https://www.abc.net.au/4corners/power-and-influence-promo/8579844.

ABC (Australian Broadcasting Corporation). 2019a. "Cash Cows: Australian Universities Making Billions Out of International Students." *Four Corners*, May 6, 2019. https://www.youtube.com/watch?v=Sm6lWJc8KmE.

ABC (Australian Broadcasting Corporation). 2019b. "How the Chinese Communist Party Infiltrated Australia's Universities." *Four Corners*, October 14, 2019. https://www.youtube.com/watch?v=JpARUtf1pCg.

ABC News. 2016. "Victorian Government to Crack Down on Melbourne's 'Dog Box' Apartments." August 13, 2016. http://www.abc.net.au/news/2016-08-14/melbourne-dog-box-apartments-targeted-in-new-design-guidelines/7732678.

Abur, William. 2012. "A Study of the South Sudanese Refugees' Perspectives of Settlement in the Western Suburbs of Melbourne." Master's thesis, Victoria University.

Ameeriar, Lalaie. 2017. *Downwardly Global: Women, Work, and Citizenship in the Pakistani Diaspora*. Durham, NC: Duke University Press.

Amin, Ash. 2002a. "Ethnicity and the Multicultural City: Living with Diversity." *Environment and Planning A: Economy and Space* 34 (6): 959–80.

Amin, Ash. 2002b. "Spatialities of Globalization." *Environment and Planning A: Economy and Space* 34 (3): 385–99.

Amin, Ash. 2004. "Regions Unbound: Towards a New Politics of Place." *Geografiska Annaler: Series B, Human Geography* 86 (1): 33–44.

Amin, Ash, and Nigel Thrift. 2017. *Seeing like a City*. Cambridge: Polity.

Amrute, Sareeta. 2016. *Encoding Race, Encoding Class: Indian IT Workers in Berlin*. Durham, NC: Duke University Press.

An Dongni 安东尼. 2008. 《陪安东尼度过漫长的岁月》 [A journey through time, with Anthony]. Wuhan: Changjiang Wenyi Chubanshe.

Anagnost, Ann. 2004. "The Corporeal Politics of Quality (*Suzhi*)." *Public Culture* 16 (2): 89–108.

Anderson, Allan, and Edmond Tang, eds. 2005. *Asian and Pentecostal: The Charismatic Face of Christianity in Asia*. Oxford: Regnum.

Anderson, Benedict. 1992. *Long-Distance Nationalism: World Capitalism and the Rise of Identity Politics*. Wertheim Lecture series. Amsterdam: Centre for Asian Studies.

Anderson, Kay, Ien Ang, Andrea Del Bono, Donald MacNeill, and Alexandra Wong. 2019. *Chinatown Unbound: Trans-Asian Urbanism in the Age of China*. London: Rowman and Littlefield.

Andersson, Magnus. 2012. "Media and Migration through the Lens of Mediatization and Transnationalism." Paper presented at International Communication Association annual conference, Phoenix, Arizona, May 24–28, 2012. http://lup.lub.lu.se/search/ws /files/40012686/media_migration_ICA_2012.pdf.

Ang, Ien. 2001. *On Not Speaking Chinese: Living between Asia and the West.* London: Routledge.

Ang, Ien, Jeffrey E. Brand, Greg Noble, and Derek Wilding. 2002. "Living Diversity: Australia's Multicultural Future." Artarmon, Sydney, Australia: Special Broadcasting Service. http://www.multiculturalaustralia.edu.au/doc/livingdiversity_1.pdf.

Aozhou Mirror 澳洲 Mirror. 2017. "那些来了澳洲的中国女人,为什么再也回不去了?" [Those Chinese women who came to Australia, why do they never go back?]. March 9, 2017. https://www.sohu.com/a/206620155_100010381.

Appadurai, Arjun. 1996. *Modernity at Large.* Minneapolis: University of Minnesota Press.

Appadurai, Arjun. 2004. "The Capacity to Aspire: Culture and the Terms of Recognition." In *Culture and Public Action*, edited by Vijayendra Rao and Michael Walton, 59–84. Stanford, CA: Stanford University Press.

Arnett, Jeffrey J. 2000. "Emerging Adulthood: A Theory of Development from the Late Teens through the Twenties." *American Psychologist* 55 (5): 469–480.

Astarita, Claudia, Allan Patience, and Sow Keat Tok. 2019. "Chinese Students in Australia: Generators of Cosmopolitanism, Evidence of Economic Necessity or Agents of Political Influence?" *Journal of Australian Studies* 43 (3): 317–32.

Augé, Marc. 1995. *Non-places: Introduction to an Anthropology of Supermodernity.* Translated by John Howe. London: Verso.

Australian Bureau of Statistics. 2016a. "Australian Census and Temporary Entrants Integrated Dataset, 2016": LFSP Labour Force Status (Hierarchical) by OCCP Occupation of Person by VISAP Visa Type, VPAFP Applicant Status, CPLP Citizenship Country and SEXP Sex. Private data purchase.

Australian Bureau of Statistics. 2016b. "2016 Census QuickStats: Box Hill (Vic.)." http://www.censusdata.abs.gov.au/census_services/getproduct/census/2016/quickstat /SSC20312.

Australian Bureau of Statistics. 2016c. "2016 Census QuickStats: Melbourne." https:// quickstats.censusdata.abs.gov.au/census_services/getproduct/census/2016/quickstat /LGA24600?opendocument.

Australian Bureau of Statistics. 2017. "Australia Today." https://www.abs.gov.au/ausstats /abs@.nsf/mf/2024.0.

Australian Bureau of Statistics. 2018. "2016 Census QuickStats: Greater Melbourne." http://www.censusdata.abs.gov.au/census_services/getproduct/census/2016/quickstat /2GMEL.

Australian Department of Education and Training. 2017. "International Student Data 2016." https://internationaleducation.gov.au/research/International-Student-Data /Pages/InternationalStudentData2016.aspx#Pivot_Table.

Australian Department of Education and Training. 2019. "International Student Enrolments in Australia 1994–2018." https://internationaleducation.gov.au/research

/International-Student-Data/Documents/INTERNATIONAL%20STUDENT%20
DATA/2018/2018%20Time%20Series%20Graph.pdf.

Australian Department of Education and Training, International Research and Analysis Unit. 2016. "China—Outbound and Inbound International Students." https://
internationaleducation.gov.au/research/Research-Snapshots/Documents/China
_outbound%20and%20inbound%20tertiary%20students.pdf.

Australian Department of Education and Training, International Research and Analysis Unit. 2017a. "Export Income to Australia from Educational Activity in 2016–17."
https://internationaleducation.gov.au/research/Research-Snapshots/Documents
/Export%20Income%20FY2016%E2%80%9317.pdf.

Australian Department of Education and Training, International Research and
Analysis Unit. 2017b. "International Student Data 2017: 2017 Pivot Tables."
https://internationaleducation.gov.au/research/International-Student-Data/Pages
/InternationalStudentData2017.aspx.

Australian Department of Education and Training, International Research and
Analysis Unit. 2017c. "International Student Enrolments in Australia 1994–2016."
https://internationaleducation.gov.au/research/International-Student-Data/Pages
/InternationalStudentData2016.aspx#Annual_Series.

Australian Department of Education and Training, International Research and
Analysis Unit. 2018. "International Student Data Monthly Summary." https://
internationaleducation.gov.au/research/International-Student-Data/Documents
/MONTHLY%20SUMMARIES/2018/Feb%202018%20MonthlyInfographic.pdf.

Australian Department of Education, Skills and Employment. 2020. "Global Reputation
Taskforce." https://internationaleducation.gov.au/News/Latest-News/Pages/Novel
-coronavirus-update-for-international-students.aspx.

Australian Department of Education, Skills and Employment. 2020. "Student Numbers."
https://internationaleducation.gov.au/research/DataVisualisations/Pages/Student
-number.aspx.

Australian Department of Home Affairs. 2019. "Points Table for Skilled Independent
Visa (Subclass 189)." https://immi.homeaffairs.gov.au/visas/getting-a-visa/visa-listing
/skilled-independent-189/points-table.

Australian Education International. 2010. *International Graduate Outcomes and Employer
Perceptions*. Canberra: Commonwealth of Australia.

Baas, Michiel. 2012. *Imagined Mobility: Migration and Transnationalism among Indian
Students in Australia*. London: Anthem.

Baas, Michiel. 2019. "The Education-Migration Industry: International Students, Migration Policy and the Question of Skills." *International Migration* 57 (2): 222–34.

Babones, Salvatore. 2019. "The China Student Boom and the Risks It Poses to Australian
Universities." China and Free Societies Analysis Paper 5, Centre for Independent Studies, Sydney. https://www.cis.org.au/app/uploads/2019/08/ap5.pdf.

Bai, Limin. 2006. "Graduate Unemployment: Dilemmas and Challenges in China's
Move to Mass Higher Education." *China Quarterly* 185:128–44.

Baidu Zhidao 百度知道. 2018. "为什么墨尔本叫墨村?" [Why is Melbourne called Melvillage?]. October 31, 2018. https://zhidao.baidu.com/question/982794219072911339.html.

Bakken, Børge. 2000. *The Exemplary Society: Human Improvement, Social Control, and the Dangers of Modernity in China.* Oxford: Oxford University Press.

Banki, Susan. 2013. "Precarity of Place: A Complement to the Growing Precariat Literature." Paper presented at the Power and Justice in the Contemporary World conference, New York, August 9, 2013. https://ses.library.usyd.edu.au/bitstream/handle/2123/9352/SusanBanki_PowerJusticePEWSConference%20Paper.pdf.

Bao, Hongwei. 2018. *Queer Comrades: Gay Identity and Tongzhi Activism in Postsocialist China.* Copenhagen: NIAS Press.

Barnett, Clive. 2005. "The Consolations of 'Neoliberalism.'" *Geoforum* 36:7–12.

Battersby, Lucy, and Christina Zhou. 2015. "Six Tonnes of Shopping Flying from Swanston Street to China Every Week." *Age,* August 21, 2015. http://www.theage.com.au/victoria/six-tonnes-of-shopping-flying-from-swanston-street-to-china-every-week-20150818-gj1vxf.html.

Beck, Ulrich. 1992. *Risk Society: Towards a New Modernity.* London: Sage.

Beck, Ulrich, and Elisabeth Beck-Gernsheim. 2002. *Individualisation: Institutionalised Individualism and Its Social and Political Consequences.* London: Sage.

Beck, Ulrich, and Elisabeth Beck-Gernsheim. 2010. "Foreword: Varieties of Individualisation." In *iChina: The Rise of the Individual in Modern Chinese Society*, edited by Mette Halskov Hansen and Rune Svarverud, xiii–xx. Copenhagen: NIAS Press.

Bélanger, Danièle, and Linh Tran Giang. 2013. "Precarity, Gender and Work: Vietnamese Migrant Workers in Asia." *Diversities* 15 (1): 5–20.

Bell, Emily. 2016. "The End of the News as We Know It: How Facebook Swallowed Journalism." Medium, March 7, 2016. https://medium.com/@TowCenter/the-end-of-the-news-as-we-know-it-how-facebook-swallowed-journalism-60344fa50962#.fiab6ge3k.

Belliappa, Jyothsna L. 2013. *Gender, Class and Reflexive Modernity in India.* New York: Palgrave Macmillan.

Bennett, W. Lance. 2004. "Global Media and Politics: Transnational Communication Regimes and Civic Cultures." *Annual Review of Political Science* 7:125–48.

Benson, Michaela, and Emma Jackson. 2013. "Place-Making and Place Maintenance: Performativity, Place and Belonging among the Middle Classes." *Sociology* 47 (4): 793–809.

Berg, Laurie, and Bassina Farbenblum. 2017. *Wage Theft in Australia: Findings of the National Temporary Migrant Work Survey.* Sydney: Migrant Worker Justice Initiative.

Berg, Laurie, and Bassina Farbenblum. 2020. *As If We Weren't Humans: The Abandonment of Temporary Migrants in Australia during COVID-19.* Sydney: Migrant Worker Justice Initiative.

Berlant, Lauren. 2011. *Cruel Optimism.* Durham, NC: Duke University Press.

Bian, Yanjie. 2002. "Chinese Social Stratification and Social Mobility." *Annual Review of Sociology* 28:91–116.

Bian, Yanjie, Ronald L. Breiger, Deborah Davis, and Joseph Galaskiewicz. 2005. "Occupation, Class and Social Networks in Urban China." *Social Forces* 83 (4): 1143–67.

Bishop, Julie. 2017. Doorstop interview. October 16, 2017. Transcript accessed October 18, 2017, subsequently removed. https://foreignminister.gov.au/transcripts/Pages/2017/jb_tr_171016.aspx?w=tb1CaGpkPX%2FlSoK%2Bg9ZKEg%3D%3D.

Blackmore, Jill, Cate Gribble, and Mark Rahimi. 2017. "International Education, the Formation of Capital and Graduate Employment: Chinese Accounting Graduates' Experiences of the Australian Labour Market." *Critical Studies in Education* 58 (1): 69–88.

Bloch, Barbara, and Tania Dreher. 2009. "Resentment and Reluctance: Working with Everyday Diversity and Everyday Racism in Southern Sydney." *Journal of Intercultural Studies* 30 (2): 193–209.

Bondi, Liz. 2005. "Working the Spaces of Neoliberal Subjectivity: Psychotherapeutic Technologies, Professionalisation and Counselling." *Antipode* 37 (3): 497–514.

Booth, Alison L., Andrew Leigh, and Elena Varganova. 2012. "Does Ethnic Discrimination Vary across Minority Groups? Evidence from a Field Experiment." *Oxford Bulletin of Economics and Statistics* 74 (4): 547–73.

Borys, Stephanie. 2020. "Universities Reject China's Claim That Australia Is Not Safe for International Students." *ABC News*, June 10, 2020. https://www.abc.net.au/news/2020-06-10/universities-reject-china-claims-international-students-unsafe/12337286.

Bourdieu, Pierre. 1986. "The Forms of Capital." In *Handbook of Theory and Research for the Sociology of Education*, edited by John Richardson, 241–58. Westport, CT: Greenwood.

Brady, Anne-Marie. 2017. "*Plus ça Change*? Media Control under Xi Jinping." *Problems of Post-Communism* 64 (3–4): 128–40.

Bregnbæk, Susanne. 2016. "Running into Nowhere: Educational Migration in Beijing and the Conundrum of Social and Existential Mobility." In *Politics of Precarity: Migrant Conditions, Struggles and Experiences*, edited by Carl-Ulrik Schierup and Martin Bak Jørgensen, 179–97. Leiden: Brill.

Brooks, Rachel, and Johanna Waters. 2011. *Student Mobilities, Migration and the Internationalization of Higher Education*. Basingstoke, UK: Palgrave Macmillan.

Brown, Wendy. 2015. *Undoing the Demos: Neoliberalism's Stealth Revolution*. Cambridge, MA: MIT Press.

Bu Jianhua 卜建华, Meng Liwen 孟丽雯, and Zhang Zongwei 张宗伟. 2018. "'佛系青年'群像的社会心态诊断与支持" [Social psychology diagnosis and support of "Buddha youth"]. 《中国青年研究》 [China youth study] 11:105–11, 61.

Buckley, Nick. 2017. "Dainty Sichuan Restaurant Group Allegedly Underpay Staff Thousands." *Broadsheet Melbourne*, July 17, 2017. https://www.broadsheet.com.au/melbourne/food-and-drink/dainty-sichuan-restaurant-group-allegedly-underpay-staff-thousands.

Bude, Heinz, and Jörg Dürrschmidt. 2010. "What's Wrong with Globalization? Contra 'Flow Speak'—towards an Existential Turn in the Theory of Globalization." *European Journal of Social Theory* 13 (4): 481–500.

Cai, Shenshen. 2019. "Talented Celebrity Rene Liu: Spokesperson of the Left-Over Women (*Sheng nu*)." In *Female Celebrities in Contemporary Chinese Society*, edited by Shenshen Cai, 105–26. Singapore: Palgrave Macmillan.

Cai, Yong, and Wang Feng. 2014. "(Re)emergence of Late Marriage in Shanghai: From Collective Synchronization to Individual Choice." In *Wives, Husbands and Lovers: Marriage and Sexuality in Hong Kong, Taiwan, and Urban China*, edited by Deborah S. Davis and Sara L. Friedman, 97–117. Stanford, CA: Stanford University Press.

Caixin. 2016. "China to Place New Taxes on Foreign Goods Bought via E-commerce." March 28, 2016. http://english.caixin.com/2016-03-28/100925526.html.

Callahan, William A. 2004. "National Insecurities: Humiliation, Salvation, and Chinese Nationalism." *Alternatives: Global, Local, Political* 29 (2): 199–218.

Cao, Nanlai. 2013. "Gender, Modernity, and Pentecostal Christianity in China." In *Global Pentecostalism in the 21st Century*, edited by Robert W. Hefner, 149–75. Indianapolis: Indiana University Press.

Cao Tongqing 曹同庆. 2018. "世界华文传媒新媒体影响力榜单发布 看看前十名都有谁" [World Chinese new media influence list released: Look who's in the top ten]. 《侨报网》 [*China Press*], May 24, 2018. Accessed September 16, 2018, subsequently removed. http://www.uschinapress.com/2018/0524/1132360.shtml.

Castells, Manuel. 1996. "Space of Flows, Space of Places: Materials for a Theory of Urbanism in the Information Age." In *The Cybercities Reader*, edited by Stephen Graham, 82–93. London: Routledge.

Castillo, Robert. 2015. "'Homing' Guangzhou: Emplacement, Belonging and Precarity among Africans in China." *International Journal of Cultural Studies* 19 (3): 287–306.

Central Propaganda Department 中宣部宣教局. 2015. "社会主义核心价值观公益广告" [Socialist core values public service advertisement]. 2:26. Uploaded by Warakorn Angsumalee วรากร อังศุมาลี, YouTube, December 5, 2015. https://www.youtube.com/watch?v=rxpGU3DRW5w.

Certeau, Michel de. 1984. *The Practice of Everyday Life*. Translated by Steven Rendall. Berkeley: University of California Press.

Chakrabarty, Dipesh. 1997. "The Time of History and the Times of Gods." In *The Politics of Culture in the Shadow of Capital*, edited by Lisa Lowe and David Lloyd, 35–60. Durham, NC: Duke University Press.

Chan, Brenda. 2005. "Imagining the Homeland: The Internet and Diasporic Discourse of Nationalism." *Journal of Communication Inquiry* 29 (4): 336–68.

Chang, Kyung-Sup. 2017. "China as a Complex Risk Society: Risk Components of Postsocialist Compressed Modernity." *Temporalités*, no. 26: 1–20.

Chang, Leslie T. 2009. *Factory Girls: From Village to City in a Changing China*. New York: Spiegel and Grau.

Chang, Shanton, Catherine Gomes, and Fran Martin. 2018. "Navigating Online Down Under: International Students' Digital Journeys in Australia." In *Transnational Migrations in the Asia-Pacific: Transformative Experiences in the Age of Digital Media*, edited by Brenda Yeoh and Catherine Gomes, 3–23. London: Rowman and Littlefield.

Chen, Juan. 2019. "Values Reconciliation: Constructing the Exemplary Ideal Personhood through Overseas Education." *Journal of Current Chinese Affairs* 48 (1): 29–49.

Chen, Minglu, and David S. G. Goodman. 2013. "Introduction: Middle Class China—Discourse, Structure and Practice." In *Middle Class China: Identity and Behaviour*, edited by Minglu Chen and David S. G. Goodman, 1–11. Cheltenham, UK: Edward Elgar.

Chen, Rou-lan. 2017. "Chinese Youth Nationalism in a Pressure Cooker." In *Taiwan and China: Fitful Embrace*, edited by Lowell Dittmer, 93–113. Oakland: University of California Press.

Chen, Xi. 2018. "Sojourner Intimacies: Chinese International Students Negotiating Dating in Sydney." Honours thesis, University of Sydney.

Chen, Xiaomei. 1995. *Occidentalism: A Theory of Counter-discourse in Post-Mao China.* Oxford: Oxford University Press.

Chen Yanmin 陈燕民, dir. 1997. 《追逐墨尔本》 [In pursuit of Melbourne]. TV series. China.

Chen Yuping 陈玉屏. 2017. "关于'祖国'和'国家'的理论思考" [A theoretical reflection on "homeland" and "nation"]. 《西南民族大学学报》 [Southwest Minzu University journal] 7:162–67.

Cheng, Yi'En, Peidong Yang, and Cora Lingling Xu. 2020. "Researching International Student Mobility into a Post-pandemic Future." *COMPAS* (blog), School of Anthropology, Oxford University, June 10, 2020. https://www.compas.ox.ac.uk/2020 /researching-international-student-mobility-into-a-post-pandemic-future-part-i/.

Cheng, Yinghong. 2011. "From Campus Racism to Cyber Racism: Discourse of Race and Chinese Nationalism." *China Quarterly* 207:561–79.

Cherlin, Andrew J. 2004. "The Deinstitutionalization of American Marriage." *Journal of Marriage and Family* 66 (4): 848–61.

Chew, Jonathan. 2019. *Economic Opportunities and Outcomes of Post-study Work Rights in Australia.* Melbourne: International Education Association of Australia (IEAA). https://www.ieaa.org.au/research/post-study-work-rights.

China Daily. 2012. "Beijing's Average Marriage Age Rises to 27." February 27, 2012. http://www.chinadaily.com.cn/china/2012-02/27/content_14704461.htm.

Chisholm, Lynne. 2014. "The Life-Course as Hypertext." In *Changing Landscapes for Childhood and Youth in Europe*, edited by Vassiliki Deliyianni, 2–13. Cambridge: Cambridge Scholars.

Chong, Gladys Pak Lei. 2013. "Chinese Bodies That Matter: The Search for Masculinity and Femininity." *International Journal of the History of Sport* 30 (3): 242–66.

Chong, Michelle, dir. 2013. 《他她它》 [3 peas in a pod]. Singapore: Huat Films.

Chow, Rey. 1991. *Woman and Chinese Modernity: The Politics of Reading between West and East.* Minneapolis: University of Minnesota Press.

Chow, Yiu Fai. 2019. *Caring in Times of Precarity: A Study of Single Women Doing Creative Work in Shanghai.* Cham: Palgrave Macmillan.

Christensen, Miyase, and André Jansson. 2015. *Cosmopolitanism and the Media: Cartographies of Change.* Basingstoke, UK: Palgrave Macmillan.

Chu, Koel. 2016. "Video: 'Totally Unacceptable': China Foreign Minister Lashes Out at Canadian Reporter for Asking about Human Rights." *Hong Kong Free Press*, June 2, 2016. https://www.hongkongfp.com/2016/06/02/totally-unacceptable -china-foreign-minister-lashes-out-at-canadian-reporter-for-asking-about-human -rights/.

Chun, Janet, dir. 2015. 《陪安东尼度过漫长岁月》 [Les aventures d'Anthony]. Beijing, China: Enlight Pictures.

City of Melbourne. 2013. "A Great Place to Study: International Student Strategy 2013–17." https://www.melbourne.vic.gov.au/SiteCollectionDocuments/internat -student-strategy-2013-17.pdf.

City of Melbourne. 2016. "City of Melbourne Tertiary Student and Education Profile." https://www.melbourne.vic.gov.au/SiteCollectionDocuments/tertiary-student -education-profile.pdf.

Clibborn, Stephen. 2018. "Multiple Frames of Reference: Why International Student Workers in Australia Tolerate Underpayment." *Economic and Industrial Democracy*, published online April 12, 2018. https://doi.org/10.1177/0143831X18765247.

Coates, Jamie. 2015. "'Unseeing' Chinese Students in Japan: Understanding Educationally Channelled Migrant Experiences." *Journal of Current Chinese Affairs* 44 (3): 125–54.

Cohen, Scott A., Tara Duncan, and Maria Thulemark. 2015. "Lifestyle Mobilities: The Crossroads of Travel, Leisure and Migration." *Mobilities* 10 (1): 155–72.

Colic-Peisker, Val, and Karen Farquharson. 2011. "Introduction: A New Era in Australian Multiculturalism? The Need for Critical Interrogation." *Journal of Intercultural Studies* 32 (6): 579–86.

Collins, Francis L. 2014. "Globalising Higher Education in and through Urban Spaces: Higher Education Projects, International Student Mobilities and Trans-local Connections in Seoul." *Asia Pacific Viewpoint* 55 (2): 242–57.

Collins, Francis L., Kong Chong Ho, Mayumi Ishikawa, and Ai-Hsuan Sandra Ma. 2017. "International Student Mobility and After-Study Lives: The Portability and Prospects of Overseas Education in Asia." *Population, Space and Place* 23 (4): 1–15.

Collins, Jock, Carol Reid, and Charlotte Fabiansson. 2011. "Identities, Aspirations and Belonging of Cosmopolitan Youth in Australia." *Cosmopolitan Civil Societies Journal* 3 (3): 92–107.

Collins, Randall. 1979. *The Credential Society: An Historical Sociology of Education and Stratification*. San Diego: Academic Press.

Comaroff, Jean, and John Comaroff. 2003. "Ethnography on an Awkward Scale: Postcolonial Anthropology and the Violence of Abstraction." *Ethnography* 4 (2): 147–79.

Connell, John. 2005. "Hillsong: A Megachurch in the Sydney Suburbs." *Australian Geographer* 36 (3): 315–32.

Connell, Raewyn. 2014. "Understanding Neoliberalism." In *Neoliberalism and Everyday Life*, edited by Susan Braedley and Meg Luxton, 22–36. Montreal: McGill-Queen's University Press.

Connelly, Rachel, Xiao-yuan Dong, Joyce Jacobsen, and Yaohui Zhao. 2018. "The Care Economy in Post-reform China: Feminist Research on Unpaid and Paid Work and Well-Being." *Feminist Economics* 24 (2): 1–30.

Conradson, David, and Alan Latham. 2005a. "Friendship, Networks and Transnationality in a World City: Antipodean Transmigrants in London." *Journal of Ethnic and Migration Studies* 31 (2): 287–305.

Conradson, David, and Alan Latham. 2005b. "Transnational Urbanism: Attending to Everyday Practices and Mobilities." *Journal of Ethnic and Migration Studies* 31 (2): 227–33.

Conradson, David, and Deirdre McKay. 2007. "Translocal Subjectivities: Mobility, Connection, Emotion." *Mobilities* 2 (2): 167–74.

Cook, Sarah, and Xiao-yuan Dong. 2011. "Harsh Choices: Chinese Women's Paid Work and Unpaid Care Responsibilities under Economic Reform." *Development and Change* 42 (2): 947–65.

Cornwall, Andrea, Jasmine Gideon, and Kalpana Wilson. 2008. "Introduction: Reclaiming Feminism: Gender and Neoliberalism." *IDS Bulletin* 39 (6): 1–9.

Couldry, Nick, and Andreas Hepp. 2017. *The Mediated Construction of Reality*. Cambridge: Polity.

Courtois, Aline. 2020. "Study Abroad as Governmentality: The Construction of Hypermobile Subjectivities in Higher Education." *Journal of Education Policy* 35 (2): 237–57.

Crime Statistics Agency Victoria. 2017. "Latest Crime Data by Area." https://www.crimestatistics.vic.gov.au/crime-statistics/latest-crime-data-by-area.

Croll, Elisabeth. 1995. *Changing Identities of Chinese Women: Rhetoric, Experience and Self-Perception in Twentieth-Century China*. London: Hong Kong University Press and Zed Books.

Csordas, Thomas J. 2007. "Introduction: Modalities of Transnational Transcendence." *Anthropological Theory* 7 (3): 257–72.

Cunningham, Stuart. 2001. "Popular Media as Public 'Sphericules' for Diasporic Communities." *International Journal of Cultural Studies* 4 (2): 131–47.

Cwerner, Saulo B. 2001. "The Time of Migration." *Journal of Ethnic and Migration Studies* 27 (1): 7–36.

Daskalova, Krassimira, Caroline Hornstein Tomic, Karl Kaser, and Filip Radunovic, eds. 2012. *Gendering Post-socialist Transition: Studies of Changing Gender Perspectives*. Vienna: LIT.

Davies, Anne, and Paul Karp. 2020. "'A Downward Spiral': Coronavirus Spins Australian Universities into Economic Crisis." *Guardian Australia*, April 14, 2020. https://www.theguardian.com/australia-news/2020/apr/14/a-downward-spiral-coronavirus-spins-australian-universities-into-economic-crisis.

Davis, Dána-Ain, and Christa Craven. 2016. *Feminist Ethnography: Thinking through Methodologies, Challenges, and Possibilities*. Lanham, MD: Rowman and Littlefield.

Davis, Deborah S., and Sara L. Friedman. 2014. "Deinstitutionalizing Marriage and Sexuality." In *Wives, Husbands and Lovers: Marriage and Sexuality in Hong Kong, Taiwan, and Urban China*, edited by Deborah S. Davis and Sara L. Friedman, 1–38. Stanford, CA: Stanford University Press.

de Kloet, Jeroen, and Anthony Fung. 2017. *Youth Cultures in China*. Cambridge: Polity.

DeLanda, Manuel. 2006. *A New Philosophy of Society: Assemblage Theory and Social Complexity*. London: Bloomsbury Academic.

Denniss, Richard. 2020. "After the Virus: Debt Warranted." *Saturday Paper* 322 (October 10–16): 7.

Denyer, Simon. 2017. "A Chinese Museum Paired Africans with Animals, Prompting Charges of Racism—and Then There's This Translation App." *Washington Post*, October 13, 2017.

Deshingkar, Priya. 2019. "The Making and Unmaking of Precarious, Ideal Subjects—Migration Brokerage in the Global South." *Journal of Ethnic and Migration Studies* 45 (14): 2638–54.

de Souza e Silva, Adriana. 2006. "From Cyber to Hybrid: Mobile Technologies as Interfaces of Hybrid Spaces." *Space and Culture* 9 (3): 261–78.

Dhanji, Surjeet. 2009. "Welcome or Unwelcome? Integration Issues and the Resettlement of Former Refugees from the Horn of Africa and Sudan in Metropolitan Melbourne." *Australasian Review of African Studies* 30 (2): 152–78.

Dikötter, Frank. 1992. *The Discourse of Race in Modern China*. Stanford, CA: Stanford University Press.

Ding Wei 丁未 and Tian Qian 田阡. 2009. "流动的家园：新媒介技术与农民工社会关系个案研究" [The mobile home: A case study of new media usage and migrant workers' social relationship]. 《新闻与传播研究》 [Journalism and communication] 1:61–70.

Dirlik, Arif. 2012. "The Idea of a 'Chinese Model': A Critical Discussion." *China Information* 26 (3): 277–302.

Donald, Stephanie H., and Yi Zheng. 2008. "Richer than Before: The Cultivation of Middle-Class Taste: Reading, Tourism and Education Choices in Urban China." In *The New Rich in China: Future Rulers, Present Lives*, edited by David S. G. Goodman, 71–82. London: Routledge.

Dovey, Kim. 2010. *Becoming Places: Urbanism/Architecture/Identity/Power*. London: Routledge.

Dow, Aisha. 2015. "Melbourne's Illegal High-Rise Rooming Houses Profit from Foreign Students." *Age*, June 21, 2015. https://www.theage.com.au/national/victoria/melbournes-illegal-highrise-rooming-Economisthouses-profit-from-foreign-students-20150611-ghl8un.html.

Du, Fenglian, and Xiao-yuan Dong. 2009. "Why Do Women Have Longer Durations of Unemployment than Men in Post-restructuring Urban China?" *Cambridge Journal of Economics* 33 (2): 233–52.

Duffy, Conor. 2020. "Government Announces Coronavirus Relief Package for Higher Education with Focus on Domestic Students." *ABC News*, April 12, 2020. https://mobile.abc.net.au/news/2020-04-12/government-announces-coronavirus-higher-education-relief-package/12142752.

Duhigg, Charles. 2013. *The Power of Habit: Why We Do What We Do in Life and Business*. London: Random House.

Dukalskis, Alexander. 2018. "The Chinese Communist Party Has Growing Sway in Western Universities." Democratic Audit UK, April 1, 2018. http://www.democraticaudit.com/2018/01/04/the-chinese-communist-party-has-growing-sway-in-western-universities/.

Dunn, Kevin, Danielle Pelleri, and Karin Maeder-Han. 2011. "Attacks on Indian Students: The Commerce of Denial in Australia." *Race and Class* 52 (4): 71–88.

Durkin, Patrick. 2019. "The Daigou Channel Is Different, Not Gone." *Australian Financial Review*, November 7, 2019. https://www.afr.com/companies/retail/the-daigou-channel-is-different-not-gone-20191106-p537ze.

Duthie, Laurie. 2005. "White Collars with Chinese Characteristics: Global Capitalism and the Formation of a Social Identity." *Anthropology of Work Review* 26 (3): 1–12.

Dutta, Mohan Jyoti, and Satveer Kaur-Gill. 2018. "Precarities of Migrant Work in Singapore: Migration, (Im)Mobility, and Neoliberal Governmentality." *International Journal of Communication* 12:4066–84.

Dziedzic, Stephen. 2017. "Government Needs to Be 'Very Conscious' of Foreign Interference in Australian Universities, ASIO Says." *ABC News*, October 25, 2017. https://www.abc.net.au/news/2017-10-25/government-very-conscious-foreign-interference-australian-unis/9082948.

Economist. 2016. "The East Is Pink: Youthful Nationalists." August 13, 2016, 30.

Edensor, Tim. 2002. *National Identity, Popular Culture and Everyday Life*. Oxford: Berg.

Elliott, Anthony, and John Urry. 2010. *Mobile Lives*. London: Routledge.

Engebretsen, Elisabeth. 2014. *Queer Women in Urban China: An Ethnography*. London: Routledge.

Engebretsen, Elisabeth. 2017. "Under Pressure: Lesbian-Gay Contract Marriages and Their Patriarchal Bargains." In *Transforming Patriarchy: Chinese Families in the Twenty-First Century*, edited by Gonçalo Santos and Stevan Harrell, 163–81. Seattle: University of Washington Press.

England, Paula, and Elizabeth Aura McClintock. 2009. "The Gendered Double Standard of Aging in US Marriage Markets." *Population and Development Review* 35 (4): 797–816.

Essed, Philomena. 1991. *Understanding Everyday Racism: An Interdisciplinary Theory*. Newbury Park, CA: Sage.

Evans, Harriet. 2002. "Past, Perfect or Imperfect: Changing Images of the Ideal Wife." In *Chinese Femininities, Chinese Masculinities: A Reader*, edited by Susan Brownell and Jeffrey N. Wasserstrom, 335–60. Berkeley: University of California Press.

Evans, Russell. 2004. *Profile of a Planetshaker*. With Dave Reardon. Adelaide: Planetshakers Ministries International.

Fan, Yiying. 2017. "Chinese Grads Return Home with Degrees and Disillusionment." *Sixth Tone*, November 11, 2017. http://www.sixthtone.com/news/1001154/chinese-grads-return-home-with-degrees-and-disillusionment.

Fang, I-chieh. 2013. "The Girls Who Are Keen to Get Married." In *Ordinary Ethics in China*, edited by Charles Stafford, 66–79. London: Bloomsbury Academic.

Fang, Kecheng, and Maria Repnikova. 2017. "Demystifying 'Little Pink': The Creation and Evolution of a Gendered Label for Nationalistic Activists in China." *New Media and Society* 20 (6): 2162–85.

Farrer, James. 2002. *Opening Up: Youth Sex Culture and Market Reform in Shanghai*. Chicago: University of Chicago Press.

Farrer, James. 2014a. "Love, Sex and Commitment: Delinking Premarital Intimacy from Marriage in Urban China." In *Wives, Husbands, and Lovers: Marriage and Sexuality in Hong Kong, Taiwan, and Urban China*, edited by Deborah S. Davis and Sara L. Friedman, 62–96. Stanford, CA: Stanford University Press.

Farrer, James. 2014b. "Youth and Sexuality in China: A Century of Revolutionary Change." In *Routledge Handbook of Sexuality Studies in East Asia*, edited by Vera Mackie and Mark McLelland, 150–61. London: Routledge.

Fenton, Natalie. 2010. "Drowning or Waving? New Media, Journalism and Democracy." In *New Media, Old News: Journalism and Democracy in the Digital Age*, edited by Natalie Fenton, 3–16. London: Sage.

Ferguson, Adele. 2005. "Prophet-Minded." *BRW*, May 26–June 1, 2005, 34–41. http://www.moriah.com.au/textarchive/AOG-Profits.pdf.

Ferguson, Hazel, and Henry Sherrell. 2019. "Overseas Students in Australian Higher Education: A Quick Guide." Parliament of Australia, June 20, 2019. https://www.aph.gov.au/About_Parliament/Parliamentary_Departments/Parliamentary_Library/pubs/rp/rp1819/Quick_Guides/OverseasStudents.

Fernando, Mayanthi L., and Susan Harding. 2020. "Practices of Relation." *The Immanent Frame: Secularism, Religion and the Public Sphere*, April 27, 2020. https://tif.ssrc.org/2020/04/27/fernando-and-harding/.

Fincher, Ruth. 2011. "Cosmopolitan or Ethnically Identified Selves? Institutional Expectations and the Negotiated Identities of International Students." *Social and Cultural Geography* 12 (8): 905–27.

Fincher, Ruth, and Kate Shaw. 2009. "The Unintended Segregation of Transnational Students in Central Melbourne." *Environment and Planning A: Economy and Space* 41 (8): 1884–1902.

Fish, Eric. 2015. *China's Millennials: The Want Generation*. Lanham, MD: Rowman and Littlefield.

Fong, Vanessa L. 2002. "China's One-Child Policy and the Empowerment of Urban Daughters." *American Anthropologist* 104 (4): 1098–109.

Fong, Vanessa L. 2004a. "Filial Nationalism among Chinese Teenagers with Global Identities." *American Ethnologist* 31 (4): 631–48.

Fong, Vanessa L. 2004b. *Only Hope: Coming of Age under China's One-Child Policy*. Stanford, CA: Stanford University Press.

Fong, Vanessa L. 2011. *Paradise Redefined: Transnational Chinese Students and the Quest for Flexible Citizenship in the Developed World*. Stanford, CA: Stanford University Press.

Fong, Vanessa L., Cong Zhang, Sang won Kim, Hirokazu Yoshikawa, Niobe Way, Xinyin Chen, Zuhong Lu, and Huihua Dang. 2012. "Gender Role Expectations and Chinese Mothers' Aspirations for Their Toddler Daughters' Future Independence and Excellence." In *Chinese Modernity and the Individual Psyche*, edited by Andrew Kipnis, 89–117. New York: Palgrave Macmillan.

Foster, Robert J. 2002. "Bargains with Modernity in Papua New Guinea and Elsewhere." *Anthropological Theory* 2 (2): 233–51.

Franquesa, Jaume. 2011. "'We've Lost Our Bearings': Place, Tourism, and the Limits of the 'Mobility Turn.'" *Antipode* 43 (4): 1012–33.

Freeman, Carla. 2001. "Is Local : Global as Feminine : Masculine? Rethinking the Gender of Globalization." *Signs* 26 (4): 1007–37.

Freeman, Carla. 2014. *Entrepreneurial Selves: Neoliberal Respectability and the Making of a Caribbean Middle Class*. Durham, NC: Duke University Press.

Freeman, Elizabeth. 2010. *Time Binds: Queer Temporalities, Queer Histories*. Durham, NC: Duke University Press.

Gaetano, Arianne M. 2014. "'Leftover Women': Postponing Marriage and Renegotiating Womanhood in Urban China." *Journal of Research in Gender Studies* 4 (2): 124–49.

Gaetano, Arianne M. 2015. *Out to Work: Migration, Gender, and the Changing Lives of Rural Women in Contemporary China*. Honolulu: University of Hawai'i Press.

Gao, Zhihong. 2015. "When Nationalism Goes to the Market: The Case of Chinese Patriotic Songs." *Journal of Macromarketing* 35 (4): 473–88.

Gao-Miles, Linling. 2017. "Beyond the Ethnic Enclave: Interethnicity and Trans-spatiality in an Australian Suburb." *City and Society* 19 (1): 82–103.

García Canclini, Néstor. 2014. *Imagined Globalization*. Durham, NC: Duke University Press.

Garnaut, John. 2017. "Our Universities Are a Frontline in China's Ideological Wars." *Financial Review*, August 30, 2017. https://www.afr.com/news/economy/our -universities-are-a-frontline-in-chinas-ideological-wars-20170830-gy74br.

Gatt, Krystle. 2011. "Sudanese Refugees in Victoria: An Analysis of Their Treatment by the Australian Government." *International Journal of Comparative and Applied Criminal Justice* 35 (3): 207–19.

Georgiou, Myria. 2011. "Media and the City: Making Sense of Place." *International Journal of Media and Cultural Politics* 6 (3): 343–50.

Gergen, Kenneth J. 2002. "Self and Community in the New Floating Worlds." In *Mobile Democracy: Essays on Society, Self and Politics*, edited by K. Nyiri, 103–14. Vienna: Passagen.

Giddens, Anthony. 1990. *The Consequences of Modernity*. Cambridge: Polity.

Giddens, Anthony. 1991. *Modernity and Self-Identity: Self and Society in the Late Modern Age*. Stanford, CA: Stanford University Press.

Giddens, Anthony. 1999. "Risk and Responsibility." *Modern Law Review* 62 (1): 1–10.

Gilbert, Melissa R. 1998. "'Race,' Space and Power: The Survival Strategies of Working Poor Women." *Annals of the Association of American Geographers* 88 (4): 595–621.

Goffman, Erving. 1959. *The Presentation of Self in Everyday Life*. New York: Anchor Books.

Goleman, Daniel. 2005. *Emotional Intelligence: Why It Can Matter More than IQ*. London: Bloomsbury.

Goleman, Daniel. 2014. *Focus: The Hidden Driver of Excellence*. London: Bloomsbury.

Gomes, Catherine. 2017. *Transient Mobility and Middle Class Identity: Media and Migration in Australia and Singapore*. Singapore: Palgrave Macmillan.

Goodman, David S. G., ed. 2008a. *The New Rich in China: Future Rulers, Present Lives*. London: Routledge.

Goodman, David S. G. 2008b. "Why China Has No New Middle Class: Cadres, Managers and Entrepreneurs." In *The New Rich in China: Future Rulers, Present Lives*, edited by David S. G. Goodman, 23–37. London: Routledge.

Goodman, David S. G. 2014. *Class in Contemporary China*. Cambridge: Polity.

Goodman, David S. G., and Xiaowei Zhang. 2008. "Introduction: The New Rich in China: The Dimensions of Social Change." In *The New Rich in China: Future Rulers, Present Lives*, edited by David S. G. Goodman, 1–20. London: Routledge.

Gordon, Avery F. 2008. *Ghostly Matters: Haunting and the Sociological Imagination*. 2nd ed. Minneapolis: Minnesota University Press.

Gorman-Murray, Andrew. 2009. "Intimate Mobilities: Emotional Embodiment and Queer Migration." *Social and Cultural Geography* 10 (4): 441–60.

Grant, Stan. 2020. "Coronavirus Has Sped Up Changes to Global Order and Sovereignty Is Making a Comeback." *ABC News*, April 13, 2020. https://mobile.abc.net.au/news /2020-04-13/coronavirus-changes-to-global-order-us-china/12139216.

Greene, Andrew, and Stephen Dziedzic. 2017. "China's Soft Power: Julie Bishop Steps Up Warning to University Students on Communist Party Rhetoric." *ABC News*, October 16, 2017. https://www.abc.net.au/news/2017–10–16/bishop-steps-up-warning-to-chinese-university-students/9053512.

Greiner, Clemens, and Patrick Sakdapolrak. 2013. "Translocality: Concepts, Applications and Emerging Research Perspectives." *Geography Compass* 7 (5): 373–84.

Gries, Peter Hayes, Qingmin Zhang, H. Michael Crowson, and Huajian Cai. 2011. "Patriotism, Nationalism and China's US Policy: Structures and Consequences of Chinese National Identity." *China Quarterly* 205:1–17.

Griffiths, M., A. Rogers, and B. Anderson. 2013. "Migration, Time and Temporalities: Review and Prospect." Centre of Migration Policy and Society (COMPAS) Research Resources Paper, March 2013. https://www.compas.ox.ac.uk/wp-content/uploads/RR-2013-Migration_Time_Temporalities.pdf.

Grigg, Angus, and Lisa Murray. 2017. "Australia's Biggest Daigou Who Can Make or Break Brands in China." *Australian Financial Review*, May 31. https://www.afr.com/companies/retail/meet-australias-biggest-daigou-who-can-make-or-break-brands-in-china-20170523-gwavsx.

Gu, Qing. 2015. "An Emotional Journey of Identity Change and Transformation: The Impact of Study-Abroad Experience on the Lives and Careers of Chinese Students and Returnees." *Learning and Teaching* 8 (3): 60–81.

Gu, Queenie. 2016. "看不惯牵手就结婚,受不了上床没结果: 陷在保守与激情夹缝中的留学生" [Can't accept getting married the moment you've held hands but can't stand going to bed with nothing to show for it: International students caught between conservatism and passion].《东成西就教育文化交流》[eastwest 100 WeChat public account], July 17, 2016. http://mp.weixin.qq.com/s?__biz=MjM5MzY1NjQzNw==&mid=2651985010&idx=1&sn=cfd6d0c05becfa35070b255e71c903e8&scene=1&srcid=071775MbCZeMy4k7OZ1KvvSZ.

Gwo, Frant, dir. 2019.《流浪地球》[The wandering earth]. Beijing: China Film Group Corporation.

Hage, Ghassan. 2009. "Waiting Out the Crisis: On Stuckedness and Governmentality." In *Waiting*, edited by Ghassan Hage, 97–106. Carlton: Melbourne University Press.

Haigh, Adam. 2016. "Blackmores CEO Downplays China E-Commerce Tax as Shares Sink." *Bloomberg*, April 11, 2016. http://www.bloomberg.com/news/articles/2016-04-12/blackmores-ceo-downplays-china-e-commerce-tax-as-shares-tumble.

Hail, Henry Chiu. 2015. "Patriotism Abroad: Overseas Chinese Students' Encounters with Criticism of China." *Journal of Studies in International Education* 19 (4): 311–26.

Hall, Stuart. 1980a. "Cultural Studies: Two Paradigms." *Media, Culture and Society* 2 (1): 57–72.

Hall, Stuart. 1980b. "Encoding/Decoding." In *Culture, Media, Language*, edited by Stuart Hall, Dorothy Hobson, Andrew Love, and Paul Willis, 128–38. London: Hutchinson.

Hall, Stuart. 1988. "The Toad in the Garden: Thatcherism among the Theorists." In *Marxism and the Interpretation of Culture*, edited by Cary Nelson and Lawrence Grossberg, 35–74. Urbana: University of Illinois Press.

Han, Huamei. 2011. "Love Your China and Evangelise: Religion, Nationalism, Racism and Immigrant Sentiment in Canada." *Ethnography and Education* 6 (1): 61–79.

Hannerz, Ulf. 2000. "Thinking about Culture in a Global Ecumene." In *Culture in the Communication Age*, edited by James Lull, 54–71. London: Routledge.

Hansen, Anders Sybrandt. 2015. "The Temporal Experience of Chinese Students Abroad and the Present Human Condition." *Journal of Current Chinese Affairs* 44 (3): 49–77.

Hansen, Mette Halskov, and Cuiming Pang. 2010. "Idealizing Individual Choice: Work, Love and Family in the Eyes of Young, Rural Chinese." In *iChina: The Rise of the Individual in Modern Chinese Society*, edited by Mette Halskov Hansen and Rune Svarverud, 39–64. Copenhagen: NIAS Press.

Hansen, Mette Halskov, and Rune Svarverud, eds. 2010. *iChina: The Rise of the Individual in Modern Chinese Society*. Copenhagen: NIAS Press.

Hanson, Susan. 2010. "Gender and Mobility: New Approaches for Informing Sustainability." *Gender, Place and Culture: A Journal of Feminist Geography* 17 (1): 5–23.

Hao, Jie. 2012. "Employability of Australian-Educated Chinese Postgraduates in China: A Study of the University of Sydney." PhD diss., University of Sydney.

Hao, Jie, and Anthony R. Welch. 2012. "A Tale of Sea Turtles: Job-Seeking Experiences of Hai Gui (High-Skilled Returnees) in China." *Higher Education Policy* 25 (2): 243–60.

Hao, Jie, Wen Wen, and Anthony Welch. 2016. "When Sojourners Return: Employment Opportunities and Challenges Facing High-Skilled Chinese Returnees." *Asia and Pacific Migration Journal* 25 (1): 22–40.

Hao, Yanbo. 2019. "Wandering at a Crossroad: An Exploration of Gendered Mobility Aspirations in the Study-to-Work Transition of Chinese Graduates at Dutch Universities." Master's thesis, Utrecht University.

Harding, Susan. 2020. "Secular Trouble: Regulating Reality in Non-fiction Literatures." *Christianity and Literature* 69 (4): 126–37.

Harman, Grant. 2005. "Internationalization of Australian Higher Education: A Critical Review of Literature and Research." In *Internationalizing Higher Education*, edited by Peter Ninnes and Meeri Hellstén, 119–40. Heidelberg: Springer.

Harrell, Stevan, and Gonçalo Santos. 2017. Introduction to *Transforming Patriarchy: Chinese Families in the Twenty-First Century*, edited by Gonçalo Santos and Stevan Harrell, 3–36. Seattle: University of Washington Press.

Harris, Anita. 2013. *Young People and Everyday Multiculturalism*. London: Routledge.

Harris, Anita, Loretta Baldassar, and Roberta Raffaeta. 2015. "Chinese Youth across Wenzhou and Prato: From Hybridity to Mobile Belongings." Paper presented at Asian Migration and Rooted Transnationalism conference, Monash Asia Institute, November 19–20, 2015.

Harvey, David. 2005. *A Brief History of Neoliberalism*. Oxford: Oxford University Press.

Healey, Patsy. 2002. "On Creating the 'City' as a Collective Resource." *Urban Studies* 39 (10): 1777–92.

Heaton, Bill. 1980. "Mormonism and Maoism: The Church and People's China." *Dialogue: A Journal of Mormon Thought* 8 (1): 40–50.

Hefner, Robert W. 2013. "Introduction: The Unexpected Modern—Gender, Piety, and Politics in the Global Pentecostal Surge." In *Global Pentecostalism in the 21st Century*, edited by Robert W. Hefner, 1–36. Indianapolis: Indiana University Press.

Heinerman, John, and Anson Shupe. 1985. *The Mormon Corporate Empire*. Boston: Beacon.

Hepp, Andreas. 2009. "Localities of Diasporic Communicative Spaces: Material Aspects of Translocal Mediated Networking." *Communication Review* 12 (4): 327–48.

Herbert, Steve. 2016. "Victorian Education Leading the Way in China." Media release from the Victorian minister for training and skills. Accessed February 15, 2017, subsequently removed. http://www.premier.vic.gov.au/victorian-education-leading-the-way-in-china/.

Hey, Sam. 2013. *Megachurches: Origins, Ministry and Prospects*. Eugene, OR: Wipf and Stock.

Ho, Christina. 2011. "Respecting the Presence of Others: School Micropublics and Everyday Multiculturalism." *Journal of Intercultural Studies* 32 (6): 603–19.

Ho, Christina. 2020. *Aspiration and Anxiety: Asian Migrants and Australian Schooling*. Carlton: Melbourne University Press.

Hobsons Australia. 2016. *The Employability of International Student Graduates in Australia*. Melbourne: Hobsons Solutions.

Hochschild, Arlie Russell. 2003. *The Managed Heart: Commercialization of Human Feeling*. 2nd ed. Berkeley: University of California Press.

Hoffman, Lisa. 2010. *Patriotic Professionalism in Urban China: Fostering Talent*. Philadelphia: Temple University Press.

Hogan, Bernie. 2010. "The Presentation of Self in the Age of Social Media: Distinguishing Performances and Exhibitions Online." *Bulletin of Science, Technology and Society* 30 (6): 377–86.

Hong Fincher, Leta. 2014. *Leftover Women: The Resurgence of Gender Inequality in China*. London: Zed Books.

Hong Fincher, Leta. 2018. *Betraying Big Brother: The Feminist Awakening in China*. London: Verso.

Hsu, Carolyn L. 2007. *Creating Market Socialism: How Ordinary People Are Shaping Class and Status in China*. Durham, NC: Duke University Press.

Hua, Wen. 2013. *Buying Beauty: Cosmetic Surgery in China*. Hong Kong: Hong Kong University Press.

Huang, Xin. 2018. *The Gender Legacy of the Mao Era: Women's Life Stories in Contemporary China*. New York: State University of New York Press.

Human Rights and Equal Opportunity Commission. 2009. *African Australians: A Report on Human Rights and Social Inclusion Issues*. Sydney: Human Rights and Equal Opportunity Commission. https://www.humanrights.gov.au/sites/default/files/content/africanaus/AFA_2009.pdf.

Human Rights Watch. 2018. *"Only Men Need Apply": Gender Discrimination in Job Advertisements in China*. New York: Human Rights Watch. https://www.hrw.org/report/2018/04/23/only-men-need-apply/gender-discrimination-job-advertisements-china.

Huppatz, Kate. 2009. "Reworking Bourdieu's 'Capital': Feminine and Female Capitals in the Field of Paid Caring Work." *Sociology* 43 (1): 45–66.

Indelicato, Maria Elena. 2018. *Australia's New Migrants: International Students' History of Affective Encounters with the Border*. London: Routledge.

Ip, David. 2005. "Contesting Chinatown: Place-Making and the Emergence of 'Ethnoburbia' in Brisbane, Australia." *GeoJournal* 64 (1): 63–74.

Ip, Penn Tsz Ting. 2018. "Female Migrant Workers Navigating the Service Economy in Shanghai: Home, Beauty and the Stigma of Singlehood." PhD diss., University of Amsterdam.

Irvine, Jessica. 2015. "Why Baby Formula Is the New Iron Ore." *Age*, November 12, 2015. http://www.theage.com.au/comment/why-infant-formula-is-the-new-iron-ore-20151112-gkxdq3.html.

Isaković, Nela Porobić. 2020. "What Has COVID-19 Taught Us about Neoliberalism?" Women's International League for Peace and Freedom, March 23, 2020. https://www.wilpf.org/covid-19-what-has-covid-19-taught-us-about-neoliberalism/?fbclid=IwAR2bhhlfr1SwX12HJEyQr6EqOS0Ac4j9Ke79w-Hlnuc5QoejXcCNwoqvKaY.

Jacka, Tamara. 2006. *Rural Women in Urban China: Gender, Migration, and Social Change*. Armonk, NY: Sharpe.

Jankowiak, William. 2013. "Chinese Youth: Hot Romance and Cold Calculation." In *Restless China*, edited by Perry Link, Richard P. Madsen, and Paul G. Pickowicz, 191–212. Lanham, MD: Rowman and Littlefield.

Jankowiak, William, and Xuan Li. 2017. "Emergent Conjugal Love, Mutual Affection, and Female Marital Power." In *Transforming Patriarchy: Chinese Families in the Twenty-First Century*, edited by Gonçalo Santos and Stevan Harrel, 146–62. Seattle: University of Washington Press.

Jankowiak, William, and R. L. Moore. 2012. "China's Emergent Youth: Gender, Work, Dating and Life Orientation." In *Adolescent Identity: Evolutionary, Cultural and Developmental Perspectives*, edited by Bonnie L. Hewlett, 277–300. New York: Routledge.

Jeffreys, Elaine, ed. 2006. *Sex and Sexuality in China*. London: Routledge.

Jeffreys, Elaine. 2015. *Sex in China*. With Haiqing Yu. Cambridge: Polity.

Ji, Yingchun. 2015. "Between Tradition and Modernity: 'Leftover' Women in Shanghai." *Journal of Marriage and Family* 77 (5): 1057–73.

Ji, Yingchun. 2017. "A Mosaic Temporality: New Dynamics of the Gender and Marriage System in Contemporary Urban China." *Temporalités*, no. 26. https://journals.openedition.org/temporalites/3773.

Ji, Yingchun, and Wei-Jun Jean Yeung. 2014. "Heterogeneity in Contemporary Chinese Marriage." *Journal of Family Issues* 35 (12): 1662–82.

Jiang, Quanbao, and Jesús J. Sánchez-Barricarte. 2012. "Bride Price in China: The Obstacle to 'Bare Branches' Seeking Marriage." *History of the Family* 17 (1): 2–15.

Jinri Chuanmei Jituan 今日传媒集团. 2015. 《今日传媒集团 Media Kit 2015》 [Media Today Group media kit 2015]. Sydney. https://mediatodaygroup.com/vip.php.

Johnson, Jessica. 2017. "Bodily Encounters: Affect, Religion, and Ethnography." In *Feeling Religion*, edited by John Corrigan, 200–222. Durham, NC: Duke University Press.

Johnson, M. Dujon. 2007. *Race and Racism in the Chinas: Chinese Racial Attitudes toward Africans and African-Americans*. Bloomington, IN: AuthorHouse.

Johnson, Mark. 2010. "Diasporic Dreams, Middle Class Moralities and Migrant Domestic Workers among Muslim Filipinos in Saudi Arabia." *Asia Pacific Journal of Anthropology* 11 (3–4): 428–48.

Johnston, Alastair Iain. 2017. "Is Chinese Nationalism Rising? Evidence from Beijing." *International Security* 41 (3): 7–43.

Kajanus, Anni. 2015. *Chinese Student Migration, Gender and Family*. Basingstoke, UK: Palgrave Macmillan.

Kam, Lucetta Yip Lo. 2012. *Shanghai Lalas: Female Tongzhi Communities and Politics in Urban China*. Hong Kong: Hong Kong University Press.

Kam, Lucetta Yip Lo. 2020. "Coming Out and Going Abroad: The *Chuguo* Mobility of Queer Women in China." *Journal of Lesbian Studies* 24 (2): 126–39.

Kandiyoti, Deniz. 1988. "Bargaining with Patriarchy." *Gender and Society* 2 (3): 274–90.

Karp, Paul. 2019. "Penny Wong Blasts 'Malicious' WeChat Campaign Spreading Fake News about Labor." *Guardian*, May 7, 2019. https://www.theguardian.com/australia-news/2019/may/07/penny-wong-blasts-malicious-wechat-campaign-spreading-fake-news-about-labor.

Kaufmann, Vincent, Manfred Max Bergman, and Dominique Joye. 2004. "Motility: Mobility as Capital." *International Journal of Urban and Regional Research* 28 (4): 745–56.

Kell, Peter, and Gillian Vogl. 2012. *International Students in the Asia Pacific: Mobility, Risks and Global Optimism*. New York: Springer.

Kelsky, Karen. 2001. *Women on the Verge: Japanese Women, Western Dreams*. Durham, NC: Duke University Press.

Kim, Youna. 2011. *Transnational Migration, Media and Identity of Asian Women: Diasporic Daughters*. New York: Routledge.

King, Russell, and Gunjan Sondhi. 2016. "Gendering International Student Migration: A Comparison of UK and Indian Students' Motivations and Experiences of Studying Abroad." Working Paper 84, University of Sussex Centre for Migration Research.

Kipnis, Andrew. 1995. "'Face': An Adaptable Discourse of Social Surfaces." *Positions: Asia Critique* 3 (1): 119–48.

Kipnis, Andrew. 2006. "*Suzhi*: A Keyword Approach." *China Quarterly* 186:295–313.

Kipnis, Andrew. 2011. *Governing Educational Desire: Culture, Politics and Schooling in China*. Chicago: University of Chicago Press.

Kleinman, Arthur, Yunxiang Yan, Jing Jun, Sing Lee, Everett Zhang, Tianshu Pan, Fei Wu, and Jinhua Guo. 2011. *Deep China: The Moral Life of the Person*. Berkeley: University of California Press.

Knowlton, David Clark. 2007. "Go Ye to All the World: The LDS Church and the Organization of International Society." In *Revisiting the Mormons: Persistent Themes and Contemporary Perspectives*, edited by Cardell K. Jacobson, John P. Hoffman, and Tim B. Heaton, 389–412. Salt Lake City: University of Utah Press.

Knudsen, Britta Timm, and Carsten Stage. 2015. "Introduction: Affective Methodologies." In *Affective Methodologies: Developing Cultural Research Strategies for the Study of Affect*, edited by Carsten Stage and Britta Timm Knudsen, 1–22. London: Palgrave Macmillan.

Kobayashi, Yoko. 2007. "Japanese Working Women and English Study Abroad." *World Englishes* 26 (1): 62–71.

Kohrman, Matthew. 2004. "Should I Quit? Tobacco, Fraught Identity, and the Risks of Governmentality in Urban China." *Urban Anthropology* 33 (2–4): 211–45.

Kong, Lily. 2013. "Christian Evangelizing across National Boundaries: Technology, Cultural Capital and the Intellectualization of Religion." In *Religion and Place: Landscape, Politics and Piety*, edited by Peter Hopkins, Lily Kong, and Elizabeth Olson, 21–38. Dordrecht: Springer.

Kunz, Sarah. 2016. "Privileged Mobilities: Locating the Expatriate in Migration Scholarship." *Geography Compass* 10 (3): 89–101.

Lahad, Kinneret. 2017. *A Table for One: A Critical Reading of Singlehood, Gender and Time*. Manchester: Manchester University Press.

Latham, Alan, and David Conradson. 2003. "The Possibilities of Performance." *Environment and Planning A: Economy and Space* 35 (11): 1901–6.

LDS. n.d. The Church of Jesus Christ of Latter-day Saints in China. Accessed July 23, 2019. http://www.mormonsandchina.org/.

LDS Newsroom. n.d. "Australia: Country Profile." Accessed July 23, 2019. https://www.mormonnewsroom.org/country/australia.

Lee, Ching Kwan. 2014. "A Chinese Developmental State: Miracle or Mirage?" In *The End of the Developmental State?*, edited by Michelle Williams, 102–25. London: Routledge.

Lee, Dong-Hoo. 2010. "Digital Cameras, Personal Photography and the Reconfiguration of Spatial Experiences." *Information Society* 26 (4): 266–75.

Lee, Emma. 2017. "Tencent Reports 58% Profit Surge on Strong Q1 Driven by WeChat and Gaming." *TechNode*, May 18, 2017. http://technode.com/2017/05/18/tencent-reports-58-profit-surge-on-strong-q1-driven-by-wechat-and-gaming/.

Lee, Jenny J. 2019. "Universities, Neo-nationalism and the 'China Threat.'" *University World News*, November 9, 2019. https://www.universityworldnews.com/post.php?story=2019110507475472.

Lefebvre, Henri. 1991. *The Production of Space*. Translated by Donald Nicholson-Smith. Oxford: Blackwell.

Lesh, Matthew. 2019. "Campus Freedom of Speech Gagged by Chinese Money." *Australian*, August 2, 2019. https://www.theaustralian.com.au/commentary/campus-freedom-of-speech-gagged-by-chinese-money/news-story/2378ac0ecc2cda7bc0c818a2d966991a.

Lewis, Hannah, Peter Dwyer, Stuart Hodkinson, and Louise Waite. 2015. "Hyper-precarious Lives: Migrants, Work and Forced Labour in the Global North." *Progress in Human Geography* 39 (5): 580–600.

Lewis, Tania, Fran Martin, and Wanning Sun. 2016. *Telemodernities: Television and Transforming Lives in Asia*. Durham, NC: Duke University Press.

Ley, David. 2004. "Transnational Spaces and Everyday Lives." *Transactions of the Institute of British Geographers* 29 (2): 151–64.

Ley, David. 2010. *Millionaire Migrants: Trans-Pacific Life Lines*. Malden, MA: Wiley-Blackwell.

Ley, David, and Justin Tse. 2013. "Homo Religiosus? Religion and Immigrant Subjectivities." In *Religion and Place: Landscape, Politics and Piety*, edited by Peter Hopkins, Lily Kong, and Elizabeth Olson, 149–66. Dordrecht: Springer.

Li, Barry. 2017. *The New Chinese: How They Are Shaping Australia*. Milton, Australia: Wiley.

Li, Cheng. 2010. "Introduction: The Rise of the Middle Class in the Middle Kingdom." In *China's Emerging Middle Class: Beyond Economic Transformation*, edited by Cheng Li, 3–31. Washington, DC: Brookings Institution Press.

Li, Chunling. 2010. "Characterizing China's Middle Class: Heterogeneous Composition and Multiple Identities." In *China's Emerging Middle Class: Beyond Economic Transformation*, edited by Cheng Li, 135–56. Washington, DC: Brookings Institution Press.

Li, Gang. 2016. "Politically Sensitive Chinese Students' Engagement with Democracy in Canada." *Journal of Chinese Overseas* 12 (1): 96–121.

Li, Wei. 1998. "Anatomy of a New Ethnic Settlement: The Chinese 'Ethnoburb' in Los Angeles." *Urban Studies* 35 (3): 479–501.

Li Yinhe 李银河. 2003. 《性文化研究报告》 [Research report on sexual culture]. Nanjing: Jiangsu Renmin Chubanshe.

Li, Zhonglu, and Shizheng Feng. 2018. "Overseas Study Experience and Students' Attitudes toward China: Evidence from the Beijing College Students Panel Survey." *Chinese Sociological Review* 50 (1): 27–52.

Lieberman, Sally Taylor. 1998. *The Mother and Narrative Politics in Modern China*. Charlottesville: University Press of Virginia.

Lin, Delia. 2017. *Civilizing Citizens in Post-Mao China: Understanding the Rhetoric of Suzhi*. New York: Routledge.

Lin, Jing, and Xiaoyan Sun. 2010. "Higher Education Expansion and China's Middle Classes." In *China's Emerging Middle Class: Beyond Economic Transformation*, edited by Cheng Li, 217–42. Washington, DC: Brookings Institution Press.

Liu, Fengshu. 2008. "Constructing the Autonomous Middle-Class Self in Today's China: The Case of Young-Adult Only-Children University Students." *Journal of Youth Studies* 11 (2): 193–212.

Liu, Fengshu. 2012. "'Politically Indifferent' Nationalists? Chinese Youth Negotiating Political Identity in the Internet Age." *European Journal of Cultural Studies* 15 (1): 53–69.

Liu, Fengshu. 2014. "From Degendering to (Re)gendering the Self: Chinese Youth Negotiating Modern Womanhood." *Gender and Education* 26 (1): 18–34.

Liu, Hailong, ed. 2019. *From Cyber-Nationalism to Fandom Nationalism: The Case of Diba Expedition in China*. London: Routledge.

Liu, Hao. 2017. "2017 Spring Commencement Student Speaker Shuping Yang." 9:25. YouTube, May 22, 2017. https://www.youtube.com/watch?v=9c8H1FcndKE.

Liu, Jieyu. 2007. *Gender and Work in Urban China: Women Workers of the Unlucky Generation*. London: Routledge.

Liu, Lisong. 2016a. "Chinese Student Migrants and American Religious Organizations." *Journal of Chinese Overseas* 12 (1): 122–53.

Liu, Lisong. 2016b. *Chinese Student Migration and Selective Citizenship: Mobility, Community and Identity between China and the United States*. London: Routledge.

Liu, Shuning. 2020. *Neoliberalism, Globalization, and "Elite" Education in China: Becoming International*. London: Routledge.

Liu, Tingting. 2018. "Digital Romance in Precarious Times: Online Dating Cultures of Chinese Rural Migrant Labourers." PhD diss., University of Queensland.

Liu, Tingting, and Zhuoyun Deng. 2020. "'They've Made Our Blood Ties Black': On the Burst of Online Racism towards the African in China's Social Media." *Critical Arts: South-North Cultural and Media Studies* 34 (2): 104–7.

Liu Wen-rong 刘汶蓉. 2010. "婚前性行为和同居观念的现状及影响因素: 现代性解释框架的经验验证" [Current situation and influencing factors of attitudes toward premarital sex and cohabitation: An empirical study with the modernity perspective]. 《青年研究 》 *Youth Studies* 2: 23–34.

Liu-Farrer, Gracia. 2011. *Labour Migration from China to Japan: International Students, Transnational Migrants*. London: Routledge.

Liu-Farrer, Gracia. 2016. "Migration as Class-Based Consumption: The Emigration of the Rich in Contemporary China." *China Quarterly* 226:499–518.

Lloyd-Damjanovic, Anastasia. 2018. *A Preliminary Study of PRC Political Influence and Interference Activities in American Higher Education*. Washington, DC: Wilson Center.

Low, Setha M. 2001. "The Edge and the Centre: Gated Communities and the Discourse of Urban Fear." *American Anthropologist* 103 (1): 45–58.

Maddox, Marion. 2012. "'In the Goofy Parking Lot': Growth Churches as a Novel Religious Form of Late Capitalism." *Social Compass* 59 (2): 146–58.

Maddox, Marion. 2013. "'Rise Up Warrior Princess Daughters': Is Evangelical Women's Submission Merely a Fairytale?" *Journal of Feminist Studies in Religion* 29 (1): 9–26.

Maddox, Marion. 2014. *Taking God to School: The End of Australia's Egalitarian Education?* Sydney: Allen and Unwin.

Maddox, Marion. 2015. "Finding God in Global Politics." *International Political Science Review* 36 (2): 185–96.

Maddox, Marion. 2016. "Transforming Australian Christianity: From Private to Public." Paper presented at Crossroads in Cultural Studies conference, Western Sydney University and the University of Sydney, December 14–17, 2016.

Madianou, Mirca, and Daniel Miller. 2012. "Polymedia: Towards a New Theory of Digital Media in Interpersonal Communication." *International Journal of Cultural Studies* 16 (2): 169–87.

Madsen, Richard P. 2008. "Religious Renaissance and Taiwan's Modern Middle Classes." In *Chinese Religiosities: Afflictions of Modernity and State Formation*, edited by Mayfair Mei-hui Yang, 295–322. Berkeley: University of California Press.

Madsen, Richard P. 2013. "The Sacred and the Holy: Religious Power and Cultural Creativity in China Today." In *Restless China*, edited by Perry Link, Richard P. Madsen, and Paul G. Pickowicz, 153–66. Lanham, MD: Rowman and Littlefield.

Mankekar, Purnima. 2015. *Unsettling India: Affect, Temporality, Transnationality*. Durham, NC: Duke University Press.

Marginson, Simon. 2007. "The Global Positioning of Australian Higher Education: Where To from Here?" Dean's Lecture series, University of Melbourne Faculty of Education, October 16, 2007. http://citeseerx.ist.psu.edu/viewdoc/download?doi=10.1.1.189.4561&rep=rep1&type=pdf.

Marginson, Simon. 2012. "Including the Other: Regulation of the Human Rights of Mobile Students in a Nation-Bound World." *Higher Education* 63 (4): 497–512.

Marginson, Simon, and Mark Considine. 2000. *The Enterprise University: Power, Governance and Reinvention in Australia*. Cambridge: Cambridge University Press.

Marginson, Simon, Christopher Nyland, Erlenawati Sawir, and Helen Forbes-Mewett. 2010. *International Student Security*. Cambridge: Cambridge University Press.

Martin, Bernice. 2013. "Tensions and Trends in Pentecostal Gender and Family Relations." In *Global Pentecostalism in the 21st Century*, edited by Robert W. Hefner, 115–48. Indianapolis: Indiana University Press.

Martin, David. 2002. *Pentecostalism: The World Their Parish*. Oxford: Blackwell.

Martin, David. 2013. "Pentecostalism: An Alternative Form of Modernity and Modernization?" In *Global Pentecostalism in the 21st Century*, edited by Robert W. Hefner, 37–62. Indianapolis: Indiana University Press.

Martin, Fran. 2014. "The Gender of Mobility: Chinese Women Students' Self-Making through Transnational Education." *Intersections: Gender and Sexuality in Asia and the Pacific*, no. 35. http://intersections.anu.edu.au/issue35/martin.htm.

Martin, Fran. 2016. "Media, Place, Sociality, and National Publics: Chinese International Students in Translocal Networks." In *Contemporary Culture and Media in Asia*, edited by Koichi Iwabuchi, Olivia Khoo, and Daniel Black, 209–26. London: Rowman and Littlefield.

Martin, Fran. 2017a. "Mobile Self-Fashioning and Gendered Risk: Rethinking Chinese Students' Motivations for Overseas Education." *Globalisation, Societies and Education* 15 (5): 706–20.

Martin, Fran. 2017b. "Overstating Chinese Influence in Australian Universities." *East Asia Forum*, November 30, 2017. http://www.eastasiaforum.org/2017/11/30/overstating-chinese-influence-in-australian-universities/.

Martin, Fran. 2017c. "Rethinking Network Capital: Hospitality Work and Parallel Trading among Chinese Students in Melbourne." *Mobilities* 12 (6): 890–907.

Martin, Fran. 2018. "Overseas Study as Zone of Suspension: Chinese Students Renegotiating Youth, Gender, and Intimacy." *Journal of Intercultural Studies* 39 (6): 688–703.

Martin, Fran. 2020. "iPhones and 'African Gangs': Everyday Racism and Ethno-transnational Media in Melbourne's Chinese Student World." *Journal of Ethnic and Racial Studies* 43 (5): 892–910.

Martin, Fran, and Ana Dragojlovic. 2019. "Gender, Mobility Regimes, and Social Transformation in Asia." *Journal of Intercultural Studies* 40 (3): 275–86.

Martin, Fran, John Erni, and Audrey Yue. 2019. "(Im)Mobile Precarity in the Asia-Pacific." *Cultural Studies* 33 (6): 815–914.

Martin, Fran, and Tania Lewis. 2016. "Lifestyle Media in Asia: Consumption, Aspiration and Identity." In *Lifestyle Media in Asia: Consumption, Aspiration and Identity*, edited by Fran Martin and Tania Lewis, 13–31. London: Routledge.

Martin, Fran, Can Qin, Caitlin Douglass, Carol El-Hayek, and Megan Lim. 2019. *Intimate Attitudes, Practices and Knowledges: Chinese-Speaking International Students in Australia*. Melbourne: University of Melbourne and the Burnet Institute.

Martin, Fran, and Fazal Rizvi. 2014. "Making Melbourne: Digital Connectivity and International Students' Experience of Locality." *Media, Culture and Society* 36 (7): 1016–31.

Massey, Doreen. 1994. *Space, Place and Gender*. Minneapolis: University of Minnesota Press.

Massey, Doreen. 2004. "The Political Challenge of Relational Space: Introduction to the Vega Symposium." *Geografiska Annaler: Series B, Human Geography* 86 (1): 3.

Massey, Doreen. 2005. *For Space*. London: Sage.

Massumi, Brian. 2015. *Politics of Affect*. Cambridge: Polity.

Matthews, Julie, and Ravinder Sidhu. 2005. "Desperately Seeking the Global Subject: International Education, Citizenship and Cosmopolitanism." *Globalisation, Societies and Education* 3 (1): 49–66.

McCarthy, Anna. 2008. "From the Ordinary to the Concrete: Cultural Studies and the Politics of Scale." In *Questions of Method in Cultural Studies*, edited by Mimi White and James Schwoch, 21–53. Hoboken, NJ: Wiley-Blackwell.

McKenzie, Lara, and Loretta Baldassar. 2017. "Missing Friendships: Understanding the Absent Relationships of Local and International Students at an Australian University." *Higher Education* 74 (4): 701–15.

McRobbie, Angela. 2020. *Feminism and the Politics of Resilience: Essays on Gender, Media and the End of Welfare*. Cambridge: Polity.

Metykova, Monika. 2010. "Only a Mouse Click Away from Home: Transnational Practices of Eastern European Migrants in the United Kingdom." *Social Identities* 16 (3): 325–38.

Meyer, Birgit. 2010. "Pentecostalism and Globalization." In *Studying Global Pentecostalism: Theories and Methods*, edited by Allan Anderson, Michael Bergunder, André Droogers, and Cornelis van der Laan, 113–32. Berkeley: University of California Press.

Miller, Elizabeth. 2015. "A Planting of the Lord: Contemporary Pentecostal and Charismatic Christianity in Australia." PhD diss., University of Sydney.

Min Dahong 闵大洪. 2004. "中国互联网上的民意表达" [Expression of Chinese public opinion on the internet]. Paper presented at the China Computer Mediated Communication Annual Conference, Nanjing, May 15, 2004. https://www.sinoss.net/qikan/uploadfile/2010/1130/3109.pdf.

Mitchell, Katharyne. 1997. "Transnational Subjects: Constituting the Cultural Citizen in the Era of Pacific Rim Capital." In *Ungrounded Empires: The Cultural Politics of Modern Chinese Transnationalism*, edited by Aihwa Ong and Donald M. Nonini, 228–56. New York: Routledge.

Moerben Weishenghuo 墨尔本微生活. 2016. "呵! 这真是个好问题,留学的姑娘为什么容易单身?" [Ha! That's a good question, why do girls who study abroad tend to stay single?]. June 19, 2016. http://mp.weixin.qq.com/s?__biz=MjM5NzcwNDA0MQ===&mid=2652784552&idx=1&sn=31d6350448ac2b69c84bfb23d75bb68a&scene=0.

Moores, Shaun. 2012. *Media, Place and Mobility*. Basingstoke, UK: Palgrave Macmillan.

Morley, David. 2003. "What's 'Home' Got to Do with It? Contradictory Dynamics in the Domestication of Technology and the Dislocation of Domesticity." *European Journal of Cultural Studies* 6 (4): 435–58.

Morley, David. 2009. "For a Materialist, Non Media-Centric Media Studies." *Television and New Media* 10 (1): 114–16.

Morris, Madeleine. 2020. "Killing the Golden Goose: How Australia's International Students Are Being Driven Away." *ABC News Breakfast*, October 5, 2020. https://www.abc.net.au/news/2020-10-05/how-australia-international-students-driven-away-during-covid-19/12721488.

Mulinari, Diana, and Kerstin Sandell. 2009. "A Feminist Re-reading of Theories of Late Modernity: Beck, Giddens and the Location of Gender." *Critical Sociology* 35 (4): 493–507.

National Bureau of Statistics of China. 2012. *Women and Men in China—Facts and Figures.* https://www.unicef.cn/en/reports/women-and-men-china.

Noble, Greg. 2009. "Everyday Cosmopolitanism and the Labour of Intercultural Community." In *Everyday Multiculturalism*, edited by Amanda Wise and Selvaraj Velayutham, 46–65. London: Palgrave Macmillan.

Nolan, David, Karen Farquharson, Violeta Politoff, and Timothy Marjoribanks. 2011. "Mediated Multiculturalism: Newspaper Representations of Sudanese Migrants in Australia." *Journal of Intercultural Studies* 32 (6): 655–71.

Nonini, Donald M. 2008. "Is China Becoming Neoliberal?" *Critique of Anthropology* 28 (2): 145–76.

Nonini, Donald M., and Aihwa Ong. 1997. "Chinese Transnationalism as an Alternative Modernity." In *Ungrounded Empires: The Cultural Politics of Modern Chinese Transnationalism*, edited by Aihwa Ong and Donald M. Nonini, 3–33. New York: Routledge.

Norton, Andrew, and Beni Cakitaki. 2016. *Mapping Australian Higher Education 2016.* Carlton, Melbourne: The Grattan Institute. https://grattan.edu.au/report/mapping-australian-higher-education-2016/.

Norton, Andrew, and Ittima Cherastidtham. 2018. *Mapping Australian Higher Education 2018.* Carlton, Melbourne: The Grattan Institute. https://grattan.edu.au/report/mapping-australian-higher-education-2018/.

Nyíri, Pál. 2001. "Expatriating Is Patriotic? The Discourse on 'New Migrants' in the People's Republic of China and Identity Construction among Recent Migrants from the PRC." *Journal of Ethnic and Migration Studies* 27 (4): 635–53.

Nyíri, Pál. 2003. "Moving Targets: Chinese Christian Proselytizing among Transnational Migrants from the People's Republic of China." *European Journal of East Asian Studies* 2 (2): 263–301.

Nyíri, Pál. 2010. *Mobility and Cultural Authority in Contemporary China.* Seattle: University of Washington Press.

Nyíri, Pál, and Juan Zhang. 2010. "China's Cosmopolitan Nationalists: 'Heroes' and 'Traitors' of the 2008 Olympics." With Merriden Varrall. *China Journal* 63:25–55.

Oakes, Tim, and Louisa Schein. 2006. "Translocal China: An Introduction." In *Translocal China: Linkages, Identities, and the Reimagining of Space*, edited by Tim Oakes and Louisa Schein, 1–35. London: Routledge.

Oblau, Gotthard. 2005. "Pentecostal by Default? Contemporary Christianity in China." In *Asian and Pentecostal: The Charismatic Face of Christianity in Asia*, edited by Allan Anderson and Edmond Tang, 411–36. Oxford: Regnum.

OECD (Organisation for Economic Co-operation and Development). 2017. *Education at a Glance 2017: OECD Indicators.* Paris: OECD. http://www.oecd.org/education/education-at-a-glance-19991487.htm.

Olliff, Louise. 2007. *Settling In: How Do Refugee Young People Fair [sic] within Australia's Settlement System?* Melbourne: Centre for Multicultural Youth Issues.

Ong, Aihwa. 1999. *Flexible Citizenship: The Cultural Logics of Transnationality.* Durham, NC: Duke University Press.

Ong, Aihwa. 2003. "Cyberpublics and Diaspora Politics among Transnational Chinese." *Interventions: International Journal of Postcolonial Studies* 5 (1): 82–100.

Ong, Aihwa. 2006. *Neoliberalism as Exception: Mutations in Citizenship and Sovereignty.* Durham, NC: Duke University Press.

Ong, Aihwa. 2007. "Neoliberalism as a Mobile Technology." *Transactions of the Institute of British Geographers* 32 (1): 3–8.

Ong, Aihwa. 2008. "Self-Fashioning Shanghainese: Dancing across Spheres of Value." In *Privatizing China: Socialism from Afar*, edited by Li Zhang and Aihwa Ong, 182–96. Ithaca, NY: Cornell University Press.

Ong, Aihwa, and Donald M. Nonini, eds. 1997. *Ungrounded Empires: The Cultural Politics of Modern Chinese Transnationalism.* New York: Routledge.

Ong, Aihwa, and Li Zhang. 2008. "Introduction: Privatizing China: Powers of the Self, Socialism from Afar." In *Privatizing China: Socialism from Afar*, edited by Li Zhang and Aihwa Ong, 1–19. Ithaca, NY: Cornell University Press.

Ong, Johnathan Corpus. 2009. "The Cosmopolitan Continuum: Locating Cosmopolitanism in Media and Cultural Studies." *Media, Culture and Society* 31 (3): 449–66.

Osburg, John. 2013. *Anxious Wealth: Money and Morality among China's New Rich.* Stanford, CA: Stanford University Press.

Overell, Rosemary. 2014. *Affective Intensities in Extreme Music Scenes: Cases from Australia and Japan.* Basingstoke, UK: Palgrave Macmillan.

Pan Suiming. 2006. "Transformations in the Primary Life Cycle: The Origins and Nature of China's Sexual Revolution." In *Sex and Sexuality in China*, edited by Elaine Jeffreys, 21–42. London: Routledge.

Pan Suiming 潘绥铭, William Parish 白维廉, Wang Aili 王爱丽, and Edward Laumann 苏曼. 2004. 《当代中国人的性行为与性关系》 [Sexual behavior and relation in contemporary China]. Beijing: Social Sciences Academic Press.

Pan Xianghui 潘祥辉. 2018. "'祖国母亲': 一种政治隐喻的传播及溯源." ["Homeland-mother": Tracing the propagation and spread of a political metaphor] 《人文杂志》 [Journal of humanities] 1:92–102.

Paret, Marcel, and Shannon Gleeson. 2016. "Precarity and Agency through a Migration Lens." *Citizenship Studies* 20 (3–4): 277–94.

Park, Kyeyoung. 1996. "Use and Abuse of Race and Culture: Black-Korean Tension in America." *American Anthropologist* 98 (3): 492–99.

Parreñas, Rhacel Salazar. 2001. *Servants of Globalization: Women, Migration and Domestic Work.* Stanford, CA: Stanford University Press.

Pei, Yuxin. 2011. "Multiple Sexual Relationships as a New Lifestyle: Young Women's Sexuality in Contemporary Shanghai." *Women's Studies International Forum* 34 (5): 401–10.

Pellegrini, Ann. 2007. "'Signaling through the Flames': Hell House Performance and Structures of Religious Feeling." *American Quarterly* 59 (3): 911–35.

Penttinen, Elina, and Anitta Kynsilehto. 2017. *Gender and Mobility: A Critical Introduction.* London: Rowman and Littlefield.

Petersen, Eva Bendix, and Gabrielle O'Flynn. 2007. "Neoliberal Technologies of Subject Formation: A Case Study of the Duke of Edinburgh's Award Scheme." *Critical Studies in Education* 48 (2): 197–211.

Pfafman, Tessa M., Christopher J. Carpenter, and Yong Tang. 2015. "The Politics of Racism: Constructions of African Immigrants in China on ChinaSMACK." *Communication, Culture and Critique* 8 (4): 540–56.

Phillips, Rick. 2006. "Rethinking the International Expansion of Mormonism." *Nova Religio: The Journal of Alternative and Emergent Religions* 10 (1): 52–68.

Pink, Sarah. 2015. *Doing Sensory Ethnography*. 2nd ed. Los Angeles: Sage.

Piper, Nicola, and Sohoon Lee. 2016. "Marriage Migration, Migrant Precarity, and Social Reproduction in Asia: An Overview." *Critical Asian Studies* 48 (4): 473–93.

Planetshakers. n.d. Accessed June 13, 2018. https://www.planetshakers.com/.

Planetshakers SOCA. n.d. Accessed June 13, 2018. https://www.planetshakers.com/soca/.

Polson, Erika. 2016. *Privileged Mobilities: Professional Migration, Geo-social Media, and a New Global Middle Class*. New York: Peter Lang.

Pomfret, John. 2020. "The Coronavirus Reawakens Old Racist Tropes against Chinese People." *Washington Post*, February 5, 2020.

Prensky, Marc. 2001. "Digital Natives, Digital Immigrants." *On the Horizon* 9 (5): 1–6. https://www.marcprensky.com/writing/Prensky%20-%20Digital%20Natives,%20 Digital%20Immigrants%20-%20Part1.pdf.

Prime Minister of Australia. 2020. "Transforming Australian Manufacturing to Rebuild Our Economy." Media release, October 1, 2020. https://www.pm.gov.au/media /transforming-australian-manufacturing-rebuild-our-economy#.

Pun Ngai. 2005. *Made in China: Women Factory Workers in a Global Workplace*. Durham, NC: Duke University Press.

Putnam, Robert. 2000. *Bowling Alone*. New York: Simon and Schuster.

Qian, Licheng, Bin Xu, and Dingding Chen. 2017. "Does History Education Promote Nationalism in China? A 'Limited Effect' Explanation." *Journal of Contemporary China* 2 (104): 199–212.

Qian Ning 钱宁. [1996] 2003. 《留学美国：一个时代的故事》[Studying in America: Tale of a generation]. Hangzhou: Zhejiang Wenyi Chubanshe.

Qin, Can. 2012. "Globalisation as Lived Reality: The Expectations, Experiences and Strategies of Chinese International Students in Australia." PhD diss., La Trobe University, Melbourne.

Qin, Dongxiao. 2009. *Crossing Borders: International Women Students in American Higher Education*. Lanham, MD: University Press of America.

Ramdas, Kamalini. 2012. "Women in Waiting? Singlehood, Marriage, and Family in Singapore." *Environment and Planning A: Economy and Space* 44 (4): 832–48.

Ramia, Gaby, Simon Marginson, and Erlenawati Sawir. 2013. *Regulating International Students' Wellbeing*. Bristol: Policy.

Ren, Hai. 2013. *The Middle Class in Neoliberal China: Governing Risk, Life-Building, and Themed Spaces*. London: Routledge.

Renmin Ribao 人民日报. 2016. "八成留学生回国发展" [Eighty percent of overseas students return to China to work]. March 29, 2016. http://www.moe.gov.cn/jyb _xwfb/xw_fbh/moe_2069/xwfbh_2016n/xwfb_160325_01/160325_mtbd01/201603 /t20160329_235747.html.

Rizvi, Fazal. 2005. "International Education and the Production of Cosmopolitan Identities." *RIHE International Publication Series* 9:1–11.

Robbins, Joel. 2004. "The Globalization of Pentecostal and Charismatic Christianity." *Annual Review of Anthropology* 33:117–43.

Robbins, Joel. 2009. "Pentecostal Networks and the Spirit of Globalization: On the Social Productivity of Ritual Forms." *Social Analysis* 53 (1): 55–66.

Robertson, Shanthi. 2013. *Transnational Student-Migrants and the State: The Education-Migration Nexus.* Basingstoke, UK: Palgrave Macmillan.

Robertson, Shanthi. 2020. "Suspending, Settling, Sponsoring: The Intimate Chronomobilities of Young Asian Migrants in Australia." *Global Networks: A Journal of Transnational Affairs* 20 (4): 677–96.

Robertson, Shanthi, Yi'En Cheng, and Brenda S. A. Yeoh. 2018. "Introduction: Mobile Aspirations? Youth Im/Mobilities in the Asia-Pacific." *Journal of Intercultural Studies* 39 (6): 613–25.

Robertson, Shanthi, Anita Harris, and Loretta Baldassar. 2018. "Mobile Transitions: A Conceptual Framework for Researching a Generation on the Move." *Journal of Youth Studies* 21 (2): 203–17.

Robertson, Shanthi, and Dallas Rogers. 2017. "Education, Real Estate, Immigration: Brokerage Assemblages and Asian Mobilities." *Journal of Ethnic and Migration Studies* 43 (14): 2393–407.

Rofel, Lisa. 1999. *Other Modernities: Gendered Yearnings in China after Socialism.* Berkeley: University of California Press.

Rofel, Lisa. 2007. *Desiring China: Experiments in Neoliberalism, Sexuality, and Public Culture.* Durham, NC: Duke University Press.

Rogers, Dallas. 2017. *The Geopolitics of Real Estate: Reconfiguring Property, Capital and Rights.* London: Rowman and Littlefield.

Rogers, Dallas, and Rae Dufty-Jones. 2015. "21st-Century Australian Housing: New Frontiers in the Asia-Pacific." In *Housing in 21st-Century Australia: People, Practices and Policies,* edited by Rae Dufty-Jones and Dallas Rogers, 221–36. Farnham, UK: Ashgate.

Rogers, Dallas, and Ilan Wiesel. 2018. "Australian Urban Geographies of Housing in the Context of the Rise of China in the 'Asian Century.'" *Geographical Research* 56 (4): 393–400.

Rose, Nikolas. 1998. *Inventing Our Selves: Psychology, Power, and Personhood.* Cambridge: Cambridge University Press.

Rosen, Stanley. 2009. "Contemporary Chinese Youth and the State." *Journal of Asian Studies* 68 (3): 359–69.

Rottenberg, Catherine. 2017. "Neoliberal Feminism and the Future of Human Capital." *Signs: Journal of Women in Culture and Society* 42 (2): 329–48.

Rottenberg, Catherine. 2018. *The Rise of Neoliberal Feminism.* Oxford: Oxford University Press.

Scannell, Paddy. 1996. *Radio, Television and Modern Life: A Phenomenological Approach.* Cambridge, MA: Blackwell.

Schierup, Carl-Ulrik, and Martin Bak Jørgensen. 2017. *Politics of Precarity: Migrant Conditions, Struggles and Experiences.* Leiden: Brill.

Schiller, Nina Glick, Linda Basch, and Cristina Szanton Blanc. 1995. "From Immigrant to Transmigrant: Theorizing Transnational Migration." *Anthropological Quarterly* 68 (1): 48–63.

Schlesinger, Larry. 2015. "Church Group Signs $1m Southbank Lease." *Australian Financial Review*, February 9, 2015. http://www.afr.com/real-estate/commercial/church-group-signs-1m-southbank-lease-20150209-139l0n.

Schneider, Florian. 2018. *China's Digital Nationalism*. Oxford: Oxford University Press.

Schneiders, Ben, and Royce Millar. 2020. "A City Divided: COVID-19 Finds a Weakness in Melbourne's Social Fault Lines." *Age*, August 8, 2020. https://www.theage.com.au/national/victoria/a-city-divided-covid-19-finds-a-weakness-in-melbourne-s-social-fault-lines-20200807-p55ji2.html.

Scutt, David. 2017. "Enter the Dragon: There's Finally Hard Data on the Huge Role of Foreign Buyers in Australian Property." *Business Insider Australia*, March 24, 2017. https://www.businessinsider.com.au/foreign-investment-in-australian-housing-2017-3.

Sedgwick, Eve Kosofsky. 1990. *Epistemology of the Closet*. Berkeley: University of California Press.

Sedgwick, Eve Kosofsky, and Adam Frank. 2003. "Shame in the Cybernetic Fold: Reading Silvan Tomkins." In *Touching Feeling: Affect, Pedagogy, Performativity*, by Eve Kosofsky Sedgwick, 193–12. Durham, NC: Duke University Press.

Seigworth, Gregory J., and Melissa Gregg. 2010. "An Inventory of Shimmers." In *The Affect Theory Reader*, edited by Melissa Gregg and Gregory J. Seigworth, 1–25. Durham, NC: Duke University Press.

Shamir, Ronen. 2005. "Without Borders? Notes on Globalization as a Mobility Regime." *Sociological Theory* 23 (2): 197–217.

Shand, Adam. 2013. "Eyeing Off God's Bounty." *Australian*, May 2, 2013. https://www.theaustralian.com.au/news/inquirer/eyeing-off-gods-bounty/news-story/0c2d7c8031ae8db24b577e7eec44d388?sv=951ef240f280c6689da1c1fd375a4195.

Sheller, Mimi, and John Urry. 2006. "The New Mobilities Paradigm." *Environment and Planning A: Economy and Space* 38 (2): 207–26.

Shi, Lihong. 2009. "'Little Quilted Vests to Warm Parents' Hearts': Redefining the Gendered Practice of Filial Piety in Rural North-Eastern China." *China Quarterly* 198:348–63.

Shih, Shu-mei. 2007. *Visuality and Identity: Sinophone Articulations across the Pacific*. Berkeley: University of California Press.

Shih, Shu-mei. 2011. "The Concept of the Sinophone." *PMLA* 126 (3): 709–18.

Sigley, Gary. 2006. "Chinese Governmentalities: Government, Governance and the Socialist Market Economy." *Economy and Society* 35 (4): 487–508.

Silverstone, Roger. 2008. *Media and Morality: On the Rise of the Mediapolis*. Cambridge: Polity.

Simons, Margaret. 2020. "Making Time." *Saturday Paper*, September 19–25, 2020, 7.

Singh, Supriya. 2013. *Globalization and Money: A Global South Perspective*. Lanham, MD: Rowman and Littlefield.

SK-II. 2016. "Marriage Market Takeover." Video advertisement, 4:16. YouTube, April 6, 2016. https://www.youtube.com/watch?v=irfd74z52Cw.

Skeggs, Beverley. 1997. *Formations of Class and Gender: Becoming Respectable*. London: Sage.

Skeggs, Beverley. 2004. "Context and Background: Pierre Bourdieu's Analysis of Class, Gender and Sexuality." In *Feminism after Bourdieu*, edited by Lisa Adkins and Beverley Skeggs, 19–34. Oxford: Blackwell.

Sklair, Leslie. 2001. *The Transnational Capitalist Class*. Oxford: Wiley-Blackwell.

Sky Post 晴報. 2016. "墨爾本街頭騷亂 20人搶劫華裔學生" [20 people rob Chinese students in Melbourne street violence]. March 14, 2016. http://millionaire.skypost.hk /港聞 / 要聞 / 墨爾本街頭騷亂％2020人搶劫華裔學生 / 209793.

Smith, Kerry. 2016. "Media's Racist Post-Moomba Rampage." *Green Left Weekly*, March 17, 2016.

Smith, Michael Peter. 2001. *Transnational Urbanism: Locating Globalization*. Malden, MA: Blackwell.

Smith, Michael Peter. 2005. "Transnational Urbanism Revisited." *Journal of Ethnic and Migration Studies* 31 (2): 235–44.

Song Shao-peng 宋少鹏. 2011. "'回家'还是'被回家'？——市场化过程中'妇女回家'讨论 与中国社会意识形态转型" [Retreating back home willingly or being unwillingly sent home?—Debates on "women-going-home" and the ideological transformation in the course of marketization in China]. 《妇女研究论丛》 [Collection of women's studies] 4 (Ser. No. 106): 5–26.

Soutphommasane, Tim. 2018. "Confronting the Return of Race Politics." Australian Human Rights Commission, August 6, 2018. https://www.humanrights.gov.au/about /news/speeches/confronting-return-race-politics.

Sparrow, Jeff. 2012. *Money Shot: A Journey into Porn and Censorship*. London: Scribe.

Stewart, Kathleen. 2007. *Ordinary Affects*. Durham, NC: Duke University Press.

Stratton, Jon. 1998. *Race Daze: Australia in Identity Crisis*. Sydney: Pluto.

Stratton, Jon. 2006. "Two Rescues, One History: Everyday Racism in Australia." *Social Identities* 12 (6): 657–81.

Sun, Shengwei, and Feinian Chen. 2015. "Reprivatized Womanhood: Changes in Mainstream Media's Framing of Urban Women's Issues in China, 1995–2012." *Journal of Marriage and Family* 77 (5): 1091–107.

Sun, Wanning. 2002. *Leaving China: Media, Migration, and Transnational Imagination*. Lanham, MD: Rowman and Littlefield.

Sun, Wanning. 2009. *Maid in China: Media, Morality, and the Cultural Politics of Boundaries*. London: Routledge.

Sun, Wanning. 2016. *Chinese-Language Media in Australia: Developments, Challenges and Opportunities*. Ultimo, Australia: Australia-China Relations Institute.

Sun, Wanning. 2018a. "How Australia's Mandarin Speakers Get Their News." *Conversation*, November 22, 2018. https://theconversation.com/how-australias-mandarin -speakers-get-their-news-106917.

Sun, Wanning. 2018b. "The Importance of Being Cosmopolitan in Australia's Global Classroom." *Communication Research and Practice* 4 (1): 67–82.

Sun, Wanning. 2018c. "Romancing the Vulnerable in Contemporary China: Love on the Assembly Line and the Cultural Politics of Inequality." *China Information* 32 (1): 69–87.

Sun Wei 孙玮. 2015. "微信：中国人的'在世存有'" [WeChat: The 'Dasein' for Chinese]. 《学术月刊》 [Academic monthly] 47 (Ser. No. 559): 5–18.

Tadiar, Neferti X. M. 2009. *Things Fall Away: Philippine Historical Experience and the Makings of Globalization*. Durham, NC: Duke University Press.

Tang, Wendy. 2016. "Report: News Consumption Shifts to News Aggregators in China." AllChina Tech, February 11, 2016. http://www.allchinatech.com/report-news -consumption-shifts-to-news-aggregators-in-china/.

Taylor, David. 2016. "Social Media Dominates Way Millennials Consume News, Prompting Alarm, Deloitte Survey Says." ABC News, August 15, 2016. http://www.abc.net.au /news/2016-08-15/social-media-dominates-millenials-consume-news,-deloitte-says /7721528.

Tehan, Dan. 2019. "Taskforce to Protect Universities from Foreign Interference." Media release, August 28, 2019. https://docs.education.gov.au/system/files/doc/other /minister_tehan_taskforce_to_protect_universities_from_foreign_interference.pdf.

Tehan, Dan, and Michaelia Cash. 2020. "Higher Education Relief Package." Joint media release, April 12, 2020. https://ministers.dese.gov.au/tehan/higher-education-relief -package.

Thelle, Hatla. 2004. *Better to Rely on Ourselves: Changing Social Rights in Urban China since 1979.* Copenhagen: NIAS Press.

Thrift, Nigel. 2006. "Space." *Theory, Culture and Society* 23 (2–3): 139–55.

Thrift, Nigel. 2008. *Non-representational Theory: Space, Politics, Affect.* London: Routledge.

Time Weekly 时代在线. 2013. "哈药再现售假门凸显营销困局：旗下药房非法销售假冒保健品 十年频爆产品质量丑闻" [More fraudulent products from Harbin Pharmaceuticals highlight a marketing dilemma. Affiliated pharmacies illegally selling counterfeit health products: A decade of frequent product quality scandals]. December 25, 2013. http://www.time-weekly.com/story/2013-12-25/131894.html.

Tomba, Luigi. 2004. "Creating an Urban Middle Class: Social Engineering in Beijing." *China Journal,* no. 51: 1–26.

Tomba, Luigi. 2009. "Of Quality, Harmony, and Community: Civilization and the Middle Class in Urban China." *Positions: East Asia Cultures Critique* 17 (3): 592–616.

Tomlinson, John. 2007. *The Culture of Speed: The Coming of Immediacy.* London: Sage.

Tran, Ly Thi, and Catherine Gomes, eds. 2017. *International Student Connectedness and Identity: Transnational Perspectives.* Singapore: Springer.

Tu, Mengwei, and Kailing Xie. 2020. "Privileged Daughters? Gendered Mobility among Highly Educated Chinese Female Migrants in the UK." *Social Inclusion* 8 (2): 68–76.

Tutou Mama Shuo Yu'er 兔头妈妈说育儿. 2018. "据说女性财务自由被分为这几个等级，你在哪个阶段？" [Apparently women's financial freedom has been divided into these stages, which stage are you at?]. February 8, 2018. http://www.sohu.com/a/221622250 _627902.

Universities Australia. 2015. *Higher Education and Research: Facts and Figures 2015.* Deakin: Universities Australia. https://www.universitiesaustralia.edu.au/australias -universities/key-facts-and-data#.Wrnq_pNuZuU.

Universities Australia. 2018. *Data Snapshot 2018.* Accessed 2018, subsequently removed. https://www.universitiesaustralia.edu.au/publication/data-snapshot/.

Universities Australia. 2020. "A Personal Message from Australia's University Community." Video advertisement, 2:25. YouTube, February 6, 2020. https://www.youtube .com/watch?v=4g3PFVxBv8I&feature=youtu.be.

Urry, John. 2000. *Sociology beyond Societies: Mobilities for the Twenty-First Century*. London: Routledge.

Urry, John. 2007. *Mobilities*. Cambridge: Polity.

Urry, John, and Jonas Larsen. 2011. *The Tourist Gaze 3.0*. Thousand Oaks, CA: Sage.

Vendassi, Pierre. 2014. "Mormonism and the Chinese State: Becoming an Official Church in the People's Republic of China?" Translated by Will Thornely. *China Perspectives* 1:43–50.

Verrender, Ian. 2020. "When Insular Replaces Open: How Could COVID-19 Affect the Global Economy?" *ABC News*, April 20, 2020. https://mobile.abc.net.au/news/2020 -04-20/how-could-coronavirus-affect-the-global-economy/12163198.

Vertovec, Steven. 2007. "Super-diversity and Its Implications." *Ethnic and Racial Studies* 30 (6): 1024–54.

Victorian Government. 2015. "China's Online Retail Boost to Jobs and Victoria's Economy." September 22, 2015. https://www.premier.vic.gov.au/chinas-online-retail-boost -jobs-and-victorias-economy.

Wade, Matthew, and Maria Hynes. 2013. "Worshipping Bodies: Affective Labour in the Hillsong Church." *Geographical Research* 51 (2): 173–79.

WalkTheChat. 2016. "WeChat Impact Report 2016 Is Finally Out!" WeChat official account post, June 26, 2016 (via mobile app).

Wallis, Cara. 2013. *Technomobility in China: Young Migrant Women and Mobile Phones*. New York: New York University Press.

Wang, Chih-ming. 2013. *Transpacific Articulation: Student Migration and the Remaking of Asian America*. Honolulu: University of Hawai'i Press.

Wang, Jianying, and Deborah Davis. 2010. "China's New Upper Middle Classes: The Importance of Occupational Disaggregation." In *China's Emerging Middle Class: Beyond Economic Transformation*, edited by Cheng Li, 157–76. Washington, DC: Brookings Institution Press.

Wang, Yuting, and Fenggang Yang. 2006. "More than Evangelical and Ethnic: The Ecological Factor in Chinese Conversion to Christianity in the United States." *Sociology of Religion* 67 (2): 179–92.

Wang, Zheng. 2008. "National Humiliation, History Education, and the Politics of Historical Memory: Patriotic Education Campaign in China." *International Studies Quarterly* 52 (4): 783–806.

Wang, Zheng. 2013. "The Chinese Dream: Concept and Context." *Journal of Chinese Political Science* 19 (1): 1–13.

Wangyi Xinwen 网易新闻. 2011. "内地'皮革奶粉'死灰复燃 长期食用可致癌" [The resurgence of 'leather milk' in the nation's interior: Long-term consumption carcinogenic]. February 17, 2011. http://news.163.com/11/0217/13/6T3LITSQ0001124J.html.

Waters, Johanna L. 2006. "Geographies of Cultural Capital: Education, International Migration and Family Strategies between Hong Kong and Canada." *Transactions of the Institute of British Geographers* 31 (2): 179–92.

Waters, Johanna L. 2007. "'Roundabout Routes and Sanctuary Schools': The Role of Situated Educational Practices and Habitus in the Creation of Transnational Professionals." *Global Networks* 7 (4): 477–97.

Waters, Johanna L. 2008. *Education, Migration, and Cultural Capital in the Chinese Diaspora: Transnational Students between Hong Kong and Canada.* New York: Cambria.

Welch, Anthony. 2002. "Going Global? Internationalizing Australian Universities in a Time of Global Crisis." *Comparative Education Review* 46 (4): 433–71.

Wellman, Barry. 2002. "Little Boxes, Glocalization and Networked Individualism." *Digital Cities II: Computational and Sociological Approaches, Lecture Notes in Computer Science* 2362:10–25.

Wenzel-Teuber, Katharina. 2016. "2015 Statistical Update on Religions and Churches in the People's Republic of China." Translated by Jacqueline Mulberge. *Religions and Christianity in Today's China* 6 (2): 20–43.

Whyte, Sarah, Eric Tlozek, and Lin Evlin. 2017. "Manus Island: Government Could Pay Compensation to Almost 2,000 Detainees over Treatment." *ABC News*, June 12, 2017. http://www.abc.net.au/news/2017-06-13/lawyers-predict-biggest-human-rights-settlement-in-australia/8610780.

Williams, Raymond. 1977. *Marxism and Literature.* Oxford: Oxford University Press.

Williams, Roman R. 2010. "God's Global Professionals: International Students, Evangelical Christianity, and the Idea of a Calling." PhD diss., Boston University.

Windle, Joel. 2008. "The Racialisation of African Youth in Australia." *Social Identities* 14 (5): 553–66.

Wise, Amanda. 2005. "Hope and Belonging in a Multicultural Suburb." *Journal of Intercultural Studies* 26 (1–2): 171–86.

Wise, Amanda. 2011. "Moving Food: Gustatory Commensality and Disjuncture in Everyday Multiculturalism." *New Formations*, no. 74: 82–107.

Wise, Amanda, and Selvaraj Velayutham, eds. 2009. *Everyday Multiculturalism.* Basingstoke, UK: Palgrave Macmillan.

Wolf, Margery. 1985. *Revolution Postponed: Women in Contemporary China.* Stanford, CA: Stanford University Press.

Wong, Alexandra. 2017. "Mobility of Asian Urbanism and the Re-configuration of Sydney's Chinatown." Paper presented at the Ausmob conference The Future of Mobilities Research in Australia and Beyond, University of Melbourne, December 7–8, 2017.

Woods, Jackson S., and Bruce J. Dickson. 2017. "Victims and Patriots: Disaggregating Nationalism in Urban China." *Journal of Contemporary China* 26 (104): 167–82.

Woolworths Limited. 2016. "Woolworths Launches on TMall Global." January 4, 2016. https://www.woolworthsgroup.com.au/page/media/Press_Releases/Archives/2016/Woolworths_Launches_on_Tmall_Global/.

World Bank. 2006. "Gender Gaps in China: Facts and Figures." http://siteresources.worldbank.org/INTEAPREGTOPGENDER/Resources/Gender-Gaps-Figures&Facts.pdf.

World Bank. 2016. "School Enrollment, Tertiary (Gross), Gender Parity Index (GPI), China." http://data.worldbank.org/indicator/SE.ENR.TERT.FM.ZS?locations=CN.

World Economic Forum. 2018. *The Global Gender Gap Report 2018.* Geneva: World Economic Forum. http://www3.weforum.org/docs/WEF_GGGR_2018.pdf.

Wu, Jing. 2012. "Post-socialist Articulation of Gender Positions: Contested Public Sphere of Reality Dating Shows." In *Women and the Media in Asia: The Precarious Self,* edited by Youna Kim, 220–36. Basingstoke, UK: Palgrave Macmillan.

Wu, Jing. 2016. "Family, Aesthetic Authority and Class Identity in the Shadow of Neo-liberal Modernity." In *Lifestyle Media in Asia: Consumption, Aspiration and Identity*, edited by Fran Martin and Tania Lewis, 50–66. London: Routledge.

Wu, Jingsi Christina. 2019. "Technology-Assisted Political Awakening among the Silent Minority: The Rise of China-Based Social Media Platforms and Their Role in the Information Environment and Opinion Space for New U.S. Immigrants." Paper presented at the seventeenth Chinese Internet Research Conference, Digital Cultures: Chinese Internet and Beyond, National University of Singapore, June 28, 2019.

Wu Xiaoying 吴小英. 2009. "市场化背景下性别话语的转型" [The transformation of gender discourse in the context of marketization]. 《中国社会科学》 [Chinese social science] 2:1–13.

Wu Xiaoying. 2010. "From State Dominance to Market Orientation: The Composition and Evolution of Gender Discourse." *Social Sciences in China* 31 (2): 150–64.

Wu, Yujun. 2012. "Modern Chinese National-Cultural Identity in the Context of Globalization." *Transtext(e)s Transcultures* 7. https://journals.openedition.org/transtexts/456?lang=en.

Xiang, Biao, and Wei Shen. 2009. "International Student Migration and Social Stratification in China." *International Journal of Educational Development* 29 (5): 513–22.

Xiao, Bang, Christina Zhou, and Iris Zhao. 2020. "How the Coronavirus Pandemic Could Shift the Multicultural Makeup of Our Society." *ABC News*, April 11, 2020. https://mobile.abc.net.au/news/2020-04-11/coronavirus-migrant-workers-international-students-australia/12130784.

Xinhua Materials. 2016. "General Secretary Xi Jinping Explicates the 'Chinese Dream.'" Translated by Ted Wang. *Chinese Law and Government* 48 (6): 477–79.

Xinhua's China Economic Information Service. 2017. "Number of Chinese Students Studying Overseas Exceeds 4.58 Mln." December 19, 2017.

Xinhua She 新华社 (Xinhua News Agency). 2018. "2017年中国公民出境旅游人次超1.3亿" [Over 130 million international tourist departures by Chinese citizens in 2017]. February 2, 2018. http://www.gov.cn/xinwen/2018-02/06/content_5264343.htm.

Yan, Hairong. 2003. "Neoliberal Governmentality and Neohumanism: Organizing *Suzhi/*Value Flow through Labor Recruitment Networks." *Cultural Anthropology* 18 (4): 493–523.

Yan, Hairong. 2008. *New Masters, New Servants: Migration, Development, and Women Workers in China.* Durham, NC: Duke University Press.

Yan, Yunxiang. 2009. *The Individualization of Chinese Society.* Oxford: Berg.

Yan, Yunxiang. 2010. "Introduction: Conflicting Images of the Individual and Contested Process of Individualization." In *iChina: The Rise of the Individual in Modern Chinese Society*, edited by Mette Halskov Hansen and Rune Svarverud, 1–38. Copenhagen: NIAS Press.

Yan, Yunxiang. 2013. "The Drive for Success and the Ethics of the Striving Individual." In *Ordinary Ethics in China*, edited by Charles Stafford, 263–91. London: Bloomsbury.

Yang, Fan, and Fran Martin. 2020. "The 2019 Australian Federal Election on WeChat Official Accounts: Right-Wing Dominance and Disinformation." *Melbourne Asia Review*, edition 5, December 15, 2020. https://melbourneasiareview.edu.au/the-2019-australian-federal-election-on-wechat-official-accounts-right-wing-dominance-and-disinformation/.

Yang, Fenggang. 1998. "Chinese Conversion to Evangelical Christianity: The Importance of Social and Cultural Contexts." *Sociology of Religion* 59 (3): 237–57.

Yang, Fenggang. 2005. "Lost in the Market, Saved at McDonald's: Conversion to Christianity in Urban China." *Journal for the Scientific Study of Religion* 44 (4): 423–41.

Yang, Fenggang. 2006. "The Red, Black and Gray Markets of Religion in China." *Sociological Quarterly* 47 (1): 93–122.

Yang, Fenggang. 2015. "The Other Chinese Miracle: Great Awakening Shifts Growth of Global Christianity to the East." *ARDA*, December 1, 2015. http://globalplus.thearda .com/globalplus-religion-in-china/.

Yang, Fenggang, and Joseph B. Tamney. 2006. "Exploring Mass Conversion to Christianity among the Chinese: An Introduction." *Sociology of Religion* 67 (2): 125–29.

Yang, Guobin. 2019. "Performing Cyber-Nationalism in Twenty-First-Century China: The Case of Diba Expedition." In *From Cyber-Nationalism to Fandom Nationalism: The Case of Diba Expedition in China*, edited by Hailong Liu, 1–12. London: Routledge.

Yang, Guobin, and Wei Wang. 2016. "The Political Styles of Online Activism in China." In *Contemporary Culture and Media in Asia*, edited by Daniel Black, Olivia Khoo, and Koichi Iwabuchi, 193–207. London: Rowman and Littlefield.

Yang, Lijun, and Yongnian Zheng. 2012. "Fen Qings (Angry Youth) in Contemporary China." *Journal of Contemporary China* 21 (76): 637–53.

Yang, Mayfair Mei-Hui. 2004. "Spatial Struggles: Postcolonial Complex, State Disenchantment, and Popular Reappropriation of Space in Rural Southeast China." *Journal of Asian Studies* 63 (3): 719–55.

Ye, Weili. 2001. *Seeking Modernity in China's Name: Chinese Students in the United States, 1900–1927*. Stanford, CA: Stanford University Press.

You, Jing, Xuejie Yi, and Meng Chen. 2016. "Love, Life, and 'Leftover Ladies' in Urban China." Munich Personal RePEc Archive (MPRA) Paper No. 70494. https://mpra.ub .uni-muenchen.de/70494/.

You, Lan. n.d. "Caught in the Split: Chinese Students in the Soviet Union, 1960–1965." Cold War International History Project (CWIHP) e-Dossier 52, Wilson Center. Accessed May 7, 2021. https://www.wilsoncenter.org/publication/caught-the-split -chinese-students-the-soviet-union-1960-1965.

Yu, Haiqing. 2020. "The Transformation of Daigou in the Post-COVID 19 Era." *Pearls and Irritations Public Policy Journal*, October 6, 2020. https://johnmenadue.com/the -transformation-of-daigou-in-the-post-covid-19-era/.

Yu, Haiqing, and Hayden Blain. 2019. "Tongzhi on the Move: Digital/Social Media and Placemaking Practices among Young Gay Chinese in Australia." *Media International Australia* 173 (1): 66–80.

Yu, Haiqing, and Lili Cui. 2019. "China's E-Commerce: Empowering Rural Women?" *China Quarterly* 238:418–37.

Zavoretti, Roberta. 2017. "Being the Right Woman for 'Mr Right': Marriage and Household Politics in Present-Day Nanjing." In *Transforming Patriarchy: Chinese Families in the Twenty-First Century*, edited by Gonçalo Santos and Stevan Harrell, 129–45. Seattle: University of Washington Press.

Zhan, Heying, and Rhonda J. Montgomery. 2003. "Gender and Elder Care in China: The Influence of Filial Piety and Structural Constraints." *Gender and Society* 17 (2): 209–29.

Zhang, Han. 2019. "The 'Post-truth' Publication Where Chinese Students in America Get Their News." *New Yorker*, August 19, 2019. https://www.newyorker.com/culture /culture-desk/the-post-truth-publication-where-chinese-students-in-america-get-their -news.

Zhang, Hong. 2017. "Recalibrating Filial Piety: Realigning the State, Family, and Market Interests in China." In *Transforming Patriarchy: Chinese Families in the Twenty-First Century*, edited by Gonçalo Santos and Stevan Harrell, 234–50. Seattle: University of Washington Press.

Zhang, Jun, and Peidong Sun. 2014. "'When Are You Going to Get Married?': Parental Matchmaking and Middle-Class Women in Contemporary Urban China." In *Wives, Husbands, and Lovers: Marriage and Sexuality in Hong Kong, Taiwan, and Urban China*, edited by Deborah S. Davis and Sara L. Friedman, 118–44. Stanford, CA: Stanford University Press.

Zhang, Li. 2010. *In Search of Paradise: Middle-Class Living in a Chinese Metropolis.* Ithaca, NY: Cornell University Press.

Zhang, Lin. 2017. "Fashioning the Feminine Self in 'Prosumer Capitalism.'" *Journal of Consumer Culture* 17 (2): 184–204.

Zhang, Meng. 2012. "A Chinese Beauty Story: How College Women in China Negotiate Beauty, Body Image, and Mass Media." *Chinese Journal of Communication* 5 (4): 437–54.

Zhang, Siqi, and Cora Lingling Xu. 2020. "The Making of Transnational Distinction: An Embodied Cultural Capital Perspective on Chinese Women Students' Mobility." *British Journal of Sociology of Education* 41 (8): 1251–67.

Zhang, Vickie. 2018. "Im/mobilizing the Migration Decision." *Environment and Planning D: Society and Space* 36 (2): 199–216.

Zhang Weiwei 张维为. 2014. "一出国，就爱国" [As soon as one leaves the country, one turns patriotic]. 《观察者》 [The observer], July 29, 2014. https://www.guancha.cn /ZhangWeiWei/2014_07_29_251359.shtml.

Zhang Xiuli 张秀丽. 2010. "九0后一代大学生特点浅析" [A brief analysis of the characteristics of the nineties generation of undergraduates]. *Du Xie Suan* 《读写算》 [Reading and writing] 1:5–7.

Zhang, Xuefeng. 2006. "How Religious Organizations Influence Chinese Conversion to Evangelical Protestantism in the United States." *Sociology of Religion* 67 (2): 149–59.

Zhang, Zhen. 2000. "Mediating Time: The 'Rice Bowl of Youth' in Fin de Siecle Urban China." *Public Culture* 12 (1): 93–113.

Zhao, Suisheng. 2005. "China's Pragmatic Nationalism: Is It Manageable?" *Washington Quarterly* 29 (1): 131–44.

Zhao, Xinyu. 2016. "Social Exclusion in the Everyday: (Re)conceptualizing Student-Migrant Experiences in Australia." In *Refereed Proceedings of TASA 2016 Conference*, edited by Mark Chou, 347–54. Melbourne: TASA. https://tasa.org.au/wp-content /uploads/2015/03/TASA_2016_Conference_Proceedings-1.pdf.

Zhao, Xinyu. 2017. "International Students and Social Exclusion in the Age of Social Media." *Transitions: Journal of Transient Migration* 1 (2): 163–75.

Zhao, Xinyu. 2019a. "Disconnective Intimacies through Social Media: Practices of Transnational Family among Overseas Chinese Students in Australia." *Media International Australia* 173 (1): 36–52.

Zhao, Xinyu. 2019b. "(Re)Making Boundaries: Chinese International Students in the Age of Social Media." PhD diss., Deakin University.

Zheng, Jiaran. 2016. *New Feminism in China: Young Middle-Class Chinese Women in Shanghai.* Singapore: Foreign Language Teaching and Research Press and Springer.

Zheng, Wang. 2003. "Gender, Employment, and Women's Resistance." In *Chinese Society, Change, Conflict and Resistance,* edited by Elizabeth J. Perry and Mark Selden, 158–82. 2nd ed. London: RoutledgeCurzon.

Zheng, Yi. 2014. *Contemporary Chinese Print Media: Cultivating Middle-Class Taste.* London: Routledge.

Zhong Yiwen 鍾怡雯. 2000. 《亞洲華文散文的中國圖象 (1949–1999)》 [The image of China in Chinese-language essays from Asia, 1949–1999]. Taipei: Wanjuan Lou.

Zhongguo Jihua Shengyu Xiehui 中国计划生育协会 [China Family Planning Council]. 2015. 《大学生性与生殖健康调查报告》 [A report of the college students' sexual and reproductive health survey 2015]. Beijing: China Family Planning Council.

Zhongguo Wang 中国网. 2010. "2008年：三聚氰胺婴幼儿奶粉事件" [Three incidents of melamine in infant formula in 2008]. Accessed October 15, 2011, subsequently removed. http://www.china.com.cn/node_7064072/content_19612595.htm.

Zhongguo Wang 中国网. 2012. "邵琪伟局长：2011年中国出境旅游人数7025万人次" [Bureau Chief Zhao Qiwei: 70,250,000 outbound travelers from China in 2011]. January 21, 2012. http://www.china.com.cn/travel/txt/2012-01/21/content_24461318.htm.

Zhu, Shanjie, and Qiaolian Zhu. 2017. "On Shanghai's Middle Class: A Preliminary Survey Report." *Inter-Asia Cultural Studies* 18 (4): 632–42.

Zurndorfer, Harriet. 2016. "Men, Women, Money and Morality: The Development of China's Sexual Economy." *Feminist Economics* 22 (2): 1–23.

Zurndorfer, Harriet. 2018. "Escape from the Country: The Gender Politics of Chinese Women in Pursuit of Transnational Romance." *Gender, Place and Culture* 25 (4): 489–506.

Index

divorce, 5, 92, 165, 172, 184–86

Dovey, Kim, 58

dream, 31, 96, 214, 260, 291–92, 295, 306n5; affective, 27–28, 122–27; Chinese, 15–16, 306n5; differential distribution of, 52–55; of education and global mobility, 1, 5, 12, 35–56; of Melbourne, 60–64, 85–96; rejection of, 276–80. *See also* aspiration

Duhigg, Charles, 198

Duthie, Laurie, 307n5

economic reform in China. *See* China: post-reforms era

education: class and, x, 4–39, 54–56, 108, 122, 127, 162–63, 174, 247, 266, 282; education-migration agency, 252; edu-tourist city, 61–64; export and commodification of, ix–x, 21–24, 57, 127, 211–14, 289–95, 298n8, 303n2 (chap. 3); outflows from China, 10, 21–24; study participants' pre-arrival educational histories, 1–2, 11, 48, 52–55; system in Australia, 22–24, 66, 127, 289–95; system in China, 11, 53–55; transnational, ix–x, 9–13, 21–24, 31–56, 161–63, 187–89, 247–84; women's participation in, 17, 23

Elliott, Anthony, 133, 286

Engebretsen, Elisabeth, 177

England, 47, 201, 298n7

English teaching and learning, 191, 194, 252. *See also* International English Language Testing System (IELTS); Pearson Test of English (PTE)

entrepreneurship, 23, 69, 116, 297nn4–5; micro-, 32, 132–44, 153–58, 252; parental occupation, 6–9, 20, 38, 260; self-entrepreneurship, 44, 56, 198, 282, 299n16. *See also* neoliberalism: neoliberal subjectivity

Essed, Philomena, 108

ethnicity, 5, 86, 183, 192; Anglo, 58, 92, 95–96, 107, 112–17, 120–23, 193, 201, 206–7, 243–44, 277, 304n3; multiethnic, 58, 79, 108, 123, 200, 204, 206, 211; representations of African Other, 32, 99, 105–12, 127. *See also* Chineseness; race

ethnography, 27–31, 192, 286–89

e-trading, 105, 229, 269, 285, 304n10; as feminine network capital, 32, 132–35, 140–58

Europe, 38, 108, 120, 143, 297n4, 299n11; racism in, 293; religion in 190, 213; as study destination, 10; as travel and immigration destination, 253, 298nn7–8

Evans, Andrew, 205–6

Evans, Ashley, 205–6

Evans, Russell, 205–6

Evans, Sam, 205–6

expatriate microworld, Chinese students', 31, 66–79, 96, 99, 101, 285, 301n3

Facebook, 24, 30, 100–101, 126, 199

Fair Work Australia, 304n6

family, 107, 130, 158, 177, 206, 213, 215–17, 221; family-focused femininity, 16–19, 162–63, 248, 280–84, 290; migrant family-owned business and property, 65, 87–88, 91, 139, 142, 145; of students, 1–4, 8, 12, 14, 20, 23, 31, 36–56, 70, 89, 144, 164, 172–73, 179, 183–88, 192, 196, 199, 200, 209, 249, 253, 260–78, 305n5; virtual communication with family, 100, 105. *See also* filial piety

Family First (political party), 205

Farbenblum, Bassina, 303n4 (chap. 4)

Farrer, James, 164–68

fazhan (development), 15, 41, 44, 229, 271

femininity. *See gender*

feminism, 16, 27, 48, 166, 283–84, 291, 304n9

Feng, Wang, 17

filial piety, 3, 49, 156, 185–86, 202, 272, 288; daughterly, 18–19, 21, 174. *See also* patriotism: filial and gendered

Fincher, Ruth, 70, 191

Fong, Vanessa L., 223, 233–35

Four Corners (news and current affairs TV program), 244

foxi qingnian (Buddha-style youth), 308n8

France, 111, 201, 298n7

Frank, Adam, 308n5

Friedman, Sara L., 165

fudaoyuan (guidance counsellor), 53, 193, 300n5

Fulian (All China Women's Federation), 17

Gaetano, Arianne M., 56

gaokao (National College Entrance Exam), 11, 53–55

Gao-Miles, Linling, 302n8

race, 5–6, 204, 288; racialization, 13, 32, 96, 99, 285. *See also* ethnicity; refugees; work

racism, 6; anti-African, 32, 106–27, 303n2 (chap. 3), 303n5; anti-Chinese, 61, 92–95, 108–26, 135–37, 141, 242–44, 250, 275, 285, 293–95, 303n2 (chap. 4), 304n3, 307n3

Raffaeta, Roberta, 301n2

reflexivity, 83, 266–69, 275; media engagement, 122–24; national identity and, 236–42

refugees, 32, 99, 107, 109–10, 118–19, 120–26, 240, 303nn5–6. *See also* race

religion, 91, 192, 160; in China, 190–93, 196–97, 200, 203, 213–14; Chinese folk, 197; transnational and translocal, 190–92, 200–214, 305n2; and welfare services, 33, 191, 194–96, 211–12. *See also* affect: religious; *and specific religions and religious organizations*

Renmin Ribao (*People's Daily*; newspaper), 4, 10, 35

risk: academic, 53, 199; economic, 8, 12, 15, 36; environmental, 12, 36–37; gendered, 31–39, 174–76, 285, 300n1; reputational, 166–69, 172–74, 209

Rizvi, Fazal, 101

Robertson, Shanthi, 70

Rofel, Lisa, 16

Rogers, Dallas, 70

Romance of the Three Kingdoms, 89

Rose, Nikolas, 299n11

Rottenberg, Catherine, 299n12

ruhua (insulting China), 216–18, 221

Salt Lake City, 92, 199

Santos, Gonçalo, 166, 299n15

Schein, Louisa 25

Sebastian, Guy, 205

Sedgwick, Eve Kosofsky, 308n5

self-advancement. *See* individualization; neoliberalism: neoliberal subjectivity

Seventh-Day Adventism, 193–94

sexuality, 4, 32, 160–89; reputational risk, 166–69, 172–74, 209. *See also* homosexuality; tomboy

Seymour, William J., 203

Shandong, 91, 170

Shanghai, 7, 40, 42, 45, 47, 90, 170, 254, 305n6; delayed marriage of women in, 17; as fieldwork site, 1, 29, 57–59, 138, 144,

156, 223, 279, 290; as postgraduation work destination, 50, 196, 256, 261, 268–69, 273, 291; youth sexual culture in, 164–65

Shaw, Kate, 70

shengnü (leftover women), 17–18, 42, 163, 169, 272

Shenzhen, 263–64, 290

Sichuan, 192, 304n6

Sidhu, Ravinder, 127

Singapore, 57, 61, 69, 142, 260; religion in, 200, 205–6, 213

singularity, concept of, 28, 157, 291, 308n4

Skeggs, Beverley, 134

Sky Post, 117

Smith, Joseph, 199

socialism. *See* China.

social theory, macroscale, 27, 34, 157, 283–89, 300n1

Southwestern University of Finance and Economics, 50

Soutphommasane, Tim, 119

Soviet Union, 110, 298n7

Spain, 52, 108, 178, 182, 276–77

Special Broadcasting Service (SBS), 303n7

Stewart, Kathleen, 28

Stratton, Jon, 109

striving, 253, 268, 277, 308n8; individual, 14–16, 18–19, 28, 35, 43, 56, 126, 182, 280–83, 299n11. *See also* individualization; neoliberalism: neoliberal subjectivity

subjectivity, 102, 197; gendered, 12–13, 26, 173, 179, 295, 304n9, 308n3

Sun, Wanning, 61, 221

Sun Wei, 102, 105, 115, 125, 303n4 (chap. 3)

superdiversity, 32, 100, 106–9, 122, 126–27. *See also* cities; multiculturalism

suzhi, 9–10, 41, 44, 230–36, 253, 287–88, 306n9, 308n3

Sydney, 158, 174, 205, 234–35, 243, 301n3, 302n7, 304n8; as fieldwork site, 29, 30, 242; as study destination, 22, 116, 123, 153, 242, 263, 267, 278

SydneyToday (WeChat public account), 116

Taipei, 90, 241

Taiwan, 69, 175, 200, 202, 239, 231; celebrities from, 227, 229; migrants in Australia, 142, 241, 304n4; relationship with China, 240–41, 306n1, 306n8, 307n10

www.ingramcontent.com/pod-product-compliance
Lightning Source LLC
Chambersburg PA
CBHW071013280326
41935CB00011B/1336